Blue Skies, Green Politics

Blue Skies, Green Politics

The Clean Air Act of 1990
and Its Implementation

Second Edition

Gary C. Bryner
Brigham Young University

A Division of Congressional Quarterly Inc.
Washington, D.C.

BDU0970-8/2

Copyright © 1995 Congressional Quarterly Inc.
1414 22nd Street, N.W., Washington, D.C. 20037

Printed in the United States of America

Cover design by Paula Anderson

Library of Congress Cataloging-in-Publication Data

Bryner, Gary C.
    Blue skies, green politics : the Clean Air Act of 1990 and its implemen-
tation / Gary C. Bryner—2nd ed.
    p.   cm.
    Includes bibliographical references and index.
    ISBN 1-56802-134-8(alk. paper)
    1. Air—Pollution—Law and legislation—United States. 2. United
States. Clean Air Act Amendments of 1990. 3. Environmental policy—
United States. Air—Pollution—United States. I. Title.
KF3812.Z9B78 1995
344.73'046342—dc20
[347.30446342]
                                                                    95-38400
                                                                        CIP

To Nicholas Stevens Bryner,
future scientist

Contents

Tables and Figures

Tables

Figures

Preface

The passage of the Clean Air Act Amendments of 1990 was an impressive political achievement: it produced the comprehensive revision (after nearly a decade of deadlock) of one of the most important statutes ever enacted by Congress. It also served as proof that divided government can work—that a legislative branch under the control of one political party can cooperate with an executive branch controlled by another party to produce major legislation.

Blue Skies, Green Politics gives readers an opportunity to examine what Congress and the executive branch were trying to do in revising the Clean Air Act. The framework I've provided enables readers to assess for themselves how well the two branches did in crafting the legislation and, in this second edition, how implementation of the law is proceeding. I hope that the information presented will encourage discussion about how to achieve cleaner air and how to ensure the effectiveness of public policies whose aim is to improve environmental quality. I encourage readers to seek their own answers to the questions posed here; my proposals are offered to stimulate their thinking.

One focus of this book is the process of policy making. Passage of the 1990 amendments to the Clean Air Act provides a useful case study of how public policies are formulated. The central questions examined include how the issue of clean air came to be put on the national policy agenda; how the policy subsequently evolved; and how successfully Congress and the executive branch dealt with the political conflicts, policy disputes, and institutional limitations that caused the deadlock. Members of Congress not only had to confront regionally divisive issues but also had to sort out the competing demands of powerful interest groups, grapple with complicated scientific and technical issues, and balance public concerns about environmental quality and economic growth.

A second focus of the book is on the outcomes of the policy process. Here the questions examined are to what extent the goals of the statute are likely to be achieved and to what extent Congress provided the policy tools and incentives necessary to achieve them. This assessment also considers whether the goals themselves are appropriate and whether they reflect an adequate understanding of the nature of air pollution and of the political, economic, and legal contexts in which regulation takes place. The ultimate public policy questions are: Will the goal of cleaner air be realized under this new statutory framework? And, if so, at what price? Much has been written about environmental law in general, and the Clean Air Act of 1970 and the 1977 amendments in particular. A review of some of these studies provides an opportunity to analyze whether Congress satisfied the criticisms of its earlier statutory handiwork in producing an improved model of clean air legislation in 1990.

A third focus of the book is on subsequent actions to implement the law. As is true of most major laws enacted by Congress, passage of the law is only the first chapter in the policy-making process. The debate then shifts to another forum, the federal and state regulatory agencies that are responsible for translating legislative mandates into effective administrative programs. In so doing, they will revisit most of the policy choices made by Congress and the executive branch when the law was passed.

Blue Skies, Green Politics begins with a discussion of environmental problems in general and some of the challenges they pose for the policy-making process; Chapter 1 also presents a model of the policy-making process. Chapter 2 explores different ways in which the problem of air pollution can be defined and understood. Chapter 3 traces the evolution of clean air policy in Congress and the executive branch and provides a detailed account of the passage of the 1990 law. Chapter 4 examines some of the important issues central to the passage of the 1990 law, which have implications for the future of environmental law and regulation in the United States. Chapter 5 reviews the first four years of the implementation of the 1990 law, and the dramatic change in implementation resulting from the 1994 election. The final chapter analyzes the prospects for successful implementation of the Clean Air Act Amendments and for achieving the goal of clean air.

Acknowledgments

I owe an enormous debt to many people who contributed to the first and second editions of this book in many ways. I benefited greatly from the opportunity to interview a number of congressional staff members, executive branch officials, and representatives of environmental organizations and industry groups. Those interviews were largely held off the record and therefore have not been acknowledged. But they were absolutely indispensable, and I greatly appreciate the time these individuals took to answer questions and explain events. They include Richard Ayres, Greg Barnett, Bill Becker, John Blodgett, Rob Brenner, David Cantour, Jeff Clark, Trent Clark, Jack Clough, Len Coburn, Mira Courpas, Kathy Cudlipp, Terry Davies, David Doninger, Blake Early, Ric Erdheim, Bill Fay, Eddie Flaherty, Dirk Forrester, Bob Friedman, David Gardiner, Theresa Gorman, Bob Grady, Melanie Griffin, Heidi Halek, David Hawkins, Ed Heidig, Kate Kimball, Jessica Laverty, Skip Luken, Chris Neme, Jimmy Powell, Bill Roberts, William Rosenberg, Philip Schiliro, Zoe Schneidner, Russ Shay, Deborah Sheiman, Mike Shields, Dan Weiss, Greg Whetstone, Ron White, and Terry Yosie.

The Brookings Institution provided office space and support when I was studying the Clean Air Act in 1990 and 1991; I especially appreciate the help of Tom Mann and the staff members at Brookings during my stay there.

I attended a number of conferences and lectures and, in particular, benefited greatly from the opportunity to attend the Inside EPA Clean Air Conferences in 1990 and 1991, as well as the Clean Air Strategy Session organized by the Natural Resources Defense Council and the Natural Resources Council of Maine.

Earlier versions of some chapters of this book were presented as papers at meetings of the American Political Science Association, the Association for Policy Analysis and Management, and the Association for Canadian Studies in the United States. I am most grateful to those who offered comments and criticism or discussed with me their views on the Clean Air Act, particularly Robert Katzmann, Paul Light, Theodore Lowi, Norm Vig, Kathy Wagner, Aaron Wildavsky, and Edward Woodhouse.

The Canadian Government Faculty Research Program; the College of Family, Home, and Social Sciences; and the Political Science Department at Brigham Young University provided resources to help finance the research. I learned much about air pollution from members of the Utah County Clean Air Coalition, officials from Region 8 of the EPA, the Division of Environmental Quality of the State of Utah, and, in particular, from the research of my colleagues at Brigham Young University C. Arden Pope III and Samuel Rushforth. Barry Balleck, John Dunn, Rex Facer, Paul Kube, David Passey, and Jon Tasso, students at Brigham Young, provided outstanding research help. Students in my public policy classes at the university helped me develop many of the ideas expressed here through their thoughtful questions about and discussions of environmental policy.

Lisa Miller's word-processing skill was indispensable to the project; Jane Stevens Bryner helped in innumerable ways throughout the project; and criticism and suggestions by reviewers greatly improved the manuscript, and I appreciate their candid assessments.

In preparing the second edition, Jayne Mardock, Ina Schlez, and John Tallmadge of the Clean Air Network provided extremely valuable information on states' implementation of the Clean Air Act, and on congressional efforts to weaken the law. Sharon Buccino, David Driesen, David Hawkins, and Deborah Sheiman Sphrentz of the Natural Resources Defense Council were very helpful in my efforts to understand better how the Clean Air Act works—and doesn't work. Michael Kraft, Barry Rabe, and Ted Sears made many thoughtful and important suggestions for improving the manuscript. Portions of the second edition were presented at recent meetings of the Association of Policy Analysis and Management, the Midwest Political Science Association, and the Western Political Science Association. While the conclusions I have drawn are my own, and I cannot implicate others, I am happy to recognize that anything of value in this book is the result of what I have learned from others.

Congressional Quarterly editor Brenda Carter marvelously balanced helpful criticism of and supportive interest in the project. Her efforts and the careful editing of Laura Carter improved immensely what I first submitted to them.

Finally, I have learned a great deal from a wide range of scholars who have written about American politics and public policy, environmental regulation in general, and air pollution in particular. I have acknowledged their outstanding work in the endnotes, but those references do not adequately express my indebtedness to them and to their knowledge, creativity, and skill.

Introduction

Congress and the executive branch had been bitterly divided on the subject of environmental regulation during most of the 1980s. The passage of the Clean Air Act Amendments of 1990 was made possible, in part, by an extraordinary set of negotiations between representatives of the executive branch and a group of senators in early 1990, when the bill had become stalled in the Senate. That tension has resurfaced, but in a different way, as the executive branch has become the protector of a strong environmental regulatory role for the federal government, while congressional leaders have become aggressive deregulators. The 1996 election may alter again this tenuous balance, and environmental law will continue to be caught in the middle of a tremendous political debate over the role of government and our reliance on "free markets."

The 1990 Clean Air Act raises, but clearly does not settle, a number of questions that are central to formulating regulatory policy and structuring administrative power, such as how much discretion should be given to agencies implementing regulatory statutes and how detailed and prescriptive statutes should be. Given the past ten years of conflict between Congress and the Environmental Protection Agency over how environmental laws are to be implemented, many members of Congress distrust executive branch officials and are seeking new ways to ensure that the goals of the laws they enact are more fully realized. Their experience with the new law illustrates the difficulties of trying to make certain that agencies faithfully adhere to congressional intent, yet are allowed sufficient flexibility to administer the law in an effective manner.

The Clean Air Act also raises fundamental questions about how responsibility for implementing regulatory legislation should be divided between the states and the federal government. Many people have argued that states should be given flexibility in deciding how to balance the improvement of environmental quality and the regulation of industrial, commercial, and individual activities. Since pollution levels are much higher in some areas, different standards and approaches may be required, depending on the seriousness of their problems. Others have argued that standards should apply uniformly throughout the United States; otherwise, some states might relax standards in an attempt to attract industries from other states.

Because the Clean Air Act of 1990, like other complex statutes, relies on a variety of policy instruments, it is also a useful vehicle for assessing the strengths and weaknesses of traditional approaches to regulation as well as alternative policy mechanisms, including the use of marketlike incentives. One of the most important provisions in the new law creates a system for reducing emissions of the pollutants responsible for acid rain. The 1990 act is a complex combination of the traditional regulatory approach that imposes technology-based limits on emissions as well as market-based innovations that will help shape the future of environmental law.

The story of the passage of the Clean Air Act Amendments of 1990, including an explanation of what Congress and the Bush administration were trying to do in producing some 400 pages of statutory language, requires the reader to confront a mass of detailed, technical information. But the technicalities cannot be avoided if one is to grasp the essential elements of the Clean Air Act, to get a sense of how Congress deals with complicated policy issues, and to assess the response of Congress and the executive branch to the problem of air pollution.

The underlying goal of the Clean Air Act is to ensure that air pollution does not continue to harm public health. Air pollution causes the premature death of thousands of people each year and requires the hospitalization and medical treatment of many more. It indirectly contributes to poor health by weakening the human immune system, thus increasing susceptibility to disease. Perhaps most significantly, it is a risk that most people expose themselves to involuntarily. The economic benefits of some pollution-producing activities, such as industrial processes, are received largely by corporate owners and workers, whereas the adverse health effects are experienced by the entire community. Children and the elderly are especially susceptible to the hazards of air pollution and often lack the resources to seek community support to protect their interests. Viewed from this perspective, reducing air pollution becomes a moral imperative.

Clean air is also compatible with other policy goals such as a strong economy. Because environmental quality affects the health of workers and consumers, its improvement is a prerequisite for efficient economic activity. Moreover, since pollution from industrial activity is waste, reducing it can reduce the costs of production. Pollution from energy sources can be reduced in ways that also conserve those sources and thus save money. Pollution reduction is often achieved by modernization and quality control improvements that also increase industrial competitiveness. The problem is that the costs of instituting cleaner processes and technologies are immediate and often narrowly focused, at least initially, whereas the benefits are frequently delayed and dispersed geographically. Those who profit from the status quo will continue to lead the fight against change; they have considerable resources and incentives to block new approaches and inhibit new research. Nevertheless, increasingly stringent environmental regulations are inevitable. Other countries, such as Germany and Japan, have concluded that improving environmental quality represents great economic opportunities. The United States may no longer be the leader in environmental regulation because of industry resistance to change and government timidity in encouraging these changes.

Although it is difficult to dispute the argument that the benefits of the Clean Air Act (or any other policy initiative) should exceed the costs of complying with them, it is also difficult to assess the Clean Air Act from that perspective alone. It is not clear, for example, how many lives will be saved by improving air quality by specific increments, since a host of other factors are involved, from personal behavior to weather patterns. We do not know how to quantify the benefits of cancer cases prevented and respiratory attacks avoided. Similarly, the costs of compliance are difficult to assess, since industrial practices are dynamic; changes in production methods, reduced use of materials, and modernization of equipment may all ultimately reduce costs. Given the moral implications of imposing the risks of pollution on involuntary victims, however, the uncertainties about costs and benefits cannot justify inaction. We buy insurance against the possibility of bad things happening, and pollution controls are simply another form of insurance against unknown hazards. That reasoning does not eliminate the possibility of weighing costs and benefits, but allows them to be viewed more realistically. Cost-benefit analysis might help us allocate resources among competing public concerns. If we spent less money on air pollution controls, we could spend more money on safer highways or research to find more efficient drugs. But at present we have no mechanism for making such comprehensive risk comparisons; therefore, most policies cannot simply be assessed and analyzed on the basis of their distribution of costs and benefits.

The expectations created by the language of the Clean Air Act greatly exceed the resources provided to implement it, and over time, this inconsistency is likely to contribute to our cynicism about government. The EPA might not meet its deadlines for issuing regulations; states might not fully implement the programs assigned them; the investments necessary to achieve compliance will be greater than what businesses believe they can afford to spend; and we will probably not reach our air quality goals. Advocates of clean air may argue that we should aim high, so that if we fall short, we have nevertheless made considerable progress. That argument may make sense solely from the perspective of improving environmental quality. But the viability of democratic government and the capacity of the policy-making process must also be considered; the Clean Air Act continues a tradition of detailed statutes that seek to force the executive branch to take actions it might not otherwise take and create expectations that are not fulfilled that, in the long run, may be damaging. Although passage of the Clean Air Act proves that divided government can work, the tension and disagreement between Congress and the president concerning the law's implementation, as well as broader political changes reflected in the 1994 congressional elections, culminated in dozens of bills introduced in 1995 to limit the implementation of the Clean Air Act or even to repeal it.

One of the great challenges we face is how to maintain the momentum for improving air quality that resulted from passage of the 1990 Clean Air Act as Congress considers legislation to change the way environmental policy making takes place and responds to critics of the Clean Air Act and its implementation by the EPA and the states. The stakes are high: air pollution is a major public health threat, but fortunately, it is a threat that we can effectively reduce by creating clear incentives for industries to produce less waste and become more efficient. Blue skies and a healthy, vibrant economy are, in the long run, compatible goals. But a green politics today is a much greater challenge than it was in 1990.

1 Challenges in Environmental Policy Making

Protecting the environment has become a major policy concern of government at all levels. Public opinion polls and other measures of public sentiment show strong support for more aggressive laws and regulations that attempt to solve pollution problems and protect natural resources. According to recent polls, more than 70 percent of Americans believe that "protecting the environment is *so* important that requirements and standards cannot be too high, and continuing environmental improvements must be made *regardless* of cost" (italics in original).[1] Political candidates have used environmental issues as a springboard to electoral success. Environmentalism played a significant role in the 1988 presidential election (it was perhaps not as central an issue in 1992) and has been an important factor in a number of other political races.

The 1994 election, which brought a new Republican Congress to Washington, did not focus directly on environmental policy, but concerns over the size of government, the reach of regulation, and the relationship between the federal government and the states were addressed by Republican candidates throughout the nation. Public dissatisfaction with congressional Democrats' inability to deal with some issues, and promises by Republican candidates to reduce federal spending and roll back government regulation produced a vote that caused a dramatic shift in power. While support for effective efforts to ensure environmental quality remains strong, governments at all levels are rethinking the way the United States regulates clean air and water and hazardous wastes.

Despite the political upheaval, environmental protection remains a major public health concern. Toxic waste dumps that contaminate drinking water, the release of hazardous chemicals into the air and water, damage to the stratospheric ozone layer that filters out harmful ultraviolet radiation, and a host of other problems threaten human health and natural resources. Air pollution is one of the most serious environmental problems in the United States and throughout the world. According to the Environmental Protection Agency's National Air Quality and Emissions Trend Report, published in 1994, 140 million Americans live in areas that have failed to meet the national air quality standard for ground-level ozone in recent years. Changes in weather, incomplete monitoring, and

1

other factors introduce great variation in the number of areas that violate the national standards in any one year, however. In 1993, for example, the Environmental Protection Agency (EPA) reported that 51 million people lived in areas reporting ozone levels that exceeded the standard.[2] We have a long way to go before we have in place a comprehensive and effective system of monitoring and regulating air pollution.

Although urban ozone is the most widespread air pollution problem, public health studies published in the early 1990s identified particulate pollution as potentially the most serious health threat from air pollution. A December 1993 study published in the *New England Journal of Medicine* by researchers at the Harvard School of Public Health tracked the health of over 8,000 individuals in six U.S. cities; after correcting for smoking, age, and other factors, the study concluded that residents of the more polluted cities had a *mortality rate 26 percent higher* than residents of the least polluted cities.[3] These and other studies discussed later translate into estimates that particulate pollution is responsible for 50,000 to 70,000 premature deaths or more each year in the United States.

The Clean Air Act[4] is one of the most important environmental laws ever enacted in the United States because it is the primary legislative means of addressing one of the nation's most serious environmental problems. The flagship of some two dozen environmental laws, it has raised widespread expectations for a remedy to the problem of air pollution. The act also has major economic consequences for virtually every sector of the economy. Given its importance, study of the passage of the Clean Air Act Amendments of 1990 can enhance our understanding of the policy-making process and shed light on the prospects for improving policy-making capabilities in environmental and other areas. This chapter examines some of the general challenges confronting policymakers attempting to solve environmental problems.

Overview of Environmental Policy Making

Environmental regulation poses a number of particularly difficult challenges to policymakers. There is considerable uncertainty surrounding the causes and consequences of pollution; furthermore, long lead times are frequently required before the adverse health effects and other consequences of pollution are discovered. Policy making must therefore include learning from experience and making adjustments, which can be particularly risky because the effects of some environmental hazards are largely irreversible, in terms of loss of human life or ecological changes.

There is little agreement concerning how much needs to be known about the health and environmental effects of pollutants and how much risk should be accepted before regulatory action is taken. A central issue is how risks should be calculated. Some argue that intervention should ensure that all people are protected, including those most susceptible to the effects of pollution; others insist that the risk posed to the community in general should be the basis of regulatory action. A second issue is how reduction of environmental risks should be balanced with other values such as individual freedom and corporate profit making.

The distribution of the consequences of technological advances is another issue facing policymakers in a democracy. Many of the adverse environmental consequences of industrial activity will be felt by future generations, whereas the benefits are largely confined to the current generation. It is not clear how future interests or those of subgroups of the population that have limited economic and political resources can be protected in a political system dominated by well-financed interest groups.

Environmental policymakers must consider both environmental and economic goals and concerns. The question they attempt to answer has often been posed in stark terms of whether priority should be given to the protection of human health and ecological systems or to economic growth and competitiveness. Environmentalists argue that protection of human health must be provided regardless of cost. Opponents are quick to argue that environmental regulations restrict the global competitiveness of U.S. industry and will simply drive jobs overseas.

Cost-benefit analysis has been widely heralded by economists, industry spokespersons, and opponents of regulation as the way to balance environmental protection and economic growth. While few argue with the commonsense notion that we should not undertake actions unless the expected benefits are greater than the likely costs, efforts to quantify costs and benefits usually emphasize costs and fail to recognize all of the benefits. There is usually little agreement about what costs and benefits to include in the calculations. Should costs be limited to pollution control equipment, for example, or should they include the impact on individuals who lose their jobs when industries cannot afford to meet regulatory requirements? The benefits in terms of lives saved or illnesses prevented are similarly difficult to measure. Disagreements over how to perform this kind of analysis also focus on how to assess the distribution of costs and benefits across generations and whether the current monetary value of costs and benefits should be discounted in comparing their long-term value. Perhaps even more pressing is the distribution of costs and benefits among members of the current generation, since minorities and others who live in economically poor areas are much more likely to suffer from the effects of pollution than are their wealthy neighbors—the problem of environmental justice. Cost-benefit analysis also provides little help in determining the advantages and disadvantages for different industries subject to regulation.

Some of the progress that has been made in reducing air pollution has been a consequence of economic growth and modernization. In many cases, when new, more efficient equipment and machinery have been put in place, pollution has diminished. Regulation can easily cement established control technologies into practice, however. One of the central challenges to environmental policymakers is to encourage continual modernization and development of more efficient, less polluting processes and equipment.

Finally, all the lawmaking and administrative rule making in the world is of little use if laws and regulations are not enforced and complied with. Regulatory programs must therefore include effective incentives for compliance. Some policymakers believe that economic or marketlike incentives (such as taxes on emissions of pollutants) are the key to increasing compliance at lower cost; others prefer traditional regulatory approaches (standards set by federal agencies and largely implemented by state officials, with federal responsibilities in some areas). Incentives for effective execution of traditional as well as market-based regulatory approaches must reach federal, state, and local regulatory officials, who are all involved in implementing environmental laws, to encourage them to make the difficult choices that are required. Perhaps most important, regulatory programs should reduce and prevent pollution rather than simply transfer it from one medium to another. These issues are explored in more detail in subsequent chapters.

The Policy-Making Process

Although observers and students of the policy-making process often disagree about how that process *ought* to take place, there is a fair amount of agreement concerning the way it actually *does* take place. Policy making is a dynamic process. Charles Lindblom has described it as a "complex analytic and political process to which there is no beginning or end, and the boundaries of which are uncertain."[5] It is also a continual process of identifying problems, formulating governmental responses or policies, organizing administrative mechanisms for carrying out the policies, and evaluating the extent to which policy objectives are achieved.

Most policy efforts are incremental rather than comprehensive; they are primarily a series of marginal adjustments of earlier efforts rather than dramatic departures from past practices. Although many scholars have defended such an approach as reasonable, given the limitations of policy analysis and the impossibility of formulating comprehensive solutions to most policy dilemmas, it may produce policies that fail to remedy the underlying problems.

The process of making public policies is not particularly precise. Since it is often difficult to identify with precision the nature of the problems to be addressed or the policy response that would most likely lead to their resolution, a lot of action may be taken with little effect. Policies often help to move society away from some of the effects of a problem yet do not really move it closer to a solution. Policy efforts may treat symptoms of problems without addressing root causes.

One of the most important characteristics of policy making is that different kinds of policies tend to be associated with different kinds of political relationships and processes. Theodore Lowi has persuasively argued that there are three primary types of policies—distributive, redistributive, and regulatory—and that each type of policy is associated with a particular political process.[6] All public policies, according to Lowi, are coercive because they seek to alter individual and societal conduct. There are different ways of controlling behavior, however, and they have different implications both for the way the policy-making process works and for the implementation of the policies that result. Complicated statutes like the Clean Air Act may incorporate all three kinds of policies.

Distributive policies include grants and subsidies that give protection to certain interests against competition and underwrite or directly provide benefits. Grants to states for pollution control equipment and programs are an example of distributive policies. The formulation and implementation of such policies are likely to be accompanied by political relationships in Congress and the executive branch that are disaggregated or individualized, that involve logrolling—the trading of votes or exchanges of support among legislators—and that are usually removed from public scrutiny. Legislation regarding implementation is likely to be quite specific and to allow little administrative discretion. The key decisions—who is to receive the benefits and how much they are to receive—are usually made by the legislators, who have a considerable interest in ensuring that recipients can clearly trace the origins of the benefits given them.

Redistributive policies are concerned with the economy and society. They include the actions of the Federal Reserve Board of Governors that affect credit and the supply of money, as well as the income tax and Social Security. Redistributive policies are ideological; they raise basic issues about the proper role of government in societal and economic matters. They usually capture the attention of both legislative and executive branches and are formulated in a more centralized manner than other policies. Some redistributive policies are only vaguely defined by law and require considerable administrative expertise and discretion in implementation; other policies are clearly defined by law and require only routine methods of administration.

Regulatory policies seek to alter individual behavior directly by imposing standards on regulated industries. Most of the provisions of the Clean Air Act fall in this category. Regulatory policies are much more likely to arouse controversy. Private interests may be significantly constrained or have compliance costs imposed upon them by regulatory actions. Powerful interest groups are likely to be organized around regulatory issues, and the interaction of these policy advocates plays an important role in determining the nature of the policy. Technical information is also likely to be important in decision making. Regulatory policies often involve complex, technical decisions or concern areas of effort for which appropriate policy actions cannot easily be determined; much time will be spent discussing technical issues and the role of experts in administrative agencies and interested groups will be paramount.

Although the policy-making process differs for different kinds of policies, some elements are present in all policy efforts. As outlined by Charles Jones and others, the policy process includes four major steps: initiation and definition, formulation and enactment, implementation, and impact and evaluation.[7] This model does not explain why policies take the shape they do, but it provides a useful way of examining the factors that determine the policy process and of organizing the ideas and concerns that have been central to the policy-making debate over how to regulate air pollution in the United States. It is also a convenient framework for examining the making of environmental policy. In the following section, a general discussion of each step in the policy-making process is followed by an analysis of the circumstances and variables that are specific to that step in the making of environmental policy.

How Environmental Policy Is Made

Initiation and Definition

The policy process begins when people identify social and economic problems that might be resolved by governmental efforts. After the problem is perceived and defined, interests are aggregated and organized in anticipation of presenting demands or proposals to government officials. (Government officials themselves, particularly administrative officials, are often involved early in this step of the process, as they seek to develop support for policies of interest to them.) Depending upon the strength of the political forces behind a proposal and government officials' perception of its importance, the proposal may become an element of the policy agenda.

Getting a proposal on the policy agenda is a major challenge, given the tremendous number of problems clamoring for attention. Interest groups may organize, mobilize their resources, and lobby elected officials, but action may not occur until a major event or "crisis" focuses widespread attention on the issue. Innovative policies are possible when there is a convergence of public attention, political interest in responding to public concern, and "policy entrepreneurs" who are able to channel the political energy toward policy changes.[8]

Policy innovations arise from several sources. Some originate from crises and then undergo the difficult process of evolving into policy response. Policies that are rapidly enacted in response to some major threat may not resolve the underlying problems. Innovations may also spring from the routine demands of the political system. Policy entrepreneurs are constantly in search of problems to be solved, and they interact with organized interests, bureaucracies, and others who have an interest in new policies. Perhaps their biggest challenge is to maintain momentum in the face of obstacles, detours arising from competing concerns, and demands for short-run fixes instead of long-run changes.[9]

The way policy problems are identified and the assumptions and values that give shape to their definitions can have a number of important consequences for the administration of public policies. Misperception of the problem (attention directed toward symptoms rather than root causes, for example) may lead to a proposed policy response that is inadequate or lacks proper focus. The political support (or lack of it) generated during this initial stage of the process can have an important effect on policy development, implementation, and evaluation. Some problems may be ignored—and attention given to other, less serious problems—simply because they fail to attract strong political support.

For more than two decades, environmental policy has been defined as a balancing of environmental quality and economic growth. Despite the broad language of some statutes that set absolute goals of clean air and water and no loss of endangered species, the reality of regulation has been that the cost of compliance with environmental regulations has been the key concern. Cost considerations, rather than achievement of the public health or environmental preservation goal, have largely determined to what extent environmental goals are met. Some presidential administrations have adjusted the balance more towards economic costs than others, but no administration has sought to implement the laws in ways that would actually achieve the goals they contain.

In a typical regulatory action, for example, the EPA estimates the level of harm posed by a chemical; chooses some acceptable level of harm, such as an increased risk of cancer of one case in a million; establishes a standard to maintain that level of risk; and requires some kind of control technology to trap pollutants and reduce emissions to meet the standard. Before they go into effect, most major regulatory initiatives are challenged in court by regulated industries that believe the regulations are too stringent and environmental groups that find them too weak.

Policymakers must balance some level of risk to society with some level of expenditures for pollution control equipment. They fear the public outcry that will result if the risks are too great or the costs too high. But they are confronted with considerable economic and scientific uncertainties even though they are bombarded with material from environmental and industry groups. Sorting out the competing and contradictory data is a daunting task.

Pollution and Public Health. Although literally hundreds of articles concerning the adverse health effects of environmental pollutants have been published in medical and scientific journals, the study of the health and ecological effects of pollution is a relatively new science. The synergistic effect resulting from the exposure to a number of different pollutants, for example, is not well understood. There is, however, compelling scientific research proving that pollution causes sickness and death in humans, adversely affects crops and farm animals, corrodes statues and buildings, damages forests and lakes, reduces visibility, and causes unpleasant odors. Studies have demonstrated a strong association between death rates and poor air quality. Sulfates and fine particulates that contain toxic metals and carcinogens are some of the most hazardous forms of air pollution in the United States.[10]

In some ways, the evolution of scientific understanding concerning the health effects of pollution is comparable with that of the health effects of smoking. Throughout the 1950s and 1960s, evidence mounted on the risks of tobacco use, but such findings were challenged as inaccurate by the tobacco industry. Many industry groups continue to challenge the idea that industrial emissions pose public health threats. Given the long latency period between exposure to some pollutants and the onset of disease, and the difficulties in tracing the source of pollutants that have done damage, many groups have demanded more research or delays before accepting imposition of control measures.[11]

Most research on the health effects of pollution falls into one of three categories: epidemiological studies, direct or laboratory human exposure, and animal testing. Epidemiological studies attempt to derive statistical correlations of the relationships between observed levels of pollution and such health effects as personal discomfort, diminished lung capacity or damage, or death. The strong correlations these studies have identified have raised major concerns about the health effects of various pollutants and have led in some cases to the imposition of federal regulations. But differences between epidemiological studies often make comparisons difficult and the aggregation of findings problematic. It is difficult to identify, define, and isolate the relevant factors or variables. And there is little information on the synergistic effect of exposure to several pollutants. Moreover, the standards of epidemiological studies are difficult to meet; they usually require a high level of statistical confidence in estimating risk. Aggressive regulatory programs are not usually launched until there are major disasters—"bodies in the streets"—that make them politically significant.[12]

Epidemiological studies are particularly useful in attempts to identify the long-term results from exposure to pollutants. But since these studies show only a statistical correlation and thus cannot *prove* that a particular pollutant causes specific health problems, they are often the target of criticism by industry officials. The response is a familiar one: despite study after study that associates tobacco use with cancer, cigarette manufacturers still argue that the health effects of smoking are uncertain.

Direct testing of the effects of pollutants on volunteers in a controlled setting provides more direct evidence than does epidemiological research of the adverse health effects associated with specific pollutants. These studies have found decreased lung functioning of healthy adults exposed to various levels of ozone, for example.[13] But such experiments usually fail to provide an adequate basis for regulation. Only healthy, relatively young people are permitted to participate in these experiments, so little data are available concerning the effects on people with existing respiratory problems or on children or elderly persons. There is also an inadequate understanding of the relationship between acute symptoms and long-term risks. Critics of regulation have dismissed research on short-term effects, arguing that people can recover from short-term respiratory exposure to pollutants without suffering permanent damage. Some health researchers, however, believe that there is a connection between acute and chronic exposure. In the case of pollution and respiratory disease, for example, short-term exposure causing inflammation of lung tissue may cause the lungs to become more "leaky." This may result in increased levels of protein in the lungs, trigger the creation of excess white blood cells, and eventually produce scarring of lung tissue and reduced lung capacity.[14]

Animal testing of chemicals is widely used because of the difficulties of conducting tests on humans. Since the physiology of some animals is quite similar to that of humans, these tests have become particularly important in determining whether certain substances should be considered carcinogens. There are also a number of difficulties with animal testing, however, including their expense (tests of one chemical can cost more than $1 million) and the pain and suffering they cause animals. The results of these tests are often controversial, since scientists disagree about how to extrapolate from the high doses given animals to produce results as rapidly as possible (humans are usually exposed to lower doses), and how to account for possible differences between animals and humans in the way cancer and other diseases develop and spread. There are also disagreements about which species and sex of animal to use for these tests, what exposure path should be used to introduce to the animal the chemical to be tested, and how many animals should be included in the test group. Laboratory tests of one chemical in isolation may not be a realistic test of environmental pollution, which exposes humans to a host of chemicals simultaneously. Such tests can, at best, only demonstrate associations between exposure to chemicals and disease; they cannot prove causality.[15]

The physiology of air pollution-induced mortality is not well understood. Rates of mortality may include deaths caused by misdiagnosis of symptoms, impact on the cardiovascular system from respiratory stress, and other factors in addition to air pollution. However, mortality studies have been conducted in several states and throughout the world. Separate studies involved the use of different models, assumptions, and demographic and other conditions. They eliminated confounding effects of weather, other pollutants, and other known factors. Associations between particulate pollution and mortality, for example, have occurred in a variety of climatic conditions and during different seasons. These results are constant across different kinds of statistical models and tests.[16]

Individual studies have been criticized for failing to account for all the possible factors that might contribute to health risks. Indeed, no one study is sufficiently comprehensive to demonstrate without question the health effects of particulates. There are different kinds of health effects, different kinds of particulates, different sensitivities among different groups of persons, and different complicating and interacting factors and conditions. But taken as a whole, this body of evidence provides overwhelming proof of the damaging effects on health from exposure to particulate pollution.[17]

Some advocates of aggressive environmental regulation argue that eliminating pollution is a moral imperative, since those who suffer the adverse effects of pollution—from industrial sources, for example—are not always the ones who benefit from the economic activity of which that pollution is a by-product. Air pollution regulation can be viewed as one of many public health measures aimed at protecting the majority from a threat posed by a group of individuals. Economists argue that polluting industries that fail to invest in pollution prevention equipment are "externalizing," or imposing their costs on others. The problem, however, is not just economic inefficiency—the prices industries charge fail to reflect the true costs of production—but the fundamental unfairness of subjecting innocent people to air pollution hazards.

Economic Competitiveness and the Costs of Regulation. Although public health goals have been an important consideration in determining the objectives of environmental policy, economic issues have dominated decisions about implementation and enforcement. The costs of compliance with environmental regulation and the consequences for employment have been major concerns throughout the policy debate, even though the economic consequences of environmental controls are often as ambiguous as the impact on health of specific sources of air pollution. There is little agreement about the impact of regulation on the competitive position of American industry in global markets, but evidence of the declining position of American industries in global markets is widespread and is largely blamed on high labor costs, poor management, faulty strategic decisions, and other factors.[18] Industries that dominated the world market two decades ago have seen their share of that market shrink dramatically in recent years. U.S. firms that developed the technology for videocassette recorders and color televisions now have less than 2 percent of the videocassette markets and 10 percent of the television markets. Japanese sales of semiconductor chips, another product developed by American scientists, have eclipsed sales by U.S. companies.[19]

The competitiveness of U.S. firms in global markets has major implications for the standard of living Americans will enjoy in the future. World economic leadership also has great symbolic importance to Americans, for it helps determine U.S. influence in international affairs.[20] The state of the economy also affects the political prospects of candidates in presidential, congressional, and state elections. The success of policymakers and industry leaders in promoting American competitiveness will determine the extent to which public and private resources will be available to pursue other important goals, such as alleviating poverty, promoting public health, protecting environmental quality, and preserving natural resources.[21]

There is, however, little information concerning the impact of pollution control costs on the competitiveness of American companies. In 1990, the public and private sectors spent nearly $100 billion to control pollution. In 1993, the EPA estimated that some $140 billion was spent by state and local governments and industry to comply with environmental laws,[22] and that figure is expected to rise above $150 billion by the end of the century, as shown in Figure 1-1. Nor is much information available concerning the cost of compliance with environmental regulations faced by industries in other nations. Some U.S. industries have moved to other countries, primarily the less developed ones, to escape stringent environmental regulations (as well as for other reasons), but some of America's major economic competitors appear to have regulatory requirements at least as stringent as those in the United States.[23] Other countries use control technologies developed in the United States.

As shown in Table 1-1, between 1972 and 1988, the majority of the expenditures for environmental quality were devoted to pollution abatement and control; only a fraction was spent on regulation and monitoring and on research and development. Industries, as one would expect, have the highest expenditures for pollution abatement and control. Although spending for pollution control equipment is undoubtedly the most expensive component of the total, the relatively small amount allocated to these

Figure 1-1 Total Expenditures for Pollution Control, Assuming Full Implementation of Laws, 1972-2000

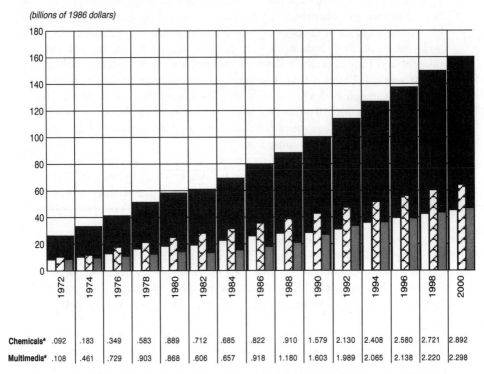

(billions of 1986 dollars)

	1972	1974	1976	1978	1980	1982	1984	1986	1988	1990	1992	1994	1996	1998	2000
Chemicals*	.092	.183	.349	.583	.889	.712	.685	.822	.910	1.579	2.130	2.408	2.580	2.721	2.892
Multimedia*	.108	.461	.729	.903	.868	.606	.657	.918	1.180	1.603	1.989	2.065	2.138	2.220	2.298

* Expenditures associated with chemicals and multimedia are too small to be represented graphically. Therefore, they are simply listed here.

■ Total   ▢ Air and Radiation   ▨ Water   ▨ Land

Source: Environmental Protection Agency, *Environmental Investments: The Cost of a Clean Environment* (Washington, D.C.: EPA, 1990), 3-1.
Note: Chemicals: hazardous chemicals that have economic value and are not simply waste products. Multimedia: more than one environmental medium (air, water, land).

other purposes means that we have limited information about pollution trends and levels, the effects of pollutants on humans and ecosystems, and options for reducing emissions. One of the key debates in environmental policy is whether a greater investment in research and data collecting would result in more effective regulatory efforts.

In 1984 and 1988, state and local governments spent about four times as much as the federal government for pollution control. Although the states have the primary responsibility for enforcing most environmental laws, they spent only about as much as the federal government did on regulation and monitoring in those years. One of the most important challenges confronting state and federal policymakers is to generate support for increased spending for research and monitoring so that air pollution problems can be better understood. Table 1-1 also demonstrates that spending to control air and water pollution were roughly equal, whereas expenditures for solid waste collection and disposal were about one-half of the amounts spent for the other two categories. Although expenditures for control of air and water pollution dominate now, projections for the end of the century indicate that spending for collection and disposal of solid waste will approach that for control of air and water pollution.

By 1994, states' frustration with "unfunded mandates"— requirements the federal government imposed on states without providing funding to meet those obligations—became a rallying cry for governors and critics of federal policies.[24] While unfunded mandates were a concern across the policy spectrum, environmental regulations were often highlighted. Table 1-2 presents the results of a widely reported study done for the U.S. Conference of Mayors that estimated the cost to cities of certain federal environmental requirements.[25] The debate over unfunded mandates largely failed to discuss the billions of dollars of federal grants to state and local governments in other areas, used figures concerning costs of compliance that were often little more than educated guesses, and failed to account for the interstate nature of pollution. Nevertheless, the demand for reducing federally imposed regulations on states was overwhelming in 1994 and 1995. In February 1995, Congress enacted legislation that made it much more difficult for the federal government to impose regulatory responsibilities on states and local governments without providing money to pay for them. New laws that include unfunded mandates on states and localities are subject to special procedural provisions that permit members of Congress to block these bills and require special votes to proceed.[26] This legislation and other actions taken by the Republican-led Congress to change environmental regulation are discussed in Chapter 6.

From a public health perspective, the costs that are most relevant are those of continued high levels of air pollution. From the perspective of economic competitiveness, however, the reduction in risk to public health is less important than the threat of lost jobs and factory shutdowns. But it is not at all clear that this balancing of costs and risks is satisfactory or inevitable. Once an acceptable level of pollution is reached, for example, there is little incentive for industry to reduce emissions further. The health hazard posed by pollution comes to be accepted by society as inevitable, even though in other areas, such as air travel or disease prevention, we continue to strive for reduced risk.

Barry Commoner, a biologist who has been one of the most visible critics of the EPA, and Gus Speth, former president of the World Resources Institute, make the case for pollution prevention from public health and

Table 1-1 Total Expenditures for Improving Environmental Quality, 1972-1988 (billions of current and constant [1982] dollars)

By Type of Activity

Year	Pollution abatement and control[a]		Regulation and monitoring		Research and development		Total	
	Current	Constant	Current	Constant	Current	Constant	Current	Constant
1972	16.7	40.3	0.4	0.8	0.8	1.9	18.1	43.0
1976	31.9	53.2	0.7	1.2	1.3	2.2	33.9	56.5
1980	50.5	58.4	1.3	1.5	1.8	2.1	53.5	62.1
1984	65.2	61.3	1.4	1.2	2.3	2.2	68.9	64.7
1988	81.5	70.0	1.7	1.3	2.8	2.3	85.9	73.7

By Type of Pollution

Year	Air		Water		Solid waste	
	Current	Constant	Current	Constant	Current	Constant
1972	5.6	14.6	8.5	19.7	3.3	7.1
1976	12.6	21.7	14.9	24.5	5.2	8.4
1980	24.7	21.3	24.7	8.8	10.7	10.7
1984	29.6	28.6	25.2	23.3	11.8	10.8
1988	31.9	29.3	32.2	27.5	18.8	14.6

By Sector[b]

Year	Pollution abatement and control					Regulation and monitoring		Research and development		
	Private/personal	Business	Federal government	State government	Local government	Federal government	State/local government	Private	Federal government	State/local government
1972	3.26	31.50	0.35	2.85	7.07	0.40	0.38	1.26	0.47	0.21
1976	6.46	33.23	0.81	2.92	9.73	0.62	0.53	1.22	0.88	0.07
1980	7.16	37.89	0.58	3.29	9.50	0.93	0.61	1.31	0.70	0.08
1984	10.57	39.50	0.88	3.51	6.87	0.68	0.55	1.58	0.55	0.02
1988	11.01	45.54	1.13	4.45	7.87	0.68	0.66	1.74	0.55	0.02

Source: Council on Environmental Quality, *Environmental Quality: 21st Annual Report* (Washington, D.C.: CEQ, 1990), Part 2, tables 9-11.

Notes: Excludes agricultural production except for feedlot operations. Interest costs are not included. Totals may not agree because of independent rounding.

a Spending for goods and services that U.S. residents use to produce cleaner air and water and to collect and dispose of solid waste.

b In billions of constant (1982) dollars.

c Spending to purchase and operate motor vehicle emission reduction devices.

Table 1-2   Current and Projected Cost of Federal Environmental
                 Requirements, per city

Mandate	Total Cost (Fiscal 1993)	Projected Cost (Fiscal 1994-1998)
Underground storage tanks	$ 161,148	$ 1,040,627
Clean Water Act/wetlands	3,612,533	29,303,379
Clean Air Act	403,820	3,651,550
Solid waste disposal	881,575	5,475,968
Safe Drinking Water Act	562,332	8,644,145
Asbestos	129,308	746,828
Lead-based paint	118,217	1,628,228
Endangered species	36,958	189,488
Americans with Disabilities Act	355,681	2,195,808
Fair Labor Standards Act	212,123	1,121,524

Source: Price Waterhouse for the U.S. Conference of Mayors. Reprinted from *Congressional Quarterly Weekly Report* 54 (December 31, 1994): 3605.

ecological preservation perspectives. Commoner argues that environmental goals are much more likely to be achieved if changes are required in industrial design. He points out that progress in remedying most environmental problems has been quite slow and much less successful than has been envisioned in virtually every environmental statute and that the only real successes have come when basic changes have been made in the means or technology of production.[27] An alternative to attempting to trap pollution with control equipment is to try to prevent it; for example, lead emissions fell by 86 percent between 1975 and 1985, primarily because lead was removed from most gasoline sold. Concentrations of polychlorinated biphenyl (PCB) in body fat declined by 75 percent a few years after its production was banned in 1979. The concentration of mercury in lake sediments decreased by 80 percent between 1970 and 1979 because of the discovery of substitutes for it in chlorine production.[28] (Nonpolluting substitutes are not available for all pollution sources, however.)

Gus Speth has also emphasized the importance of promoting "rapid and far-reaching technological change." Economic growth and environmental sustainability will occur only "if there is a transformation in technology; a shift, unprecedented in scope and pace, to technologies— high and low, soft and hard—that facilitates economic growth while sharply reducing the pressures on the natural environment." Environmental considerations must be "integrated into the basic design of our transportation, energy, and other systems." Regulation must ensure that the "major sectors of the U.S. economy—manufacturing, agriculture, transportation, housing, and energy—[are] redesigned in the years ahead so that they fulfill economic needs without destroying our national and global environments."[29]

Many companies have found that the public health or ecological preservation perspective also makes economic sense. Pollution is ultimately waste and reducing it saves money. This idea was codified in the Pollution Prevention Act of 1990, which encouraged companies to prevent waste generation and to recycle waste whenever "feasible."[30] In some cases, however, imposing controls or making changes in a manufacturing process may be more expensive than simply producing waste. Moreover, the materials might themselves be underpriced if the real cost of producing them is not reflected in their price. In other cases, companies may simply lack the information or technology to improve their operations or meet other investment priorities. The costs of dealing with pollution and the demands of consumers for "greener" products can also have a powerful effect on corporate decision making.[31] The costs of disposing of hazardous waste, and the liability costs imposed through litigation, are major expenses in some industries. Liability for cleaning up toxic waste sites can be ascribed to virtually any company that had any involvement with operations, including those that merely lent money. Responsibility can be retroactive and can be based on ability to pay rather than on the amount of waste produced. There are tremendous opportunities for technological entrepreneurs who can develop cleaner sources of energy, more effective ways of recycling, and more environmentally friendly products. Industries that are ahead of their competitors in this regard can introduce new pollution control technologies according to their own schedule, gain further market advantages, and help shape the requirements that will likely be reflected in regulation since regulatory requirements are often based on existing controls.[32]

Environmental quality is increasingly viewed as a precondition for a healthy, sustainable economy.[33] An engineer for a Swedish firm emphasized industry's inevitable interest in the environment this way: "We treat nature like we treated workers a hundred years ago. We included then no cost for the health and social security of workers in our calculations, and today we include no cost for the health and security of nature." [34] In some countries, environmental regulation may follow the pattern of social regulation. Although one can argue about its ultimate consequences for the economy, environmental regulation, like social welfare, will come to be seen as a prerequisite for all economic activity.

Some believe that a transformation toward an ecologically based commerce is about to occur, that businesses are on the verge of reconstructing commerce and creating an economy that will "restore ecosystems and protect the environment while bringing forth innovation, prosperity, meaningful work, and true security."[35] For others, economic rationality is not enough to produce a movement to an environmentally sustainable econo-my. For them, a new paradigm is required, a "higher and more thorough rationality" that links our well-being with that of others, and with the well-being of other life forms and the biosphere itself.[36]

Chemical companies in the United States and Europe appear to be undergoing the most dramatic transformation in environmental con-sciousness, for they are allocating a large percentage of their spending to environmental protection. One of the most striking aspects of this change is the extent to which some companies have gone beyond minimum regu-latory requirements. Both Monsanto and DuPont have voluntarily reduced emissions of hazardous air pollutants and have pledged to eliminate them entirely. Some companies have also embraced the idea of zero emissions as a parallel to having no product defects. These companies have found that environmental damage is more cheaply thwarted through prevention than through installation of equipment at the end of the pipe or, even worse, cleaning up pollution after emission.[37] By basing arguments for regulation on economic benefits—true costs, expanding market shares, money saved from reduced use of raw materials, long-run economic viability—it may be easier to attract industry support and overcome opposition. The economic case for pollution control is clear and persuasive, particularly from a long-run perspective. But the public health perspective is also a powerful one. Will it lose some of its moral force if it is reduced to an appeal for compa-nies to act in ways that are in their self-interest?

Although many people continue to resist regulation as inconsistent with economic growth, it is becoming increasingly clear that environmental quality and economic health can be compatible policy goals. Attainment of environmental goals requires economic resources; healthy economies have many more resources to invest in achieving and preserving environmental quality than do faltering economies. Modernization of industrial processes can improve the quality of products as well as reduce air and water pollu-tion. In the short run, regulation imposes costs that may be quite burden-some, but in the long run regulation can contribute to modernization, increased efficiency, and global competitiveness. Companies that develop cleaner, more environmentally sensitive processes have access to lucrative worldwide markets. The regulatory requirements imposed on some indus-tries have created new markets and customers for producers of pollution control equipment. One of the greatest challenges in environmental policy making, and one of the clearest criteria by which the Clean Air Act and other statutes can be assessed, is the development of specific policy interventions that balance environmental protection with long-run economic viability.

Some companies are changing. Twenty years ago, 3M developed its Pollution Prevention Pays program, an integrated effort to redesign man-ufacturing to reduce emissions. By 1990, the company had saved $537 million and reduced air pollution by 120,000 tons; wastewater by 1 billion gallons; and solid waste by 410,000 tons. In 1986, the plan was amended to include the goal, which was achieved, of eliminating all emissions by the 1990s. Other companies are coming to see that industrial processes that produce waste are more costly in the long run than cleaner processes. Environmental protection can be part of an innovative, growing, successful industrial strategy.[38]

Despite their success, however, these efforts only scratch the surface. Public policies need to combine with these industrial innovations to create strong incentives for maintaining and expanding these efforts and to see that they occur on an international basis. International agreements are critical for ensuring that all industrial activities take place under common rules. But international agreements will need to include decentralized implementation and enforcement mechanisms that are based on true cost pricing, which requires companies to include all the costs of production, including pollution prevention, in the prices they charge. "Green" taxes are essential for internalizing more of the total costs of production and creating incentives for designers to produce products that are environmentally safer. Market prices need to be adjusted to include all the costs of production; current market prices do not recognize the damage resulting from production, since market competition favors producers who offer the lowest prices, not those whose price reflects all the costs production. Costs that should be internalized include the spillover effects, the damage to the environment or public health caused by the release of dangerous by-products, and the costs to future generations of pollution and resource loss.[39]

Formulation and Enactment

The second step in the policy process includes formulating a program to respond to the demand for action, getting it on the policy agenda of the governing body that is to take action, enacting legislation to authorize the program's implementation, and appropriating sufficient funds for implementation. This requires the interaction of the legislature, the groups advocating the proposal, and the executive branch agency that will ultimately be responsible for implementing the policy. Proposals that are supported by interests with political clout and large financial resources for congressional campaign contributions and other efforts are much more likely to be acted upon and implemented than those that are not.

The coalition building and compromise that are central to the legislative process often result in laws that are imprecise and leave much room for interpretation by administrative officials. Difficult choices might be deferred to the agency implementing the policy, thus deflecting the political controversy from the legislative process to the administrative process. The political environment in which agencies operate is thus highly charged because agencies end up making basic policy decisions that are expected to satisfy the various interests affected. Even legislation that is quite specific usually gives agencies responsibilities that greatly exceed their resources, requiring that they set priorities and make choices. An assessment of the Clean Air Act requires some reflection on the general process of translating policy demands into laws. Public policies are influenced by political factors; political motivations, calculations, and concerns thus usually overwhelm technical analyses in importance. The success of policymakers in accurately defining the nature and causes of problems and in developing and implementing effective solutions is a function of policy analysis as well as political acumen and luck.

Environmental law and regulation are at a critical point in their development in the United States. Considerable progress has been made in cleaning up some of the most egregious and visible forms of air and water pollution. There is in place a complex infrastructure of agencies, legislation, regulations, and enforcement mechanisms for protecting the environment. Government (federal, state, and local), regulated industry, the scientific community, and public interest groups have all invested significant resources in addressing the challenges of assessing environmental and health risks and enforcing laws and regulations.

The environmental and health hazards that remain are among the most difficult to address. Regulating these pollutants frequently means increasingly larger compliance costs for increasingly smaller increments of protection and hazard reduction. Some problems, such as atmospheric pollution, transcend national boundaries and require international cooperation on an unprecedented scale.

The current policy debate is dominated by basic questions such as how much authority, flexibility, and responsibility should be given to the EPA and other federal and state agencies and how environmental statutes might be restructured in a way that will permit more effective and potentially more comprehensive policy making. It is not at all clear that the regulatory system (environmental laws, EPA regulations, and state enforcement programs) now in place is capable of addressing these increasingly complex environmental problems.[40]

Some critics of regulation argue that more protection should be given to private property rights, and that a system of private property rights, enforced by lawsuits, is more efficient and effective than the conventional approach to regulation. The more complex the world, Richard Epstein argues, the less likely are lawmakers and rule writers to know how things interact and to be able to anticipate possible problems. As a law becomes more complex, it becomes increasingly bureaucratic and rigid, and less efficient and effective. A legal framework based on principles of the common law, according to Epstein, can address 90 to 95 percent of the disputes and problems that regulation tries to address, but at much lower cost and with much greater individual freedom. These principles include private ownership of virtually everything of value, tort law to protect individuals against harm from others, the right to contract with others for virtually any transaction, and the taking of private property by government in a few cases of overwhelming public necessity along with compensation to private property owners when government actions take or reduce the value of property. Environmental regulation, under Epstein's approach, can largely be reduced to "polluter-pays" laws that rely on markets in pollution rights.[41]

There is also an important debate over the success of different statutory approaches in achieving the most effective implementation of environmental policies to attain policy goals. A common assumption is that the approach of all environmental laws resembles that of the Clean Air Act of 1970, the oldest major environmental law. A closer examination, however, reveals that some statutes include clear and specific delegations of authority to administrative agencies, whereas others allow more agency flexibility.

Environmental statutes enacted in the late 1970s and early 1980s and designed in response to the congressional abdication of policy-making power that characterized regulatory statutes enacted during the New Deal have placed a variety of checks on agency actions. The paralyzing effect of these fetters may not have been anticipated by congressional advocates of the programs affected, but the efforts to ensure greater agency accountability also limit the ability of administrative agencies to accomplish the tasks delegated to them.[42]

Others have argued that environmental and other laws have become too prescriptive, too detailed, and too anxious to anticipate every possible problem and prevent all harms. This results in delay, excessive compliance costs, paralysis, and frustration with government. People are fearful of fraud, waste, and abuse of discretionary powers, and believe that detailed rules and regulations can prevent them from happening; they thus try to anticipate every eventuality, ensure consistency and uniformity, and avoid—at almost any cost—discretion by regulatory officials. As Philip K. Howard has argued,

> We seem to have achieved the worst of both worlds: a system of regulation that goes too far while it also does too little. This paradox is explained by the absence of the one indispensable ingredient of any successful human endeavor: use of judgment. In the decades since World War II, we have constructed a system of regulatory law that basically outlaws common sense.[43]

Regulators *need* to be given flexibility and discretion so that they can use judgment in applying general rules to specific situations. We must give regulatory officials clear goals and then hold them accountable for achieving them. If there is no flexibility for regulators, there will be inadequate flexibility for regulated industries.[44] A 1995 report commissioned by Congress and completed by the National Academy of Public Administration concluded that Congress needs to give the EPA more flexibility and discretion in order to accomplish the nation's environmental goals.[45] Similarly, the EPA must give more decision-making authority to the states and local governments and to regulated industries. According to the report, there should be more attention focused on results and less on mandates for how those results are to be obtained:

In the past two decades, the United States has made extraordinary progress in reducing pollution from the biggest and most obvious sources. To continue to make environmental progress, the nation will have to develop a more rational, less costly strategy for protecting the environment, one that achieves its goals more efficiently, using more creativity and less bureaucracy.[46]

Most environmental statutes are extremely broad and ambitiously promise to reduce or eliminate virtually all environmental and health hazards, but they reflect little consideration of the costs of achieving that goal. Some statutes include very specific mandates for the implementing agencies, particularly the EPA. These statutes read much like agency regulations: they sometimes include emission standards, or impose deadlines for agency actions; some include "hammer" provisions, which go into effect if the agency does not issue a regulation by a certain deadline to deal with specified problems. Although there are certainly many areas in which environmental problems are poorly understood, even when solutions are relatively clear the policy-making process often fails to develop and implement effective remedies.[47]

Regulation and the Structure of Government. In designing the American political system, the framers of the Constitution intended policy making to be inefficient, to check the power of policymakers, and to permit action only when there is widespread support among different constituencies and their representative institutions. Deliberative democracy, once defended as an ideal, is now frequently afflicted by institutional deadlock, causing elected officials to resign or retire in frustration. Many people believe the institutional obstructions to coherent, unified, and effective policy making prevent the United States from responding to the challenges confronting it. Divided government, in which the legislative and executive branches are dominated by leaders of different political parties whose primary goal is the political defeat of the opposition, makes effective policy making extremely difficult at best, and often impossible.[48]

There is little agreement on how policy making can best proceed in a system of divided government.[49] A tradition of bipartisanship in foreign policy offers some hope that the divisiveness of political competition can be overcome as environmental pollution comes to be viewed universally as a major threat to U.S. interests.[50] Other examples of domestic policy making demonstrate the ability of Congress and the president to work together when major problems must be addressed.[51] Charles O. Jones's analysis of the passage of twenty-eight major pieces of legislation during the past fifty years illustrates great variety in congressional-presidential relationships and a great deal of creativity and flexibility as Congress and the president find ways to work together in passing laws.[52] David Mayhew's study of 267 major laws passed by Congress during the last quarter-century also provides compelling evidence that a system of separated powers and politically divided government can work in ways that are consistent with our constitutional expectations.[53]

Some partisans urge confrontational, hardball politics that highlight differences. For presidents, the strategy is often to use their institutional prerogative and address the nation directly, sometimes coupling this with aggressive use of the veto power. Members of Congress can use their institutional prerogative to produce legislation that is extremely detailed and leaves a minimum of flexibility and discretion to the executive branch.[54]

The tension that is part of divided government and political competition, along with the separation of powers and competing institutional prerogatives, has implications for the kind of legislation that Congress enacts. Some scholars have long argued the importance of statutes that give implementing agencies unambiguous direction, preserve a commitment to the rule of law, and limit bureaucratic discretion. Others argue that the price of political compromise and policy complexity is the passage of statutes that blur distinctions and permit differing interpretations.[55] The tension between the two branches of government during the 1980s and 1990s has focused debate on how specific statutes ought to be. Should they minimize administrative discretion, so that congressional will is more likely to prevail? Should they include deadlines for executive action and legislative hammer provisions? Or should laws give administrative officials the kind of discretion and freedom that will permit flexible and, it is hoped, efficient administration?[56] Such a debate has been taking place throughout government, but it has been particularly sharp in Congress with regard to environmental legislation because of the deep frustration many members had with the EPA during the early years of the Reagan administration, when the ranking agency officials defied their congressional overseers and rejected traditional interpretations of congressional intent concerning many environmental statutes.

Federalism. Environmental regulation is further complicated by the politics of federalism. The structure of federal-state relations is at the heart of the implementation of environmental regulation. Scholars have developed models of federalism that help illuminate the way in which environmental and other laws are implemented. James P. Lester, for example, has argued that federal-state relationships take several forms, and offers a four-fold typology: (1) states and the federal government form a partnership, with interdependent relations aimed at facilitating or enhancing state capacity; (2) states are dependent on the federal government for resources and assistance; (3) states have some independence from federal agencies and have their own resources, institutions, and programs; or (4) states are disengaged from the federal government and resist its intrusion.[57]

Patricia McGee Crotty describes regulatory federalism as "centrally directed sharing," in which the federal government determines the rules for states and federal powers preempt state powers. Intergovernmental relations "are neither cooperative nor competitive but rather regulative."[58] States are far from powerless: they can use their implementation efforts as bargaining chips in dealing with the EPA. The EPA, in turn, can threaten to impose sanctions such as ordering a cutoff of highway funds.

David M. Welborn uses the term "conjoint federalism" to emphasize the blending of federal and state authority. Most environmental laws fall into this category: the EPA establishes national standards, and responsibility for implementation rests with the states, although concurrent enforcement efforts can occur. Welborn argues that conjoint federalism is the only reasonable structural adaptation in the modern regulatory state since there is a need for national policy making but total federal preemption is impossible.[59] "Picket-fence" federalism describes state governments as independent, balkanized bureaucracies that make coordination of policy efforts difficult and insulate bureaucratic officials from broader political control.[60]

These and other models of intergovernmental relations emphasize the tension that arises between the federal and state governments in the implementation of environmental laws. At the state level, citizen groups have lobbied for legislation that is more protective of health and the environment, sponsored ballot initiatives when state legislatures have failed to take action, organized boycotts of products sold by companies that fail to protect the environment or that otherwise increase health risks, conducted research on environment-related health problems, and established communication networks for victims of environmental hazards and other concerned individuals. Enforcement of laws and regulations may not occur or standards may be lowered as a result of state politics[61] or state efforts to remedy local problems may be impeded by rigid national standards.[62] Many state officials resent federal intrusion in their affairs, fearing that the enlargement of federal authority threatens the viability of federalism and state government. Others seek provisions permitting states to opt out of certain federally mandated programs if local conditions warrant such exceptions.

Further, state legislatures may fail to delegate sufficient authority to regulatory bodies for them to effectively implement environmental laws and may fail to provide adequate staffing of state regulatory agencies. Some state officials fear that effective enforcement of environmental laws will discourage investment and development. The level of compliance among regulated industries and state and local governments is often minimal, a result of ineffective implementation of federal laws by state regulatory agencies as well as federal bureaucratic problems.[63] Evan J. Ringquist's study of state environmental protection efforts emphasized that although technical conditions limit state efforts to some degree, the primary limitation is government's limited ability to change social norms and values in ways that lead to more environmentally sensitive behaviors.[64]

There is considerable tension in states between demands for environmental protection and efforts to promote economic growth. As noted earlier, most Americans surveyed in nationwide polls say that protecting the environment is so important that it should be done regardless of cost, but there are also real fears among many Americans that environmental regulation will result in layoffs and plant shutdowns. Despite the existence of national standards, states may engage in bidding wars to attract new industries that may raise questions of how stringent state environmental regulations and enforcement are. But states are not monolithic; environmental regulation officials and their allies in the state legislatures and governors' offices may compete with economic development agencies and their political proponents. Some states have largely settled this issue one way or the other, but in others the battle goes on.[65]

The debate over the role of states in policy formation and implementation shifted dramatically in 1994 as Republicans made major gains in capturing statehouses and found allies in the new Republican leadership in Congress. This issue is discussed in more detail in Chapter 6. But the demands by states to be given more latitude in devising their own solutions to environmental and other public problems have become a groundswell. Criticism of, and frustration with, federal bureaucrats and regulations, and the ambition of governors who have aggressive policy agendas and seek the freedom to pursue them, have combined to create powerful pressure for devolution of power to the states. But the federal role in environmental regulation grew in the 1970s and 1980s because of the failure of states to act on pollution problems, and because of the interstate nature of pollution. Can states really be free to be authors of their own environmental policies when their neighbors upstream or upwind have a different set of priorities?

Implementation

Implementation, the third step in the policy process, is often a long, complicated procedure that includes interpreting congressional intent, balancing statutory and presidential priorities, creating administrative structures and processes, reviewing congressional debates on policy formulation as regulations are devised, and building political support for enforcement of regulatory requirements. This model of the policy process assumes a simple relationship between policy formulation and implementation that largely mirrors the separation of powers: Congress makes the policy choices and the executive branch and the states implement them. It reflects a widely held perception that major policy decisions are the responsibility of elected representatives. In reality, the line between making and implementing policies is blurred and there is much overlap; those who implement laws are often required to make policy choices.

Implementation can be simply defined as the carrying out of public policies, the achievement of the consequences promised when policies are formulated, or the forging of the required links in a causal chain that will accomplish the goals articulated for the policies.[66] Implementation includes those events and activities, such as the effort to administer the policy and the substantive impact a policy will have on people and events, that occur after the issuing of authoritative public policy directives. This definition encompasses not only the behavior of the administrative body that has responsibility for the program and for the compliance of target groups, but also both the web of direct and indirect political, economic, and social forces that bear on the behavior of all those involved and, ultimately, the impact—the intended and unintended consequences—of the program.[67]

There are a great number of reasons why implementation of public policies in general is so difficult. Some implementation fails to achieve its objectives because of a lack of political will or agreement. Other efforts suffer from inadequate funding or authority. Environmental goals must compete with other policy objectives. Even within a given policy area, there are multiple goals that often conflict with each other. The price of political compromise is often vagueness, and there may be little agreement over what exactly the goals of a particular policy are. Implementation is a continuation of the politics of policy formulation, but with some new actors, procedures, and institutional settings. As implementation efforts proceed, administrators become aware of new problems, constraints, and opportunities, and resources and goals are constantly in flux. Unintended consequences pervade policy implementation efforts.[68]

One of the most important challenges in formulating environmental policy is to structure the law in such a way that it will be effectively implemented. Incentives, ranging from sanctions and other penalties to subsidies and technical assistance, can be used to induce compliance by regulated industries. All recent presidential administrations, from Ford's to Clinton's, have emphasized the advantages of cooperation and consensus building rather than confrontation in implementing regulations. Government agencies do not have the resources to monitor every source, so the willingness of regulated industries to comply with regulations is important. Compliance might be enhanced if industry officials are allowed to participate in formulating standards, thus encouraging a sense of shared responsibility for making them work. But the fundamental nature of regulation cannot be disguised; it is designed to get industries to do things they otherwise would probably not do. There are clear incentives for industry to delay implementation of regulations, so an agency committed to consensus building and cooperation is faced with a real challenge.

At the heart of implementation are the inevitable trade-offs, such as choosing either more centralized control and consistency or decentralized flexibility, community control, and decentralization.[69] As a consequence of these and other competing concerns, implementation often seems to be unsuccessful in accomplishing the policy goals expected of it. Much criticism has centered on the means by which the EPA and other agencies that choose centralized-control approaches pursue environmental goals, and particularly on the inefficiency resulting from national standards that are imposed on all sources regardless of local conditions and environmental needs.

Traditional Approaches to Regulation. The most common regulatory approach employed by the EPA and other agencies to implement and enforce statutes and regulations is often described as "command and control." The agency sets specific requirements with which sources of pollution must comply, and enforcement responsibilities are turned over to the states. One advantage of this combination of national standard setting and decentralized enforcement is that expertise and knowledge concerning basic requirements are concentrated in the federal agency, but local variations and needs can be accommodated.

The command-and-control approach has been widely criticized, however, for being excessively rigid and insensitive to geographical and technological differences and for being inefficient. Uniform standards are more expensive than they need to be for some facilities, and there is no provision of incentives for polluters to develop more effective means of reducing emissions—rather, past polluters are inadvertently rewarded. Aggressive enforcement by a state may encounter political opposition because it discourages investment in new facilities that are more efficient and less damaging to the environment.

One way of characterizing this debate over statutory strategies is to differentiate between goal-oriented and rule-oriented statutes.[70] Some statutes are expressions of broad goals that give general guidance and direction to regulatory agencies and require that they develop policy details, whereas others provide specific rules that agencies are to administer. Some strategies are more compatible with certain kinds of environmental problems. The formulation and enactment of environmental statutes must be guided by a careful consideration of the imperatives of implementation and enforcement. Agencies must be given enough flexibility to permit rational administration, yet not so much discretion that the rule of law is threatened and congressional intent jeopardized.

Marketlike Incentives. One way government regulations can be made more effective is to increase the incentives for compliance—that is, to provide positive inducements for reducing pollution rather than relying on fear of penalties. Market, or economic incentives have been increasingly heralded as the most effective mechanism for accomplishing environmental goals. Since the costs of controlling pollution vary so widely among firms, efficiency demands that "the degree by which individual sources have to reduce their pollution discharges should vary."[71] If sources of pollution are permitted to find the cheapest way of reducing emissions, the costs of pollution control will be minimized.

Incentives are also championed as being essential to "harnessing the 'base' motive of material self-interest to promote the common good."[72] It is simply not effective to condemn polluters as being immoral or selfish; what is needed are clear incentives to encourage them to change their behavior, to ensure that they take actions that are consonant with the public good. Regulatory policies that rely on economic incentives include:

1. Taxes levied on emissions of pollutants or on inputs to activities producing pollutants;
2. Fees that are part of pollution discharge permits or other regulatory requirements;
3. Emission allowances that can be traded, banked, or saved for future use, or sold by polluting companies as long as limits on total emissions are not exceeded;
4. Tax concessions or direct subsidies for antipollution control investments;
5. Deposits and refunds on products;
6. Legal liability and associated fines for certain kinds of pollution.[73]

One important market-oriented innovation developed by the EPA in 1974 was an emissions trading program that allows companies to receive credit for reducing emissions in some areas that can be used for higher emissions elsewhere. The EPA views total emissions from each industry plant as encapsulated within a large "bubble" rather than attempting to regulate individual smokestacks. Regulatory officials establish maximum total allowable emissions and allow plant managers to determine emissions from individual sources. Sources can "bank" emissions for future credits or sell them to new sources that need to purchase offsets of existing emissions in order to operate.[74]

Another way in which economic incentives are harnessed to improve environmental quality is through imposing a pollution tax. The regulatory agency first places a limit on the amount of each pollutant to be emitted. Permits to release a pollutant up to the level allowed by the regulatory agency are either auctioned to the highest bidder or sold at a fixed price, and companies are prohibited from emitting pollutants without a permit. The number of permits or amount of each emission can be reduced over time, thereby diminishing total emissions. The agency may also tax each unit of pollutant emitted; the tax can be higher for emissions that exceed levels provided for in the permit. The permit system ensures that air quality standards are met, and the tax provides an incentive for polluters to reduce their emissions further than is required. Revenue from the permits and tax can be used to fund the regulatory program, sponsor research on the health effects of air pollution, treat individuals suffering from respiratory diseases, and subsidize efforts to develop less polluting industrial processes.

A pollution tax or fee, if it is high enough, can encourage companies to reduce their emissions below permitted levels in whatever way is most efficient for them—closing down some operations, using cleaner fuels, investing in control technologies, or changing work practices. Under the traditional approach to regulation, companies gained no economic advantage from emitting less pollution than was legally permitted them; with the pollution tax, they save money every time they reduce emissions. Pollution taxes are considered a cost factor in production; they preserve the flexibility and autonomous decision making that are important to businesses, as well as minimize the need for coercion. Agency officials are also given important incentives to enforce the law if pollution tax revenues remain with the agency. Companies that are complying with the law support strong enforcement efforts aimed at ensuring that their competitors also pay the required taxes.

The 1986 Emergency Planning and Community Right-to-Know Act, a separate law that is technically Title III of the Comprehensive Environmental Response, Compensation, and Liability Act of 1980 (the "Superfund" law, which was aimed at the cleanup of hazardous wastes), is another good example of the way market forces can encourage companies to reduce emissions. The law requires companies to publicly disclose their emission of hazardous air pollutants, thus creating an incentive to reduce emissions to avoid generating public fears and criticism.

The use of economic incentives to reduce pollution may represent a middle ground that is important in public debate. Conservatives can champion an approach that tries to make markets work, is consistent with a market economy, and promotes autonomy for business decision makers. Liberals who favor environmental protection can get more of it for the same level of expenditure. Pollution taxes and emissions permit charges are a form of user fees that ensures that those who benefit from the use of a natural resource pay for those benefits.[75]

Market-oriented approaches are not the solution to every environmental problem in every economy. A combination of market incentives and other approaches such as technological control mandates and bans on certain activities will likely be required in comprehensive regulatory programs. But market incentives are believed by many to be the key to ensuring that environmental goals are achieved at lower costs than are possible using bureaucratic, centralized approaches. Most important, they are central in moving toward an economy where the total social costs of production are reflected in the prices charged.[76]

There are, however, considerable barriers to overcome in relying on economic incentives. Critics argue that the environment is an endowment that is shared by everyone. Placing the values of this endowment in a market would ultimately result in their unequal distribution and eventual devaluation.[77] Furthermore, such incentives fail to recognize the importance of preventing pollution. Barry Commoner, for example, emphasizes that technological changes that reduce or eliminate emissions, rather than a focus on treatment and disposal, are needed. For Commoner, the creation of a free market in pollution simply allows companies to buy permits when they choose not to install mechanisms to control or prevent pollution. Giving polluters a certain quantity of pollution they can emit

is a perverse parody of the "free market." . . . Instead of goods—useful things that people want—being exchanged, "bads" that nobody wants are traded. It is a market that cannot operate unless it is provided with what it is supposed to exchange—pollutants. This is a proposal that not only fails to prevent pollution but actually *requires* it.[78]

Marketlike incentives may send the signal that pollution is acceptable if the polluter is wealthy enough to pay for it. Moreover, regulators usually lack sufficient information about the economic status of individual firms to permit them to set pollution taxes at the optimal level. And industry groups, usually vigorous proponents of market incentives that do not cost them anything, like emissions trading, quickly withdraw their support when pollution taxes or fees are proposed.

The debate over marketlike approaches to regulation reinforces the importance of devising effective means of implementing policies. An analysis of policy implementation should focus on questions such as the extent to which the provisions of the act are likely to be implemented, the major challenges that will confront those who will be involved in implementing it, and whether federal and state officials have been given the tools they need to achieve the policy goals assigned them. Recent environmental statutes have been ambitious in their goals, yet specific in their mandates. Regulatory agencies such as the EPA are expected to fulfill the expectations that have been raised, yet have been given only limited discretion and resources to do so.

Impact and Evaluation

Policy evaluation or analysis is not simply the last step in the policy-making process; it plays a role throughout the entire process. Congress and the executive branch oversee the implementation of the law or policy and regularly assess the effectiveness of its major provisions, including the clarity with which policy goals are expressed. They also consider the extent to which policy objectives have been achieved and reformulate policies as necessary. Administrators are expected to make a politically neutral professional judgment, but policy evaluation by legislators is a very political undertaking, pursued by politicians for a variety of purposes.

Central to the policy-making process is the ability of policymakers to assess the strengths and weaknesses of existing policies and alter them when necessary. Policy analysis in general rests on the expectation that the technical assessment of competing policy options will be separated from the political calculations of the policymakers, and that there will be an objective, nonpolitical assessment of policy options before the inevitable political calculations shape the decisions eventually made. Careful policy analysis should precede the application of narrow political pressure and ensure that policies producing the greatest net gains in social welfare will be pursued. In practice, of course, policy making is a very political exercise.

The reliance of most analytic techniques on measures of economic efficiency and utility may clash with other values such as distributive justice.[79] Reliance on analytic techniques may give the illusion of precision, certainty, and objectivity, when in fact decisions must be made on much more subjective grounds. Policy analysis may enhance the role of experts at the expense of elected officials, thus reducing the accountability of policy making to the people.[80] This model of rational policy analysis and policy making often falls short in providing guidance for policy making that takes place under conditions of uncertainty and in situations where trial and error are inevitable.[81]

Assessing environmental policies is particularly challenging because policy making so often rests on limited knowledge and on scientific and economic analyses that are still being widely debated.[82] Environmental laws give little guidance to federal and state agencies about how to measure and balance costs and benefits in making the ultimate political decisions. Furthermore, the executive and legislative branches of government frequently disagree about the direction environmental regulation should take. (Recent Republican presidents were preoccupied with the health of the economy, whereas a Democratic majority in Congress emphasized a broad range of domestic policies.) For many congressional sponsors of environmental legislation, reducing hazards is the primary goal; costs are secondary. Officials in the executive branch have sought to achieve a balance between economic and environmental policies. The environmental hazards and plant shutdowns that are blamed on expensive regulations can have important electoral consequences. Tension also results from the competition between members of opposing political parties, who are bent on defeating each other. Moreover, there have been judicial challenges to virtually every major regulation issued, delays in issuing regulations, and charges of minimal enforcement and compliance with laws and regulations. Although the debate has been carried on in the media, political campaigns, academic journals, and blue ribbon panels, it might be best understood by reviewing the struggle in the federal government during the past decade over the stringency of environmental regulation and the prioritization of economic growth, pollution reduction, and protection of health. Despite overwhelming public support for environmental quality, there has been a vigorous debate over how that goal is to be achieved and how it interacts with other public policies. The debate reached a kind of culmination in the mid-1990s, as discussed in Chapter 6, but the debate in the 1970s and 1980s provided background for the 1990s as well as for passage of the Clean Air Act Amendments of 1990, and is briefly reviewed below.

Criticisms of Excessive Regulation.   Environmental regulations, particularly those aimed at air pollution, have been widely criticized as being too stringent and unjustified when their expected costs are compared with the benefits they promise. These criticisms are rooted in analyses of the costs and benefits of regulation that were initiated by the Ford administration and continued under President Jimmy Carter. In 1981, President Ronald Reagan directed that the regulatory review process be centered in the Office of Management and Budget (OMB) and established the Presidential Task Force on Regulatory Relief.[83] The Bush administration continued these presidential initiatives and in 1989 created the Council on Competitiveness to oversee regulatory reform efforts. The Clinton administration abolished the council in 1993 but maintained a more modest regulatory review program in the OMB. The debate over risk assessment eventually shifted to Congress in 1993, as discussed in Chapter 6. Despite these shifts, the issues have remained quite constant.

Many OMB officials have been relentless critics of the EPA and other regulatory agencies and, by implication, Congress, for their failure to provide adequate justification for clean air regulations and other regulatory initiatives.[84] These officials have argued that agencies should not take regulatory actions unless sufficient scientific evidence is available to justify them—that is, until scientific uncertainties and ambiguities are reduced or eliminated. In a recent compilation of regulatory actions proposed by several agencies, the OMB summarized its indictment of regulatory agencies: "risk-assessment practices continue to rely on conservative models and assumptions that effectively intermingle important policy judgments within the scientific assessment of risk." As a result, senior agency officials are forced to make regulatory decisions "based on risk assessments in which scientific findings cannot be readily differentiated from embedded policy judgments." Not only does this "make it difficult to discern serious hazards from trivial ones, and distort the ordering of the Government's regulatory priorities," but it may even "increase health and safety risks" by regulating less serious problems and ignoring more serious ones.[85]

The OMB officials also charge that agencies adopt upper bounds of estimates rather than the most likely projections, treat benign tumors as malignant, use the most sensitive species and sex in laboratory tests and in determining acceptable exposure levels, and apply the most cautious models in extrapolating from animals to humans and from low to high exposure levels. Although such conservative approaches may not be particularly unreasonable individually, the cumulative effect is to produce assessments of risks that have "extremely conservative biases" and "do not provide decisionmakers with the information they need to formulate an efficient and cost-effective regulatory strategy." [86]

According to the OMB, a reliance on conservative or worst-case assumptions and analyses may overstate risks by several orders of magnitude. Assessments usually include "margin of safety" factors and upper-bound estimates that really represent policy choices rather than scientific assessments. Although it may make sense to use such approaches initially as screening devices to exclude risks that are shown to be insignificant even in the worst-case scenarios, the OMB complains that agency officials continue to rely on these biased estimates and thus greatly overstate the benefits that would result from regulatory intervention. Given the uncertainties surrounding animal bioassays, agency officials have considerable discretion in determining how results are used. These officials often rely on tests using the most sensitive animals available and expose the animals to such high doses that some response is inevitable. Models used to extrapolate human risks from animal tests, according to the OMB, are from nine to thirty times more likely to produce false positives (the test erroneously appears to demonstrate an effect) than false negatives (the test mistakenly indicates no effect). Models used to extrapolate low doses from high doses require the use of the upper limit of a 95 percent confidence level (so that there is only a 5 percent chance that the real risk exceeds the estimate), rather than the use of an unbiased estimate. The OMB cites differences in modeling that produce estimates of the risk from dioxin, for example, that vary by a figure as high as 5,000.[87]

Risk assessments serve as the basis for calculating the costs and benefits of regulatory options. The OMB has criticized the EPA and other agencies for failing to provide adequate analyses of the benefits and costs of regulations they want to impose. The OMB and other agencies have differed over the calculation of both costs and benefits. Benefits are particularly difficult to determine, as they often rely on minimal information concerning the levels of exposure to the regulated substance and the nature of the exposure-response relationship. But the calculation of costs also requires choices that are not strictly technical. Costs may be limited to direct expenditures for compliance or may include allowances for the projected impact on prices and competitiveness and on unemployment, and for other possible consequences of increased expenditures by the regulated industries. Basic assumptions and beliefs concerning the appropriateness and value of regulations cannot help but color the way in which actual dollar values are assigned in the cost-benefit analysis. Agencies have failed to rely on market-based measures such as the "willingness to pay" that are, for the OMB, the only real means of "comparing alternative sources of value to individuals . . . and allocating goods and services to the highest-valued use."[88]

Cost-benefit analysis is generally understood to require the quantification of all costs and benefits and the calculation of their dollar values in a numerical ratio. These calculations are, of course, extremely controversial when estimating the value of human life or protection of ecosystems. Therefore, calculations of their cost effectiveness means comparing alternative regulatory strategies or different regulations without requiring explicit value calculations. A cost-effective standard requires that the goal be achieved at the lowest cost or that the most good be achieved with the resources available. Cost-benefit analysis, however, requires that the policy goal be justified by showing that the projected benefits exceed the anticipated costs. Agencies may select a regulatory option with the highest cost-effective ratio, and may compare the cost effectiveness of different regulations in deciding whether to pursue them. Problems with this approach remain, and OMB officials have criticized the EPA (and other agencies) because the cost effectiveness of regulations varies greatly.[89]

The OMB and the regulatory agencies have also differed over the selection of discount rates for computing the effects of regulations over time. In many areas of regulatory activity, benefits and costs develop on different time schedules, but their net present values are determined so that alternative regulatory actions can be compared. The net present value is dependent upon the discount rate selected; the higher the rate used, the greater the incentive to defer the effective date of regulations. In general, OMB officials appear to prefer a higher rate than do agencies, thus making it difficult to justify new regulations. Agencies have been hesitant to discount costs and benefits, and that biases decisions in favor of regulatory interventions.[90]

Reports of the president's Council of Economic Advisers (CEA) have also been part of the debate over the costs and benefits of regulation. Markets and the legal system of liability, CEA officials argue, provide sufficient incentives for safety in most cases. Markets "accommodate individual preferences for avoiding risk and produce information that helps people make informed choices." Since many of the most significant risks to health, such as smoking, are a result of individual choice, "government regulation can never replace the need for responsible individual action."[91] The costs of regulation are particularly serious, including "restricting freedom of individual choice" and "retarding innovation, investment, and economic growth." Regulations with the "highest expected net gains should be undertaken first." All statutes and regulations of the federal government should be consistent in their minimization of risk so that the most cost-effective strategy can be pursued. Congress is at fault here, CEA officials believe, because "statutory language sometimes impedes the realization of consistency by setting goals that do not take into account costs."[92]

Many economists also argue that we cannot afford the inefficiency inherent in traditional regulatory schemes and criticize regulation that insulates some companies from competitive forces. They also reject national standards as being inefficient. The diversity of the American economy means that pollution problems are more serious in some areas than in others; therefore, such standards will only perpetuate arbitrariness, inequity, and waste.[93]

Bruce Ackerman and William Hassler, in their criticism of the 1977 Clean Air Act, charge that imposing technological controls on all new stationary sources made policy "in an ecological vacuum—without a sober effort to define the costs and benefits of designing one or another technology into the plants of the future."[94] Robert Crandall has contended that votes on environmental issues demonstrate that members of Congress representing declining industrial areas see regulation as a way to protect their constituents by imposing costs on new facilities locating in the sunbelt. Standards imposed on stationary sources, he argues, "do not generate pollution reduction at the lowest possible cost."[95] For Lester Lave and Gilbert Omenn, "regulation of air pollution imposes costs and causes economic inefficiencies and social disruption. Society desires pristine air, but is not willing to sacrifice much of the standard of living to achieve it."[96] Paul Portney has reviewed studies assessing the costs and benefits of clean air regulation and has concluded that, although there is great uncertainty and wide variation in the estimates of costs and benefits, there is general agreement that it is possible to "substantially reduce the costs of meeting the nation's current air quality goals. . . . By reallocating control effort away from high-cost and toward low-cost sources," he has asserted, "the total cost of pollution control can be reduced while emissions of air pollutants remain constant, or even decline."[97] Bruce Yandle has bemoaned the "rent-seeking" behavior of polluters who use regulation to gain artificial economic advantage (or "rents") by pushing for new source standards that are "set very high, while allowing existing polluters to operate older plants that continue to pollute the environment."[98]

Environmental Politics and Regulatory "Unreasonableness." Environmental policy has been blamed for the inefficiency or "unreasonableness" of environmental regulation. Critics argue that environmentalists have made wildly exaggerated claims to arouse fears as part of their strategy of attacking corporate power to enhance their own political influence and gain passage of strict laws.[99] They are effective at getting commitments from politicians to champion basic positions, but their political base cannot easily direct the details of administration. They captured the agenda-setting power in the 1970s and 1980s, and until recently neither Congress nor the executive branch has been willing to challenge their claims and advocate a more realistic set of expectations and objectives. Environmentalists have convinced the public that the costs of regulation can easily be financed by industry's deep pockets. They, and their allies in Congress, the bureaucracy, the courts, and the media, are willing to impose tremendous regulatory burdens for marginal, hypothetical benefits. Presidents have been unwilling to push for real statutory reform of environmental laws to ensure that they establish mechanisms for balanced policy making; they have only tinkered with short-run administrative changes.[100]

Critics also argue that Congress has passed, and EPA officials have been unwilling to challenge, statutes that provide unrealistic criteria for policy making and raise unreasonable expectations that greatly exceed what the EPA and the states have actually accomplished. Both legislators and bureaucrats have failed to educate the public about the nature and inevitability of health hazards, the complexity of risk assessment, the costs of trying to eliminate risks, and other trade-offs. They have also failed to structure debate over environmental quality so that the policy choices are clearer to the public; been insensitive to the impact of the regulations on state and local governments; and been unable and unwilling to integrate environmental health problems with broader concerns, such as the quality of life in urban areas, that affect people directly and immediately.[101]

Many critics also believe that federal courts should bear some responsibility for pressuring the EPA to issue more stringent regulations, since they forced the EPA and other agencies to take more aggressive action in the 1960s and 1970s. In his study of the 1977 Clean Air Act, Shep Melnick found that judges "commonly criticized administrators for being too timid in their wielding of public authority rather than encroaching on private property." They insisted that agencies interpret their "nondiscretionary duties" broadly. Rather than restraining administrative power, activist judges "pushed agencies to be more aggressive in protecting citizens' 'fundamental personal interests in life, health, and liberty.' "[102] Activist courts required agencies to provide more documentation for their actions. Rather than deferring to agency expertise, courts took a "hard look" at or made a "searching and careful review" of agency decision making.[103] One impact of the heightened judicial scrutiny (some 80 percent of major EPA rules are contested in court) has been that agencies have exaggerated the health risks that will be reduced in order to have a strong case when the regulation is challenged in court.

Failure to Regulate Aggressively Enough. On the other hand, the federal government has been criticized for not going far enough to regulate environmental risks in the past two decades. Regulators have generally been unwilling to impose regulations that would close down factories and cause widespread job loss. Even though a large number of chemicals have been identified as causing cancer in animals, making them candidates for risk assessment to determine whether they pose hazards to humans, the EPA has taken few regulatory actions other than those forced on it by statutory deadlines.

Environmental, health, and safety regulations have been of particular interest to the White House, because of their high compliance costs. But it is not at all clear that there is too much government intervention in these areas and that the number of regulations should be dramatically reduced. Environmental and health hazards are continually reported in books, journals, and newspapers, and on television programs. According to a 1987 review by the Office of Technology Assessment, the EPA has analyzed only a small number of the chemicals within its regulatory jurisdiction.[104] By 1990, the Agency, under authority of the Clean Water Act of 1972, had established toxic effluent standards for six categories of pollutants, and it has since agreed to prepare standards for sixty-five more categories. But of the twenty-nine nonbinding water quality criteria documents the agency has prepared for the states, only seven have been adopted, and only one has been adopted by more than one-fourth of the states. As authorized by the 1974 Safe Drinking Water Act, the EPA has issued maximum contaminant levels for nine chemicals, but many of the drinking water standards that are in effect are based on 1962 guidelines of the Public Health Service. Environmental statutes enacted by Congress in the 1980s provided clear evidence of congressional dissatisfaction with the scope and pace of EPA regulation setting. In its 1986 reauthorization of the Safe Drinking Water Act, for example, Congress set deadlines for the EPA to regulate eighty-three chemicals.

Almost all the authors of a collection of essays on the topic "Protecting the Earth: Are Our Institutions Up to It?" published in a 1989 issue of *EPA Journal*, criticized the EPA and other agencies for not adequately protecting the environment. Gladwin Hill, former environmental correspondent for the *New York Times*, observed that despite some progress, we are "still in a reactive mode, avoiding collective action until it is forced upon us.[105] Arthur Koines, an official in the EPA Office of Policy Analysis, argued that the "system for providing environmental protection is on overload, and it isn't going to improve on its own. Our episodic efforts as a society to respond to environmental threats have led to institutions lacking in unified direction and efficient organization."[106] Former EPA administrator William K. Reilly emphasized that regulatory efforts should focus on pollution prevention so that emissions are not simply transferred from one medium to another and so that improved environmental quality will be economically advantageous to industry.[107]

Walter Rosenbaum, in a 1991 assessment of environmental politics and policy, laments the "continuing failure of environmental institutions and policies to achieve many essential goals. Regulatory failure . . . is especially serious in the management of toxic and hazardous substances, in solid waste management, and in air and water pollution abatement." One of the key causes of this failure, he notes, is the EPA's "lack of a large and dependable research and development (R&D) budget through which it can generate information and schedule future research appropriately for its statutory responsibilities and institutional needs."[108]

Causes of Limited Regulatory Activity.   One reason for the limited progress in accomplishing environmental goals is that the EPA has been constrained by recent administrations concerned about controlling inflation and increasing the competitiveness of American firms in international markets. The executive branch, particularly since 1984, has insisted that reducing environmental and health risks is only one of several competing social goals. Michael Kraft and Norman Vig analyzed the impact of appointments in the early 1980s of officials who were hostile to the agency's mission, and of the reduction, in constant dollars, of nearly one-third in the EPA's pollution control budget and one-fourth in outlays for research between 1981 and 1984.[109] These reductions significantly limited the EPA's operational capacity. Later Reagan, Bush, and Clinton appointments have done much to restore agency morale and capability, but the EPA's budget has had only nominal increases in recent years.[110]

The tension that existed between Congress and the White House over environmental regulation in the early to mid-1980s is an essential element in explaining the politics of clean air in the late 1980s and early 1990s. However, by 1995, the roles were reversed: Congress as a whole became critical of environmental regulation, and a beleaguered executive branch sought to protect the Clean Air Act and other environmental laws from members of Congress determined to repeal or modify those statutes and limit their enforcement. The politics of environmental regulation in the 1980s that culminated in the passage of the Clean Air Act Amendments of 1990 was dramatically reversed as a result of the 1994 elections.

The roots of this transformation were evident in the 1980s, and their foundation was laid by Ronald Reagan. The Reagan administration restrained the growth of regulation by insisting on OMB review of all proposed and final regulations. The regulatory review process at that time concentrated mainly on the EPA; one-third of all regulations submitted by the agency to the OMB have been changed or eventually withdrawn. Earlier administrations also pressured the EPA and other agencies to limit regulations (although not to the same extent as the Reagan administration did).[111]

The regulatory review process was oriented toward relief rather than reform and toward reducing costs rather than improving regulations. The form developed by the OMB to monitor compliance with the regulatory review process outlined in Executive Order 12291 of February 17, 1981, for example, included four categories of costs but no provision for calculating benefits.[112] The agenda of many senior EPA and OMB officials, when the process was instituted, was simply to reduce research, rule making, and enforcement rather than to reshape policy. Analysis was seen not as a tool for improved policy making, but as a means of limiting agency action. Susan Tolchin and Martin Tolchin observed that the review process gave business interests an opportunity to block regulatory initiatives with which they disagreed. The primary concern was to "alleviate the burdens of excessive regulation." The Reagan administration's regulatory "reform" effort was an "exercise in national self-deception because of the singularity of its dominant goal: short-term relief for business."[113]

A second reason for the limited regulatory activity is the length and complexity of the EPA's rule-making process. Virtually every regulation of consequence is challenged in court. Extremely stringent regulations that can withstand rigorous review by federal courts are expensive and time-consuming, for the agency must invest considerable resources in developing regulations and defending them in litigation. The resources required in such regulatory proceedings are tied up for years and thus not available to respond to other problems. Given limited agency budgets (in part due to the unwillingness of administrations to expand agency activity), few major regulatory initiatives can be undertaken. The agreements reached are often only tentative steps for which the parties involved anticipate ultimate judicial determination; major regulations intended by Congress to be agreed upon within a few months take from three to ten years to promulgate. Although the EPA has begun to experiment with alternative processes, such as regulatory negotiations (the agency convenes a series of meetings with interested parties to develop the provisions of a regulation), rule making will probably continue to be a politically contentious and difficult undertaking.[114]

Third, although regulations require that the level of risk approach zero, the costs of achieving this goal tend to increase much faster than the benefits, so that marginal benefits are decreasing while marginal costs are increasing, often exponentially. Reducing health risks to zero may be compatible with the other policy goals that governments must pursue (when safe products can be substituted or other technological processes are available), but in many cases, trade-offs are inescapable. If the goal of reducing health risks outweighs other policy concerns, then a conservative approach may be noncontroversial. If, however, the costs that regulatory agencies can impose are limited, such an approach will likely collide with other policy concerns.

Failure to Regulate the Most Serious Risks. The EPA itself has provided the most detailed criticism of its regulatory agenda in reports prepared by an agency task force and by the agency's Science Advisory Board. A 1990 Science Advisory Board report also indirectly criticized Congress and environmental laws in general.[115] The board called the EPA a largely "reactive" agency, insufficiently oriented toward "opportunities for the greatest risk reduction." It pointed out that not all risks can be reduced, but that not all problems are equally serious, and the agency had failed to set priorities for reducing the most important problems. The board also called on the EPA to pursue a much broader agenda than it had in the past, and to take responsibility for "protecting the environment, not just for implementing environmental law" by addressing "the most serious risks, whether or not Agency action is required specifically by law."[116] The EPA needed to ensure, according to the report, "a more rigorous, scientifically defensible comparison and merging of environmental risks and alternative strategies for reducing them." Interestingly, the board did not criticize the agency for excessive conservatism, as previously discussed.[117] According to the report, the agency had failed to employ a broad range of policy tools to reduce environmental risks. It had usually imposed "end-of-pipe controls that often cause environmental problems of their own" rather than "preventing pollution at the source—through the redesign of production processes, [and] the substitution of less toxic production materials," for example.[118] Agency officials had failed to ensure that "environmental considerations are a part of the policy framework at other Federal agencies whose activities [in such areas as energy production, agriculture, taxation, transportation, and foreign relations] affect environmental quality directly or indirectly." The EPA "must work to ensure that environmental considerations are incorporated into policy discussions across the Federal government."[119]

A panel convened by the EPA in 1992 to examine ways the EPA can best use "sound science" in its decision making concluded that the agency "does not have a coherent science agenda and operational plan to guide scientific efforts throughout the Agency." As a result, it lacks the scientific support for a regulatory program aimed at relatively high-risk environmental problems. The panel noted that the EPA has not communicated to those outside the agency, or even within it, that high-quality science is a priority; the panel also noted that the process of ensuring that science informs policy decisions "is not well defined or coherently organized within EPA." The agency "often does not evaluate the impact of its regulations" and thus loses the opportunity to examine the impact of regulation on pollution. In addition, the panel concluded that the EPA needs to make the work of its scientists better known, encourage its scientists to interact with the broader scientific comunity, and remedy problems in its academic grants and centers so that it has access to the best quality research available.[120]

This debate over how to assess environmental risks and about what priorities for environmental regulation might result from such a comparison of hazards shifted to Congress in early 1995. Proponents of cutting federal regulations led the charge against what they termed the "exaggerated risks" resulting from current risk assessment approaches; others demanded more "rational" regulatory efforts. A number of bills were introduced to change the process by which the EPA assesses risks in preparing regulations, to require the EPA to use comparative risk assessment in establishing new priorities, and to mandate cost-benefit analyses before new regulations are issued.[121] These issues are discussed further in Chapter 2.

Fragmentation in the Regulation of Environmental Problems. Many of the criticisms of the Science Advisory Board in 1990 really pertained to statutory problems that affect the EPA. The agency was not created by statute but was part of a reorganization plan that consolidated a variety of programs spread throughout the executive branch. The EPA is currently responsible for implementing more than a dozen major environmental statutes, including the Clean Air Acts of 1970, 1977, and 1990; the Clean Water Act of 1972 (also known as the Federal Water Pollution Control Act); the Toxic Substances Control Act of 1976; the Federal Insecticide, Fungicide, and Rodenticide Act of 1972; the Resource Conservation and Recovery Act of 1984; and the Comprehensive Environmental Response, Compensation, and Liability Act of 1980 (also known as the "Superfund" law). There is little interaction between the program offices, each of which is responsible for administering laws concerning a particular environmental medium, and little incentive for such interaction, which is necessary for more comprehensive environmental policy making. This fragmentation limits the flexibility of federal, state, and local governments to alter their resource allocation or coordinate their efforts in response to changing environmental threats.

Figure 1-2 Operating Budget of the Environmental Protection Agency, 1987-1993

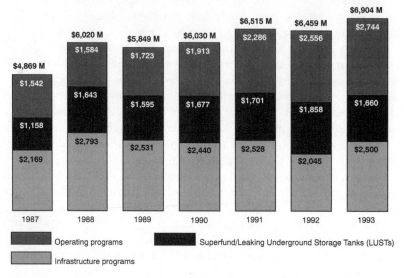

Source: Environmental Protection Agency, *Summary of the 1994 Budget* (Washington, D.C.: EPA, 1993),10.

More interaction is needed because the elements of the environment are interconnected. Regulations requiring treatment and removal of toxic substances in one environmental medium may merely result in their transfer to another environmental medium (for example, substances filtered from the air may be deposited on the land or water). Such regulations might not reduce risk; they subject industry to competing and contradictory regulatory requirements and needless expense, consuming resources that could be better employed elsewhere.

The political pressures and incentives that have led Congress to launch expansive regulatory programs have not prompted it to ensure their aggressive implementation. Industry groups participate very effectively in the administrative process, where the discourse is technical, detailed, and largely out of public view. As a result, industry concerns often prevail.

The EPA's budget and resources are overwhelmed by the areas of responsibility Congress and the White House continue to place under the agency's jurisdiction, by changes in technology, and by increases in industrial activity. Hazardous wastes accumulate and new chemicals and pesticides are introduced; yet the agency's budget and work force have decreased. In 1980, the EPA's budget for pollution control and abatement was $6.374 billion (in 1987 dollars) and the agency had a work force of 13,078; in 1985, despite new legislation that gave the agency additional responsibilities, the budget was $4.496 billion and the work force had decreased to 9,998. By 1993, the agency's budget remained smaller in real (1987) dollars—$5.557 billion—than it had been in 1980.[122] As shown in Figure 1-2, the EPA's budget largely goes for grants to states for pollution control infrastructure, and for cleanup of hazardous waste sites and leaking underground storage tanks (LUSTs) under the "Superfund" law.

The Outlook for Environmental Policy Making

Environmental policy making has taken place amid the contention of warring interest groups, partisan politics, and wrangling between the president and Congress. It has also been hindered by scientific uncertainty and lack of data. The debate over whether environmental laws have been too strict or not strict enough and whether regulatory efforts have been misdirected continues. Innumerable analyses are available to Congress and the executive branch concerning ways to address environmental problems and the shortcomings of existing regulatory efforts. Members of Congress must consider a host of factors in formulating environmental laws.

Contradictory expectations are inescapable. Policymakers should allow those responsible for implementing a law the flexibility to make the adjustments necessary to solve evolving problems and to learn from trial and error. But elected officials should make basic policy decisions and hold agencies accountable for implementing them. Congress and the executive branch should also be willing to learn from experience when they review and revise laws, preferably on a regular basis. But the press of new legislative business, reelection campaigns, constituent service, and other demands limit time and resources. Policy evaluation requires clear goals and standards against which policy implementation efforts can be measured. But that kind of clarity is often lacking, and when it exists, the regulatory tasks may overwhelm available resources.

Perhaps most important, policymakers and citizens alike must ask whether environmental laws are consistent with government's ability to achieve the goals they establish. These laws continually heighten public expectations, yet the government continually falls short in its attempts to meet them. Each law passed by Congress, particularly a major statute like the Clean Air Act, has a cumulative impact on future efforts to devise effective solutions to environmental problems. Government's unwillingness or inability to succeed may ultimately erode the public's faith in collective efforts and the institutional capacity to resolve pressing public problems.

The Clean Air Act Amendments of 1990 are placed in their political and historical contexts in Chapter 3. The challenges involved in regulating air pollution deserve additional exploration, however, and they are the subject of Chapter 2.

Notes

1. Robert Cameron Mitchell, "Public Opinion and the Green Lobby: Poised for the 1990s?" in Norman J. Vig and Michael E. Kraft, eds., *Environmental Policy in the 1990s* (Washington, D.C.: CQ Press, 1990), 85. See also Riley E. Dunlap, "Public Opinion in the 1980s: Clear Consensus, Ambiguous Commitment," *Environment* 33, no. 8 (October 1991): 32.
2. Environmental Protection Agency, *National Air Quality and Emissions Trends Report, 1993* (Research Triangle Park, N.C.: EPA, 1993), 97.
3. Douglas W. Dockery et al., "Mortality Risks of Air Pollution: A Prospective Cohort Study," *New England Journal of Medicine* 329 (1993): 1753-1759.
4. The Clean Air Act was enacted in 1970; major amendments were added in 1977 and 1990. This book is primarily concerned with the act as amended in 1990.
5. Charles E. Lindblom, *The Policy-Making Process* (Englewood Cliffs, N.J.: Prentice Hall, 1968), 4.
6. See, generally, Theodore Lowi, "Four Systems of Policy, Politics, and Choice," *Public Administration Review* 33 (July-August 1972): 298-310.
7. This section is largely based on Charles O. Jones, *An Introduction to the Study of Public Policy* (Monterey, Calif.: Brooks/Cole, 1984). See also B. Guy Peters, *American Public Policy: Promise and Performance*, 3d ed. (Chatham, N.J.: Chatham House, 1991); and James Anderson, *Public Policy-Making* (New York: Praeger, 1975).
8. John W. Kingdon, *Agendas, Alternatives, and Public Policies*, 2d ed. (New York: HarperCollins, 1995).
9. For an interesting study of policy innovation, see Nelson W. Polsby, *Policy Innovation in America: The Politics of Policy Initiation* (New Haven, Conn.: Yale University Press, 1984).
10. U.S. Congress, Office of Technology Assessment, *Acid Rain and Transported Air Pollutants* (Washington, D.C.: Government Printing Office, 1984), 13.
11. For a review of the debate concerning the ecological and health risks of pollution, see the Conservation Foundation, *State of the Environment: A View toward the Nineties* (Washington, D.C.: Conservation Foundation, 1987); Lester Lave, *The Strategy of Social Regulation* (Washington, D.C.: Brookings Institution, 1981); National Research Council, *Risk Assessment in the Federal Government: Managing the Process* (Washington, D.C.: National Academy Press, 1983); Edith Effron, *The Apocalyptics: Cancer and the Big Lie* (New York: Simon and Schuster, 1984); and H. W. Lewis, *Technological Risk* (New York: Norton, 1990).
12. Office of Management and Budget, *Regulatory Program of the United States Government, April 1, 1990-March 31, 1991* (Washington, D.C.: Government Printing Office, 1990), 13-26.
13. U.S. Congress, Office of Technology Assessment, *Catching Our Breath: Next Steps for Reducing Urban Ozone* (Washington, D.C.: Government Printing Office, 1989), 39-78.
14. Becky Bascom, "Clean Air Strategy Session" (lecture delivered at a conference sponsored by the Natural Resources Council of Maine and the Natural Resources Defense Council, Washington, D.C., May 28, 1991).
15. For a discussion of animal testing, see Lester B. Lave, "Methods of Risk

Assessment" in Lave, ed., *Quantitative Risk Assessment in Regulation* (Washington, D.C.: Brookings Institution, 1982), 37-48. For a skeptical view, see Elizabeth Whelan, *Toxic Terror* (Ottawa, Ill.: Jameson, 1985).

16. See, for example, Joel Schwartz and Douglas W. Dockery, "Increased Mortality in Philadelphia Associated with Daily Air Pollution Concentrations," *American Review of Respiratory Disease* 145 (1992): 600-604; and Dockery, Schwartz, and John D. Spengler, "Air Pollution and Daily Mortality: Associations with Particulates and Acid Aerosols," *Environmental Research* 59 (1992): 363-373.

17. See, generally, C. Arden Pope III, Douglas W. Dockery, and John D. Spengler, "Respiratory Health and PM_{10} Pollution: A Daily Time Series Analysis," *American Review of Respiratory Disease* 144 (1991): 668-674; C. A. Pope III, "Respiratory Disease Associated with Community Air Pollution and a Steel Mill, Utah Valley," *American Journal of Public Health* 79 (1989): 623-628; Joel Schwartz, "Lung Function and Chronic Exposure to Air Pollution: A Cross-sectional Analysis of NHANES II," *Environmental Research* 50 (1989): 309-321.

18. For more on this debate, see Ira C. Magaziner and Robert B. Reich, *Minding America's Business* (New York: Vintage, 1983); Henry R. Nau, *The Myth of America's Decline: Leading the World Economy into the 1990s* (New York: Oxford University Press, 1990); and Graham K. Wilson, *Business and Politics: A Comparative Introduction* (Chatham, N.J.: Chatham House, 1985).

19. Department of Commerce, *The Competitive Status of the U.S. Electronics Sector* (Washington, D.C.: Government Printing Office, April 1990), 7-10.

20. John A. Young, "Technology and Competitiveness: A Key to the Economic Future of the United States," *Science* 252 (July 15, 1988): 314.

21. See Gary C. Bryner, ed., *Science, Technology, and Politics: Policy Analysis in Congress* (Boulder, Colo.: Westview Press, 1992), chap. 10.

22. Keith Schneider, "New View Calls Environmental Policy Misguided," *New York Times*, March 21, 1993, 1.

23. This issue is explored in David Vogel, *National Styles of Regulation: Environmental Policy in Great Britain and the United States* (Ithaca, N.Y.: Cornell University Press, 1987).

24. See, for example, Susan Eckerly, "The Environment," in The Heritage Foundation, *Issues '94: The Candidate's Briefing Book* (Washington, D.C.: Heritage Foundation, 1994), 71-88.

25. David Hosansky, "The Time May Be Ripe For Mandates Bill," *Congressional Quarterly Weekly Report* 54 (December 31, 1994): 3605.

26. See S.1, 104th Congress; U.S. Senate, Committee on Governmental Affairs, *Unfunded Mandate Reform Act of 1995*, Senate Report 104-1 (January 11, 1995); Pub. L. No. 104-4.

27. Barry Commoner, "Let's Get Serious about Pollution Prevention," *EPA Journal* 15 (July-August 1989): 15.

28. Barry Commoner, "Failure of the Environmental Effort," *Environmental Law Reporter* 18 (June 1988): 10195-10199.

29. Gus Speth, "EPA and the World Clean-up Puzzle," *EPA Journal* 15 (July-August 1989): 26.

30. For a discussion of the law, see Council on Environmental Quality, *Environmental Quality* (Washington, D.C.: Government Printing Office, 1992), 151-158.

31. "The Environment: An Enemy, and Yet a Friend," *The Economist* 320 (September 8, 1990): 3-26.
32. Ibid., 9.
33. "Growth vs. Environment," *Business Week*, May 11, 1992, 66-78.
34. Quoted in "The Environment: An Enemy and Yet a Friend," 4.
35. Paul Hawken, *Ecology of Commerce* (New York: HarperCollins, 1993), 2.
36. David W. Orr, *Ecological Literacy: Education and the Transition to a Postmodern World* (Albany, N.Y.: State University of New York Press, 1992), 182.
37. Some examples of industries that seek a much more aggressive policy to reduce regulation are given in Bruce Smart, *Beyond Compliance: A New Industry View of the Environment* (Washington, D.C.: World Resources Institute, 1992).
38. Hawken, *Ecology of Commerce*, 60-61.
39. For perhaps the earliest argument for pollution taxes, see Nicolas Pigou, *A Study in Public Finance* (London: Macmillan, 1928). See also Hawken, *Ecology of Commerce*, 75-90.
40. For a thoughtful critique of the EPA, see Marc K. Landy, Marc J. Roberts, and Stephen R. Thomas, *The Environmental Protection Agency: Asking the Wrong Questions* (New York: Oxford University Press, 1994).
41. Richard Epstein, *Simple Rules for a Complex World* (Cambridge, Mass.: Harvard University Press, 1995).
42. For a further discussion of this issue, see Gary C. Bryner, *Bureaucratic Discretion: Law and Policy in Federal Regulatory Agencies* (New York: Pergamon, 1987).
43. Philip K. Howard, *The Death of Common Sense* (New York: Random House, 1994), 11.
44. Ibid., 180.
45. National Academy of Public Administration, *Setting Priorities, Getting Results* (Washington, D.C.: National Academy of Public Administration, 1995).
46. Ibid., 1.
47. Zachary A. Smith, *The Environmental Policy Paradox*, 2d ed. (Englewood Cliffs, N.J.: Prentice Hall, 1995).
48. See, generally, Burke Marshall, ed., *A Workable Government? The Constitution after 200 Years* (New York: Norton, 1987); Donald L. Robinson, *Reforming American Government: The Bicentennial Papers of the Committee on the Constitutional System* (Boulder, Colo.: Westview Press, 1985); Robert E. Hunter, Wayne L. Berman, and John F. Kennedy, *Making Government Work: From White House to Congress* (Boulder, Colo.: Westview Press, 1986); James MacGregor Burns, *The Power to Lead: The Crisis of the American Presidency* (New York: Simon and Schuster, 1984); and James L. Sundquist, *Constitutional Reform and Effective Government* (Washington, D.C.: Brookings Institution, 1986).
49. See James L. Sundquist, "Needed: A Political Theory for the New Era of Coalition Government in the United States," *Political Science Quarterly* 103 (Winter 1988): 614; and John E. Chubb and Paul E. Peterson, eds., *Can the Government Govern?* (Washington, D.C.: Brookings Institution, 1989).
50. For a review of the making of foreign policy, see Thomas E. Mann, ed., *A Question of Balance: The President, the Congress, and Foreign Policy* (Washington, D.C.: Brookings Institution, 1990).

51. One example is given in Paul Light, *Still Artful Work: The Continuing Politics of Social Security Reform* (New York: Random House, 1995).
52. Charles O. Jones, *The Presidency in a Separated System* (Washington, D.C.: Brookings Institution, 1994).
53. David R. Mayhew, *Divided We Govern: Party Control, Lawmaking, and Investigations, 1946-1990* (New Haven, Conn.: Yale University Press, 1990).
54. For a helpful discussion of the politics of divided government, see Thomas E. Mann, "Breaking the Political Impasse," in Henry J. Aaron, ed., *Setting National Priorities: Policy for the Nineties* (Washington, D.C.: Brookings Institution, 1990), 293-317.
55. For more on this debate, see Theodore J. Lowi, *The End of Liberalism* (New York: Norton, 1979); Richard A. Harris and Sidney M. Milkis, *The Politics of Regulatory Change: A Tale of Two Agencies* (New York: Oxford University Press, 1989); Cass R. Sunstein, *After the Rights Revolution: Reconceiving the Regulatory State* (Cambridge, Mass.: Harvard University Press, 1990); and Gary C. Bryner, *Bureaucratic Discretion.*
56. See, generally, Lawrence Dodd and Richard Schott, *Congress and the Administrative State* (New York: Wiley, 1979); Energy and Environment Study Institute, "Statutory Deadlines in Environmental Legislation: Necessary but Need Improvement" (Washington, D.C.: EESI, 1985); National Academy of Public Administration, *Congressional Oversight of Regulatory Agencies: The Need to Strike a Balance and Focus on Performance* (Washington, D.C.: NAPA, 1988).
57. James P. Lester, "New Federalism and Environmental Policy," *Publius* 16 (Winter 1986): 149-165.
58. Patricia McGee Crotty, "The New Federalism Game: Primary Implementation of Environmental Policy," *Publius* 17 (Spring 1987): 53, 66.
59. David M. Welborn, "Conjoint Federalism and Environmental Regulation in the United States," *Publius* 18 (Winter 1988): 27-43.
60. Deil S. Wright, *Understanding Intergovernmental Relations* (Pacific Grove, Calif.: Brooks/Cole, 1988): 83-84.
61. Crotty, "The New Federalism Game," 67.
62. Welborn, "Conjoint Federalism," 33-37.
63. Barry Commoner, *Making Peace with the Planet* (New York: Pantheon, 1990).
64. Evan J. Ringquist, *Environmental Protection and the State Level* (Armonk, N.Y.: M. E. Sharpe, 1993).
65. See, generally, Walter Rosenbaum, *Environmental Politics and Policy,* 3d ed. (Washington, D.C.: CQ Press, 1995).
66. Jeffrey Pressman and Aaron Wildavsky, *Implementation,* 3d ed. (Berkeley: University of California Press, 1984), xii-xiii.
67. Paul Sabatier and Daniel Mazmanian, *Implementation and Public Policy* (Glenview, Ill.: Scott Foresman, 1983), 4.
68. Pressman and Wildavsky, *Implementation,* 168-180.
69. Ibid., 232-233.
70. See David Schoenbrod, "Goals Statutes or Rules Statutes: The Case of the Clean Air Act," *UCLA Law Review* 30 (1983): 740-828.
71. Allen V. Kneese and Charles L. Schultze, *Pollution, Prices, and Public Policy* (Washington, D.C.: Brookings Institution, 1975), 16.
72. Charles L. Schultze, *The Public Use of Private Interest* (Washington, D.C.:

Brookings Institution, 1977), 18.

73. Offices of Sen. Timothy Wirth and Sen. John Heinz, *"Project '88,"* 1988.

74. See Richard A. Liroff, *Reforming Air Pollution Regulation: The Toil and Trouble of EPA's Bubble* (Washington, D.C.: Conservation Foundation, 1986).

75. Many countries have imposed emissions fees for the release of pollutants into lakes and streams. Germany has made wider use of effluent taxes and fees than has the United States, particularly for water pollution. One of the earliest policies was enacted in 1976 when the Bundestag passed a law that set annual charges for the emission of five pollutants; receipts are given to the *Länder* (states) to offset the costs of administering the program and to finance pollution abatement projects. France has also begun to include economic incentives in its environmental statutes. *International Environmental Reporter* (February 2, 1986): 53-55. See, generally, Robert Repetto et al., *Green Fees: How a Tax Shift Can Work for the Environment and the Economy* (Washington, D.C.: World Resources Institute, 1992).

76. Robert N. Stavins, "Harnessing Market Forces to Protect the Environment," *Environment* 31 (January-February, 1989): 5-35.

77. Steven Kelman, *What Price Incentives?* (Boston: Auburn House, 1981).

78. Commoner, *Making Peace with the Planet,* 188.

79. See, for example, Robert Nozick, *Anarchy, State, and Utopia* (New York: Free Press, 1974); and John Rawls, *A Theory of Justice* (Cambridge, Mass.: Harvard University Press, 1971).

80. See M. E. Hawkesworth, *Theoretical Issues in Policy Analysis* (Albany, N.Y.: State University of New York Press, 1988); and Giovanni Sartori, *Democratic Theory* (Detroit: Wayne State University Press, 1962).

81. For an elaboration of these issues, see Bryner, ed., *Science, Technology, and Politics.*

82. Kathryn Wagner, "Congress, the Environment, and Technology Assessment," in Bryner, ed., *Science, Technology, and Politics,* 43-64.

83. For a review of these efforts, see National Academy of Public Administration, *Presidential Management of Rulemaking in Regulatory Agencies* (Washington, D.C.: NAPA, 1987).

84. Office of Management and Budget, *Regulatory Program of the United States Government, 1990-91* (Washington, D.C.: Government Printing Office, 1990), 33, 35.

85. Ibid., 14.

86. Ibid.

87. Office of Management and Budget, *Regulatory Program of the United States Government, April 1, 1985-March 30, 1986* (Washington, D.C.: Government Printing Office, 1986), xxii-xxvi.

88. Ibid., 36-37.

89. Ibid., xxi.

90. Ibid., 40.

91. Council of Economic Advisers, *Economic Report of the President* (Washington, D.C.: Government Printing Office, 1987), 207.

92. Ibid., 183. Other offices in the executive branch, such as the Council on Environmental Quality, have lined up more closely with the EPA. In 1984, the Office of Science and Technology Policy issued a "framework" for assessing cancer risks that included a review of scientific knowledge concerning cancer

and a set of thirty-one principles that agencies could rely on in risk assessment; it generally paralleled the EPA's approach.

93. Kneese and Schultze, *Pollution, Prices, and Public Policy.*

94. Bruce Ackerman and William Hassler, *Clean Coal/Dirty Air* (New Haven, Conn.: Yale University Press, 1981), 12.

95. Robert W. Crandall, *Controlling Industrial Pollution: The Economics and Politics of Clean Air* (Washington, D.C.: Brookings Institution, 1983), 110-130.

96. Lester B. Lave and Gilbert S. Omenn, *Clearing the Air: Reforming the Clean Air Act* (Washington, D.C.: Brookings Institution, 1981), 5.

97. Paul R. Portney, "Air Pollution Policy," in Portney, ed., *Public Policies for Environmental Protection* (Washington, D.C.: Resources for the Future, 1990), 87.

98. Bruce Yandle, *The Political Limits of Environmental Regulation* (New York: Quorum, 1989), 104.

99. Harris and Milkis argue that the "ideas behind environmentalism were especially attractive to reformers who sympathized with the radicalism of the 1960s, because these ideas offered a powerful indictment of the capitalistic foundation of American society." Environmentalists have been joined by others who seek to bring about a "radical reorientation of American values" by attacking capitalism as leading to "ecological ruin." Harris and Milkis, *Politics of Regulatory Change,* 233. See also Ronald Bailey, ed., *The True State of the Planet* (New York: Free Press, 1995); Wallace Kaufman, *No Turning Back: Dismantling the Fantasies of Environmental Thinking* (New York: Basic Books, 1994); and Gregg Easterbrook, *A Moment on the Earth: The Coming Age of Environmental Optimism* (New York: Viking Books, 1995).

100. George Eads and Michael Fix, *Relief or Reform: Reagan's Regulatory Dilemma* (Washington, D.C.: Urban Institute Press, 1984).

101. Landy, Roberts, and Thomas, *The Environmental Protection Agency,* 279-281.

102. R. Shep Melnick, *Regulation and the Courts* (Washington, D.C.: Brookings Institution, 1981), 3, 11-12.

103. Ibid., 11.

104. Office of Technology Assessment, *Identifying and Regulating Carcinogens* (Washington, D.C.: Government Printing Office, 1987), 12-15.

105. Gladwin Hill, "A Management Job for the Human Race," *EPA Journal* 15 (July-August 1989): 3.

106. Arthur Koines, "Under the Environmental Regulation Layer Cake," *EPA Journal* 15 (July-August 1989): 19.

107. William K. Reilly, "The Greening of EPA," *EPA Journal* 15 (July-August 1989): 8-10.

108. Walter Rosenbaum, *Environmental Politics and Policy,* 2d ed. (Washington, D.C.: CQ Press, 1991), 301, 304.

109. Norman J. Vig and Michael E. Kraft, "Environmental Policy from the Seventies to the Nineties: Continuity and Change," 3-32, and "Conclusion: Toward a New Environmental Agenda," 369-389, in Vig and Kraft, eds., *Environmental Policy in the 1990s.*

110. Vig, "Presidential Leadership: From the Reagan to the Bush Administration," in Vig and Kraft, eds., *Environmental Policy in the 1990s,* 33, 58.

111. National Academy of Public Administration, *Presidential Management of*

Rulemaking.

112. Harris and Milkis, *Politics of Regulatory Change,* 257.

113. Susan J. Tolchin and Martin Tolchin, *Dismantling America: The Rush to Deregulate* (Boston: Houghton Mifflin, 1983), 58, 266.

114. See, generally, Gail Bingham, *Resolving Environmental Disputes: A Decade of Experience* (Washington, D.C.: Conservation Foundation, 1986); and Cornelius M. Kerwin, *Rulemaking: How Government Agencies Write Law and Make Policy* (Washington, D.C.: CQ Press, 1994).

115. Environmental Protection Agency, Science Advisory Board, *Reducing Risk: Setting Priorities and Strategies for Environmental Protection* (Washington, D.C.: EPA, 1990).

116. Ibid., 16.

117. Ibid., 17.

118. Ibid., 22.

119. Ibid., 23.

120. Environmental Protection Agency, Expert Panel on the Role of Science at EPA, *Safeguarding the Future: Credible Science, Credible Decisions* (Washington, D.C.: EPA, 1992), 4-9.

121. Margaret Kriz, "Risky Business," *National Journal* 27 (February 18, 1995): 417-421; Louis Jacobson, "Risky Assessments," *National Journal* 27 (March 4, 1995): 550-551; Adam Babich, "What Next?" *The Environmental Forum* (November-December 1994): 48-55; and Terry Davies, "Congress Discovers Risk Analysis," *Resources* (Winter 1995): 5-8.

122. Environmental Protection Agency, Office of the Comptroller, "Budget Justifications of Appropriation Estimates for Committee on Appropriations" (Washington, D.C.: Government Printing Office, selected years); and Office of Management and Budget, *Budget of the United States Government, Fiscal Year 1993* (Washington, D.C.: Government Printing Office, 1992).

2 The Problem of Air Pollution

The different kinds of air pollution pose distinct policy-making problems. A key step in the policy-making process, outlined in Chapter 1, is to define the problem to be remedied since subsequent policy efforts may be misguided if there is not an adequate understanding of the problem. Air pollution occurs when gases and particles are combined or altered in such a way that they degrade the air and form substances that are harmful to humans, animals, and other living things. There may be as many as 7,000 air pollutants; no place on earth is really free of them. Some pollution is a result of natural processes, such as forest fires and volcanoes, or is caused by windblown dust. Other kinds result from human intervention and include emissions from automobiles, wood-burning stoves, heating units, and industrial sources such as power plants and ore reduction. More than half the air pollution in the United States comes from motor vehicle exhaust. The glossary at the end of the book provides additional information on air pollution.

The air we breathe is a mixture of nitrogen (78.084 percent), oxygen (20.948 percent), argon (0.934 percent), and carbon dioxide (0.032 percent); it also includes traces of neon, helium, krypton, hydrogen, xenon, methane, and nitrous oxide. With the exception of carbon dioxide, the concentration of these chemicals remains constant in unpolluted air. Nitrogen, oxygen, and carbon dioxide are essential to plant and animal life. Nitrogen is a precursor of nitrate oxygen, a component of proteins, nucleic acids, and chlorophyll, which are essential to living things. Oxygen in the atmosphere is a basic element of the biochemical reactions that are necessary for all higher forms of life to exist. The other chemicals are inert and do not play a major role in the atmosphere. All of these gases are held by gravity in the troposphere, seven to ten miles above the earth's surface, just below the stratosphere.[1]

A number of atmospheric gases (such as sulfur dioxide and nitrogen dioxide) vary in concentration. Water vapor is the most variable, ranging from 0 to 4 percent by volume in the lower troposphere. A greenhouse gas, it forms clouds that help radiate sunlight back into space and that constitute a source of water. Carbon dioxide, a key raw material for photosynthesis and food production, also absorbs heat radiated from the earth's surface and, along with greenhouse gases such as water vapor, helps to warm the atmosphere. Oxygen is transformed into ozone, which forms a stratospheric layer that protects life on earth from dangerous ultraviolet light. Ozone also occurs at low altitudes (but is harmful to humans and plant-life there). Ammonia, methane, hydrogen sulfide, carbon monoxide, sulfur dioxide, and traces of other gases are produced by biological and geological processes.[2]

Air pollution has been defined as a group of chemical compounds that "are in the wrong place or in the wrong concentrations at the wrong time. As long as a chemical is transported away or degraded rapidly relative to its rate of production, there is no pollution problem. Pollutants that enter the atmosphere through natural or artificial emissions may be degraded not only in the atmosphere but also by natural processes in the hydrocycle and geochemical cycles."[3]

Two of the most common forms of air pollution are smog and haze. In London and other European cities, fog from the North Sea and smoke from coal-burning stoves and factories form grey air, or smog. In Los Angeles, another kind of smog is formed when automobile exhaust and other gases are trapped by the surrounding mountains and warmed by sunshine. The gases undergo a photochemical reaction, producing brown air, or photochemical smog. Smog in other cities is usually a combination of automobile exhaust and smoke from the burning of fuels. Haze is much like smog, but the term usually refers to wide-scale, low-level pollution that obstructs visibility. It has become an increasingly serious problem in national parks and other rural areas as well as a chronic urban problem.[4]

The heart of air pollution regulation in the United States has been the requirement, in the Clean Air Act, that the EPA establish national ambient air quality standards, or NAAQS (acceptable levels of concentration in the ambient, or outside, air), for six major pollutants—carbon monoxide, ozone, particulate matter, sulfur dioxide, nitrogen dioxide, and lead. Emission standards were to be established at the level required to provide "an ample margin of safety to protect the public health."[5] (The standard for lead was added in 1977. A standard for hydrocarbons was issued under the 1970 law but was deleted in 1978 as unnecessary since hydrocarbon emissions are a major component of ozone and are regulated under that standard.) These pollutants differ considerably in terms of their sources, levels of concentration in the atmosphere, and health impacts, and in the control measures that have been developed to reduce their concentration in the air. Urban ozone (in contrast to the stratospheric ozone layer) has been the most pervasive and difficult to regulate; levels of carbon monoxide and particulate matter in the ambient air exceeded the national standards in many of the nation's urban areas in the early 1990s. Table 2-1

Table 2-1   Effects of Ambient Air Pollutants Regulated by the Clean
Air Act

Pollutant	Effects
Ozone	Respiratory tract problems such as difficulty in breathing, reduced lung function, possible premature aging of lung tissue, and asthma; eye irritation, nasal congestion, and reduced resistance to infection; damage to trees and crops
Particulate matter	Eye and throat irritation, bronchitis, lung damage, impaired visibility, cancer
Carbon monoxide	Impairment of blood's ability to carry oxygen; damage to cardiovascular, nervous, and pulmonary systems
Sulfur dioxide	Respiratory tract problems, including diminished lung capacity and permanent damage to lung tissue; primary component of "killer fogs"; precursor of acid rain, which damages trees, vegetation, and aquatic life
Nitrogen dioxide	Respiratory illnesses and lung damage; damage to immune system; precursor of acid rain
Lead	Brain damage and retardation, especially in children

Source: Adapted from Environmental Protection Agency, *Environmental Progress and Challenges: EPA's Update* (Washington, D.C.: EPA, 1988), 13.

shows the environmental and health effects of traditional or ambient air pollutants regulated by the Clean Air Act.

The second regulatory effort focuses on another category—toxic or hazardous air pollutants. Air toxics vary significantly in the threats they pose to human health. Many of them are carcinogens; others cause neurological damage or destroy organ tissue. As is true for other kinds of pollutants, little information is available concerning the health effects of air toxics, and we have little understanding of the relationship between exposure to pollutants and contraction of disease. Different population groups exhibit significant differences in sensitivity to chemicals and pollutants, and not much is known about the synergistic or interactive effect of exposure to a variety of potentially harmful substances. The variety of substances involved, the large number and diversity of sources, and the cost of regulatory controls have made regulation particularly challenging. These are chemicals for which no ambient air quality standard has been developed and that are determined by the EPA to "reasonably be anticipated to result in an increase in mortality or an increase in serious irreversible, or incapacitating reversible illness." By the time the act was amended in 1990, the

Table 2-2   Health Effects and Major Sources of Hazardous or Toxic Air
Pollutants Regulated by the 1990 Amendments

Pollutant	Health effects	Major sources
Asbestos	A variety of lung diseases, especially lung cancer	Vehicle brakes, buildings
Benzene	Leukemia	Gas, solvents
Vinyl chloride	Lung and liver cancer	Chemical manufacturing
Beryllium	Primarily lung disease; also damage to liver, spleen, kidneys, and lymph glands	Foundries, incinerators
Mercury	Damage to the brain, kidneys, and bowels	Chemical manufacturing
Radionuclides	Cancer	Nuclear power, fossil fuel combustion
Arsenic	Cancer	Incinerators, coal

Source: Adapted from Environmental Protection Agency, *Environmental Progress and Challenges: EPA's Update* (Washington, D.C.: EPA, 1988), 13.

EPA had only issued seven such standards (for asbestos, benzene, vinyl chloride, beryllium, mercury, radionuclides, and arsenic) and had merely proposed a standard for coke oven emissions, which were also classified as a hazardous air pollutant. The major sources and health effects of these pollutants are shown in Table 2-2. Table 2-3 gives the major source categories and subcategories for air pollutants.

Two global air pollution issues that emerged in the late 1970s and 1980s have been added to the clean air agenda: acid rain and stratospheric ozone layer depletion. Acid rain threatens the health of trees and other plant and aquatic life, and also poses a serious threat to human health. Similarly, destruction of the ozone layer threatens aquatic life and triggers skin cancer and cataracts in humans. This chapter outlines some of the issues concerning these different kinds of air pollution and the regulatory challenges they pose.

Traditional or Ambient Air Pollutants

In 1988, the EPA estimated that 112 million people lived in areas where at least one national ambient air quality standard was violated. That figure declined to 74.4 million people in 1990 and 59.1 million people in 1993.[6] Although there has been some improvement, this trend may be only temporary. Such figures, regularly reported in the press, are somewhat misleading, since nonattainment of air quality standards is measured over sev-

Table 2-3 Major Source Categories and Subcategories for Air Pollutants

Transportation

Highway vehicles (gasoline and
    diesel-powered)
Aircraft
Railroads
Vessels
Off-highway vehicles and machinery

Stationary Source Fuel Combustion

Electric utilities
Industrial boilers
Commercial and institutional boilers
    and furnaces
Residential furnaces and space
    heaters

Miscellaneous

Forest fires
Other burning (agricultural burning,
    coal refuse burning, and structure
    fires)
Miscellaneous organic solvents
    evaporation

Solid Waste Disposal

Incineration
Open burning

Fugitive Dust PM_{10} Sources

Roads (paved and un-
    paved)
Agricultural tilling
Construction activity
Mining and quarrying
Wind erosion

Industrial Processes

Chemical manufacturing
Petroleum refining
Primary and secondary
    metals
Iron and steel mills
Mineral products
Food production and agriculture
Industrial organic solvent use
Petroleum product production
    and marketing

Source: Environmental Protection Agency, *National Air Pollutant Emission Estimates 1940-1990* (Washington, D.C.: EPA, 1991), 4.

eral years. The EPA has reported that 140 million Americans live in areas that have failed to meet the national air quality standard for ground-level ozone in recent years, although in 1993, the most recent year for which data are available, the EPA reported that 51 million people lived in areas reporting ozone levels that exceeded the standard.[7] Meteorological conditions affect ambient air quality; the hot, dry summer of 1988, particularly in the East, stimulated the formation of ozone. Pollution levels are also a function of changes in technology (as industrial and commercial facilities modernize and become more efficient, their emissions usually decrease); the implementation and enforcement of environmental laws and regulations by state and federal officials; and compliance efforts by regulated industries. Figure 2-1 shows the number of people living in counties where ambient air quality does not meet national standards.

Trends in Emissions of Traditional Pollutants

Carbon monoxide (CO) emissions in the United States peaked about 1970 and have fallen noticeably since then, largely as a result of automo-

Figure 2-1 Number of People Living in Counties That Fail to Meet National Ambient Air Quality Standards, 1993

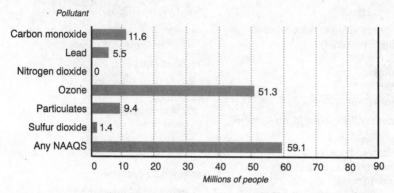

Source: Environmental Protection Agency, *National Air Quality and Emissions Trends Report, 1993* (Research Triangle Park, N.C.: EPA, 1994), 15.
Note: Figures are based on 1990 population data and 1993 air quality data.

bile emission controls. Residential coal and wood burning significantly increased carbon monoxide levels until about 1970. Coal has largely been replaced as a household fuel, but residential wood burning has increased since the late 1970s as wood-burning fireplaces have grown in popularity. Emissions of volatile organic compounds (VOCs), the primary constituent of ozone pollution, also peaked around 1970, but showed little decline throughout the 1980s. Emissions of total suspended particulates (TSPs) peaked around 1950, declined steadily until 1980 (primarily as a result of increased use of cleaner fuels and controls placed on fuel burning), and have remained relatively stable since then. Monitoring of fine particulates began only in about 1985. Nitrogen oxide (NO_x) emissions have held constant since the late 1970s. The most dramatic change has been the reduction in lead emissions as a result of the phasing out of leaded gasoline. Such technological changes hold tremendous promise for reducing pollution. Regulatory strategies that attempt to prevent pollution are generally much more desirable than those that seek to control it, through installation of equipment on smokestacks and auto tailpipes, for example. Pollution control equipment may break down or still result in some emissions, while prevention eliminates the pollutants. Figure 2-2 compares the emissions of six major pollutants in 1970 and 1993.

Although there have been some major acute air pollution disasters, chronic exposure to pollutants has had a much greater impact on human health and on ecological systems. When oxides of sulfur and nitrogen, for example, are transformed in the atmosphere to sulfate and nitrate particles, they fall to earth in dry form or as rain, making soils and water more

Figure 2-2 Emissions of Six Major Pollutants, 1970 and 1993

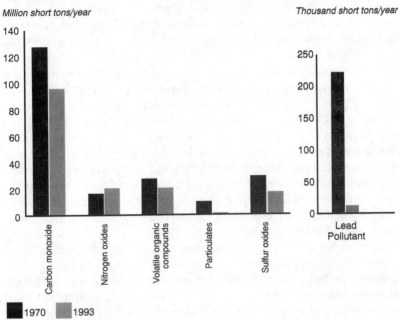

Million short tons/year

Thousand short tons/year

1970   1993

Source: Environmental Protection Agency, *National Air Quality and Emissions Trends Report, 1993* (Research Triangle Park, N.C.: EPA, 1994), 14.

acidic, killing some species, and damaging human lung tissue. Carbon dioxide does not directly cause human health problems but is classified as a pollutant because of concerns that its increasing concentration in the atmosphere is contributing to global climatic change.

Air pollution-related diseases include asphyxiation, pulmonary irritation, systemic toxicity, and cancer. Human respiratory tract defenses—nasal hairs, ciliated cells lining the upper airways, coughs and sneezes, and the sense of smell—are often overwhelmed by air pollutants. People with chronic respiratory problems such as emphysema, asthma, and bronchitis suffer increased damage to lung tissue that is already extremely sensitive when they come in contact with these pollutants. Air pollution can also damage other parts of the body because some pollutants are absorbed into the bloodstream and are carried to sensitive organs. Air pollution also affects body tissues; two of its most general consequences are the formation of scar tissue and the accumulation of fluid, particularly in the lungs. High levels of pollutants can also weaken the immune systems of individuals who might otherwise be healthy, making them more susceptible to colds, infections, and other diseases seemingly unrelated to air pollution.[8]

Researchers have compared the incidence of respiratory diseases such as bronchitis and chronic cough among children living with mothers who smoke at least one pack of cigarettes a day and children living in cities with high pollution levels. Children living in such cities are up to three times more likely to suffer from respiratory problems than children whose mothers smoke, thus demonstrating the seriousness of the health threat posed by community air pollution. In controlled experiments, human subjects who breathe acid compounds and other particulates for short periods of time at levels commonly found in urban areas experience decreased lung capacity and other respiratory problems. Hospitalization of children for respiratory problems during periods of high levels of particulate pollution occurs at a rate three times that observed when such levels are below the national standard. People suffering from coronary heart disease suffer chest pains, reduced flow of oxygen to the blood, and decreased physical strength when exposed to levels of carbon monoxide that are lower than those found in many cities.[9]

Other studies that have compared mortality rates in cities with different average levels of particulate pollution estimated that 3 percent to 9 percent of deaths in those cities could be attributed to particulate pollution. Separate studies involved the use of different models, assumptions, and demographic and other conditions.[10] Nevertheless, they have been quite consistent in finding strong associations between particulate pollution and mortality. Such studies suggest that particulates emitted from combustion are a greater risk than dust or other naturally occurring particles.[11] A landmark study tracing death rates among more than 8,000 adults in six U.S. cities found that, after controlling for age, sex, smoking, and other factors that contribute to risk, mortality in the most air-polluted city was 26 percent higher than in the least air-polluted city.[12] A study published in 1995 examined the health of a cohort of 1.2 million people in 151 metropolitan areas in the United States from 1982 to 1989. More than a half-million people in the study lived in cities where information on particulate air pollution was available. The study found that people living in the city with the highest level of air pollution had a 17 percent greater risk of mortality than those in the least polluted city. While smoking continues to be a much greater health threat than air pollution, the increased risk of death from air pollution is significant, even after adjusting for individual differences.[13]

Regulating Ambient Air Pollutants

Measuring the impact of regulations on air quality is fraught with difficulties. The reduction in emissions achieved by pollution controls might be offset by changes in meteorological conditions that result in increased levels of ambient air pollutants. Concentrations of ambient air pollutants may decrease as a result of a downturn in economic activity that causes the closing of polluting factories, and increase during periods of economic growth. Emissions and ambient air quality are also affected by changes in the relative cost of different forms of energy.[14]

The rate of emissions, the size of the airshed (or air quality region) into which they are emitted, and the circumstances under which they are emitted—including such variables as wind, rain, temperature, and geography—all significantly determine the impact of pollutants. For example, the formation of temperature inversions in mountain valleys, which occurs when a layer of warm air traps a layer of cold air beneath it, blocking the normal convection of air upward as the surface of the earth is heated, limits the vertical movement of polluted air. The mountains limit horizontal movement, and emissions of pollutants from stationary and mobile sources thus build to unhealthy levels.

Emissions from stationary and mobile sources have generally decreased over the past few decades, and ambient air quality has improved in many areas. But it is not clear how much of this progress can be attributed to the Clean Air Act, or why more progress has not been made, or how the act should be reformed or improved. Those engaged in the debate over the Clean Air Act during the past decade have taken two basic positions: The Clean Air Act should be strengthened to ensure that it protects human health and environmental quality and updated so that it regulates new risks; and the Clean Air Act should be reformed so that the costs of complying with its provisions are reduced.

In a 1991 study, the EPA attempted to estimate the effect of controls imposed under the Clean Air Act of 1970 by comparing projected 1988 emissions based on levels of control existing in 1970 with actual 1988 emissions. The results of this study are shown in Figure 2-3. Emissions of lead, particulates, and carbon monoxide appear to have been most affected by control efforts resulting from the 1970 act. Installation of auto tailpipes was clearly effective in reducing lead and carbon monoxide emissions. Reductions in particulate emissions might be more a function of industrial modernization than of regulatory efforts, but the relative impact of different factors is difficult to determine. Although the EPA concluded that the Clean Air Act has resulted in the reduction of pollution, its goal—protecting public health with an adequate margin of safety—is far from being achieved.

Carbon Monoxide.   Carbon monoxide is a colorless, odorless, invisible gas that is produced primarily by the incomplete combustion of organic (carbon-containing) material. Although carbon monoxide is generally viewed as being the ambient pollutant that is least potentially hazardous to the health of the population as a whole, there is increasing evidence that it does represent a serious health risk. At high levels, carbon monoxide reduces attention span, problem-solving ability, sensory ability, and visual

Figure 2-3 Actual 1988 Emissions as a Percentage of Projected 1988 Emissions Using 1970 as a Control

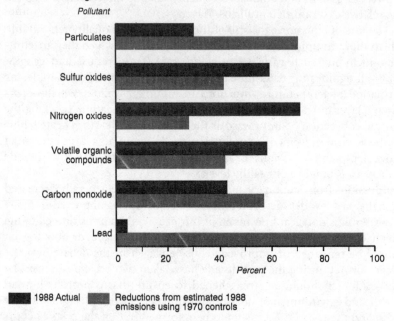

Source: Environmental Protection Agency, *Economic Investments: The Cost of a Clean Environment* (Washington, D.C.: EPA, 1991), 5-3.

acuity.[15] While these effects usually disappear after a few hours, CO has been implicated in accidents resulting from decreased attention and sensory ability. There is also some evidence that it causes or contributes to the severity of respiratory diseases such as asthma and bronchitis and reduces respiratory function.[16]

The most serious health threat from exposure to carbon monoxide, especially in urban areas, is the reduction in the capacity of blood to deliver oxygen throughout the body. Animal studies have shown that CO can damage the central nervous systems of offspring that had chronic prenatal exposure to the pollutant.[17] Acute high doses can cause asphyxiation, heart and brain damage, and impaired perception. Chronic exposure to carbon monoxide can cause an increased density of red blood cells, leading to decreased blood flow in veins and arteries, weakness, fatigue, and headache.[18] Such exposure has also been associated with heart and arterial disease and with angina.[19] At very high concentrations it is lethal.[20]

Both natural processes and human activity produce carbon monoxide, but there is little agreement over the magnitude of the relative contribution of the two sources.[21] Natural sources include volcanoes, forest fires, and electrical storms; CO is also found in marsh and mine gases and in the surface layers of the ocean. Human activity is the source of automobile exhaust, smoke from residential fireplaces and cigarettes, and fumes from industrial processes. Concentrations of CO range from 1 to 30 parts per million (ppm) in urban air to 20,000 to 60,000 ppm in cigarette smoke and 30,000 to 80,000 ppm in exhaust from older motor vehicles.[22] Industrial emissions of carbon monoxide have decreased somewhat since 1970, largely because reductions in emissions from a few high-polluting processes have exceeded increases in other areas of industrial output. Air pollution controls installed since 1970 have reduced emissions from solid waste disposal. Forest fires produced significant levels of CO in the 1940s, but as fire prevention efforts have improved, this source of carbon monoxide emissions has also decreased.[23]

Motor vehicles are the primary source of CO emissions. Residential wood burning, the second largest source, accounts for about 10 percent of such emissions. Figure 2-4 shows the trend in carbon monoxide emissions from 1940 to 1990. Although some estimates of pollution levels before 1970 may be misleading because of problems with measurements, these figures nevertheless provide a useful historical perspective on the progress that has been made over the past half-century as newer, cleaner production technologies for industrial sources and less polluting motor vehicles have been developed. The figures also highlight the difficulties encountered during the 1980s in reducing pollution levels further.

Ozone. Ozone, a colorless gas with a pungent odor, occurs naturally in the atmosphere. Its peak concentration is in the upper atmosphere (the stratosphere). A form of oxygen composed of three atoms of oxygen, ozone is highly reactive and combines with virtually all types of molecules with which it comes in contact. Ozone is produced when sunlight triggers chemical reactions between pollutants (such as volatile organic compounds and nitrogen oxides) and the gases that occur naturally in the atmosphere.

As noted in Chapter 1, ozone in the stratosphere provides a protective layer that absorbs most of the ultraviolet rays from the sun, thereby shielding life on earth from their harmful effects. If it reached the earth, such radiation would damage biological molecules, including DNA, and bring about increases in the incidence of skin cancer and cataracts. Without the protection the stratospheric ozone layer provides, life as we know it would probably not exist at all. (The problem of depletion of the stratospheric ozone layer is discussed later in this chapter.) In contrast, ozone at low altitudes is a noxious pollutant. It belongs to a broad group of pollutants, photochemical oxidants, that pose risks both to human health and to ecological systems. It can break down body tissues (particularly lung tissue)

Figure 2-4   Emissions of Carbon Monoxide, 1940-1990

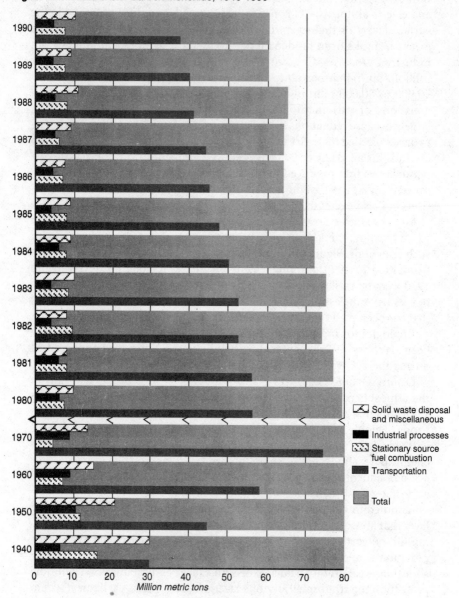

Source: Environmental Protection Agency, *National Air Pollutant Emission Estimates, 1940-1990* (Washington, D.C.: EPA, 1991), 12.
Note: See Table 2-3, which gives major source categories and subcategories for air pollutants.

and cells, and is highly toxic when inhaled, causing or contributing to several pulmonary diseases, including emphysema, bronchitis, pulmonary edema, and asthma, as well as premature aging of lung tissue. Ozone also irritates mucous membranes of the nose and throat and impairs lung-clearance mechanisms.[24] It has been shown to reduce the body's resistance to disease and to decrease the ability to engage in physical activity. Acute high-level exposure can cause stress to the heart; chronic exposure can result in heart failure.[25] Ozone can also harm trees and crops and damage fragile aquatic ecosystems.

There is considerable debate among scientists and physicians over whether the national ambient air quality standard for ozone is low enough to protect human health. In the fall of 1991, the American Lung Association sued the EPA for its failure to review the ozone standard in the face of new evidence concerning the adverse health effects of exposure at levels below the standard. A congressional Office of Technology Assessment report indicated that meeting the ozone standard would likely eliminate "several hundred million episodes of such respiratory symptoms as coughing, chest pain and shortness of breath," and "8-50 million days of restricted activity . . . days when someone feels ill enough to limit the day's activities, if not necessarily to stay in bed or home from work." No estimates were given, however, of the benefits of reducing the chronic effects of exposure to ozone.[26]

Volatile organic compounds, the primary constituent of ozone, are formed in part by hydrocarbons, a particularly important subset of VOCs. Several hydrocarbons—benzene, for example—are known carcinogens.[27] Part of the challenge in meeting the ozone standard has been that the largest sources of VOC emissions are small stationary sources and motor vehicles. In 1985, for example, motor vehicles produced 11.0 million tons of VOCs, small stationary sources (such as dry cleaners and paint shops) released 10.6 million tons, large stationary sources (such as chemical manufacturing plants and oil refineries) released only 2.1 million tons, and other means of transportation (such as air and rail) produced 1.4 million tons.[28] Before passage of the 1990 amendments, emissions from small sources had generally not been regulated.

Ozone levels are usually highest in the summer, when the weather is warmest, sunlight is most intense, and traffic levels are highest.[29] Peak ozone readings are highly correlated with maximum daily temperatures and with days that have temperatures above 90° Fahrenheit. High temperatures in-crease the evaporation of VOCs and also stimulate the chemical reactions that produce urban ozone. Figure 2-5 shows the trend in emissions of volatile organic compounds from 1940 to 1990. Total emissions decreased slightly between 1979 and 1988, despite a 33 percent increase in vehicle miles traveled during that period, as a result of regulation and other factors.[30]

Figure 2-5   Emissions of Volatile Organic Compounds, 1940-1990

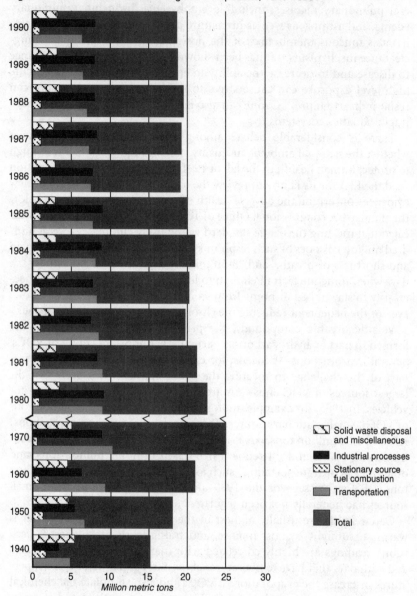

Source: Environmental Protection Agency, *National Air Pollutant Emission Estimates, 1940-1990* (Washington, D.C.: EPA, 1991), 11.

Note: See Table 2-3, which gives major source categories and subcategories for air pollutants.

Ozone has been one of the most difficult pollutants to regulate. Every major urban area in the United States except Minneapolis-St. Paul—some ninety-four metropolitan areas—has failed to meet the ozone air quality standard. More people live in areas that fail to meet the air quality standard for ozone (51.3 million in 1993) than live in areas failing to meet the standard for any other pollutant. Despite the formulation and implementation of state cleanup plans and the imposition of increasingly stringent control requirements, air quality levels have not appreciably improved. Gains in the use of cleaner technologies and processes have been offset by growth in the number of sources. The summers of 1986 to 1990 were five of the eight warmest summers ever recorded in the United States, and if this trend continues, meeting the ozone air quality standard will remain an elusive goal.

Particulate Matter. Particulate matter (usually referred to as PM-10 or PM_{10}) is a broad category of pollutants that includes a variety of chemicals and particles, ranging from dust to particles of heavy metals (such as chromium and nickel) and radioactive particles. Primary particulates include dust, dirt, soot, smoke, and liquid droplets that are emitted directly into the air by factories, power plants, and wood-burning stoves, as well as naturally occurring windblown dust. Secondary particulates are formed when gases such as sulfur dioxide and volatile organic compounds are transformed in the atmosphere into tiny particles. Until 1987, the national ambient air quality standard for particulates regulated levels of total suspended particulates. On July 1, 1987, the EPA promulgated a national ambient air quality standard for particulate matter that has an aerodynamic diameter of 10 micrometers or less. (A micrometer, or micron, is approximately 1/25,000th of an inch; 10 micrometers are about one-tenth the diameter of a human hair.)

Researchers studying the health effects of pollution throughout the 1970s and 1980s concluded that fine particulates with a diameter of 10 micrometers or less pose a much greater risk to human health than do larger particles.[31] Larger particles are usually filtered out by the body's defense mechanism in the nasal-pharynx region; fine particles, which are much more difficult for the body to filter out, bypass defense mechanisms and travel deep into the lungs. Some small particles, 0.05 micrometers in diameter or less, may remain in the lungs at the deepest level (the alveoli level) for the life of the individual. Particulates of heavy metals, arsenic, asbestos, sulfates, nitrates, hydrocarbons, and other chemicals, as well as radioactive particles, diesel exhaust particles, and particles in smoke are dangerous when they become imbedded in lung tissue. Deep penetration of the lungs is especially dangerous if high concentrations of other pollutants (especially sulfur oxides and nitrogen oxides) are also inhaled. Pollen grains and fungal spores may also be 10 micrometers or less in diameter and can cause significant human health problems, especially allergic reactions.

The health risks posed by particulate pollution appear to be greater than for other kinds of air pollution. Particulates are a major cause of, and contributor to, respiratory diseases, and many are known carcinogens. In one of the earliest epidemiological studies, hospital admissions for pneumonia, bronchitis, and asthma were found to be statistically correlated with high levels of particulate matter in the lungs. Such admissions were two to three times more numerous in the winter, when levels of pollution were high, than in periods when pollution levels were low. These relationships were clearly present even after adjustment for temperature inversions and other factors.[32] Other studies have demonstrated adverse health effects of particulate matter at levels well below the national ambient air quality standard.[33] The respiratory systems of animals have shown similar damage as a result of exposure to particulate pollution. Animals exposed to bacterial infections and air pollutants are likely to die sooner than animals that have the same infections but are not exposed to pollutants.

Several studies have concluded that for each 10 microgram per cubic meter ($\mu g/m^3$) increase in PM_{10} concentration, mortality rates increase from 0.7 to 1.6 percent, with a weighted mean of 1.0 percent. Stronger associations were found for cardiovascular disease (1.4 percent per 10 $\mu g/m^3$ of PM_{10}) and for respiratory disease (3.4 percent per 10 $\mu g/m^3$ of PM_{10}). These results obtain after controlling for weather and the presence of other pollutants, and are consistent across different kinds of statistical models and tests.[34] This consistency across a wide range of geographic areas and conditions is evidence that the health effects of PM_{10} are significant and pose a serious threat to human health.

Most significant, strong associations between pollution and increased mortality are demonstrated in these studies even at pollution levels below the national air quality standard. The causes of death in these studies included both respiratory and cardiovascular disease. Mortality studies have been conducted in several states and throughout the world, and associations between particulate pollution and mortality have occurred in a variety of climatic conditions and during different seasons. Taken as a whole, these studies have eliminated the confounding effects of weather, other pollutants, and other factors.[35] No safe level of pollution—no threshold below which no health effects occur—has been identified in these studies. Adverse health effects occur immediately after exposure to high levels of pollution as well as for several days following exposure.

Major industrial sources of PM_{10} are steel mills, smelters, power plants, cotton gins, and cement plants. Diesel engines, road dust, demolition, construction, and wood-burning stoves and fireplaces also produce particulates.[36] Figure 2-6 shows the trend in emissions of total suspended particulates from 1940 to 1990. Despite tremendous economic growth, progress in reducing such emissions was made even before the first major Clean Air

Figure 2-6 Emissions of Total Suspended Particulates[a], 1940-1990

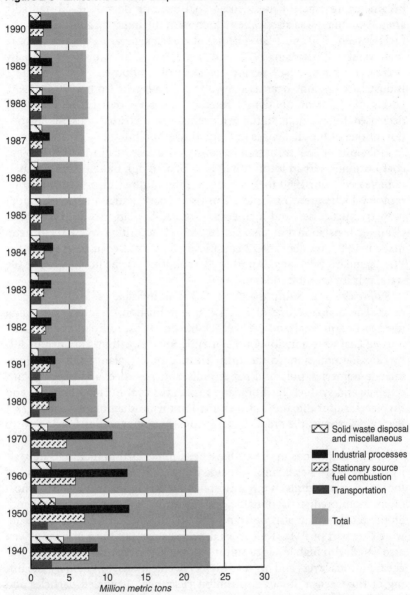

Source: Environmental Protection Agency, *National Air Pollutant Emission Estimates, 1940-1990* (Washington, D.C.: EPA, 1991), 7.
Note: See Table 2-3, which gives major source categories and subcategories for air pollutants.
[a]Although the EPA and the states continue to monitor total suspended particulate emissions, the national ambient air quality standard applies only to PM_{10}.

Act was passed, between 1950 and 1970, as industries and power plants became more efficient. Residential coal-burning decreased substantially after 1940; there was also some reduction in the industrial use of coal as a fuel between 1940 and 1990. The use of coal in generating electricity more than doubled between 1970 and 1990, but TSP emissions actually decreased during that period as control equipment was installed. Industrial emissions decreased by about 75 percent from 1970 to 1990. Levels of different pollutants interact: as some particulate emissions decreased, for example, sulfur oxide emissions increased, a useful illustration of one of the challenges in regulating air pollution.

Emissions of TSP from mobile sources decreased from 1940 to 1960 as coal-burning railroad locomotives were phased out, but emissions actually increased from 1960 to 1988 because the number of miles traveled by motor vehicles grew. Emissions from stationary source fuel combustion, industrial processes, and incineration of solid waste also decreased after clean air legislation was enacted in 1970.[37] According to EPA estimates made in 1987, residents of 72 counties in 20 states live in areas where the PM_{10} standard is violated. Another 110 counties may be in violation of the standards if current trends continue.

Sulfur Dioxide. Sulfur dioxide (SO_2) is an invisible gas with a pungent odor. The major source of SO_2 is the combustion of sulfur-containing fuels, primarily coal and fuel oil. Until the 1950s, railroad engines that burned coal were a major source of emissions. Two-thirds of current sulfur dioxide emissions come from electric power plants. Other sources include refineries, pulp and paper mills, smelters, steel and paper plants, oil shale and synfuels facilities, and residential coal-burning furnaces and fireplaces; sulfur dioxide is also emitted in the production of oil and gas.[38] Figure 2-7 shows the trend in emissions of sulfur oxides from 1940 to 1990.

Sulfur compounds in the air have been implicated in increased mortality in several studies.[39] Sulfur dioxide is generally not the most harmful of the sulfur compounds in the atmosphere, even though it is the form most often monitored; it is nonetheless a serious environmental problem.[40] Sulfur dioxide may also be transformed into sulfates and sulfuric acid, which are part of PM_{10}. Killer fogs in various parts of the world have been associated with high levels of sulfur oxides. Sulfur dioxide can thicken tracheal mucous layers and, in very high concentrations, can damage the lining of the trachea. It can also inhibit clearance of inhaled particles and cause bronchial constriction. Acute exposure to high levels of sulfur dioxides can cause edema (accumulation of fluid in tissue), bronchial spasms, shortness of breath, irritation of the respiratory tract, impaired pulmonary function and lung clearance, and increased susceptibility to disease. Sulfur dioxide can trigger asthma attacks and has been shown to cause or exacer-

Figure 2-7 Emissions of Sulfur Oxides, 1940-1990

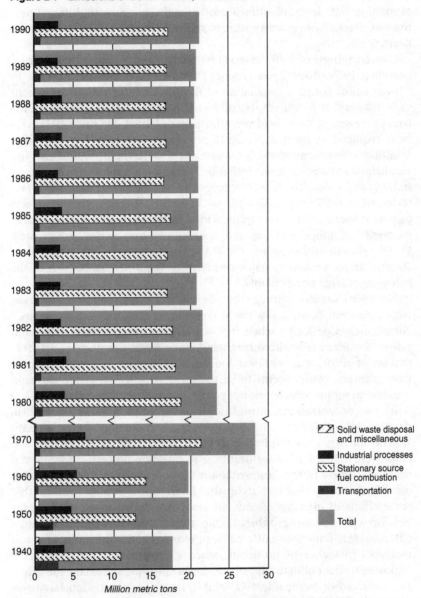

Source: Environmental Protection Agency, *National Air Pollutant Emission Estimates, 1940-1990* (Washington, D.C.: EPA, 1991), 9.

Note: See Table 2-3, which gives major source categories and subcategories for air pollutants.

bate emphysema.[41] One study found that schoolchildren who were exposed to high levels of sulfur dioxide for five to ten years suffered permanent effects.[42] Chronic exposure to sulfur dioxide can exert stress on the heart.[43]

Concentrations of sulfur dioxide have decreased by more than 25 percent since 1970, primarily as a result of the use of coal and other fuels with a lower sulfur content, installation of flue gas desulfurization equipment or "scrubbers" at power plants and factories, and other changes in industrial processes. Sulfuric acid manufacturing plants built since 1972 have been required to meet more stringent regulations issued by the EPA, resulting in lower emissions. Increased use of western, low-sulfur coal has also helped reduce SO_2 levels.[44] In order to disperse sulfur dioxide concentrations and reduce the threat to people living near power plants and factories, these facilities installed tall stacks in the 1970s. The pollutant was dispersed locally, but it was transformed to sulfates and fell to the earth hundreds of miles away as acid rain. Only one major urban area, Pittsburgh, currently exceeds the NAAQS. The standard is exceeded in counties in about sixteen states, primarily in the Midwest, because of the existence of large power plants.[45]

Nitrogen Dioxide. Nitrogen dioxide (NO_2) is a yellow-brownish-red gas with a pungent odor. It is a major component of ozone and acid rain.[46] Nitrogen dioxide forms when fuel is burned at high temperatures and nitrogen oxides are oxidized through gaining oxygen molecules. The formation of nitric acid, nitrates, and other pollutants in the atmosphere from nitrogen oxides seems to be the greatest concern. Major emission sources are motor vehicles, power plants, and industrial boilers.

In low concentrations, nitrogen dioxide can impair the sense of smell, damage cell membranes and tissue, irritate and damage the pulmonary system, and aggravate respiratory diseases such as asthma, bronchitis, and emphysema. In high concentrations, it causes pulmonary edema and death. Relatively little is known about the long-term effects of nitrogen dioxide at current ambient air quality levels. Some studies indicate that some effects of nitrogen dioxide are reversible and that a tolerance may develop with repeated exposure.[47] One study found that schoolchildren in Chattanooga, Tennessee, suffered from reduced respiratory function and increased incidence of bronchitis when exposed to nitrogen dioxide.[48] Exposure to the pollutant appears to lower the body's resistance to infection. Like carbon monoxide, NO_2 inhibits the ability of blood to carry oxygen to the body. Some studies have shown that NO_2 concentrations are associated with increases in heart disease and mortality.[49]

Emissions of nitrogen oxides increased rapidly from 1940 to 1970, peaked about 1980, and remained fairly constant throughout the 1980s, as shown in Figure 2-8. Controls on emissions of motor vehicles and coal-

Figure 2-8 Emissions of Nitrogen Oxides, 1940-1990

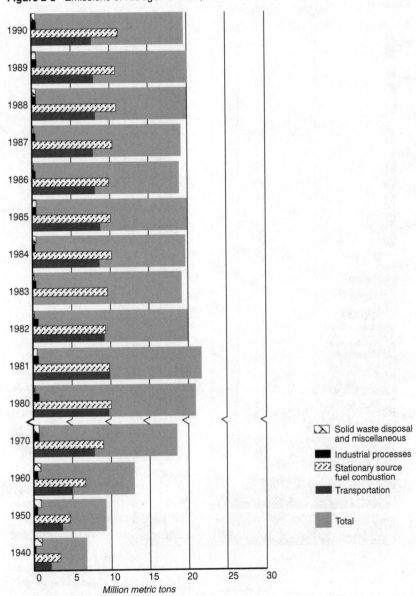

Million metric tons

Source: Environmental Protection Agency, *National Air Pollutant Emission Estimates, 1940-1990* (Washington, D.C.: EPA, 1991), 10.
Note: See Table 2-3, which gives major source categories and subcategories for air pollutants.

Figure 2-9 Emissions of Lead, 1970-1990

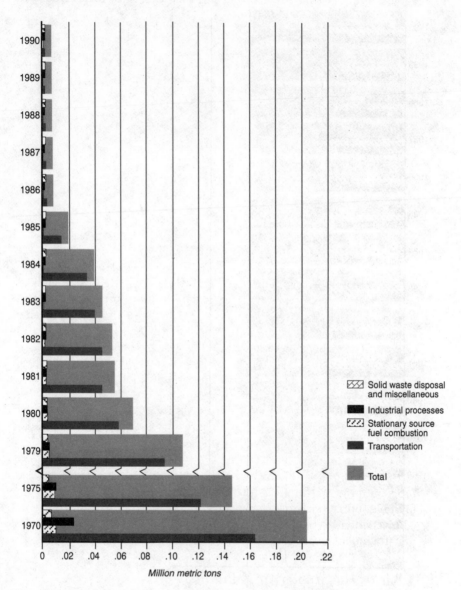

Million metric tons

Source: Environmental Protection Agency, *National Air Pollutant Emission Estimates, 1940-1990*
(Washington, D.C.: EPA, 1991), 13.
Note: See Table 2-3, which gives major source categories and subcategories for air pollutants.

Table 2-4   Ten U.S. Manufacturing Sites Releasing Most Toxic Chemicals, 1989

Site	Company	Pounds released (millions)
Alvin, Texas	Monsanto	206.5
Westwego, Louisiana	American Cyanamid	192.4
Tooele, Utah	Magnesium Corporation of America	119.1
Wichita, Kansas	Vulcan	92.3
Beaumont, Texas	DuPont	88.1
Port Lavace, Texas	British Petroleum	65.5
New Johnsonville, Tennessee	DuPont	57.4
Chicago, Illinois	Inland Steel	57.3
Lima, Ohio	British Petroleum	56.7
Wichita, Kansas	Atochem	54.5

Source: John Holusha, "The Nation's Polluters—Who Emits What," *New York Times,* October 13, 1991, F10.

fired electric power plants have moderated the increase in emissions of nitrogen oxides despite the growth in transportation and industrial activity. Los Angeles is the only area where the national ambient air quality standard was exceeded in the 1980s and early 1990s.

Lead. The primary sources of lead emissions have been motor vehicles. For many years, this toxic metal was added to gasoline as an antiknock compound. Cars using lead-free gasoline were introduced in 1975, however, and the amount of lead in leaded gas has also been reduced. As a result, lead emissions have been cut dramatically; they decreased 93 percent between 1979 and 1988, as shown in Figure 2-9. Lead poses a major health risk at high levels. It decreases red blood cell production; affects the central nervous system, thus causing loss of sensation; and retards the mental development of young children. High levels of lead emission are still a problem, primarily in areas where lead smelters are located; lead is also found in sources such as lead-based paint, which deteriorates and is ingested by children. Twelve areas of the United States have been designated as nonattainment areas for lead.[50]

Toxic or Hazardous Air Pollutants

The 1986 Emergency Planning and Community Right-to-Know Act, also known as Title III of the Superfund law, aimed at cleaning up toxic waste sites, requires manufacturers of some 300 different chemicals to report annually to the EPA and to the states in which they operate the amount of chemicals they release directly to the air, water, or land.

Figure 2-10 Release of Toxic Chemicals into the Environment, 1992

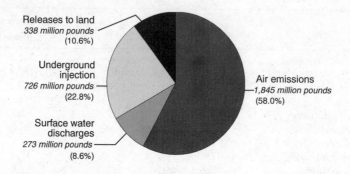

Releases to land
338 million pounds
(10.6%)

Underground
injection
726 million pounds
(22.8%)

Surface water
discharges
273 million pounds
(8.6%)

Air emissions
1,845 million pounds
(58.0%)

Source: Environmental Protection Agency, *1992 Toxics Release Inventory* Washington, D.C.:
EPA, 1994), 24.

Facilities with ten or more employees that manufacture or process more
than 25,000 pounds of the reportable chemicals, or that use more than
10,000 pounds of them, are required to file reports. The annual publication of the EPA's *Toxics Release Inventory,* based on the data culled from
manufacturers' reports, as well as major accidental releases of chemicals
(such as the toxic leak from a Union Carbide Company chemical plant in
Bhopal, India, in 1984 that killed thousands of people), generated widespread concern about air toxics in the mid-1980s and increased support
for strengthening the Clean Air Act's provisions. Table 2-4 lists the ten
worst manufacturing sites in the United States in terms of the total amount
of toxic chemicals released.

Most of the information concerning the environmental and health hazards posed by air toxics comes from laboratory tests with animals; conclusions based on it are thus, at best, only tentative. Epidemiological data
on which regulatory action might be based are often incomplete or incon-
clusive, because of conditions in the environment in which the exposure
occurs. According to one estimate, only partial or minimal toxicity information is available regarding about 15 percent of the 13,000 chemicals
that are produced in large quantities (more than a million pounds a year)
in the United States. Another 22,000 chemicals are estimated to be
released in unknown quantities, and little or no information is available
on their toxicity.[51]

The EPA reported in its 1992 inventory that more than 3.4 billion
pounds of toxic chemicals were released to the air, water, or land, or inject-
ed underground in 1992. An additional 4.3 billion pounds of toxic chem-

Figure 2-11 Release of Toxic Chemicals into the Environment, 1988-1992

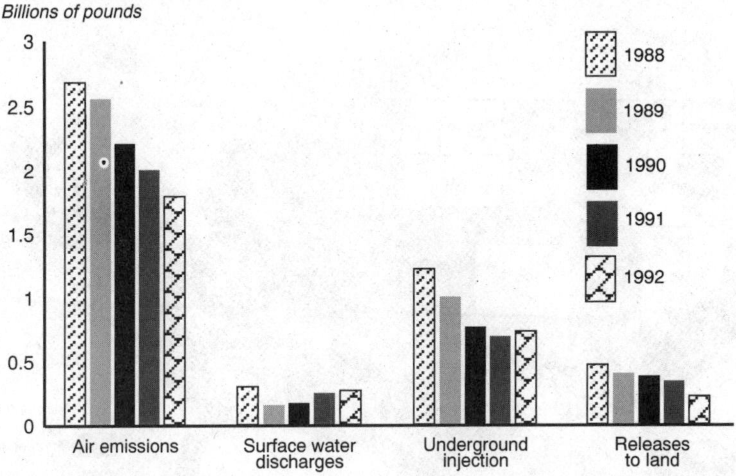

Billions of pounds

Source: Environmental Protection Agency, *1992 Toxics Release Inventory* (Washington, D.C.: EPA,

icals were produced and then transferred to recycling, energy recovery, treatment, disposal, and other facilities. As shown in Figure 2-10, most of the toxic emissions reported by businesses were released into the air. From 1987 (when the first inventory was compiled and published) to 1992, reported releases decreased by some 35 percent, even though more companies were reporting in 1992 and there was an increase in industrial production.[52] Figure 2-11 shows the results of the first five years of the inventory. These figures are only rough estimates, however, since monitoring of toxic releases is still in its infancy; there is no enforcement mechanism to ensure accurate or complete reporting, for example. Consequently, the inventory may significantly understate the amount of air toxics released each year.

Figure 2-12 indicates where toxic releases are concentrated in the United States. The highest concentrations are found primarily in the central southern and northern Midwest states. Table 2-5 lists the ten toxic chemicals that are known or suspected carcinogens that were released into the air in the largest amounts in 1992. Table 2-6 inventories toxic air emissions by industry. Many of the air toxics that are found in the greatest quantity (such as ammonia, a colorless gas with a strong odor; toluene, a liquid hydrocarbon similar to but less toxic than benzene; methanol, an alcohol made from wood or methane; and acetone, an organic compound) are used in liquid form as solvents. The vast majority of air toxics are released by chemical manufacturers—followed by paper, primary metals, and plastics industries; and transportation equipment manufacturers. Like the criteria pollutants discussed earlier, these pollutants pose serious health haz-

Figure 2-12   Release of Toxic Chemicals into the Environment, by State, 1992

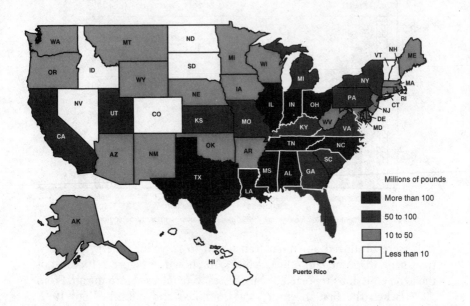

Source: Environmental Protection Agency, *1992 Toxics Release Inventory* (Washington, D.C.: EPA, 1994), 30.

ards, especially in high concentrations. Most of them can irritate the nose, throat, mouth, eyes, and lungs. Some chemicals are associated with specific health problems. Toluene, for example, can cause dizziness and headaches; damage bone marrow, the liver, and the kidneys; and damage the developing fetus. Ammonia and chlorine can burn the skin and eyes, sometimes causing permanent damage, and can cause pulmonary edema. Acetone can irritate the eyes, nose, and throat and burn the skin. Despite the problems they can cause, these four pollutants are not generally considered to be the most serious air toxics.

Controlling air toxics was a major concern of the authors of the Clean Air Act Amendments of 1990. As indicated in Table 2-7, they faced a tremendously diverse set of sources, making regulation particularly difficult. About two-thirds of all industrial emissions come from point sources (major facilities such as power plants); the rest are released from nonpoint

Table 2-5 Top Ten Known or Suspected Carcinogens Released
into the Air, 1992

Chemical compound	Total air emissions (pounds)
Dichloromethane	73,963,205
Styrene	32,334,616
Chloroform	17,034,926
Benzene	12,384,579
Tetrachloroethylene	12,311,235
Formaldehyde	10,903,035
Acetaldehyde	6,416,121
1,3-Butadiene	3,843,700
1,2-Dichloroethane	3,165,207
Acrylonitrile	1,600,071

Source: Environmental Protection Agency, 1992 Toxics Release Inventory
(Washington, D.C.: EPA, 1994), 78.

sources (area, or fugitive, sources—small facilities such as bakeries and dry
cleaners) that are widely dispersed and difficult to monitor and regulate.
The Toxics Release Inventory only reports emissions from relatively large
industrial sources. The total amount of emissions in 1989 was more than
double the 5.7 billion pounds that were estimated before the first reports
were received, since motor vehicle emissions account for more than half of
all air pollution in the United States. Regulation of tailpipe exhaust, discussed in Chapter 4, helps reduce such emissions. Shifting to alternative
fuels and reformulated gasoline may also help, although in the case of
some of these fuels, one set of air toxics is merely substituted for another.

Table 2-6 Top Ten Industries Producing Toxic Air Releases, 1992

Industry	Fugitive or nonpoint air emissions (pounds)	Stack or point air emissions (pounds)
Chemicals	151,023,884	398,012,277
Transportation equipment	42,072,256	91,994,680
Plastics	40,117,459	93,324,489
Petroleum	38,493,819	22,590,400
Primary metals	35,266,082	100,323,898
Fabricated metals	38,306,338	61,765,403
Printing	23,262,751	17,206,225
Paper	23,197,469	176,641,208
Machinery	13,547,039	19,832,183
Electrical	15,722,687	35,713,523

Source: Environmental Protection Agency, 1992 Toxics Release Inventory (Washington, D.C.:
EPA, 1994), 206-208.

Table 2-7   Major Sources of Toxic Air Pollutants and Percentages
Emitted, 1988

Source	Percent of total emissions
Area	
Motor vehicles	56
Treatment, storage, and disposal works	5
Secondary formaldehyde, nonpoint	5
Wood-burning smoke	4
Asbestos, demolition	4
Gasoline marketing	3
Solvent use/degreasing	1
Other/unspecified	2
Total	80
Point	
Electroplating	6
Cooling towers in power plants	3
Chemical users/producers	2
Secondary formaldehyde, point	2
Iron and steel production	1
Coal and oil combustion (nonresidential)	1
Other/unspecified	6
Total*	20

Source: Environmental Protection Agency figures, reported in George Hager, "The
'White House Effect' Opens A Long-Locked Political Door," *Congressional Quarterly
Weekly Report,* January 20, 1990, 143.
*Percentages do not add to total because of rounding.

The EPA's regulation of air toxics under the Clean Air Act of 1970 was
widely viewed as a failure. The agency was either unable or unwilling
to define safe levels of exposure for these substances and issued emission
standards for only a handful of substances. In contrast, during the 1970s
and 1980s the Occupational Safety and Health Administration had
regulated some 500 workplace toxic chemicals, and the states had regulated more than 700 air toxics.[53] The clear failure of regulation efforts
under the existing law, combined with widespread public fear of the
health threat posed by air toxics (generated largely by the publicity
given to chemical accidents), kept pressure on Congress to pass new
legislation regulating emissions. In addition, the chemical industry,
traditionally opposed to regulation, was by 1990 more willing to support
some kind of legislation because of the growing public relations problem;
some companies had already committed themselves to massive reductions in emissions.

Figure 2-13 Acid Rain Concentrations in the United States and Canada, as Measured by pH Values, 1985

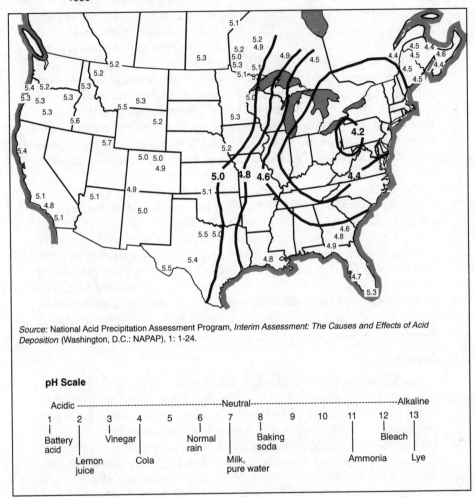

Source: National Acid Precipitation Assessment Program, *Interim Assessment: The Causes and Effects of Acid Deposition* (Washington, D.C.: NAPAP), 1: 1-24.

Acid Rain

Acid deposition (or, more commonly, acid rain) is a by-product of the burning of fossil fuels, which produces sulfur dioxide (SO_2) and nitrogen oxides (NO_x). These gases are transformed in the atmosphere into sulfuric acid and nitric acid, which usually remain in the atmosphere for weeks and may travel hundreds of miles before settling on or near the earth as dry particles or precipitation. Acidic particles and gases can also be formed at ground level and are absorbed directly by plants or oxidized into sulfates and nitrates and absorbed by the soil.

Most of the concern surrounding acid rain has focused on its danger to forests and aquatic resources. Studies conducted throughout the 1980s indicated that acid rain is a threat to watersheds, lakes, and streams in New England; forests and coastal plains in the mid-Atlantic region; and forests in northern Florida. Acid rain pollution is believed to harm red spruce and pine trees in the eastern and southeastern United States (low-level ozone pollution is also a threat to trees). The precipitation in many of the eastern states and Canadian provinces is thirty to forty times more acidic than it was in the 1980s.[54] The Office of Technology Assessment concluded in 1984 that acidic aerosols (fine droplets composed of sulfur, nitrogen, and chlorine compounds and other chemicals) pose a serious threat to individuals with respiratory problems and may be responsible for as many as 50,000 deaths in the United States each year.[55]

The acidity of a substance is indicated by its pH factor, which is measured on a logarithmic scale. A change of one unit on the scale represents a tenfold increase or decrease in acidity. As shown in the scale at the bottom of Figure 2-13, battery acid has a pH rating of 1, lemon juice has a pH rating of approximately 2, and milk and pure water have a rating of 7, the neutral point. Natural sources cause rainfall that is otherwise unpolluted to have a pH factor of 5.5 to 7.0. Rain rated below a pH factor of 5.6 is generally considered to be sufficiently acidic to have negative environmental consequences. Figure 2-13 shows acid rain concentrations in the United States and Canada.

Sources

The primary source of acid rain is sulfur oxides. Approximately 20 million tons of SO_x are emitted each year in the United States: approximately 75 percent from electric utility power plants that burn fossil fuels, 20 percent from industrial sources, and 5 percent from transportation sources. Fifty power plants, primarily older facilities not subject to the regulations for new sources issued under the Clean Air Act, are responsible for one-half of all SO_x emissions.[56] Figure 2-14 shows emissions of sulfur and nitrogen oxides by coal-fired power plants from 1940 to 1988 that confronted Congress and the Bush administration as they designed the acid rain provisions of the Clean Air Act Amendments of 1990. Unlike other pollutants, emissions of these two chemicals from power plants had greatly increased between 1950 and 1970. Emissions of sulfur oxides decreased by about 20 percent after 1977, even though the consumption of coal has increased significantly. As a result of the 1977 act, utility companies have been spending about $10 billion a year on air pollution controls.

Nitrogen oxides are the second major source of acid rain. In the United States, approximately 43 percent of NO_x emissions are from motor vehicles, 33 percent are from utilities, 15 percent are from other industrial

Figure 2-14 Emission of Sulfur Oxides and Nitrogen Oxides from Electric Utility Coal Combustion, 1940-1988

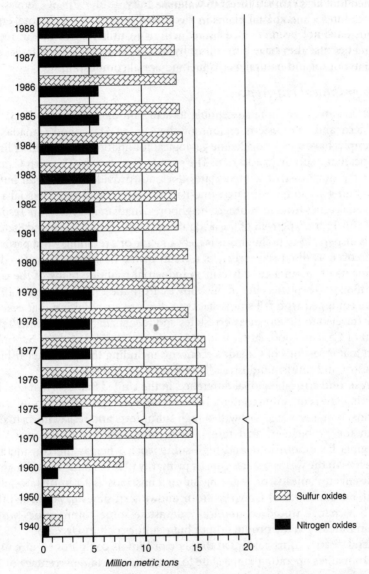

Million metric tons

Source: Environmental Protection Agency, *National Air Pollutant Emission Estimates, 1940-1990* (Washington, D.C.: EPA, 1991), 57.

combustion, and 9 percent are from all other sources. These emissions are diverse and widely dispersed, and therefore are difficult to regulate. Both SO_x and NO_x emissions increased significantly until 1970. SO_2 emissions peaked in 1976 and 1977 and have decreased since then.[57] NO_x total emissions have not been affected by reductions in utility emissions in recent years because they have been offset by increased motor vehicle travel and the use of oil and natural gas to fuel industrial combustion.[58]

Geographical Differences

Some areas are more susceptible to acid rain damage than others. The western and midwestern regions of the United States and Canada, for example, have a natural alkaline geological foundation, composed of limestone, that neutralizes acid rain. The granite foundation of eastern Canada and the northeastern United States does not provide that natural buffer. According to some estimates, one-half of all the acid rain that falls on Canada comes from its southern neighbor; Canadian industries are responsible for 15 to 25 percent of the acid rain in the northeastern United States.[59] This dispersion of pollutants is largely a factor of prevailing wind patterns. Moreover, as discussed earlier, as a result of the health concerns faced by residents of urban areas adjacent to industrial facilities, many of the coal-burning power plants built in the Midwest from the 1950s to the early 1970s were equipped with tall smokestacks to disperse air pollution that eventually traveled to the northeastern states and to Canada.[60] More than 90 percent of Canada's population is located within 150 miles of the U.S. border, and major sections of Canada's economy, including the freshwater fishing, forestry, and tourism industries, have been affected by acid rain.[61]

A second critical regional difference, in the United States, is that coal has varying levels of sulfur content. Indiana, Illinois, Ohio, West Virginia, and Pennsylvania produce coal with a high sulfur level and resist efforts to deal with the problem of acid rain by switching fuels. Kentucky and West Virginia have both low- and high-sulfur coal, whereas the considerable reserves in the western states consist primarily of low-sulfur coal. The most cost-effective means of reducing sulfur emissions is to burn low-sulfur coal, but members of Congress from midwestern states have warned that such a change would economically devastate some communities whose main industry is the production of high-sulfur coal. In December 1993, a federal district court ruled that the state of Illinois could not require utility companies operating in the state to purchase a certain percentage of the coal they consume from in-state sources.[62]

The northeastern United States has long relied on oil-fired facilities and nuclear power plants, and both the Northeast and Canada rely on hydroelectric power. Midwestern critics of proposals to control acid rain have argued that Canadians have tried to sell more electricity to their neighbors to the south.[63] Environmental laws and regulations, in general, have been more stringent in the Northeast than in the Midwest.

Fossil fuel combustion not only contributes to acid rain but is also the major source of carbon dioxide, a greenhouse gas implicated as a primary factor in theories of global climatic change. Nitrogen oxide emissions from automobiles also contribute to the formation of the urban ozone that plagues most large cities in the United States. Regulations limiting motor vehicle emissions will help reduce acid rain, and that, in turn, will contribute to progress in resolving these other environmental problems.

The Stratospheric Ozone Layer

The depletion of the stratospheric ozone layer is an air pollution problem that, like acid rain, is global in scope and impact and is the subject of international agreements and treaties as well as national legislation. Significant decreases in ozone levels have been discovered throughout the stratosphere, particularly at the North and South poles, and observations taken each year find that the problem is growing.[64] Some scientists have estimated that for every 1 percent decline in atmospheric ozone, there is a 2 percent increase in the amount of ultraviolet radiation that reaches the earth's surface. The EPA calculates that a 1 percent decline in atmospheric ozone could result in a 5 percent increase in cases of nonmalignant skin cancer and a 2 percent increase in cases of malignant skin cancer (melanoma), which claims over 5,000 American lives each year. The EPA has warned that if ozone destruction continues unchecked, there will be more than 155 million additional cases of skin cancer and more than 3.2 million additional cancer deaths over the next century. Increased levels of ultraviolet radiation resulting from depletion of the ozone layer may lead to serious adverse consequences for marine and coastal ecosystems, plants, and animals, and pose a serious potential threat to future food production throughout the world.[65]

Causes of Stratospheric Ozone Depletion

In the 1960s, scientists found some evidence that ozone was being destroyed in the atmosphere. This destruction was generally attributable to ultraviolet radiation, which, during periods of high solar intensity, was believed to bombard ozone molecules and break them down. When this radiation lessened, the ozone was allowed to regenerate itself. In 1971, researchers became concerned that a U.S.-European-proposed fleet of supersonic transport (SST) aircraft would damage the ozone layer because emissions of water vapor and nitrogen oxides from the SSTs had been shown to attack ozone. The SST fleet never came to fruition, but rising levels of nitrous oxides (NO_x), a result of increased combustion and increased use of nitrogen-rich fertilizers, led to similar concerns in the early 1970s that the ozone layer was being destroyed.

In 1974, Mario J. Molina and F. Sherwood Rowland, scientists at the University of California at Irvine, proposed that the increasing use of compounds known as chlorofluorocarbons (CFCs) posed a new threat to the ozone layer that overshadowed all previous concerns. These compounds (which, as the name suggests, consist of chlorine, fluorine, and carbon) were discovered in the early 1930s when the struggling refrigerator industry was searching for a reliable, nontoxic, and nonflammable coolant.

Chlorofluorocarbons constitute one of the most reliable groups of chemicals developed in the past half century and have a variety of industrial and commercial applications; for example, they are used as coolants for air conditioners and refrigerators, propellants for aerosol sprays, blowing agents to produce foam and insulation, and cleansers for computer microchips and other electronic parts. Their usefulness is a function of their chemical properties: CFCs are highly stable and nonreactive and are therefore nontoxic.

Ironically, it is these characteristics of CFCs that make them so dangerous to ozone in the stratosphere. Since they are not broken down at the earth's surface, CFC molecules rise intact into the upper atmosphere. At levels above 25 kilometers—roughly the place where ozone is at its highest concentration—the normally stable CFC molecules are bombarded by intense ultraviolet light, which breaks them into more reactive forms, such as chlorine atoms. Each chlorine atom can destroy as many as 100,000 ozone molecules before it is inactivated or returned to the troposphere by precipitation or other processes.[66]

Researchers fear that the release of millions of tons of CFCs into the atmosphere will cause an accumulation in the stratosphere capable of damaging the ozone layer. The problem is especially acute because CFCs can remain in the atmosphere for decades. (Two of the major varieties of CFCs, CFC-11 and CFC-12, have atmospheric lifetimes of approximately seventy-five and one-hundred years, respectively.) Even if the release of CFCs into the atmosphere were halted today, the destruction of ozone would continue well into the next century.

Some researchers suggest that CFCs may not be the only source of stratospheric ozone depletion.[67] One theory is that particles in the stratospheric clouds that form over the Antarctic region in the winter (when the absence of sunlight frequently results in very low temperatures) might stimulate the conversion of chlorine reservoirs into active chlorine: "It is possible that these particles trap and slowly modify the major chlorine reservoirs, preparing chlorine monoxide to make a rapid escape when the sun begins to shine."[68] Recent research, however, has clearly indicated that human-made chemicals are a major threat to the ozone layer.

International Agreements to Protect the
Stratospheric Ozone Layer

The research conducted by scientists in the mid-1970s led to the first international agreement to protect the ozone layer. International initiatives concerning ozone began in March 1977, when the secretariat of the United Nations Environment Programme convened a meeting of experts designated by governments and by intergovernmental and nongovernmental organizations. As a result of that meeting, an initiative entitled "A World Plan of Action on the Ozone Layer" was adopted and an international Coordinating Committee on the Ozone Layer was established.[69] In 1978, the United States, Canada, and several Scandinavian countries agreed to restrict or ban nonessential aerosol uses of CFCs. By 1983, regulatory action and voluntary industry restrictions in several CFC-producing countries had resulted in a reduction in CFC production of 21 percent below the peak level of 1974.[70]

In May 1981, the United Nations established a working group to draw up a framework for a general convention on the protection of the ozone layer. Despite the group's failure to agree on a specific provision for CFCs, its draft convention was adopted in 1985 as the Vienna Convention for the Protection of the Ozone Layer, which was signed by twenty nations. The convention consists of twenty-one treaty articles and two technical annexes, or additions. The major provisions of the agreement emphasize the general responsibility of states for preventing environmental harm caused by human interference with the ozone layer; specify the duties of states with regard to intergovernmental cooperation, including monitoring, information exchange, and the harmonization of national measures; and create new international institutions (including a subsequent conference of the parties to the convention and a secretariat) to implement the agreement and to develop more specific rules in the form of protocols, technical annexes, and financial and procedural provisions.[71]

The Vienna Conference was only the beginning of international efforts to protect the ozone layer. New concerns arose over the seemingly accelerated rate at which the ozone layer was being depleted. In late 1985, a British research team published a report stating that springtime amounts of ozone over Antarctica had decreased by more than 40 percent between 1977 and 1984. Other research groups confirmed the conclusions of the British report and showed that the region of depletion was wider than the continent of Antarctica and spanned much of the lower stratosphere. In effect, they suggested the existence of a "hole" in the earth's protective layer of ozone. This theory prompted a search for the cause of the ozone loss. Most researchers returned to an explanation that had been proposed in the mid-1970s: that human-made chemicals, specifically CFCs, were depleting the

Table 2-8   Status of International Efforts to Regulate CFCs, 1994

CFC	Status
CFC 11, 12, 113, 114, 115	Phase out in 1996
Halon 1211, 1301, 2402	Phase out in 1994*
Carbon tetrachloride	Phase out in 1996
Methyl chloroform	Phase out in 1996
HCFCs	Freeze at 1989 levels in 2004; phase out in 2030
Methylbromide	Freeze at 1991 levels in 1995*
Other CFCs (ten)	Phase out in 1996

Source: Alexandre Kiss and Dinah Shelton, International Environmental Law (Irvington-on-Hudson, N.Y.: Transnational Publishers, Inc., 1994), 125.
*These regulations took effect as scheduled.

ozone layer. Laboratory studies had previously shown that chlorine destroys ozone, and the millions of tons of CFCs that had been released into the atmosphere for decades were sufficient to produce the kind of damage that had been identified.

In 1986, delegates from fifty-four nations met in Geneva, Switzerland, to discuss limitations on the production and use of CFCs. The result of that meeting was the Montreal Protocol on Substances That Deplete the Ozone Layer, which was signed by thirty-one nations on September 16, 1987 in Montreal. It limited the production of five CFC compounds (11, 12, 113, 114, and 115) and three forms of halon—a chemical commonly used in fire extinguishers that, although used in smaller quantities than CFCs, is more effective in destroying ozone. Also provided was a graduated reduction schedule that would bring a 50 percent decline in CFC usage by 1999 for industrialized nations and a smaller reduction for developing countries.[72]

The Montreal Protocol called for an assessment of efforts to curb CFC production beginning in 1990. Barely a month after it was signed, however, a National Aeronautics and Space Administration expedition brought back definitive proof of a hole in the ozone layer, which demonstrated the inadequacy of the protocol's provisions and renewed calls for a total ban of CFCs. Findings released in 1988 by the Global Ozone Trends Panel, an international group of more than one hundred scientists, showed that ozone depletion was occurring at two to three times the rate predicted by computer models. This meant, according to the scientists, that the world had already suffered more ozone depletion than was thought would occur by the year 2050 if nations observed the reduction schedule of the Montreal Protocol.[73] In June 1990, eighty-six nations agreed to go beyond the terms of the protocol and eliminate CFCs by the year 2000.[74] Significantly, the Western industrialized countries and Japan agreed to help the third world nations achieve such a reduction,[75] although only part of the money pledged has actually been provided, and some of the money allocated has not been spent because of difficulties in finding and approving suitable projects.[76] The current status of international efforts to regulate CFCs is presented in Table 2-8.

Global Climate Change

Although the Clean Air Act Amendments of 1990 mention global climate change only in a minor provision, that issue helped form the context in which the amendments were passed. The United Nations Framework Convention on Climate Change, negotiated for the 1992 Earth Summit in Rio de Janeiro, called on the parties involved to stabilize the concentrations of greenhouse gases in the atmosphere

at a level that would prevent dangerous anthropogenic interference with the climate system . . . within a time frame sufficient to allow ecosystems to adapt naturally to climate change, to ensure that food production is not threatened and to enable economic development to proceed in a sustainable manner.[77]

All parties are required to publish on a regular basis "national inventories of anthropogenic emissions by sources and removals by sinks of all greenhouse gases not controlled by the Montreal Protocol"; to formulate and implement national and, where appropriate, regional plans to "mitigate climate change"; and to take the threat of climate change into account in "relevant social, economic and environmental policies and actions." [78] The developed countries agreed to protect carbon reservoirs (primarily forests) and limit greenhouse gas emissions "by the end of the present decade . . . to their 1990 levels of . . . anthropogenic emissions of carbon dioxide and other greenhouse gases not controlled by the Montreal Protocol" and to "provide new and additional financial resources to meet the agreed full costs incurred by the developing country Parties in complying with their obligations."[79] The convention, then, provides no specific targets or timetables and makes the effort voluntary; the only enforcement mechanism provided is an agreement by the participating states to report periodically on their progress in achieving the target.

The convention was approved in the U.S. Senate in 1992 and was ratified by the requisite fifty nations in 1994. Each country is to publish an action plan including an inventory of greenhouse gas emissions and sinks and a "general description of steps taken or envisaged by the Party to implement the Convention."[80] In October 1993 the Clinton administration, as required by the convention, released its "Climate Change Action Plan,"[81] which promises to reduce levels of greenhouse gas emissions by the year 2000 to 1990 levels of about 1.5 billion tons. Those levels are equivalent to a reduction of 1993 emissions by some 110 million tons. Progress will be measured every two years.[82]

Challenges in Regulating Air Pollution

Regulating air pollution is a complex policy task, given the wide variety in the kinds and sources of pollutants. Many of the adverse environmental consequences of industrial activity will fall on future generations, while the benefits are largely confined to the current generation. National and global environmental problems are intricately interrelated. Ozone and other low atmospheric pollutants pose immediate health risks to humans as well as acting as greenhouse gases. Chlorofluorocarbons damage the stratospheric ozone layer as well as contributing to global warming. Sulfur and nitrogen oxides threaten human health and are also precursors of acid rain.[83] Regulations far too often serve only to transfer pollution from one medium to another. Efforts to reduce one form of emissions (acid rain emissions through the use of scrubbers, for instance) may increase other kinds of emissions (greenhouse gas emissions produced because more coal is required to produce the same amount of electricity).

Although progress has been made in eliminating or reducing some forms of pollution, those that remain are, in general, among the most difficult and expensive to address because the costs of reducing the final increments are much greater than those required to achieve earlier reductions. The development of new chemical and nuclear industries and technologies poses a further problem in that relatively minute levels of their emissions can result in environmental and health hazards.

Environmental concerns sometimes seem to be of very recent vintage, but there has been widespread discussion of many of these problems for decades. However, only modest progress has been made. Some problems, like high levels of traditional air pollutants, for example, have been partially reduced through innovations in control technologies, modernization of plant and equipment, and enforcement efforts. That is no small accomplishment, given the growth in population and the economy. But compliance with air quality standards is still to a great extent a function of the weather, the health of the economy, and other factors apart from regulatory activity, and we are not much closer to remedying environmental problems than we were a quarter of a century ago when environmental regulation first became a national priority.

Our limited understanding of the nature of the environment and threats to it is an essential ingredient in the failure to make progress in these areas. Policymakers must make decisions in the face of considerable uncertainty about the causes and consequences of pollution. Many problems are characterized by long lead times before adverse health effects and other consequences are discovered. Policy making must therefore include learning from experience and making adjustments. Some environmental hazards are especially severe because their effects are largely irreversible, either in terms of loss of human life or in terms of ecological changes.

The level of scientific knowledge about environmental problems is growing but is still minuscule compared with what scientists and policymakers would like to know. The range of potential policy actions for these problems is immense. For some problems, such as the destruction of the stratospheric ozone layer, there is general scientific agreement concerning the need for action. For other concerns, such as global climate change, there may not be clear evidence of warming until it actually begins, at which point it is irreversible. How should policy making proceed when there is considerable scientific uncertainty? How much agreement among scientists is necessary before action should be taken?

In these situations, there are at least two kinds of strategies that policymakers can pursue, other than simply prohibiting every action with a projected or hypothesized risk. The first approach is to do nothing—to leave to private institutions and actors the responsibility for responding to environmental challenges. Such a position may be the result of a number of different concerns and motivations. Policymakers may opt to wait until research findings are sufficiently clear to compel action; such a position, however, can also be used as a stalling technique by politicians unwilling to impose new costs on their constituents or as a convenient dodge in escaping responsibility for potentially difficult or unpopular actions. A more responsible position is to argue that policy interventions can be more efficient and effective if additional research is completed before policies are designed.[84]

A more sophisticated justification for taking no action asserts that regulatory intervention designed to "play it safe" by seeking to anticipate and thus prevent uncertain environmental and other risks is more dangerous than coping with problems as they develop. Aaron Wildavsky has argued that the costs of intervening to anticipate harms are not always well recognized or appreciated; the resources exhausted "in a futile effort to anticipate the future" would otherwise be available to "bounce back" and mitigate effects once they occur. According to Wildavsky, society should invest resources in fostering its resilience rather than in trying to anticipate potential danger before damage occurs. Resilience does not mean simply doing nothing and waiting for a problem to occur; it requires "preparing for the inevitable . . . by expanding general knowledge, technical facility, and command over resources," rather than directing scarce resources toward preventing specific but hypothesized harms.[85]

A second strategy is to take preventive action when there is a high probability of harm occurring, or when there is a low probability of an event occurring but the risks associated with its occurrence are so great that anticipatory action is justified. The traditional idea of insurance provides conceptual guidance here. Environmental threats are no different than other challenges confronting human beings. It is prudent to insure against possible adverse changes, particularly against those whose consequences might be serious or even irreparable. The kinds of changes associated with a rapid rise in the average temperature of the earth, some have argued, are simply so cataclysmic that the risk of such developments must be minimized. Similarly, construction safety codes for highways, bridges, and buildings require architects and construction companies to prepare for contingencies such as earthquakes. This raises construction costs considerably but is viewed as a prudent precaution.

In situations where uncertainty is great but the consequences of errors are likely to be catastrophic, policymakers can set priorities to ensure that the most critical uncertainties receive the most attention, take action to protect against the worst consequences of error, and establish mechanisms to monitor phenomena and research efforts so that they can learn from experience. Good decision making cannot simply rest on the hope that analysis will be able to produce a clear decision. Policymakers must avoid actions that pose unacceptable costs and must take aggressive steps to monitor, interpret, and learn from experience and errors.[86]

In many cases, regulatory actions taken to insure against one hazard may also mediate against other harms. Reducing emissions of chlorofluorocarbons may reduce the threat of global warming, but will very likely also reduce the loss of the stratospheric ozone layer. Steps to increase energy efficiency will lead to lower energy prices and, consequently, to lower prices for manufactured goods, less dependence on imported oil, reduced health hazards from local air pollution, diminished acid rain emissions, and decreased amounts of carbon dioxide released into the atmosphere. Investments that yield these kinds of multiple benefits are clearly worthwhile. The question may not be whether or not to buy insurance (or invest in actions to reduce the likelihood or magnitude of change), but how much of it to purchase.[87]

The 1990 Clean Air Act is an important public health statute. Reducing the health effects of air pollution is one of the most important public health initiatives we can undertake as a society. The threat is serious and the possibilities for reducing risk are enormous. That is the good news of air pollution—it *can* be reduced, and, as indicated in Chapter 1, that reduction can contribute to a healthy economy. One of the tasks in the following chapters is to assess how well the framework of the Clean Air Act is helping us increase our ability to protect public health. Chapter 3 describes the evolution of clean air policy.

Notes

1. Thad Godish, *Air Quality* (Chelsea, Mich.: Lewis, 1991), 1-4.
2. Ibid.
3. Edward A. Keller, *Environmental Geology* (Columbus, Ohio: Merrill, 1987), 496.
4. Godish, *Air Quality*, 25-26.
5. Clean Air Act, sec. 112, 42 U.S.C. sec. 7412 (1990).
6. Environmental Protection Agency (EPA), *National Air Quality and Emissions Trends Report, 1990* (Research Triangle Park, N.C.: EPA, 1991), 1-3; and *National Air Quality and Emissions Trends Report, 1993* (Research Triangle Park, N.C.: EPA, 1994), 15.
7. EPA, *National Air Quality and Emissions Trends Report, 1993*, 97.
8. See, generally, Charles E. Kupchella and Margaret C. Hyland, *Environmental Science: Living within the System of Nature* (Boston: Allyn and Bacon, 1989).
9. D. W. Dockery, J. H. Ware, B. G. Ferris Jr., F. E. Speiser, N. R. Cook, and S. M. Herman, "Changes in Pulmonary Function in Children Associated with Air Pollution Episodes," *Journal of the Air Pollution Control Association* 32 (1982): 937-942; and C. Arden Pope III and Douglas W. Dockery, "Acute Health Effects of PM_{10} Pollution on Symptomatic and Asymptomatic Children," *American Review of Respiratory Disease* 145 (1992): 1123-1128.
10. For a review of a number of studies, see James S. Cannon, *The Health Costs of Air Pollution: A Survey of Studies Published 1978-1983* (Washington, D.C.: American Lung Association, 1985).
11. B. Bobak and D. A. Leon, "Air Pollution and Infant Mortality in the Czech Republic, 1986-1988" *Lancet* 340 (1992): 1010-1014.
12. D. W. Dockery et al., "Mortality Risks of Air Pollution: A Prospective Cohort Study," *New England Journal of Medicine* 329 (1993): 1753-1759.
13. C. Arden Pope III et al., "Particulate Air Pollution as a Predictor of Mortality in a Prospective Study of U.S. Adults," *American Journal of Respiratory Critical Care Medicine* 151 (1995): 669-674.
14. For further discussion, see Paul Portney, "Air Pollution Policy," in Paul Portney, ed., *Public Policies for Environmental Protection* (Washington, D.C.: Resources for the Future, 1990), 49-52.
15. C. H. Conolly, *Air Pollution and Public Health* (New York: Dryden Press, 1973); and Alan J. Krupnick, Winston Harrington, and Bart Ostro, "Ambient Ozone and Acute Health Effects: Evidence from Daily Data" (Washington, D.C.: Resources for the Future, 1989), discussion paper QE 89-01.
16. S. M. Ayers, Robert Evans, David Licht, Jane Griesbach, Felicity Reimold, Edward F. Ferrand, and Antoinette Criscitiello, "Health Effects of Exposure to High Concentrations of Automotive Emissions," *Archives of Environmental Health* 27 (1973): 168-178.
17. L. D. Fechter and Zoltan Annau, "Toxicity of Mild Prenatal Carbon Monoxide Exposure," *Science* 197 (1977): 680-682.
18. Kupchella and Hyland, *Environmental Science*.
19. Paul Astrup, Knud Kjeldsen, and John Wanstrup, "Effects of Carbon Monoxide Exposure on the Arterial Walls," in *Biological Effects of Carbon Monoxide, Annals of the New York Academy of Science* 174 (1970): 294-300; and Michael T. Kleinman, Dennis M. Davidson, Richard B. Vandagriff, Vincent J.

Caiozzo, and James L. Whittenberger, "Effects of Short-term Exposure to Carbon Monoxide in Subjects with Coronary Artery Disease," *Archives of Environmental Health* 44 (1989): 361-369.

20. L. R. Babcock and N. L. Nagada, "Cost Effectiveness of Emission Control," *Journal of the Air Pollution Control Association* 23 (1973): 173-179.

21. D. J. Spedding, *Air Pollution* (Oxford: Clarendon Press, 1974), 58-62.

22. Utah County Clean Air Coalition, "Health Effects of Carbon Monoxide," 1991; World Health Organization, *Environmental Health Criteria 13: Carbon Monoxide* (Geneva: WHO, 1979).

23. EPA, *National Air Pollutant Emission Estimates, 1940-1988* (Washington, D.C.: EPA, 1990), 4, 5, 60.

24. C. T. Stewart, *Air Pollution, Human Health, and Public Policy* (Lexington, Mass.: D. C. Heath, 1979); Kupchella and Hyland, *Environmental Science.*

25. D. L. Coffin and Herbert E. Stokinger, "Biological Effects of Air Pollutants," in Arthur C. Stern, ed., *Air Pollution,* 3d ed. (New York: Academic Press, 1977); and Theodore D. Sterling, Seymour V. Pollack, and J. Weinkam, "Measuring the Effect of Air Pollution on Urban Morbidity," *Archives of Environmental Health* 18 (1969): 485-494. See, generally, Natural Resources Defense Council, *Out of Breath: Children's Health and Air Pollution in Southern California* (New York: Natural Resources Defense Council, 1993); and American Lung Association, *Danger Zones: Ozone Air Pollution and Our Children* (New York: American Lung Association, March 1995).

26. U.S. Congress, Office of Technology Assessment (OTA), *Catching Our Breath: Next Steps for Reducing Urban Ozone* (Washington, D.C.: Government Printing Office, 1988), 8-9.

27. Godish, *Air Quality,* 41-48.

28. OTA, *Catching Our Breath,* 13.

29. EPA, *Environmental Progress and Challenges: EPA's Update* (Washington, D.C.: EPA, 1988), 18-19; and EPA, *National Air Quality and Emissions Trends Report, 1988* (Washington, D.C.: EPA, 1990), 65.

30. EPA, *National Air Quality and Emissions Trends Report, 1988,* 65-73.

31. David F. S. Natusch and John R. Wallace, "Urban Aerosol Toxicity: The Influence of Particle Size," *Science* 186 (1974): 695-699.

32. C. Arden Pope III, "Respiratory Disease Associated with Community Air Pollution and a Steel Mill, Utah Valley," *American Journal of Public Health* (May 1989): 623-628.

33. C. Arden Pope III, Joel Schwartz, and Michael Ransom, "Daily Mortality and PM_{10} Pollution in Utah Valley," *Archives of Environmental Health* 47 (May-June, 1992): 211-217.

34. See Joel Schwartz and D. W. Dockery, "Increased Mortality in Philadelphia Associated with Daily Air Pollution Concentrations," *American Review of Respiratory Disease* 145 (1992): 600-604; and Schwartz and Dockery, "Particulate Air Pollution and Daily Mortality in Steubenville, Ohio," *American Journal of Epidemiology* 135 (1992): 12-19.

35. Dockery et al., "An Association Between Air Pollution and Mortality in Six U.S. Cities," *New England Journal of Medicine* 329 (1993): 1753-1759.

36. EPA, *Environmental Progress and Challenges,* 21.

37. EPA, *National Air Pollutant Emission Estimates, 1940-1988,* 3, 51-52.

38. EPA, *Environmental Progress and Challenges,* 26-27.

39. See, for example, Lester B. Lave and E. P. Seskin, *Air Pollution and Human Health* (Baltimore: Johns Hopkins University Press, 1977). Other studies, however, have not shown this association. See, for example, R. B. Engdhal, "A Critical Review of Regulations for the Control of Sulfur Oxide Emissions," *Journal of the Air Pollution Control Association* 23 (1973): 364-375.

40. The national ambient air quality standards are for SO_2 and NO_2, but the EPA monitors emissions of SO_x and NO_x. Emissions data thus include all oxides, but monitoring is limited to SO_x and NO_x.

41. S. Ishikawa, D. H. Bowen, V. Fisher, and J. P. Wyatt, "The 'Emphysema Profile' of Two Midwestern Cities in North America," *Archives of Environmental Health* 18 (1969): 660-666.

42. Carl M. Shy, Victor Hasselblad, Robert M. Burton, Cornelius J. Nelson, and Arlan A. Cohen, "Air Pollution Effects on Ventilatory Function of U.S. School Children," *Archives of Environmental Health* 27 (1973): 124-128; and William H. Durham, "Air Pollution and Student Health," *Archives of Environmental Health* 28 (1974): 241-254.

43. Kupchella and Hyland, *Environmental Science.*

44. EPA, *National Air Pollutant Emission Estimates, 1940-1988*, 55-56.

45. EPA, *National Air Quality and Emissions Trends Report, 1988*, 26.

46. EPA, *National Air Quality and Emissions Trends Report, 1989* (Washington, D.C.: EPA, 1991), 3-20.

47. For example, W. D. Wagner, Burris R. Duncan, Paul G. Wright, and Herbert E. Stokinger, "Environmental Study of Threshold Limit of NO_2," *Archives of Environmental Health* 10 (1965): 455-456.

48. Carl M. Shy, John C. Creason, Martin E. Pearlman, Kathryn E. McClain, Ferris B. Benson, and Marion M. Young, "The Chattanooga School Children Study: Effects of Community Exposure to Nitrogen Dioxide," *Journal of the Air Pollution Control Association* 20 (1970): 539-545.

49. See, for example, Lave and Seskin, *Air Pollution and Human Health;* and Kupchella and Hyland, *Environmental Science.*

50. EPA, *National Air Quality and Emissions Trends Report, 1992*, 1-4.

51. Conservation Foundation, *State of the Environment: An Assessment at Mid-Decade* (Washington, D.C.: Conservation Foundation, 1984), 64. For a fuller discussion of these and related issues, see National Research Council, *Risk Assessment in the Federal Government: Managing the Process* (Washington, D.C.: Government Printing Office, 1983).

52. EPA, *1992 Toxics Release Inventory* (Washington, D.C.: EPA, 1994), 8.

53. David Durenberger, "Air Toxics: The Problem," *EPA Journal* 17 (January-February 1991): 30-31.

54. Cecie Starr and Ralph Taggart, *Biology*, 5th ed. (Belmont, Calif.: Wadsworth, 1989), 795.

55. EPA, *Acid Rain and Transported Air Pollutants: Implications for Public Policy* (Washington, D.C.: Government Printing Office, 1984).

56. EPA, *National Air Quality and Emissions Trends Report, 1990* (Research Triangle Park, N.C.: EPA, 1991), 3-13.

57. EPA, *National Air Quality and Emissions Trends Report*, 3-22.

58. Philip Shabecoff, "An Emergence of Political Will on Acid Rain," *New York Times*, February 19, 1989, A1.

59. John Carroll, *Acid Rain: An Issue in Canadian-American Relations* (Washing-

ton, D.C.: National Planning Association, 1982).

60. Section 123 of the Clean Air Act of 1970 was amended in 1977 to prohibit companies from relying on dispersal of pollutants by means of tall smokestacks to meet national ambient air quality standards rather than adhering to emission limits.

61. Tom McMillan, "Why Canadians Worry about Acid Rain," *EPA Journal* 12 (June-July 1986): 8-10.

62. *Alliance for Clean Coal v. Illinois Commerce Commission*, U.S. District Court for the Northern District of Illinois, 93C-4391 (December 15, 1993).

63. Sydney G. Harris, "Canadian Positions, Proposals, and the Diplomatic Dilemma: Acid Rain and Emerging International Norms," *Toledo Law Review* 17 (Fall 1985): 130-131.

64 See, generally, Cynthia Pollock Shea, *Protecting Life on Earth: Steps to Save the Ozone Layer*, Worldwatch Paper 87 (Washington, D.C.: Worldwatch Institute, 1988).

65. EPA, *Reducing Risk: The Report of the Ecology and Welfare Subcommittee, Appendix A* (Washington, D.C.: EPA, September 1990), 40-42.

66. Chlorine is believed to be at the root of the ozone depletion problem. Ozone (O_3) is created when an intact oxygen molecule (O_2) is struck by ultraviolet light. An ultraviolet photon splits the molecule into two highly reactive oxygen atoms (O). These atoms quickly combine with intact oxygen molecules to form ozone. This gas then readily absorbs ultraviolet light and is disassociated into its component parts (O_2 and O); the freed oxygen atom subsequently joins with another oxygen molecule to re-form ozone. This ozone is continually broken apart and re-formed until it collides with a free atom of oxygen, thereby forming two stable oxygen molecules. Ozone will thus reach a steady state in which its rate of formation is equal to its rate of removal, if constant conditions are maintained.

   Chlorine, however, upsets this balance and reduces the amount of ozone by hastening the formation of stable oxygen molecules (O_2). When a chlorine atom (C1) collides with an ozone molecule (O_3), the chlorine "steals" the third oxygen atom of ozone, resulting in the formation of a chlorine monoxide radical (ClO) and an oxygen molecule. Radicals, which are molecules that have an odd number of electrons, are quite reactive. When the chlorine monoxide radical meets a free oxygen atom, the oxygen atom in the chlorine monoxide becomes highly attracted to the free oxygen atom and breaks away to form a new oxygen molecule. This frees the chlorine atom to begin ozone destruction anew. See National Academy of Sciences, *One Earth, One Future: Our Changing Global Environment* (Washington, D.C.: National Academy Press, 1990), 104-110.

67. Mark R. Schoeberl, a scientist at the Goddard Space Center, contends that chlorine has little or nothing to do with the ozone "hole" and theorizes that "unusual atmospheric winds create the hole simply by shoving the ozone around." Photographs taken by Goddard's Nimbus 7 satellite that show an increase of ozone at lower latitudes when the hole appears at higher latitudes support this theory, for they suggest that the ozone is simply pushed from one region to the next. Ellen Ruppel Shell, "Watch This Space," *Omni* 9 (August 1987): 80.

68. Richard S. Stolarski, "The Antarctic Ozone Hole," *Scientific American* 258 (January 1988): 35.

69. Ibid., 40.
70. Peter H. Sand, "The Vienna Convention Is Adopted," *Environment* 27 (June 1985): 20.
71. Ibid.
72. Mike Mills, "Ozone Pact OK'd, But Some Say It's Not Enough," *Congressional Quarterly Weekly Report* 46 (March 19, 1988): 706.
73. David D. Doninger, "Global Emergency," *Environmental Forum* (July-August 1988): 17.
74. The Soviet Union's representative told the meeting that his country would abide by the Montreal Protocol but that it would not support a drive led by the United States and the European Community for a total ban on CFCs by the turn of the century.
75. For a discussion of the history of the Montreal Protocol and of its provisions, see Richard E. Benedick, *Ozone Diplomacy* (Cambridge, Mass.: Harvard University Press, 1991).
76. "Holes Galore," *The Economist* 333 (October 15, 1994): 114.
77. United Nations Framework Convention on Climate Change, Article 2.
78. Ibid., Article 4, section 1.
79. Ibid., Article 4, section 2, a, b; section 3.
80. Ibid., Article 12, section 1, a, b.
81. President William J. Clinton and Vice President Albert Gore, Jr., "The Climate Change Action Plan" (October 1993).
82. "The Climate Change Action Plan," 9.
83. World Resources Institute, *The Crucial Decade: The 1990s and the Global Environmental Challenge* (Washington, D.C.: WRI, 1989).
84. The debate over policy options to address acid rain in the United States provides examples of both approaches. Some Reagan administration officials clearly did not want to impose new regulatory burdens, hence the call for more research as a delaying tactic. Others believed that policies should not be fully designed until the federal government completed its decade-long assessment of acid rain, slated for completion in 1990. For more on that view, see Michael S. McMahon, "Balancing the Interests: An Essay on the Canadian-American Acid Rain Debate," in John E. Carroll, ed., *International Environmental Diplomacy* (New York: Cambridge University Press, 1988), 147-171.
85. Aaron Wildavsky, "The Secret of Safety Lies in Danger," in Gary C. Bryner and Dennis Thompson, eds., *The Constitution and the Regulation of Society* (Ithaca, N.Y.: State University of New York Press/Brigham Young University Press, 1988), 51-52.
86. For thoughtful discussions of these issues, see Joseph G. Morone and Edward J. Woodhouse, *Averting Catastrophe: Strategies for Regulating Risky Technologies* (Berkeley: University of California Press, 1986); and Morone and Woodhouse, *The Demise of Nuclear Energy: Lessons for Democratic Control of Technology* (New Haven: Yale University Press, 1989).
87. For development of the argument on insurance, see Stephen H. Schneider, *Global Warming: Are We Entering the Greenhouse Century?* (San Francisco: Sierra Club Books, 1989), 283-285.

3 From the Clean Air Act of 1970 to the 1990 Amendments

The passage of the Clean Air Act Amendments of 1990 was a remarkable political event and a landmark achievement in the making of environmental policy. The stage was set in 1989 for a fundamental change in the politics of clean air in Congress and a break in the legislators' decade-long deadlock. The summer of 1988 had been the hottest on record, intensifying fears of global warming and reminding Americans that they were not giving sufficient attention to protecting the environment. Environmental awareness was heightened in March 1989 by the Exxon *Valdez* Alaskan oil spill. The fact that many urban areas continued to fail to meet cleanup goals gave renewed impetus to demands that Congress update the 1970 law, even though the EPA had decided not to impose sanctions as long as Congress was considering clean air legislation.[1]

The debate over the Clean Air Act brought together two powerful forces—an alliance of environmental groups and a coalition of major U.S. industries—in a classic test of political power. Their resources and strategies differed in important ways. Environmentalists were able to frame most of the issues as clear choices for or against clean air. Industry representatives enjoyed ready access to many members of Congress and were able to shape many details of the bills they considered. Both groups were able to evoke powerful images—of job loss and economic devastation, of ecological damage and human health risks.

The politics of clean air is not only a conflict between environmentalists and proponents of industry. Just as divisive have been regional conflicts. Northeasterners blame air pollution from the Midwest for the damage done via acid rain to their forests and lakes. Midwestern coal miners compete with westerners to gain enactment of legal provisions that encourage the use of their resources. (A shift away from the high-sulfur coal found largely in the eastern states increased demand for the low-sulfur coal abundant in western states.) Heavily polluted communities such as Los Angeles require the most stringent controls possible, whereas other areas resist pollution controls that they may not need and cannot afford. "Clean" states, in regions such as the sunbelt, where industrial and utility facilities are relatively new or where investments in pollution control equipment have already been made, resist proposals that they share in the cleanup costs, claiming they should be borne by the midwestern and northea: in which emissions are greatest. These states, which have ex aging industrial infrastructure, are supportive of regulatory resti ..., on new pollution sources, which effectively impede industrial investment in clean states.[2]

The legislative process is influenced to a large degree by legislators' personalities, personal motivations and priorities, and interpersonal and negotiating skills. The history of the clean air bill would probably have been different if the congressional leaders had been different. One important event in the evolution of the clean air bill was the replacement in 1989 of Senate Majority Leader Robert Byrd (D-W. Va.), champion of his state's high-sulfur coal miners and of midwestern utility companies, by Sen. George Mitchell (D-Maine), a major proponent of acid rain regulations. Byrd had blocked clean air bills from reaching the Senate floor for several years, so Mitchell's leadership aroused hopes that the bill could finally be brought to a vote. (Byrd continued to be a major force as chairman of the Senate Appropriations Committee.) Mitchell had a long-standing commitment to the legislation, dating from his service as chairman of the Senate Committee on Environment and Public Works' Subcommittee on Environmental Protection in 1987-1988. The debate over the bill was a major test of Mitchell's leadership ability and that of Speaker of the House Thomas Foley. Foley, although not known as an advocate of clean air legislation, seemed determined that disputes among Democrats in Congress would not be blamed for the demise of such a major piece of legislation. Rep. John Dingell (D-Mich.), chairman of the House Energy and Commerce Committee and a tireless champion of the auto industry, carefully controlled Democratic appointments to his committee throughout the 1980s to protect his constituents in Detroit from new regulatory requirements. The constituency of Rep. Henry Waxman (D-Calif.), chairman of the House Energy and Commerce Committee's Subcommittee on Health and the Environment, which had initial jurisdiction over the bill, included Los Angeles, a city with serious air pollution problems. Waxman led the efforts to extend the life of the Clean Air Act in the early 1980s. The hearings of his subcommittee and those of the Senate Committee on Environment and Public Works were a major source of ideas for the 1989 bills.

It is useful to put the Clean Air Act Amendments of 1990 in historical context by briefly reviewing their evolution, beginning in 1970, and examining how they were affected by developments in the 1980s. The issues surrounding clean air policy have been debated in Congress for two decades, and many of them are still matters of controversy. The conflict that developed in the early 1980s between members of the Reagan administration and congressional Democrats over how the Clean Air Act and other environmental laws were to be implemented and enforced created an atmosphere of distrust that continued for the remainder of the decade.

The Clean Air Act of 1970

Early Efforts to Control Pollution

The first clean air laws in the United States were enacted by cities. Chicago and Cincinnati passed ordinances in the 1880s to limit smoke emissions. By the 1940s, the health effects of pollution had become a concern of public health officials. In Los Angeles, state and local officials and industry leaders launched a research program to study the health effects of air pollution. Heavy fogs (pollution from burning coal trapped during a temperature inversion) in Donora, Pennsylvania, in 1948 (and also in London in 1952) resulted in thousands of deaths. In 1962, Oregon became the first state to establish a comprehensive air pollution program.[3]

The federal government's involvement in improving air quality began in 1955 when the Public Health Service was authorized to conduct research on air pollution.[4] The first Clean Air Act, enacted in 1963, was a very modest response to the initial concern in the nation about air pollution. It increased the funds earmarked for research and established a legal process by which municipalities, states, and the federal government could take regulatory action against sources of pollution.[5] Much of the attention was focused on motor vehicle emissions of carbon monoxide, hydrocarbons, and nitrogen oxides, which were blamed for 60 percent of all air pollution. Stationary sources, especially those emitting sulfur oxides and particulates, were responsible for the remaining 40 percent. In 1965, Congress authorized the secretary of the Department of Health, Education, and Welfare (HEW) to establish standards for emissions of hydrocarbons and carbon monoxide by new motor vehicles. The regulations were issued in 1966 and took effect in the 1968 model year.[6]

Between 1955 and 1970, the federal government became increasingly involved in helping to fund state efforts to regulate air pollution. Congress was reluctant to give any real regulatory power to federal officials, however, even though the states were doing relatively little and many air pollution problems transcended state boundaries.[7] A major expansion of regulatory authority was achieved with passage of the Air Quality Act of 1967. Under the act, the federal government was to establish metropolitan air quality regions throughout the United States. States were authorized to establish air quality standards and to develop plans to achieve them. If they failed to do so, HEW was authorized to issue and enforce federal standards.[8] By 1970, no state had put in place a complete set of standards for any pollutant and the federal government had designated less than one-third of the metropolitan air quality regions that had been projected.

Public Controversy and Governmental Debate

In his State of the Union Address in January 1970, Richard Nixon called for "comprehensive new regulations" to protect the environment.[9] The Nixon administration also proposed legislation to strengthen the 1967 Air Quality Act. Part of the administration's motivation was a concern that having regulation in some states but not in others put regulated industries at a competitive disadvantage. In its version of the bill, the administration proposed that HEW be authorized to establish national ambient air quality standards for pollutants it determined were health risks. Authority would remain with the states to develop implementation plans to ensure that federal health standards were met. The proposals contributed to a wave of public concern over the environment in 1970 that led to the first Earth Day in April, widespread demands for increased protection of air quality (including the demand that Congress proclaim "the right of each individual to an unpolluted environment,"[10] demonstrations that included ceremonial burial of new cars because their emissions endangered public health, and creation of the Environmental Protection Agency (EPA) by a presidential reorganization plan.[11]

Much of the controversy surrounding the bill centered on whether standards for new vehicle emissions would be set by the EPA (the Nixon administration's position) or written into the law, as proposed by both the House and Senate. The auto industry launched a major lobbying effort to allow the EPA to set emission standards. The auto industry also fought hard against inclusion of stringent tailpipe emission standards in the law, arguing that the proposed standards could not be met with existing technology. The industry's defenders in Congress, particularly Sen. Robert P. Griffin (R-Mich.), charged that Congress was "hold[ing] a gun at the head of the American automobile industry in a very dangerous game of economic roulette." Deadlines for meeting the tailpipe emission standards were the most contentious issue throughout the debate in Congress.[12]

On June 3, the House Interstate and Foreign Commerce Committee reported a bill that was quite similar to the administration's version, introduced in February. The House passed the bill on June 10 after efforts to make it more stringent were defeated. Several House members had pressed for a number of amendments to require stricter auto emission and fuel efficiency standards, charging that the committee had "ben[t] over backward to accommodate the auto and oil industries." [13]

The Senate Environment and Public Works Committee's bill, reported out in September, was much more aggressive than the House or administration versions. It authorized more money for research and grants, mandated stricter penalties for violations, required a 90 percent reduction in auto emissions by 1975 (with provisions for a one-year extension if needed), gave the EPA broad discretion to regulate use of fuels, and permitted citizen suits against polluters and the EPA. The House-Senate conference accepted some of the Senate's provisions, such as the 1975 deadline, stricter enforcement penalties, and EPA regulation of fuel emissions. Other provisions, such as funding levels, warranties for pollution control equipment, and testing standards for vehicle emissions, were compromises between the House and Senate bills.[14]

The clean air bill was passed in December 1970.[15] Although Nixon championed the legislation as a cooperative, bipartisan effort, his administration eventually came to see that the issue of clean air could be used to political advantage. The leading proponent of clean air legislation in Congress, Sen. Edmund S. Muskie (D-Maine), was not invited to the presidential signing ceremony, apparently because he was rumored to be a candidate for the Democratic party's 1972 presidential nomination. The competition between Muskie and Nixon for leadership on clean air opened a window of opportunity that helped strengthen the bill that was eventually passed.[16]

Main Provisions of the Act

The Clean Air Act of 1970 was an ambitious attempt by Congress to protect every American from the health risks of polluted air. Its stated aim was "to protect and enhance the quality of the Nation's air resources so as to promote the public health and welfare and the productive capacity of its population." [17] To achieve the goal of cleaning up the nation's air within five years, it established national ambient air quality standards and gave the states responsibility for developing and enforcing implementation plans to meet those standards. Stationary pollution sources were to come into compliance with state implementation plans by 1975, with one extension of two years permitted. The act made federal funds available to states for the development of implementation plans and increased funding for research on the health effects of airborne pollutants. Such plans were to be submitted to the EPA within nine months of the issuance of the standards. The EPA was to ensure that each plan included emission limitations and monitoring requirements for pollution from stationary sources, a program for the regulation of new sources of pollution, inspection and testing of motor vehicles for emissions, and provision of adequate state resources to implement and enforce the plan. If the states failed to submit acceptable plans, the EPA was authorized to amend them or formulate a federal plan to achieve national ambient air quality standards. State implementation plans were to achieve compliance with the federal standards within three years of their approval, but a three-year extension could also be granted by the EPA. Motor vehicle emissions of carbon monoxide and hydrocarbons were to be reduced by 90 percent from 1970 levels beginning with the 1975 model year. Emissions of nitrogen oxides were to be cut by 90 percent from a 1971 baseline level by 1976. Emission standards were to be met for five years or 50,000 miles, whichever was less. Anyone removing pollution control devices was subject to a $10,000 fine. The EPA was authorized to test new vehicles for compliance with the mandated emission reductions, to set standards for pollution control equipment warranties, and to regulate use of fuel additives that endangered public health.[18]

The 1970 law provided both enforcement powers and penalties. The EPA was authorized to seek injunctions to halt emissions that endangered public health. Citizens could initiate suits against the EPA for failure to take nondiscretionary actions, and against polluters who violated federal standards. Enforcement actions against polluters who knowingly violated provisions of state implementation plans could result in fines of up to $25,000 a day and up to one year in prison for each violation.

The Nixon administration continued to generate political support for reauthorizing and strengthening clean air legislation. Industry representatives also lobbied for one set of federal standards rather than a variety of state provisions. They prevailed on Congress to prohibit the states (except California, since it had already developed stringent auto emission and fuel standards) from imposing more aggressive regulation than provided in the Clean Air Act of 1970.

The Clean Air Act of 1977

The Clean Air Act of 1970 was amended in 1971, 1973, 1974, and 1976, primarily to provide waivers for the motor vehicle emission standards.[19] Congress decided to take action in 1976 to amend the Clean Air Act for a number of reasons. The 1975 deadline for achieving national ambient air quality standards and enforcing state implementation plans had passed with thousands of sources still not in compliance. The deadlines for meeting auto tailpipe emission standards had been extended three times, twice by the EPA and once by Congress, and were to apply to the 1978 model year, but auto industry representatives argued that they needed an additional five years to find ways of meeting the emission standards, particularly that for nitrogen oxides, without adversely affecting fuel economy. Under the 1970 act, metropolitan air quality regions with high levels of pollution were to have in place by 1977 transportation control measures that would include the extremely unpopular (and thus not thoroughly enacted) program of gas rationing. Finally, research findings were published in the mid-1970s concerning damage to the stratospheric ozone layer that some scientists believed had resulted from the release of fluorocarbons used as refrigerants and aerosol propellants.[20]

One of the most controversial issues in clean air policy, the prevention of deterioration of relatively clean air (commonly referred to as prevention of significant deterioration), arose as a result of conflicting interpretations of the 1970 act by the judicial and executive branches. In 1974, the EPA issued regulations that divided metropolitan clean air regions into three categories. The air in class I areas, such as national parks, would be protected against any deterioration. The law specified certain amounts of additional pollution that would be permitted in class II areas, and pollution would be permitted in class III areas until national ambient air quality standards were met. These regulations were challenged in federal court, and the EPA put them on hold in anticipation of congressional reauthorization of the Clean Air Act. The Ford administration, the oil industry, electric utility and paper companies, real estate and construction interests, and other business groups all opposed the deterioration prevention provisions.

Both the House and Senate ended up passing Clean Air Act Amendments in 1976 that extended deadlines for meeting auto emission limits, national ambient air quality standards, and guidelines for protecting areas with relatively clean air. The auto industry aggressively opposed the original legislation, although it was a filibuster by western senators that actually killed the bill. Led by Sen. Jake Garn (R-Utah), the senators argued that the bill would limit economic growth and energy exploration. When Congress adjourned in October of 1976, the filibuster still had not been broken.[21]

Advocates of more stringent provisions were in no hurry to bargain. Auto industry officials warned that the 1978 model cars, scheduled for production beginning in August 1977, would not meet the existing tailpipe emission standards. They threatened to close down assembly lines rather than subject their companies to a fine of up to $10,000 for every car failing to meet the standards. Realizing the possible economic consequences of plant shutdowns, President Carter urged Congress to pass the amendments before the August congressional recess. Congress amended the Clean Air Act in the summer of 1977. Motor vehicle emission standards continued to be the most difficult issue to resolve. The amendments gave the auto industry two more years to meet tailpipe emission standards, but more stringent standards were mandated for 1980 and subsequent years. The EPA was given discretion to waive the stricter standards if the technology to achieve them was not available.

Congress resolved the other contentious issue, deterioration of air quality in areas with relatively clean air, by accepting the three area categories defined by the EPA. A compromise was struck that established maximum allowable increases of particulates and sulfur dioxide for each category. Variances were permitted for up to eighteen days a year in the cleanest (class I) areas. Nonattainment areas were given until the end of 1982 to meet national ambient air quality standards. Cities with severe ozone and carbon monoxide problems were given an extension to 1987. All areas were required to demonstrate "regular, consistent emission reductions" until compliance was achieved. Penalties for noncompliance by stationary sources were increased in an attempt to make the cost of noncompliance exceed the expenditure required to come into compliance. Civil penalties of up to $25,000 a day were authorized for violations of the act; criminal sanctions were to be imposed on those who knowingly violated the act. States were also required to collect permit fees from major stationary sources. In a key compromise, new fossil-fuel-burning power plants were required to utilize "the best technological system of continuous emission reduction," understood to mean "scrubbers." Scrubbing of the sulfur dioxide emissions was required even if companies used low-sulfur coal, thus removing much of the incentive to replace high-sulfur coal with low sulfur and protecting the high-sulfur coal industry.[22]

The Clean Air Act in the Reagan Era

Some progress in cleaning the air was achieved during the 1970s, particularly in reducing levels of particulates, sulfur dioxide, and carbon monoxide. But ozone and nitrogen dioxide levels remained high, and most environmentalists believed that the EPA had not implemented the Clean Air Act as vigorously as it should have, for many sources of pollution were not being effectively regulated. Industry group representatives and Reagan administration officials, in contrast, argued that the law was too stringent and burdensome. Authorization for the Clean Air Act terminated in 1981, and Congress funded its implementation throughout the 1980s by passing appropriations resolutions. Political maneuvering to amend the act lasted for a decade.

In March 1981, the National Commission on Air Quality, created by the 1977 amendments to the Clean Air Act,[23] recommended that the attainment deadlines be extended, that tailpipe emission standards be lowered, and that the prevention of significant deterioration program be significantly weakened.[24] The Reagan administration's draft reauthorization proposal went even further and made enforcement lawsuits optional, eliminated the prevention of significant deterioration program, doubled allowable tailpipe emissions, and eliminated the durability requirements for motor vehicle emission control equipment. Industry representatives hailed the proposals; as one lobbyist said, "I don't see anything we'd object to yet." [25]

Participants in the Amending Process

Industry groups formed an umbrella organization, the Clean Air Working Group, led by William Fay, a coal company executive, to coordinate lobbying efforts. The resources these groups brought to bear on the clean air debate in Congress were enormous. Because clean air legis-lation threatened to impose new regulatory burdens on virtually every industry, they were able to mobilize concerned citizens in every congres-sional district.

Environmental groups, organized in the early 1980s as the National Clean Air Coalition under the leadership of Chairman Richard Ayres, began lobbying for a stronger, more comprehensive Clean Air Act. Member groups included representatives of local units and national offices of the Sierra Club, the Environmental Defense Fund, the National Wildlife Federation, and the Audubon Society; church groups and labor unions, particularly the United Steelworkers Union; and groups such as the U.S. Public Interest Research Group and the American Lung Association, whose interests went far beyond environmental regulation. Lawyers and scientists at the Natural Resources Defense Council (in particular, Ayres, David Hawkins, and David Doninger) were indispensable sources of expertise to congressional leaders in drafting the details of environmental law.[26]

The challenge for the members of this coalition was in some ways like that for industry: to decide what stance should be taken, given the com-promise that is inevitable in the legislative process. Should they be aggres-sive in making their demands, vehemently criticizing any compromise, in order to ensure that the final product would be close to their liking, or should they try to help congressional and White House negotiators by coming up with reasonable compromise positions?

Policy making for the goal of clean air was further complicated by the division of responsibilities. The economic costs of environmental regula-tion brought in agencies and officials concerned with economic policy, ranging from the Council of Economic Advisers to the White House Domestic Policy staff. In addition to the EPA and the Nuclear Regulatory Commission, several branches of the Executive Office of the President, including the Council on Environmental Quality and the Office of Management and Budget, share responsibility for environmental law and regulation. Several cabinet departments, including the Departments of the Interior (public lands, energy, minerals, national parks); Agriculture (forestry, soil conservation); Commerce (oceanic and atmospheric moni-toring and research); State (international environmental agreements); Justice (environmental litigation); Energy; Transportation; Housing and Urban Development (urban parks, planning); Health and Human Services (public health); and Labor (occupational health) also have responsibility.

A large number of congressional committees share jurisdiction over environmental law. The House Ways and Means Committee and the Senate Finance Committee have responsibility for environmental laws that include tax provisions. The House Appropriations Committee, the Senate Government Affairs Committee, and the House Government Operations

Committee are the primary overseers of the implementation of environmental statutes, but the EPA has identified thirty-four Senate committees and subcommittees and fifty-six House committees and subcommittees that exercise jurisdiction over that agency.[27] The key roles, however, were played by the leaders of the Senate and its Environment and Public Works Committee, and leaders of the House Energy and Commerce Committee.

Table 3-1 lists some of the major participants in the amendment process in the 1980s that culminated in the Clean Air Act Amendments of 1990. Table 3-2 provides an overview of the major events in the evolution of clean air legislation, and Table 3-3 summarizes the major issues that were debated in Congress during the period leading up to enactment of the 1990 law.

In 1981, critics of the Clean Air Act, including economists, legal scholars, political scientists, and industry officials, focused on four major concerns. First, they believed that the national ambient air quality standards should be revised so that, in general, the costs of pollution control equipment could be balanced with the benefits of cleaner air. Second, they pressed that acceptable pollution levels should protect the general population, not only those who were most susceptible to the effects of pollution. Under the existing law, national ambient air quality standards were to protect everyone, with an ample margin of safety, but costs were not to be considered in setting them. Third, they argued that the process of obtaining permits for new construction was too slow and expensive and thus stymied economic growth. The provisions of the act aimed at protecting clean air (the prevention of significant deterioration program) were particularly complicated. Fourth, the auto industry wanted the tailpipe emission standards for carbon monoxide and nitrogen oxides relaxed to enable them to reduce costs, produce more diesel engines, and simplify their efforts to increase fuel efficiency.[28]

Advocates of strengthening the law made several demands on Congress: include an amendment regulating emissions from coal-burning utility plants that were implicated in acid rain; accelerate the EPA's regulation of airborne toxic emissions; and push the EPA to regulate fine particulates—those less than 1/1,000th of an inch in diameter—which pose more serious health threats, in general, than larger particulates.[29]

The Reagan administration had promised to submit to Congress revisions of the law, but it eventually decided to provide only a set of guiding principles. Bills to delay the imposition of tailpipe emission standards and ease regulation of stationary sources were introduced in the House and soon became mired in committee politics. Henry Waxman, chairman of the Subcommittee on Health and the Environment, led the members who sought to protect the law against industry lobbying; he proposed minor changes both to tighten provisions and to broaden them to regulate acid rain. But he was apparently in no hurry to urge passage of the amend-

Table 3-1 Major Players in Amending the Clean Air Act of 1990

Environmental Groups

National Clean Air Coalition
  Sierra Club
  Natural Resources Defense Council
  Environmental Defense Fund
  U.S. Public Interest Research Group
  American Lung Association
  National Wildlife Federation
  Audubon Society
  United Steelworkers Union
  National Council of Churches

Industry Groups

Clean Air Working Group
  Business Roundtable
  National Association of Manufacturers
  Trade associations (coal, electric utilities, steel, chemicals, and automobile
    industries)

State and Local Officials

State and territorial air pollution program administrators
Local air pollution control officials
Representatives of individual states

Executive Branch

Office of Management and Budget
Domestic Policy Staff
Chief of staff
Environmental Protection Agency
Department of Energy
Department of the Interior
Department of Transportation

Legislative Branch

House

  Speaker
  Committee on Energy and Commerce
    Subcommittee on Health and the Environment
    Subcommittee on Energy and Power

Senate

  Majority leader and minority leader
  Committee on Environment and Public Works
    Subcommittee on Environmental Protection

Table 3-2 The Evolution of Clean Air Policy

Air Pollution Control Act of 1955

Provided first federal air pollution law
Established a research program and grants to states

Clean Air Act of 1963

Required the federal government to establish health-based standards for air
  pollution
Encouraged states to adopt them

Air Quality Act of 1967

Required states to establish air quality regions and develop plans for meeting
  national standards; federal government to provide technical assistance

Clean Air Act of 1970

Provided the basic structure for the current law:
  Federal government to establish national standards
  States to develop state implementation plans to achieve those standards by
    1975
  New sources of pollution to meet more stringent standards than existing ones
  New cars to meet emission limits

Clean Air Acts of 1971, 1973, 1974, and 1976

Provided waivers for meeting auto emission standards

Clean Air Act of 1977

Extended the deadlines for meeting air quality standards to 1982 (and to 1987
  for areas with serious pollution)
Established new technology-based standards that stationary sources were to
  meet
Limited the construction of new pollution sources in areas with clean air

Clean Air Act Amendments of 1990

Extended the deadlines for meeting air quality standards into the twenty-first
  century for areas with serious pollution problems
Established several new requirements for state implementation plans, including
  incremental reductions
Tightened motor vehicle emissions standards and extended them to new classes
  of vehicles
Required new emission standards be issued for air toxins
Updated enforcement measures
Established a new operating permit program
Created new programs to regulate acid rain and protect the ozone layer

---

Table 3-3   Key Issues in the Debate over Clean Air, 1980-1990

Technology forcing

How can federal and state governments encourage industries to develop cleaner, less polluting technologies? Motor vehicle emission standards are a good example of this and are one of the real successes of the 1970 and 1977 acts, but industries resist efforts to enact more aggressive standards and argue that such standards will drive them out of business.

Federal versus state roles

Since pollution is often an interstate problem, and states might devise less stringent standards than their neighbors in order to attract new business, national standards are essential. But what should be the relative roles of federal and state agencies? How much discretion should states be given to develop plans to achieve the national standards and respond to their varying environmental conditions?

Motor vehicle versus stationary sources

Both stationary and mobile sources must be regulated to reduce pollution levels. What should be the relative demands placed on the two kinds of sources? Should the most cost-effective strategies be employed (producing the greatest reductions in emission per dollar spent), regardless of the distribution of the burdens across different kinds of sources?

Health- versus technology-based standards for air toxins

The health-based approach to regulating air toxins had bogged down under legal challenges in the 1980s. Should regulation center on reducing risk to health, or should it focus on establishing emission standards with which all sources of air toxic must comply?

Acid rain and the regional nature of pollution

Acid rain damage is centered in the Northeast, while the major sources of acid rain are located in the Midwest. How should the cost of addressing the problem be distributed across the regions affected? Nowhere is this situation more poignant than in coal-mining communities that produce high-sulfur coal, where tighter air quality controls would mean shutting down some mines.

Jobs and the environment

Concerns about the impact of environmental protection provisions on employment pervade the debate. Business interests are able to use the threat of job loss and industry shutdowns. Environmental groups are effective in focusing attention on the protection of public health and endangered ecosystems. Improved efficiency from newer, cleaner technologies reduces costs and contributes to air quality goals. But there are some disruptions, and short-run costs increase in many cases. How can industry be encouraged to make the investments that in the long run would make economic and environmental sense?

International competitiveness and domestic regulation

The Clean Air Act Amendments of 1990 become the vehicle by which the United States enforces its obligations under international agreements to protect the stratospheric ozone layer. Environmentalists see the issue as an opportunity for the United States to provide some leadership in global environmental protection. Should the United States make unilateral concessions in order to push global efforts along, or would such actions disadvantage U.S. firms competing in the global marketplace?

Administrative discretion versus congressional control

By the early 1980s Congress has come to mistrust the EPA and the executive branch in general. Members believe that the new clean air law must be as prescriptive as possible in order to force the executive branch to comply with the law. But the more detailed the provisions, the more Congress locks the EPA into technologies and approaches that might quickly become obsolete. How can the flexibility required for the EPA to adapt to a dynamic economy and a constantly changing environment be balanced with the demands for limiting its discretion?

Command-and-control versus market incentives

The traditional form of regulation rests on a centralized, bureaucratic approach: the federal government establishes national standards applicable to all relevant sources, and states enforce them. In contrast, market instruments such as taxes, fees, tradable permits, and other devices can be used to provide regulated industries some flexibility in reducing their pollution. While the arguments for market instruments have been made for decades, Congress is slow to respond. What are the advantages and disadvantages of market instruments in environmental regulation? Are they the most cost-effective means of achieving environmental goals?

Studying legislative politics

The legislative process is at the heart of the American system of governance. Personality, institutional structures, elections, media attention, and other political characteristics make the politics surrounding each major piece of legislation enacted by Congress unique. But can patterns or generalities be observed within the rich detail of case studies of legislative politics? And how do political developments interact with the substantive, technical, and scientific issues in a bill like the Clean Air Act? How can observers identify the key political developments without becoming inundated in technical issues and jargon?

ments, having calculated that as the 1982 elections approached, members of Congress would be unwilling to cast votes that could be construed as being anti-environment. John Dingell, chairman of the Committee on Energy and Commerce, led a bipartisan coalition of members who wanted major changes, including reduction of tailpipe emission standards. A third group consisted of Republicans who sought to defend industrial sources from more stringent regulation and as a consequence supported tighter tailpipe emission standards.[30] The subcommittee reported out a bill in March that relaxed tailpipe emission standards, extended compliance deadlines, and weakened regulations protecting the relatively clean air in national parks. In the full Energy and Commerce Committee, however, Dingell's package (reduction in tailpipe emission standards, easing of controls imposed on industrial sources, and retention of the scrubbing requirement for coal-burning utilities) was picked apart by Waxman and his allies, who believed that Dingell did not have control over his committee and that members were hesitant to cast votes that signified a retreat from a clean air position. The Dingell coalition prevailed in its efforts to lower tailpipe emission standards but lost on other issues, and its plan to rewrite the bill had collapsed by the fall. In contrast, the Senate Committee on Environment and Public Works, clearly controlled by supporters of the existing law, had by August completed a modest revision of the Clean Air Act. Committee members were generally content with the Clean Air Act and were interested only in limiting the EPA's discretion. There was, however, little support in the Senate leadership for consideration of their version, and it never reached the floor.[31]

In February 1983, the EPA announced that 218 areas had not met national ambient air quality standards and would be subject to sanctions, a threat that provided some motivation for Congress to amend the Clean Air Act. Acid rain also received increased attention in 1983 following reports by three major scientific committees that had examined the problem. Neither faction was willing to compromise, however: northeasterners and other members favored controls to reduce acid rain; those representing the Midwest and high-sulfur-coal states opposed any controls. The stalemate continued throughout the year, eventually prompting an amendment to an appropriations bill that imposed a one-year moratorium on EPA sanctions.

Congress was extremely apprehensive about the direction the EPA was taking during the Reagan presidency as much of its attention was diverted from legislation to oversight. Part of the administration's strategy to stimulate the economy was to cut back on the enforcement of environmental laws and regulations. EPA Administrator Ann Gorsuch and other top administration officials were defiant in their criticisms of the existing law, and the EPA had made clear its intent to work closely with industry representatives to help them solve pollution problems so that aggressive enforcement measures could be avoided.[32] This lack of trust between the executive and legislative branches presented a seemingly insurmountable barrier. The amendments to the Clean Air Act that were eventually passed reflected congressional frustration with the unwillingness of the EPA and many Reagan administration officials to ensure that the law was implemented as forcefully as demanded by Democrats. Until 1989, both houses of Congress handled the complex issues of pollution by dealing with each pollution problem (acid rain, air toxics, and smog) in a separate bill. Senate Environment and Public Works Committee bills generally favored imposition of more environmental controls, reflecting the concerns of environmental groups and state and local air quality officials, many of whom pointed to California's experience in going beyond national requirements to develop its own solutions to the state's air pollution problems.

Acid Rain and Congressional Deadlock

By 1984, the problem of acid rain had become the main stumbling block to amending the Clean Air Act. The Reagan administration was firmly opposed to anything more than continued research. Every Democratic contender in the 1984 presidential campaign criticized the president's inaction on the issue, but he was easily reelected and continued to oppose any new regulatory or statutory initiatives throughout his second term. The Senate Environment and Public Works Committee reported out a bill in 1984 that would have imposed stronger controls on midwestern power plants than were included in the bill the Senate passed in 1982 and tightened other provisions of the law, but the Senate leadership refused to bring it to the floor. The House version never got out of subcommittee. Midwestern members deleted the acid rain provision from the bill being marked up, despite efforts of Waxman and members from the Northeast to distribute the costs of cutting pollution by imposing a tax on the energy produced by burning coal.[33]

The stalemate continued through 1986 as members of the Senate Committee on Environment and Public Works waited to see if the Dingell-Waxman logjam in the House could be broken. The Subcommittee on Environmental Protection reported out an acid rain bill, but it died in the full committee. In 1987, the threat of EPA sanctions for nonattainment areas again prompted congressional attempts to reauthorize the Clean Air Act. The Senate committee, now under the control of the Democrats as a result of the 1986 elections, once again passed amendments to the act that would have given states additional time to reduce urban smog and added new regulatory programs to combat acid rain and air toxics. Democratic Majority Leader Robert Byrd refused to bring the bill to the floor, however, because he opposed sulfur dioxide emission controls that would threaten coal mining jobs in his state.

The political dynamics by this time had shifted somewhat in the House. John Dingell and other members of Congress responsive to industry concerns were not in any hurry to amend the law since the changes were no longer likely to be provisions to weaken the law but rather to strengthen it. Auto makers had met tailpipe emission standards, despite their warnings to the contrary, and Waxman and others were pushing for a new round of more stringent provisions. Opponents of acid rain controls continued to block action in the Waxman subcommittee. In a major vote that showed the strength of environmentalists, the House agreed to a Waxman-backed extension to August 31, 1988, for meeting national ambient air quality standards and defeated Dingell's proposal, which had been expected to pass, to prohibit the EPA from imposing sanctions until 1989. Environmentalists believed that Congress would be more likely to pass a bill to their liking in 1988, an election year, than in 1989, and wanted to use the threat of sanctions to force passage of amendments that would include new regulatory initiatives.[34]

Despite the August 1988 deadline, Congress failed again to amend the Clean Air Act. Sen. George Mitchell had taken over leadership of the clean air bill in the Environment and Public Works Committee in 1987, but he collided with Majority Leader Byrd and was unable to bring the committee's bill to the floor. Progress had been made in talks between Mitchell and the United Mine Workers and a tentative agreement had been struck. But opposition from environmentalists, who argued that the deal would not provide sufficient protection to human health and ecological systems, and from westerners, who believed it favored the use of high-sulfur coal at the expense of the low-sulfur coal mined in their states, killed the bill and precipitated an outburst by Mitchell, who faulted "extremists" on both sides of the issue for being unwilling to compromise.[35]

Consideration of clean air amendments in the House Subcommittee on Health and the Environment extended from February to the summer of 1988. Many of the votes on amendments to the bills proposed by Waxman and by Rep. Gerry Sikorski (D-Minn.) to address nonattainment and acid rain problems were rejected by votes of 10-10 or passed 11-9. Eventually, nine moderate-to-conservative members of the Energy and Commerce Committee tried to break the legislative gridlock with a compromise plan for urban smog. The proposal of the Group of Nine was important because these members held the balance of power in the committee, but neither Dingell nor Waxman could be persuaded to agree to it. Dingell sent the group a fifteen-page letter—on one page were listed items with which he agreed, and on fourteen pages were outlined those with which he did not. The governors of New York and Ohio proposed a plan to reduce acid rain and distribute the cleanup costs among the states. The Senate was fairly close to agreement on an acid rain proposal, and members of the House claimed to be ready to reach an agreement on ozone as soon as the Senate was ready on acid rain.[36] But no breakthrough occurred. More members were becoming familiar with the intricacies of clean air legislation and increasingly frustrated with the polarization and paralysis that afflicted Congress.[37]

The free flow of money helped stiffen the opposition of some members to a more stringent clean air bill. Members of the House Energy and Commerce Committee, for example, were the recipients in 1989 (a non-election year) of nearly $612,000 from political action committees (PACs) formed by industries interested in the bill. As many as 154 PACs were identified as having a "significant stake in the outcome of the clean-air bill." About 5 percent of all money raised by all members of Congress in 1989 came from PACs interested in securing passage of clean air legislation—an average of $14,570 per member. Republican members averaged more than $17,278 in contributions; Democrats averaged $12,729. The PAC money from clean air interests constituted as much as one-third of all PAC money received by some members. The most generous contributors were the electric utilities, who gave more than $150,000 to members of the House Energy and Commerce Committee. They were followed by the oil, natural gas, automobile, and chemical industries; gas utilities; coal and steel industries; diversified energy companies; construction; and farm equipment manufacturing. Although the amount of PAC money contributed to members supporting clean air was relatively small in terms of total PAC giving, it is illustrative of the way campaign spending chases hot legislative issues. For members such as Rep. Al Swift (D-Wash.), receiving PAC money was not a problem: "There is so damn much money out there that anybody who gives anybody anything for it is an idiot." For industry, PAC contributions have become a cost of doing business, a prerequisite for ensuring that its voice will be heard in committee decision making.[38]

Campaign contributions raised fears that industry lobbying might weaken key provisions of the bill. In October 1989, the House Subcommittee on Health and the Environment passed, by a 12-10 vote, an amendment to weaken a provision in the bill mandating the use of alternative fuels, an amendment for which the auto and oil industries had vigorously lobbied. The twelve members who voted in favor of it received an average of $6,021 from oil and auto industry PACs; the ten members who voted against it took an average of $2,755 from these PACs.[39] Some PAC contributions, of course, may be nothing more than a recognition of the already established policy views of members. But many observers and participants alike agree that they pose profound problems for the legislative process.[40]

1989: Clean Air Breakthroughs

The 1990 Amendments to the Clean Air Act were the result of the drafting of numerous bills and countless attempts to negotiate compromise throughout the 1980s. The replacement of Ronald Reagan by George Bush in November 1988 turned out to be a key event in breaking the logjam over clean air. Bush effectively used environmental issues to distance himself from the Reagan administration, since those issues continued to command widespread public support despite President Reagan's hostility to most governmental regulation. Bush and his campaign advisers had also had some success in co-opting traditional Democratic leadership in support of environmental protection. Bolstered by presidential promises, Congress renewed its efforts to amend the Clean Air Act early in 1989. The second breakthrough that year occurred in the Senate when George Mitchell replaced Robert Byrd as majority leader. The Senate Committee on Environment and Public Works promised to produce a package of bills concerning acid rain, air toxics, and urban area nonattainment by the summer. House Speaker Jim Wright promised to make clean air legislation a top priority, although he was then forced to resign in 1989 as a result of a financial scandal and was replaced by Thomas Foley. A number of bills that mirrored proposals of earlier years were introduced in the House. House Republicans began pressuring the White House to show that Republicans could take the lead on environmental protection issues.[41] An outline of the president's bill was introduced on June 12; the bill itself was released on July 21.

The Bush Administration's Clean Air Bill

The president's bill was the result of a major effort by the White House and the EPA to accomplish several things. The EPA had a growing list of reforms and improvements to the existing law that it felt were necessary. Some provisions, such as the enforcement title, were merely designed to update the Clean Air Act and make it consistent with other environmental laws. Other provisions pertained to the development of alternative-fuel vehicles, a particular interest of some key White House officials. The acid rain provisions emphasized an innovative marketlike approach to environmental regulation.

The administration was in a politically delicate position. If its bill was to have any legitimacy in Congress, it had to be as aggressive in attacking air pollution as other bills proposed by members of Congress. But if it was too aggressive, it would alienate important business constituencies. On the other hand, if it was too weak, it would be dismissed as irrelevant to what the president had repeatedly promised to do. Some members of Congress and representatives of environmental groups had argued that the president's bill would have to propose a reduction in sulfur dioxide emissions of at least 10 million tons in order to be taken seriously. Whichever bill he introduced would likely become the minimum position for the bill that Congress would finally enact. As Robert Beck of the Edison Electric Institute put it, "I think whatever George Bush sends up to the Hill is worse than the budget, it's dead before arrival. It becomes merely the floor." [42] The president's June 12 statement was widely heralded in Congress and by environmentalists as the breakthrough in clean air that everyone had been waiting for. When the bill was actually issued, however, it was immediately attacked by environmentalists as too weak and as signifying a retreat from the promises made earlier, and by industry groups as too expensive and inconsistent with the regulatory flexibility that they were expecting.[43]

In contrast to the usual practice, in which the agency drafts a bill and sends it to presidential aides for review, the bill had been prepared by a team of officials from the White House, the Office of Management and Budget, the Department of Energy, and the EPA.[44] This ensured that economic and energy issues would be central considerations in the formulation of environmental policy. The chairman of the National Clean Air Coalition viewed this approach to policy making as a mixed bag:

The fact that the White House is involved in one sense is a positive sign because it says they regard this issue as one of the big national policies. In another sense, it makes one worry, because a lot of people who are not operating from the base of environmental commitment that the EPA administrator is, are involved in shaping this policy.[45]

The president's bill included three major initiatives concerning nonattainment of national ambient air quality standards, air toxics, and acid rain, and additional provisions concerning permit requirements for sources of pollution and enforcement by the EPA and the states. The most aggressive provision, the one pertaining to acid rain, became the centerpiece of the president's bill and was politically attractive for at least two reasons. First, the public viewed acid rain as one of the most serious environmental problems and there were thus significant political advantages to proposing a strong acid rain program. Candidate Bush had promised to go beyond the Reagan administration's position of simply studying the problem further. Acid rain was compatible with the new president's interest in foreign policy, and his first foreign trip was to Canada for meetings with Prime Minister Brian Mulroney, in which acid rain was a major topic of discussion. Furthermore, the initiative adversely affected only a relatively limited number of coal-fired power plants in the Midwest—an industry group that had been the object of widespread congressional condemnation for failing to support any compromise in the 1980s. (One of the many ironies was that the bill that finally passed required much less cost sharing among Midwest utilities than earlier bills that Congress had considered but rejected because of industry opposition.)

Second, the acid rain provision's reliance on a marketlike scheme of emissions trading made it the kind of initiative that industry-oriented and conservative members of Congress could accept. It was based on an argument that critics of regulation had been making for decades—that government intervention needed to be more decentralized, flexible, and efficient. The initiative afforded a promising opportunity to demonstrate that environmental law could actually be "reformed" in practice, a goal that many members of Congress, White House officials, and others had come to champion.[46] It also had the endorsement of the Environmental Defense Fund, which was critical in gaining congressional acceptance. And it recommended a higher rate of reductions in the level of sulfur dioxide emissions than had been specified in most of the bills Congress had considered.

The nonattainment and air toxics provisions were important because they helped to structure the debate in Congress. Critics of the president argued that many provisions in his bill were weaker than the existing law. Sen. Max Baucus (D-Mont.), chairman of the Environment and Public Works Committee's Subcommittee on Environmental Protection, complained that "unfortunately, the president stepped up to the problem, blinked, and stepped back" and warned that the bill would "significantly tarnish his . . . effort to be the environment president." During the negotiations between the Senate and the administration, discussed later in detail, there was even some discussion about dropping the air toxics provisions because compromise was so difficult to reach. The announcement that John Dingell would sponsor the administration's bill in the House stirred fears that the motor vehicle emission provisions were tied too closely to the auto industry's wish list. Lower tailpipe emission standards meant that controls on stationary sources would have to be tightened to make up the difference. The zero-sum emissions game pitted auto industry-oriented members of Congress (and later those from oil-producing states affected by demands for cleaner fuels) against members representing districts with other major industries. Dingell tried to reach an agreement between these two groups and midwesterners concerned about the costs of acid rain controls, but it became increasingly difficult for him and industry coalition leaders to maintain a united front and to prevent some industries and members of Congress from making separate deals.[47]

The 1986 Emergency Planning and Community Right-to-Know Act required industries to report to local officials and the EPA the amount of certain chemicals they release each year. When Rep. Henry Waxman released an initial estimate of air toxic releases by industry in 1987, industry officials derided his figures as wildly excessive. But when the 1987 *Toxics Release Inventory* was made available in 1988, it became clear that Waxman's estimates were only a fraction of actual emissions. According to the inventory, more than 2.7 billion pounds of air toxics had been released in 1987, but emissions were widely viewed as being underreported because there was no mechanism to ensure that companies reported them.[48] Chemical industry officials, apparently sensing that they had a major public relations problem, dropped their opposition to the new legislation and began working with members of Congress (although not without major differences) to put together legislation that would require major cuts in emissions. The death of Rep. Mickey Leland (D-Texas) in a plane crash while on a humanitarian mission to Africa in 1989 was a major blow to such efforts, for he championed a strong air toxics provision, and his death prodded members of Congress to enact a new air toxics program.

Clean Air Act Amendments in Congress

The House. Clean air legislation in the House fell primarily within the jurisdiction of the Energy and Commerce Committee's Subcommittee on Health and the Environment. John Dingell, chairman of the full committee, was careful to pack the subcommittee with members who supported his efforts to block a stringent clean air bill, especially one aimed at reducing auto emissions. Support for an aggressive clean air bill was therefore weakest in the subcommittee despite the vigorous efforts of the subcommittee chairman, Henry Waxman. Waxman and his supporters were convinced that once the bill got out of committee, they would find much stronger support for their position because votes lost in the subcommittee and committee would be reversed on the floor. Waxman's subcommittee began marking up the clean air bill on September 19, 1989. Sponsored by Dingell and Rep. Norman Lent (R-N.Y.), the ranking minority member of the Energy and Commerce Committee, the bill was basically the Bush bill with thirty-two changes aimed at satisfying the concerns of environmentalists and a number of relatively minor changes or "technical corrections." Strong White House lobbying had resulted in the defeat of several Waxman amendments designed to move up the deadlines for attainment of national ambient air quality standards and to increase tailpipe emission limits. The Energy and Commerce Committee's moderates (the Group of Nine) occasionally altered the balance of power between Dingell and Waxman—for example, they successfully challenged Dingell's proposal that the auto manufacturers be able to meet emission standards by averaging emissions from all vehicles, rather than requiring that every vehicle meet them.[49]

An agreement on the length of warranties for motor vehicle pollution control equipment, although it concerned a relatively minor issue, signaled that industry could not continue to assume that it could block clean air legislation. Subcommittee members were stunned in early October when Dingell and Waxman announced a compromise on tailpipe emission standards, one of the most contentious issues. Waxman had wanted higher standards and a shorter timetable for achieving them than had been proposed by Dingell and Lent. For more than a decade Waxman and Dingell had been arguing over what should be required of the auto industry. Waxman viewed cleaning up auto emissions as the most important step in reducing air pollution in southern California. It was also a major step that needed to be taken to improve public health, and Waxman was the leading proponent of revised health legislation in the House. Dingell thought the auto industry had already borne more than its share of the burden for cleaning up the air and that there were real limits to the regulatory costs that could be imposed on U.S. industries without harming their competitiveness in global markets and causing job losses.[50]

The agreement on tailpipe emission standards was a key development; after the agreement the prospects for passage of the amendments improved considerably. Many people believed that Dingell's subcommittee victories would be short-lived and that Waxman would likely prevail in floor votes, but that outcome was still uncertain, and it would not necessarily determine the conference vote. Committee members disliked having to choose between the powerful committee and subcommittee chairmen and continually pressured them to come up with a compromise. Dingell and Waxman agreed to bind themselves to the compromise throughout the subsequent House-Senate conference committee deliberations and not push for further concessions.[51] This compromise was particularly significant because it also produced some political capital for both that could be used in future debates over clean air and other issues.

The second battle in the House subcommittee was fought over clean fuels. When tailpipe emission standards were increased, attention naturally turned to fuels that polluted less and that could be used in older cars not subject to the new tailpipe emission limits. In one skirmish in September, Waxman, the environmentalists, and EPA Administrator William Reilly were pitted against Dingell, Detroit, and White House Chief of Staff John Sununu. The Bush administration had included in its bill a requirement that one million clean-fuel vehicles be produced each year by 1997. Waxman embraced the proposal, but strong lobbying by the auto industry caught the White House in a bind. Waxman reported that he had spoken with Reilly shortly before the subcommittee meeting and that he had voiced support for the production mandate. Ranking minority member Lent reported that he had just spoken with Sununu, who supported an amendment to strike the mandate. Members then debated over who was better able to represent the president's views—Reilly, calling from a phone booth in Chicago, or Sununu, calling from his desk next to the Oval Office. The Lent-Sununu position prevailed in a 12-10 vote. The White House was quick to argue that the administration remained united and that there had only been a misunderstanding.[52]

The House subcommittee had lost its momentum by mid-October, and a number of contentious issues remained unresolved. The Energy and Commerce Committee's Subcommittee on Energy and Power had jurisdiction over the acid rain provisions in the clean air bill. Philip R. Sharp (D-Ind.), subcommittee chairman, led midwestern members in an attempt to stall the legislation so they could generate support for the notion that cleanup costs should be distributed broadly, not just borne by utilities and ratepayers in their districts.[53] The midwesterners, originally aligned with the Dingell-Lent team, began complaining that nothing was being done to solve their problems and let it be known that they would lend their support in key committee votes on other issues to whatever faction would best help them minimize the costs of acid rain controls. Coalition building in the committee was further complicated by the opposition of members from "clean" states, primarily westerners, who feared a limit on sulfur dioxide emissions that would inhibit local economic growth.[54] The conflict reached a peak in November 1989 when Dingell warned that the "public bloodletting" in his committee threatened to "turn close friends into lasting enemies, and divide [the committee] on many issues for years to come." But midwesterners led by Sharp warned that "this time we're talking about high stakes for us." Sharp's threats were explicit: "Perhaps there are going to be other costs to be paid . . . on this or other legislation, if [rolling the Midwest] is going to be the game." [55] Members and lobbyists were asking each other if Dingell's complex deal making on so many different issues could produce results. The House leadership did not push for action on clean air, given other legislative priorities and the rush to adjourn by Thanksgiving.

The Senate. The clean air bill moved much more quickly in the Senate. Throughout the history of the Clean Air Act, both industry and environmental lobbyists have perceived the Senate Committee on Environment and Public Works as a bastion of support for environmental regulation. To industry, the committee was (and continues to be) "a wholly owned subsidiary of the environmental community"; industry lobbyists have gone outside the committee to find sympathetic ears in the Senate. To environmentalists, the committee was "the conscience of the Senate on environmental matters." The committee's majority and minority staffs, particularly Katharine Kimball and Jimmie Powell, who directed the Senate bill through the committee debates, negotiations, floor debate, and House-Senate conference, were virtually indistinguishable in terms of their commitment to aggressive environmental regulation. Some observers believe the committee's clout was, paradoxically, somewhat diminished by its fierce bipartisan dedication to environmental protection. There was relatively little need for compromise when the committee did markups, but, of course, the makeup of the committee did not reflect the range of views in the entire Senate. When the committee's bills were attacked on the floor, its influence was further diluted. As one industry lobbyist pointed out, "[T]hey don't have to cut any compromises in committee level . . . [but] that makes their job twice as hard when they get to the floor." [56] The committee's clean air bill, many believed, had simply failed to be subjected to any real test, and it had to be extensively revised in negotiations with the White House.

The Subcommittee on Environmental Protection began marking up three separate bills—air toxics, acid rain, and urban smog—in mid-October. The air toxics bill, with more stringent provisions than those in the president's bill, was passed with the subcommittee's usual bipartisan cooperation on October 19. The nonattainment provisions of the urban smog bill took the subcommittee less than an hour to approve on October 26. The first big split in the subcommittee occurred in November, when a Republican proposal—patterned after the Bush administration's initiative—to include an alternative fuels program in the smog bill was rebuffed by the Democrats, who were eager to report a bill before Thanksgiving. In general, the Democrats on the subcommittee favored tougher tailpipe emission standards; the Republicans emphasized alternative fuels and the development of new cars that used them. The Democrats prevailed in a series of close votes, and the bill was reported out to the full committee. An acid rain bill was reported on November 14 after a half day of discussion. The full committee, under pressure from Majority Leader Mitchell, combined the three bills into one and passed it in less than a day.[57] Yet, despite the rapid movement of the bill in the Senate, many observers doubted that a coalition could ever be put together to break the House deadlock.[58]

1990: Toward the Finish Line

The Senate took the lead in pushing the clean air bill forward in 1990, and Senate Majority Leader Mitchell made it his top legislative priority. The bill, managed by Max Baucus, arrived on the Senate floor on January 23. Minority whip and Environment and Public Works Committee member Alan Simpson (R-Wyo.) had warned that the floor debate would be a "riotous occasion" full of "anguish and horror." The main criticism of the bill was that the costs of compliance made it simply too expensive. Forty senators, led by Steve Symms (R-Idaho), had written to the Congressional Budget Office, the Congressional Research Service, and the Office of Technology Assessment asking for cost estimates. Industry calculations put the cost as high as $104 billion a year, but environmentalists argued that the health costs of air pollution were just as high.[59] The major issues to be resolved included how to lessen the impact of acid rain controls on midwestern utility consumers and high-sulfur coal miners and whether the production and sale of alternative fuels and clean-fueled vehicles should be mandated by law.[60]

By the second week of floor consideration, White House officials, industry lobbyists, and Senate critics were arguing that the committee's bill was much more expensive than the president's version but that it offered no real additional environmental benefit. Members, staff, and lobbyists for both sides began counting votes in anticipation of a motion to end a filibuster that many believed to be inevitable. Majority Leader Mitchell and Senator Baucus believed that they had enough votes to pass the bill but not enough to cut off a filibuster. Even if the bill passed, however, a presidential veto loomed. The EPA estimated that the cost of the committee bill was more than double that of the administration bill, and Bush had promised to veto any bill whose estimated compliance costs exceeded those of his version (estimated at $20 billion) by more than 10 percent. The administration identified twenty-four "priorities" for amending the Senate bill.[61]

The White House-Senate Summit

Fearing a filibuster, Mitchell withdrew the bill from the floor and called a series of extraordinary closed-door meetings with Bush administration officials for a second markup of the bill. Environmentalists were quick to oppose the process, because their strength lies in identifying the pro-environment votes and holding members publicly accountable for their votes on certain issues. Many members were glad to escape that accountability and used the closed-door process to obtain concessions for important interests in their states that would have been difficult to obtain in the open. This process clearly favors certain interests and weakens the influence of others. Its defenders legitimately argue that, at least in theory, private talks free participants from the need for political posturing and may facilitate the kind of negotiations that are essential to resolve highly contentious issues. But skeptics fear that the process favors industry interests at the expense of broader public concerns.

The negotiations that began on February 2 in Mitchell's office were intense and contentious; an impasse on mobile source limits, for example, was broken only after a full day of hard bargaining. Discussion continued for one month (some two dozen meetings spanning more than 250 hours) and took an enormous amount of the majority leader's time. He presided over the talks, apparently because of his sincere interest in and commitment to the bill but also because Senator Baucus was believed to lack sufficient familiarity with the complicated bill to be able to manage it. Some members of the Senate Environment and Public Works Committee and a few key White House and EPA officials were the major participants (dubbed by some the Group of Fifteen), but hundreds of staff members and dozens of administration officials participated at some point; nearly half of the Senate membership came in at one time or another to ask for concessions important to their states or to satisfy their objections.[63] The agenda was set primarily by administration demands for changes in the committee bill so that the total cost of the final package could be estimated.[64] Central to the White House strategy was the threat to veto a bill that was too expensive. Some believed that the "environmental" president would never carry out such a threat, particularly when there was such strong support for the Clean Air Act among the public and in Congress. Nevertheless, it seemed to be a useful mechanism by which administration negotiators could avoid provisions they did not want included in the package. The White House was in a strong position because it had delivered on its promise to propose a clean air bill, and it was in no hurry to accept a bill that included provisions it did not want. If the bill died, the Senate Democrats, not the president, would bear the brunt of criticism. Another key White House strategy was to bind senators to an agreement not through the conference with the House of Representatives but through the final Senate vote. The White House apparently believed that it was in a strong position to get what it wanted in the House, where ally John Dingell was in control of the legislation.

Industry groups were relieved that the two bills had been taken into closed-door negotiations; they argued that the issues were too volatile for public debate and that environmentalists would vilify anyone who proposed changes in the committee's bill. Environmentalists, anxious for the bill to remain on the floor because they feared that negotiations would only weaken it, had canvassed the Senate, hoping to garner the sixty votes needed to invoke cloture on the filibuster, but were not able to obtain enough commitments.[62] Not everyone had assumed that a filibuster was inevitable; many believed that Mitchell and Baucus should have forced floor votes. Environmentalists were hesitant to criticize the two senators for failing to do so and tried to place the blame on Bush for weakening the committee bill; nevertheless, their criticism of the majority leader's strategy angered Mitchell and Baucus.

Mitchell believed that the president's bill was not strong enough or broad enough to deal with the problems of air pollution. His strategy was to push for passage of an aggressive committee bill that could then be used to pressure the president to support a stronger legislative package than the one he had proposed. He viewed the committee bill as including about 80 percent of what the president had introduced, with stronger provisions regulating air toxics, stratospheric ozone, and motor vehicle emissions. But Mitchell was caught off guard by the opposition of environmental groups, for whom the Environment and Public Works Committee's bill was the minimum acceptable measure. "Rather than praising the Committee for getting the president to move beyond his bill," Mitchell complained, "they criticized us for accepting anything less than our bill." The media joined in the attack on the secret negotiations, making it harder, according to Mitchell, to get the bill passed.[65]

By February 23, the negotiations had produced agreements on regulations concerning toxic air pollutants, the use of alternative fuels, and stationary sources of air pollution. Mitchell had set February 26 as the deadline for completion of the talks. On March 1, he and the other negotiators emerged with a substitute bill that was somewhere between the bill passed by the committee and the Bush administration's proposal. It delayed the phase-in time for meeting motor vehicle emission standards, provided a less stringent means of assessing the risks posed by air toxics, added a requirement that alternative fuels be used in the most polluted cities, gave additional time and incentives for midwestern utilities to reduce emissions, and deleted proposed increases in fuel efficiency standards aimed at reducing carbon dioxide emissions that were thought to contribute to global warming. Industry groups were generally pleased with the proposed changes. Leaders of environmental groups debated whether to support the substitute bill or to try and defeat it, and then organized a grass-roots effort to push for strengthening the amendments.[66]

The Bill Returns to the Senate Floor

An initial canvas of senators by the National Clean Air Coalition identified 225 possible amendments to the substitute bill, but only a few posed major challenges. Several senators, backed by industry groups, proposed a series of amendments that would have weakened the air toxics provisions and the permit program, a central element of the bill that would have required all major stationary sources of pollution to have operating permits that expressly indicated the kinds and quantities of pollutants they could release.[67] (The permit program is discussed more fully in Chapter 4.)The National Clean Air Coalition concentrated on passage of two key amendments: one that would raise the tailpipe emission and clean fuel standards, and one that would bolster the nonattainment provisions. The Senate leadership's strategy was to defend the compromise by attacking these and other amendments as "deal-busters" that would kill the bill if passed since the changes would increase the cost of the legislation beyond the limit set by the president. The committee bill, for example, had required a second round of higher tailpipe emission standards that were to take effect in the year 2003. The substitute bill proposed that the second round of standards not take effect unless at least twelve cities failed to meet national ambient air quality standards for ozone. Many senators believed that the second round was inevitable; White House officials predicted that it would not be needed. Because these standards were contingent on future decisions, they were not considered mandatory and thus were not included in the cost estimates.

Members of the Environment and Public Works Committee now found themselves in the awkward position of opposing amendments that they had put in their own bill a few months earlier. Some unusual political coalitions were produced by the votes on these deal-buster amendments, particularly the vote on an amendment to restore the second round of tailpipe emissions standards and require clean fuels in sixty to seventy cities rather than the nine mandated in the substitute bill. Sponsored by Senators Tim Wirth (D-Colo.) and Pete Wilson (R-Calif.), the amendment was viewed by the National Clean Air Coalition as the key environmental vote of 1990—a classic, clear-cut choice between industry and environmental interests. The Senate leadership thought passage of the Wirth-Wilson amendment would kill the substitute bill and defeat any chance for revising the clean air legislation. Some senators who normally took a position in favor of environmental protection voted against the Wirth-Wilson amendment in order to preserve the chances of getting a bill; proponents of the amendment dismissed the president's veto threat as a political impossibility. Members who found the substitute bill still too burdensome and expensive voted for the amendment, hoping that it was indeed a deal-buster. Farm state senators supported the amendment because it promoted the use of ethanol, a clean fuel made from grain. Champions of small business voted for it as a way to reduce pressure for controls on industry. Particularly irritating to some members was the warning from environmental lobbyists that this was a scorecard vote—one that would be used by the League of Conservation Voters to evaluate members. Labeling votes in that way had become an increasingly common tactic used to pressure members.[68]

In the end, strong lobbying by the administration and EPA officials who buttonholed members on their way to vote enabled the Senate leaders to keep their deal together. The Wirth-Wilson amendment was shelved by a 52-46 vote to table the motion. For many members, the key argument was that if the deal broke apart, the hope for revising clean air legislation would vanish into dirty air. Other amendments that ran counter to provisions in the substitute bill were passed once they were defined as non-deal-breakers. But the defeat of the Wirth-Wilson amendment still required some serious arm twisting by Mitchell and Minority Leader Robert Dole (R-Kan.). "You could hear the arms snapping all the way down the Mall," said Wirth. "I know of seven guys who switched in the last hour." [69]

A couple of Senate votes in late March entailed more complicated maneuvers than simply trying to protect the substitute bill from deal-breaking amendments. An amendment proposed by Sen. Tom Daschle (D-S.D.) requiring that reformulated gasoline be used by all vehicles in the nine most polluted cities (rather than used only by new vehicles in those cities) was passed despite warnings that it was a deal-breaker.[70] The White House had lobbied for another amendment to ease the requirements for the permit program and enforcement by the states, but Mitchell, Baucus, and John Chafee opposed it as an unacceptable weakening of the law. On the morning of March 27, a motion to table the amendment lost by a vote of 47-50. When the amendment came to a vote, several members had reversed their votes as a result of hours of patient work by Mitchell and others, and the amendment itself was defeated by the same 47-50 count.[71]

The final obstacle to Senate passage of the substitute bill was Sen. Robert Byrd's amendment to give job training and other assistance to miners who would lose their jobs as a result of new clean air legislation. Byrd had helped block passage of clean air amendments for years in order to protect the jobs of West Virginia miners, whose high-sulfur coal was a key element in the production of acid rain. He viewed this effort as critical to the survival of their communities. Byrd held the floor during much of the week of March 19, describing in detail the lives and deaths of coal miners. He had originally proposed that displaced miners be given from 50 percent to 100 percent of their average salary and benefits over a six-year period, at a cost to the government of nearly $1.4 billion. By the end of March Byrd had twice scaled down the cost of his proposal. He noted that the White House, which had been outspoken in its criticism of his amendment, refused to negotiate with him.[72]

The debate dragged on, and Mitchell issued an ultimatum: by April 3 the Senate would vote on the clean air bill. Senators would convene on evenings and weekends until all amendments had been proposed and voted on. As former Senate majority leader and now president pro tempore and chairman of the Appropriations Committee, Byrd had many political chits to call in. Mitchell viewed Byrd's amendment as the final challenge to the bill he had so painstakingly nurtured for so long. Passage of the clean air bill was a test of his leadership and a measure of how well he was filling the job Byrd had just vacated. Members squirmed as they faced choosing between the majority leader and the Appropriations Committee chairman. Minority whip Simpson lamented in a speech on the Senate floor that members who voted against Byrd would still have to petition him for money for projects in their states. This was one issue where industry and environmental alliances did not have much influence.[73] The National Clean Air Coalition, after a series of lengthy discussions, decided to endorse the amendment as the kind of accommodation that was generally necessary to ensure the passage of environmental legislation, and as a recognition of the importance of organized labor in the coalition.

Neither Byrd nor Mitchell would yield. On April 3 the Senate voted on Byrd's amendment to authorize an appropriation of $500 million over three years to be paid to miners as job loss benefits and retraining assistance. Byrd believed he had fifty votes lined up, including that of Spark M. Matsunaga (D-Hawaii), who was dying of cancer and had been brought from the hospital to the Senate chamber in a wheelchair to cast his vote. Byrd lost the vote of Bennett Johnston (D-La.), who had gone home to attend a funeral and was delayed in returning because of bad weather. "Three of my votes took wings," Byrd later mourned, "with the help of the boys downtown." The White House veto threats had been repeated by Senate Minority Leader Dole, although he softened somewhat in warning that the amendment would "probably lead" to the president's veto. As Sen. Joseph Biden (D-Del.) entered the chamber to vote, he was ushered to the cloakroom, where Chief of Staff John Sununu's phone call was waiting. Sununu, Biden said later, "guaranteed me the president would veto the bill." [74] Sen. Steve Symms (R-Idaho) initially voted for the amendment, believing that it would kill the bill. He was then convinced by Sununu that the amendment would not lead to a veto but would simply make what was, in Symms's view, a bad bill worse, and he switched his vote. [75] That made the vote 49-49; Sen. Alfonse D'Amato (R-N.Y.), a member of the Appropriations Committee, voted against its chairman and the amendment lost by one vote. [76] The Senate voted to approve its clean air bill on April 3.

Meanwhile, Back in the House

Many White House officials were confident that a powerful committee chairman such as John Dingell would protect their interests as well as those he represented. [77] House negotiations centered on efforts to strike political deals to gain passage of legislative packages. Members who wanted to weaken provisions affecting the coal-fired power plants blamed for acid rain, for example, were willing to exchange votes of support with other members who wanted to protect the oil industry from demands for reformulated fuels that would be expensive to produce. Other proposals, such as the stratospheric ozone depletion initiative, were dealt with individually.

The House clean air bill resurfaced for markup in February 1990, after four months of negotiations among House members. Discussion of acid rain controls lasted only a half day in the Energy and Commerce Committee's Subcommittee on Energy and Power. No votes were taken, but it was clear that there was little support for the kind of cost sharing that subcommittee chairman Philip R. Sharp and other midwesterners wanted. Some subcommittee members, such as Jim Cooper (D-Tenn.), argued that the bill already included cost sharing in the form of grants for research on clean coal technology and extra allowances to midwestern utility companies. Sharp and his allies had failed to support Waxman earlier in full committee votes, thus preventing the formation of a coalition by those two groups.[78] Midwesterners worked to no avail for another month to get support for cost sharing. The subcommittee finally decided not to mark up the bill, and it went to the full committee for markup on March 14.

One week later, after three days of negotiations among the members and their staffs concerning nonattainment of air quality standards, the Energy and Commerce Committee made a surprise announcement that an agreement had been reached on urban air quality. Title I of the House bill was now almost as aggressive as the similar title in the Senate Environment and Public Works Committee bill, and it included provisions that had been voted down on the Senate floor as deal-breaking amendments. Industry and administration officials had expected Chairman Dingell to prevail in the House negotiations, and everyone was surprised to see that the House bill beginning to take shape was in some respects more stringent than the Senate version. Dingell, Waxman, and Lent agreed to support the agreement through the conference. This title, along with the provision on tailpipe emission standards that had been agreed to in the fall, significantly increased the prospects for House passage of the bill.[79]

Committee members again retreated behind closed doors to review the alternative fuels provisions the subcommittee had agreed to in October. White House officials did not participate in these negotiations as they had in the Senate. On March 29, committee members emerged without having reached a compromise and began voting on amendments. One amendment, requiring the sale of reformulated gas in more than thirty of the most heavily polluted cities, was defeated by a vote of 21-22. A substitute provision concerning alternative fuels and related programs, offered by Reps. Ralph Hall (D-Texas) and Jack Fields (R-Texas), who had close ties to the oil industry, finally passed, but some members warned that they would try again for more aggressive amendments on the floor.[80]

Intensive talks were then held among Energy and Commerce Committee members and staff. Members reached a compromise regarding toxic air pollutants that increased the sources covered in a first round of technological controls, but eased the controls required in a subsequent round of regulations that might be required to reduce any residual risk to health. Representatives of both industrial and environmental groups were pleased with the deal, favoring it over the Senate version. The full committee approved the deal by a 43-0 vote. Two days of round-the-clock talks were then held on acid rain, involving as many as thirty-five of the forty-three members of the committee. The session that started at 10:00 a.m. on April 4 continued until 4:30 a.m. the next day. After a break of a few hours, the talks resumed and an agreement was reached early in the afternoon. But the staffs discovered some problems with the agreement, and the details were not worked out until 8:00 p.m. A markup meeting was hastily called to approve the acid rain title. Sharp and his allies had finally relented;

no express cost sharing would be included in the bill, but midwestern and clean states would be given additional allowances to help soften the impact of controls. The negotiations had been driven by fatigue as much as anything else as the committee struggled to meet a deadline Dingell had agreed to with the Speaker for completing markup of the bill.[81]

The progress made in the House was largely the result of guesses Waxman and Dingell made about how much success they would have on the floor. Both seemed confident that they would prevail in key votes, but both were willing to hedge their bets by striking a deal in committee. Dingell was in a strong position when he went to the House-Senate conference because both the committee and the House were united behind him. Some members believed that his ability to obtain some concessions in a bill that was destined to pass enhanced his power in the committee.[82] Waxman tried to avoid the uncertain developments of a contentious floor vote by locking Dingell into positions before the conference. In so doing, he also won the gratitude of members who were not forced to choose between him and Dingell.[83]

The House votes were anticlimactic. The members took only two days to pass the bill, and they spent much of that time making speeches in which they congratulated each other for their willingness to compromise and expressed relief that there were no tough votes. One of the few recorded votes (274-146) was on an amendment to create a five-year, $250 million assistance program for workers displaced as a result of the Clean Air Act. The White House had fought hard and successfully to delete a similar provision from the Senate bill, but House members largely ignored White House threats to veto the bill if the program was included. Other amendments to require use of reformulated gas, maintain visibility in national parks, and protect the stratospheric ozone layer were added with little controversy. Dingell and Waxman spent several hours in a corner of the House chamber arguing over the unresolved issue of whether to include the clean-fuel vehicles mandate that had been part of the original Bush bill. Speaker Tom Foley sat and listened passively to the two antagonists and their staffs as they argued, refusing to leave until they had come up with a deal both could support. The Speaker did not threaten or cajole, but did roll his eyes once at the bickering. As one staff member described the scene, "It looked like he wasn't going to leave until there was a deal. That's a powerful influence. It's like when someone's sitting on your throat." When the deadlock was finally broken, the bill was quickly passed by a 415-15 vote.[84]

The House-Senate Clean Air Conference

The conference chairmanship alternates between the House and Senate in each major category of legislation (such as environmental regulation) discussed. The chairman of the Senate Committee on Environment and

Public Works, eighty-two-year-old Quentin Burdick (D-N.D.), had been largely uninvolved in the debates leading to passage of the bill in the Senate and was not believed to be up to the challenge of directing the proceedings of the Senate conference committee. Instead, the task was assumed by Max Baucus, chairman of the Senate Subcommittee on Environmental Protection of the Environment and Public Works Committee. Baucus was widely viewed as relatively inexperienced and no match for the chairman of the House conference committee, John Dingell, however.

The House passed its clean air bill on May 23, but conferees were not named until June 28. The delay was a result of disagreements between John Dingell and members of his committee over who would be permitted to participate. House tradition calls for the chairman of the committee with jurisdiction over the legislation to select the conferees and for the Speaker to ratify the selection. The chairman is to be constrained in the selection, however, and is to choose members whose views reflect the basic orientation of the bill to be passed. Dingell claimed that the list he had submitted was geographically balanced and represented the diversity of interests of members of the Energy and Commerce Committee. But Dingell had again proved to be a tough negotiator, as he did not choose members of his committee who had earlier challenged his position. Some members whose names had been omitted appealed to Speaker of the House Tom Foley to force Dingell to include them. Only as a result of the Speaker's unusual intervention were Gerry Sikorski of Minnesota and Mike Synar of Oklahoma, both Democrats who had crossed Chairman Dingell earlier in the clean air debate, included in the conference.[85] Despite Foley's help, Henry Waxman, leader of the members who wanted the most stringent provisions to protect the environment, could count on only five solid votes for his position among the 26 conferees from the Energy and Commerce Committee. The House group also included about 140 members from eight committees: the Public Works; Ways and Means; Education and Labor; and Science, Space, and Technology committees each sent 26 members; the Interior and Merchant Marine committees each sent 5 members; and two other committees each named one member to work on specific amendments and to be given limited participation rights in the conference. In contrast, the nine Senate conferees came from two committees: Environment and Public Works, and Finance.

Political Motivations. Dingell's motives were questioned frequently throughout the conference. He had been the primary proponent in the House of minimal regulation of industry, but his efforts in the early 1980s to obtain enactment of legislation that would weaken provisions of the Clean Air Act had been stymied by Waxman and others. Some thought he was now making a last attempt to scuttle the clean air bill. Environmentalists feared that he planned to delay the conference and pressure those with opposing views to accept his positions as the price of the bill's passage. Delay would play into his hands, according to this view, since he would be content to have no bill emerge, whereas champions of the bill would be willing to compromise whenever necessary in order to gain passage. But Dingell's motives were more complex. Because he had been widely blamed for the failure of Congress to update the Clean Air Act and would bear the brunt of criticism if it failed again, there was a clear incentive for him to show that he could lead and not just obstruct.[86] The fact that the amendments were passed, and that they included a host of provisions in response to industry concerns, is evidence of Dingell's considerable legislative power. He was able to accommodate many industry demands and yet was also credited with gaining passage of the bill.

There were notable differences between the House and Senate delegations. The Senate Environment and Public Works Committee, from which conferees were taken, was dominated by members favoring environmental protection. The bill that was passed by the Senate committee in the fall of 1989 was the most aggressive version passed by any subcommittee or any committee during the sixteen-month odyssey of the Clean Air Act Amendments. Although senators had made numerous concessions to the White House in negotiations held during the winter of 1990, those agreements were not binding beyond the Senate vote. In some cases, the conference committee senators sought stronger language than had been in the Senate bill. Waxman later wrote that the administration's insistence that the Senate agreement not be binding through the conference with the House (it apparently assumed that industry interests would dominate in the House bill) was "one of the most striking miscalculations of the clean air fight. . . . As a result, key Senators from the Environment and Public Works Committee were free to pursue the strongest environmental bill possible at Conference." [87]

The Senate conferees' demands were tempered, however, by two political considerations. First, Baucus was up for reelection in 1990 and faced a strong challenger. His positions were shaped by a disquieting sense that some provisions might be unpopular in Montana. Second, western senators had threatened to filibuster and block a final vote on the compromise if it included the House provision intended to protect the relatively clean air in national parks. Sen. Jake Garn (R-Utah) had blocked final passage of the clean air bill that had been approved by both houses in 1976 and claimed credit for eliminating a strong visibility provision in 1990.

In contrast, the House conferees were bound through the conference to agreement on several issues, including the plan to reduce smog and air toxics; this meant that they could change their position in conference only as a group. Some members believed that the agreement on tailpipe emission standards and acid rain was also binding, but others disagreed.[88] When they had some leeway, the Dingell-led majority opposed efforts by Waxman's minority contingent and the Senate conferees to adopt the more aggressive positions of the House and Senate versions.

A preliminary question that had to be resolved was the role of the White House in the conference. Norman F. Lent, the ranking House Republican at the conference, requested that White House domestic policy adviser Roger Porter be permitted to take part in the negotiations on the regulation of chlorofluorocarbons. In 1990, the United States had participated in talks to amend the 1987 Montreal Protocol on CFCs, and Lent and others wanted to be able to compare what the White House had agreed to with the congressional provisions. Waxman and others feared that Dingell and Lent would use a formal White House presence to strengthen their hand, as they had done at the 1986 conference on Superfund legislation by giving EPA head Lee M. Thomas a role in the talks.[89] The conferees eventually decided not to permit White House participation beyond availability on the sidelines to consult with conferees.

Nevertheless, the White House tried to maintain some influence by regularly reminding the conferees of the president's threat to veto the bill if its projected costs exceeded those of the president's original bill by more than 10 percent. The executive branch was somewhat divided in its view of the clean air bill; apparently most advisers favored its passage, but a few were responsive to industry lobbyists and others who argued that it was simply too expensive. Projections of high costs and the threats of a veto were an important political strategy. Cost estimates that put the total over the president's ceiling put pressure on conferees to reject the more stringent options being considered, for they feared that the president might veto the bill. But there was also a countervailing pressure to underestimate the probable costs of compliance with the bill so that the "environmental" president would sign it.

The clean air conference was unusual in two respects. The first was that both House and Senate conferees were familiar with the legislation. House members usually enjoy an advantage in conference because they have fewer committee assignments and are likely to be more familiar with the legislation than members of the Senate. But in this case, senators had engaged in intensive negotiations with the White House and were thus familiar with the legislation. Second, the structure and key provisions of the House and Senate bills were quite similar; although there were many differences, most pertained to details such as dates for compliance or the number of allowances permitted different sources. Legislation often changes markedly as it winds its way through the House and Senate labyrinths, because members of the two chambers fiercely guard their institutional prerogative to shape legislative provisions to their own liking. These two bills had developed in roughly the same time periods, and lobbyists had furthered the cross-fertilization of basic approaches and ideas between the two chambers.

Proposals and Counterproposals. The conference had to resolve a number of contentious issues raised by each major title of the bill. The nonattainment provisions differed concerning the responsibility of the EPA to step in when states failed to act to reduce urban smog. With regard to motor vehicle emissions, three important questions were still unanswered: (1) How strict should the requirements be for alternative fuels and the vehicles using them? (2) Should a specific formula for reformulated gas be included in the bill or should oil companies simply be given a goal to meet? (3) Should a second round of stricter emission standards be imposed on new motor vehicles early in the next century? The key issues pertaining to sources of toxic air emissions were how the residual risk existing after technological controls are in place should be regulated, and how the emission allowances that were part of the acid rain cleanup provisions should be distributed among the states.

When the conference opened on July 13, the senators made offers on two sections of the bill (stratospheric ozone depletion and permits and enforcement) that were similar in the House and Senate versions, in the hope that a quick agreement might generate some momentum and result in early completion of the conference.[90] The senators' request for a response from the House within a week was rebuffed by Dingell, and the House did not make a counteroffer until July 25. The Senate made another offer two days later, and staff members then met to hammer out a compromise, which was announced on August 3.[91] The slow pace of negotiations was attributed in part to the House conferees' unfamiliarity with the CFC provisions, since they had been added to the bill on the House floor. Dingell had effectively killed the provisions in his committee by arguing that the United States should not go beyond the provisions of the Montreal Protocol on Substances That Deplete the Ozone Layer.

The conference adjourned and Congress recessed in mid-August for its Labor Day holiday. Staff meetings resumed during the week of August 27 and conference members came to an agreement on provisions to reduce urban smog and to reduce permits on September 14. The urban smog package was largely the one passed by the House, including the requirement that the EPA issue cleanup plans if states did not and an extension of areas within states that could be encompassed by cleanup plans. During its January-February negotiations with the Senate, the administration had rejected the suggestion that members be bound by agreements through conference, so Senate conferees were free to accept the more ambitious House provisions. Since that agreement had been between the Senate negotiators and the administration, other senators did not perceive the conferees' acceptance as a breach of an agreement with fellow senators. For many senators, the greater concern was the impact on their states of the emission allowances for acid rain that had been painstakingly allocated in Senate talks in the spring; they hoped that, in the words of conferee Sen. John H. Chafee (R-R.I.), a "mood of reciprocity" would result from the urban smog compromise.[92]

The back-and-forth process of making offers and counteroffers continued throughout September. The House delegation led with an offer on tailpipe emission limits; the Senate delegation responded with its own suggestions, and the House delegation then took eleven days to renegotiate the language in its own bill concerning alternative fuels, since many conferees believed they were bound only to the tailpipe emissions agreement for motor vehicles. Lobbyists were giving no better than 50-50 odds that a bill would emerge before the October recess. A breakthrough occurred when negotiators agreed to work from the House title on motor vehicles and alternative fuels and the Senate air toxics provisions.[93]

The primary roadblock was that the House conferees representing oil states demanded that the House position be changed to require that only reformulated gas be sold in the nine smoggiest cities, that oil companies be given three additional years to produce cleaner fuels, and that the EPA be able to delay or weaken other requirements. Oil company lobbyists argued successfully that some of the provisions in both the House and the Senate bills were not technologically feasible. Dingell had demanded that only the EPA, and not the states, be authorized to enforce the California tailpipe emission standards, a provision that was in neither bill. After an all-night session on October 6 and 7, the House conferees accepted the oil delegation's demands. Dingell dropped his proposal in exchange for other concessions. The Senate conferees then accepted the provisions worked out among the House members.[94]

The chaos surrounding the budget talks in the fall of 1990 generated increased pressure for congressional Democrats to show they could legislate effectively, and the clean air bill was one of the most visible pieces of draft legislation that still had a chance of passage. Congress extended its session to complete the budget talks, thus giving the clean air conferees additional time to position themselves to get what they wanted before Congress adjourned. The strategy of the Dingell-led House conferees was clear: to delay issuance of counterproposals to offers made by others as long as they could.

When the Speaker imposed a deadline of midnight October 14 for completion of their work, the conferees began moving more quickly to review the hundreds of pages of bills that remained. The House delegation again became deadlocked, this time over a special extension given to the steel industry to clean up coke oven emissions. There were only minor differences between the House and Senate provisions that called for technological controls on air toxics. But the Senate bill included a less stringent residual risk provision and a special thirty-year exemption for the steel industry. In an unusual reversal, the Senate conferees favored the House provisions, whereas Dingell and the House conferees representing midwestern states wanted the weaker Senate version. The deadlock was finally broken in an early morning (3 o'clock) meeting; the steel industry was given a thirty-year extension in exchange for some additional controls to be imposed in the next several years.[95]

All-night negotiating sessions focusing on acid rain controls continued through the middle of October; House conferees resisted acceptance of the Senate version favored by the senators and the administration. (Waxman later joked that the key to passage of the Clean Air Act Amendments of 1990 was that three members of his staff—administrative assistant Philip Schiliro and subcommittee counsel Philip Barnett and Gregory Wetstone—were in better physical shape than other staff members with whom they negotiated and simply outlasted them. Some of the best deals they made, observed Waxman, were in the early morning hours when other staff members were exhausted.)

In a session that concluded at about 5:00 a.m. on October 22, the conferees gave midwesterners some additional allowances to ease the cleanup required in their states and largely accepted the Senate acid rain package. Two contentious issues remained. The first was the provision in the House bill establishing a five-year, $250 million program to assist displaced workers, to which the Bush administration had objected. The conferees accepted the provision but added language that limited participation in the program; White House officials then signaled from outside the conference room that they were not opposed. The second issue, a measure to protect air quality in national parks, was dropped because of opposition by key senators, who were backed by threats from western senators that they would filibuster if the compromise included it.[96] The House overwhelmingly passed the bill on October 26 by a vote of 401-25, and the Senate passed it the next day, 89-10. President Bush signed the clean air bill on November 15, 1990.[97]

The Politics of Clean Air

The passage of the bill was a remarkable event after a decade of deadlock, particularly in view of the bill's scope and the stringency of its provisions, in comparison with earlier versions. The provisions concerning vehicle emission standards in the 1990 act, for example, are more stringent and cover more vehicles than the provisions of the clean air bill introduced in the 100th Congress (1987-1988).[98] The act also includes a new clean fuels package. The auto industry had argued that "achievement of the mobile source requirements in [the earlier bill] is simply beyond the reach of any known or envisioned technology." Oil companies complained that the bill was "cumbersome, expensive, and unworkable" and would "trigger economic downturns in many areas." [99] Industry and Reagan administration opposition delayed passage of clean air legislation in the 1980s, but, ironically, resulted in a much more ambitious bill than had been proposed before 1989.

Given industries' economic clout, ranging from honoraria paid to members to campaign contributions, one might expect that lobbyists could have freely worked their will in the legislative process. But business lobbying is rarely, if ever, united, since competitive pressures cut in many different directions. Small businesses might fight regulations that larger businesses have the resources to accommodate, and big companies seek to ensure that the regulatory costs they have borne are shared by all their competitors. The interests of producers of pollution control equipment are obviously different from those of the polluting industries. Every requirement that control equipment be installed in some industry also means sales for the companies that produce such equipment. Heightened public concern over environmental protection in recent years has also fragmented industry unanimity.

Chemical companies have borne the brunt of public criticism and fear concerning air toxics, frequently manifested by consumer backlash. They have recently been uncharacteristically aggressive in arguing that they now want to clean up, and they have become rather willing participants in the clean air debate. Company reputations have been damaged by adverse publicity concerning toxic waste dumps and the accidental release of massive amounts of chemical pollutants into surrounding communities.[100] Utilities, in contrast, are widely perceived as having resisted acid rain controls too long. The utilities' intransigence despite relatively generous accommodations to them ultimately resulted in a bill that was much less sympathetic to their concerns than any earlier version.

In drawing some conclusions about the events of the 1980s that culminated in the 1990 amendments, Chapter 6 assesses the politics of clean air legislation and explores further the interaction of Congress and the White House in enacting legislation, the importance of personalities, and the relative strength of environmental and industry interests in environmental politics. Before that discussion and the review in Chapter 5 of the implementation of the amendments, Chapter 4 explores some of the major issues central to the passage of the 1990 amendments.

Notes

1. George Hager, "Smog Bill Toughens Standards for Car, Truck Emissions," *Congressional Quarterly Weekly Report,* 47 (May 13, 1989): 1113.
2. Bruce A. Ackerman and William T. Hassler, in *Clean Coal/Dirty Air* (New Haven, Conn.: Yale University Press, 1981), discuss how some of these themes were reflected in the 1977 amendments to the Clean Air Act of 1970.
3. Environmental Protection Agency (EPA), *Environmental Progress and Challenges: EPA's Update* (Washington, D.C.: EPA, 1988), 13.
4. Pub. L. No. 84-159, 69 Stat. 322 (1955).
5. Pub. L. No. 88-206, 77 Stat. 392 (1963).
6. Pub. L. No. 89-272, 79 Stat. 992 (1965).
7. For a review of these efforts, see Charles O. Jones, *Clean Air: The Policies and Politics of Pollution Control* (Pittsburgh: University of Pittsburgh Press, 1975); and Paul Portney, "Air Pollution Policy," in Paul Portney, ed., *Public Policies for Environmental Protection* (Washington, D.C.: Resources for the Future, 1990): 27-96.
8. Pub. L. No. 90-148, 81 Stat. 485 (1967).
9. *New York Times,* January 23, 1970, 22.
10. Testimony of James W. Jeans at a hearing of the Senate Public Works Subcommittee on Air and Water Pollution, March 23, 1970, quoted in *Congressional Quarterly Almanac, 1970* (Washington, D.C.: Congressional Quarterly Inc., 1971), 480.
11. Reorganization Plan no. 3, 1970 5 U.S.C.A. App. (Supp. 1992).
12. Congressional Quarterly Inc., *Congressional Quarterly Almanac, 1970,* 482-483.
13. Ibid., 478.
14. Ibid., 485-486.
15. Ibid., 472-488.
16. Ibid., 472.
17. 42 U.S.C. sec. 7401(a) (1988, Supp. 1990).
18. *Congressional Quarterly Almanac, 1970,* 472-474.
19. Pub. L. No. 92-157, 85 Stat. 464 (1971); Pub. L. No. 93-15, 87 Stat. 11 (1973); Pub. L. No. 93-319, 86 Stat. 249, 256, 261, 265 (1974); and 90 Stat. 2069 (1976).
20. *Congressional Quarterly Almanac, 1976* (Washington, D.C.: Congressional Quarterly Inc., 1977), 128-132.
21. Ibid., 132.
22. See Ackerman and Hassler, *Clean Coal/Dirty Air.*
23. National Commission on Air Quality, *To Breathe Clean Air* (Washington, D.C.: Government Printing Office, 1981). Regarding establishment of the National Commission on Air Quality, see 42 U.S.C. sec. 7409(a) (1988).
24. National Commission on Air Quality, *To Breathe Clean Air,* 55-56.
25. Quoted in Henry A. Waxman, "An Overview of the Clean Air Act Amendments of 1990," *Environmental Law* 21 (1991): 1724-1725.
26. See *Wall Street Journal,* April 4, 1990, A1 for a profile of the Natural Resources Defense Council.
27. EPA, Office of Legislation, "List of Committees and Subcommittees of Interest to EPA" (Washington, D.C.: EPA, 1987).
28. *Congressional Quarterly Almanac, 1981* (Washington, D.C.: Congressional

Quarterly Inc., 1982), 505-507.

29. Ibid.

30. Ibid. The balance of this chapter is based largely on interviews with a number of House and Senate staff members who were involved in the evolution of the clean air bills in Congress. They specified that their comments were not for attribution.

31. *Congressional Quarterly Almanac, 1982* (Washington, D.C.: Congressional Quarterly Inc., 1983), 425-434.

32. In 1983, some key members of the Reagan administration began to favor action. William Ruckelshaus, who was appointed EPA administrator in May to replace the embattled Ann Gorsuch, tried to develop support for an acid rain program. However, opposition to controls by other members of the administration, including OMB Director David Stockman, who ridiculed an expensive regulatory program aimed at saving fish, killed the initiative.

33. *Congressional Quarterly Almanac, 1984* (Washington, D.C.: Congressional Quarterly Inc., 1985), 340-342. "Marking up" a bill refers to the revision process in committee, which includes careful examination and editing of every detail.

34. *Congressional Quarterly Almanac, 1987* (Washington, D.C.: Congressional Quarterly Inc., 1988), 299-302.

35. *Congressional Quarterly Almanac, 1988* (Washington, D.C.: Congressional Quarterly Inc., 1989), 145, 148.

36. Richard E. Cohen, "Breaking through the Political Smog," *National Journal* 21 (February 18, 1989): 421.

37. *Congressional Quarterly Almanac, 1988,* 144-148.

38. Chuck Alston, "As Clean-Air Bill Took Off, So Did PAC Donations," *Congressional Quarterly Weekly Report* 48 (March 17, 1990): 811-813.

39. Ibid., 813-817.

40. See, for example, Brooks Jackson, *Honest Graft* (Washington, D.C.: Farragut Publishing, 1990); and David B. Magleby and Candice J. Nelson, *The Money Chase* (Washington, D.C.: Brookings Institution, 1990).

41. George Hager, "Acid Rain Controls Advance on Both Sides of Aisle," *Congressional Quarterly Weekly Report* 47 (April 1, 1989): 688-691.

42. Quoted in Margaret E. Kriz, "Politics in the Air," *National Journal* 21 (June 5, 1989): 1102.

43. George Hager, "Bush Sets Clean-Air Debate in Motion with New Plan," *Congressional Quarterly Weekly Report* 47 (June 17, 1989): 1460-1464.

44. White House officials who played a key role included Roger B. Porter, assistant to the president for economic and domestic policy; Boyden C. Gray, the president's counsel; and Chief of Staff John H. Sununu. Also influential were Robert E. Grady, associate director for natural resources, energy, and science at OMB; Robert W. Hahn, senior staff economist at the Council of Economic Advisers; Secretary of Energy James D. Watkins; EPA Administrator William K. Reilly; and Assistant EPA Administrator for Air and Radiation William G. Rosenberg.

45. Quoted in Kriz, "Politics in the Air," 1100.

46. "Project 88, Harnessing Market Forces to Protect Our Environment: Initiatives for the New President," a report written by a panel of academics, environmentalists, corporate executives, and government officials and sponsored by

Sens. Tim Wirth (D-Colo.) and John Heinz (R-Pa.), helped to focus attention on market-oriented approaches to regulation.

47. George Hager, "Critics Disappointed by Details of Bush Clean-Air Measure," *Congressional Quarterly Weekly Report* 47 (July 22, 1989): 1852-1853.

48. George Hager, "Clean-Air Package, Part 1: Toxic Air Pollutants," *Congressional Quarterly Weekly Report* 47 (April 22, 1989): 888-889.

49. George Hager, "Bush Scores Early Victory in Clean Air Markup," *Congressional Quarterly Weekly Report* 47 (September 23, 1989): 2451-2452.

50. George Hager, "Energy Panel Seals Pact on Vehicle Pollution," *Congressional Quarterly Weekly Report* 47 (October 7, 1989): 2622-2623.

51. Ibid., 2621-2624.

52. George Hager, "Bush's Plan for Cleaner Fuels Scaled Back by House Panel," *Congressional Quarterly Weekly Report* 47 (October 14, 1989): 2700.

53. George Hager, "Tougher Air-Toxics Standards Get Quick Nod from Panel," *Congressional Quarterly Weekly Report* 47 (October 21, 1989): 2783-2784.

54. George Hager, "Senate Panel One-Ups Bush on Clean Air Controls," *Congressional Quarterly Weekly Report* 47 (October 28, 1989): 2864-2865.

55. George Hager, "Bush's Tough Acid Rain Bill Puts Midwest on the Spot," *Congressional Quarterly Weekly Report* 47 (November 4, 1989): 2934-2937.

56. Quoted in Margaret E. Kriz, "The Impassioned Panel," *National Journal* 23 (June 15, 1991): 1504-1505.

57. George Hager, "Clean-Air Bill Loses Steam in Rush to Adjournment," *Congressional Quarterly Weekly Report* 47 (November 11, 1989): 3045-3046.

58. Christopher Madison, "Clean Air Plans Go Up in Smoke," *National Journal* 21 (November 18, 1989): 2832.

59. George Hager, "Senate Takes Up Clean Air But Doesn't Get Very Far," *Congressional Quarterly Weekly Report* 48 (January 27, 1990): 230.

60. George Hager, "The 'White House Effect' Opens a Long-Locked Political Door," *Congressional Quarterly Weekly Report* 48 (January 20, 1990): 141.

61. George Hager, "Senate's Clean-Air Struggle Goes Behind Closed Doors," *Congressional Quarterly Weekly Report* 48 (February 3, 1990): 324.

62. George Hager, "Closed-Door Talks on Clean Air Anger Environmental Groups," *Congressional Quarterly Weekly Report* 48 (February 10, 1990): 386-387.

63. George Mitchell, *World on Fire* (New York: Scribners, 1991), 1-11.

64. Hager, "Closed-Door Talks on Clean Air," 386-387.

65. Mitchell, *World on Fire*, 1-11.

66. George Hager, "Senate-White House Deal Breaks Clean-Air Logjam," *Congressional Quarterly Weekly Report* 48 (March 3, 1990): 652-654.

67. Ibid., 654.

68. George Hager and Phil Kuntz, "Senate-White House Deal Survives Another Test," *Congressional Quarterly Weekly Report* 48 (March 24, 1990): 900-906.

69. Quoted in Phil Kuntz, "The 'Super-Tuesday' of Clean Air: Nothing but a Quirky Footnote," *Congressional Quarterly Weekly Report* 48 (March 24, 1990): 902-903.

70. Phil Kuntz and George Hager, "Showdown on Clean-Air Bill: Senate Says 'No' to Byrd," *Congressional Quarterly Weekly Report* 48 (March 31, 1990): 986-987.

71. Ibid.

72. Byrd said that he had therefore been forced to negotiate with himself.

Although these negotiations had been "rather amicable," he wryly observed, "I think I have voluntarily retreated about as far as I can go backward." One morning, Byrd observed that many of his colleagues had gone home before he had completed his speech late the night before, so he repeated it, noting simply that "I feel that they are entitled to some enlightenment." George Hager, "Byrd vs. Byrd," *Congressional Quarterly Weekly Report* 48 (March 24, 1990): 901.

73. George Hager, "Clean-Air Deal Survives First Senate Assaults," *Congressional Quarterly Weekly Report* 48 (March 10, 1990): 738.

74. Quoted in Kuntz and Hager, "Showdown on Clean-Air Bill," 984-985.

75. Phil Kuntz, "Was Senator Byrd's Plan Veto Bait? Sununu Signaled Yes and No," *Congressional Quarterly Weekly Report* 48 (April 14, 1990): 1136-1137.

76. Kuntz and Hager, "Showdown on Clean-Air Bill," 985.

77. Some members of Congress where expected to represent a wide range of interests in the debate on each major issue. The interests represented by Rep. Terry Bruce (D-Ill.), for example, ranged from environmentalists who were active in a movement centered at local universities to managers of coal-powered electric plants. Members oriented toward industry sometimes had to choose between the demands of large industries and the concerns of small businesses. But in general, the members represented specific industries or economic interests and the task was to put together majority coalitions concerning key issues. Environment-oriented members usually took their cues from the positions championed by the National Clean Air Coalition. See Julie Kosterlitz, "Twin Powers," *National Journal* 23 (June 15, 1991): 1431.

78. George Hager, "House Makes No Headway," *Congressional Quarterly Weekly Report* 48 (February 10, 1990): 387.

79. Hager and Kuntz, "Senate-White House Deal," 900-902.

80. Kuntz and Hager, "Showdown on Clean-Air Bill," 985-987.

81. George Hager, "Clean Air: War About Over in Both House and Senate," *Congressional Quarterly Weekly Report* 48 (April 7, 1990): 1057-1063.

82. Janet Hook, "By Shifting Tactics on Clean Air, Dingell Guarded His Power," *Congressional Quarterly Weekly Report* 48 (May 12, 1990): 1453-1456.

83. George Hager, "Easy House Vote on Clean Air Bodes Well for Bill's Future," *Congressional Quarterly Weekly Report* 48 (May 26, 1990): 1643-1645.

84. Ibid.

85. George Hager, "Clean Air Conferees Finally Named," *Congressional Quarterly Weekly Report* 48 (June 30, 1990): 2044.

86. George Hager, "Cannons of the Conference Room Draw Clean Air Battle Lines," *Congressional Quarterly Weekly Report* 48 (July 21, 1990): 2291-2293.

87. Waxman, "An Overview," 1739.

88. Hager, "Easy House Vote on Clean Air," 1644.

89. George Hager, "Conferees in Holding Pattern over Clean Air Proposals," *Congressional Quarterly Weekly Report* 48 (July 28, 1990): 2399-2400.

90. George Hager, "Clean Air Conference Opens with Two Senate Offers," *Congressional Quarterly Weekly Report* 48 (July 14, 1990): 2214.

91. George Hager, "Compromise on CFCs First Step in Slow-Moving Conference," *Congressional Quarterly Weekly Report* 48 (August 4, 1990): 2507.

92. Alyson Pytte, "Conferees Reach Agreement on Urban Smog Provision," *Congressional Quarterly Weekly Report* 48 (September 15, 1990): 2903.

93. Alyson Pytte, "Clean Air Conferees to Talk But Differences Loom," *Congressional Quarterly Weekly Report* 48 (October 6, 1990): 3210.
94. Alyson Pytte, "Clean Air Conferees Agree on Motor Vehicles, Fuels," *Congressional Quarterly Weekly Report* 48 (October 13, 1990): 3407-3409.
95. Alyson Pytte, "Clean Air Conferees Agree on Industrial Emissions," *Congressional Quarterly Weekly Report* 48 (October 20, 1990): 3496-3498.
96. Alyson Pytte, "A Decade's Acrimony Lifted in the Glow of Clean Air," *Congressional Quarterly Weekly Report* 48 (October 27, 1990): 3587-3592.
97. Pub. L. No. 101-549 (S. 1630), 104 Stat. 2399 (November 15, 1990). See *Congressional Record,* October 26, 1990, S-17118-17125, S-17232-17256, H-13101-13203; *Congressional Record,* October 27, 1990, S-16878-16999, S-18264-18268, E-3663-3714.
98. H. R. 3054, introduced by Representatives Henry A. Waxman and Jerry Lewis (R-Calif.).
99. Waxman, "An Overview," 1812.
100. Interview with Bill Roberts, senior attorney for the Environmental Defense Fund, April 9, 1990. See, generally, the text of advertisements by the Chemical Manufacturers Association in the *Washington Post* throughout the clean air debate in 1990.

4   Issues in Formulating Clean Air Policy

The evolution of air pollution regulation in the United States, recounted in Chapter 3, provides a useful illustration of how policy making takes place. At the highest level of politics, the interaction between Congress and the White House when the Bush administration introduced legislation, during the passage of the bills in the two chambers, and during the conference committee's work had a significant impact on the final policy. Despite partisan differences and differing concerns about the projected costs of compliance with the provisions, the two branches were able to work together reasonably well. Both had a major stake in producing legislation, and some provisions of the final product, such as the acid rain title, are more aggressive than one would have expected given the history of the debate in the 1980s.

Beyond the broad issues of law making and the separation of powers, however, are the policy issues central to regulating air pollution and improving air quality, and the political relationships surrounding them. The 1990 Clean Air Act is an intricate mix of traditional approaches to environmental regulation and important innovations. Because it is such a complicated and detailed piece of legislation, full examination of all of its provisions is beyond the scope of this book. The main titles or sections of the law concern some of the most difficult policy issues in environmental regulation.

This chapter explores the most important issues and problems addressed by the 1990 act and their implications both for environmental policy and for public policy making in general. It focuses on the policy goals that Congress and the White House sought to achieve in passing the Clean Air Act Amendments; Chapter 5 examines what actually happened as the law was implemented.

Challenges in Regulating Air Pollution

Five issues are particularly important in understanding the formation of clean air policy. These issues were emphasized in the debate over clean air throughout the 1980s in response to the perceived failures of the existing laws, the evolution of scientific knowledge about air pollution, devel-

141

opments in state clean air regulation, and broader issues of national and international politics.

First is the issue of how detailed environmental laws should be. The 1990 amendments push back compliance dates for achieving the national air quality standards from the 1977 act; in exchange for the additional time states are given to achieve these goals, and in order to increase the likelihood that they would eventually meet the standards, Congress imposed a tremendous array of specific requirements on the states. Given states' reluctance to reduce pollution levels, due in part to the interstate nature of pollution and the need for all states to develop effective measures, a strong, prescriptive approach seems unavoidable. But considerable political and regulatory costs result from that approach, and a heavy federal hand is necessarily balanced by differences among the states and their independent political status as well as by changes in control technologies.

Similarly, the differences among the states in terms of the levels of pollution require that they be given some flexibility in devising their regulatory strategies. The more diverse the requirements, however, the greater the challenge for companies marketing products nationwide in meeting those demands. As has been true for other areas of regulation, industries are demanding that federal environmental regulation preempt state requirements: it is better to face one (perhaps) stringent set of mandates, the thinking goes, than a patchwork of fifty different standards.

A second issue is how far Congress can push regulated industries to develop cleaner processes and technologies. Technology forcing has worked well in reducing auto emissions, but Congress has been less than willing to extend it into other areas, fearing job losses and plant shutdowns that could be blamed on environmental laws. There are significant advantages to technology forcing: all firms are required to comply as a matter of fairness; enforcement can be monitored simply by ensuring that equipment is in place; pollution levels decrease; and incentives are created for firms to develop and market control technologies in the United States and throughout the world. But some facilities will shut down and workers will be displaced if compliance costs are too high; a market-based approach to regulation might achieve the same goals at a much lower price. The acid rain program of the 1990 amendments is the leading test case in the development of economic instruments in environmental regulation. If successful, it will likely stimulate a great expansion of market-based approaches in other regulatory endeavors.

Third, the formation of effective political coalitions is an essential part of policy formation. The traditional division of environmentalists on one side and regulated industry trade associations on the other masks much of the political landscape for clean air regulation. State and local political and regulatory officials are an important set of constituents. They sometimes line up with environmental groups, and other times with regulated industries. Large corporations with the resources to understand and comply with complex and expensive environmental regulations often view regulation much differently than do small businesses struggling to survive. Some grassroots environmental activists are more aggressive in their demands and more impatient with politics as usual than are their counterparts in the Washington, D.C., offices of the large environmental groups, who believe that compromise and negotiation are essential. Environmental protection is a bipartisan issue, but traditional Republican business constituencies and proponents of limited government have given Democrats the opportunity to take the lead in environmental policy. But since much, if not all, politics in Congress is local, regional differences may at times be more important than partisan politics.

International trade and global competitiveness are additional considerations that must be factored into policy-making calculations. The provisions of the Clean Air Act Amendments of 1990, designed to write into national law the obligations the United States assumed under international agreements, raised an important debate concerning the costs and benefits of international leadership and unilateral actions in global environmental affairs.

Fourth, one of the central debates in clean air policy, and in environmental regulation as a whole, focuses on the assessment of risk. Risks permeate our lives from the foods we eat to the mode of transportation we choose. Given our scarce economic and political resources, which risk reduction efforts should be given priority? Many scientists and policymakers believe that we do not know enough about risks to be able to compare them with any precision. Risks that are imposed on people without their knowledge or consent might be given much greater attention than those voluntarily undertaken. But as environmental laws have become increasingly prescriptive, they have inhibited the ability of the executive branch to set priorities for reducing risk even when analysis is available to guide that effort. The tremendous difficulties encountered in trying to assess risks collide with rough comparisons of the costs and benefits of specific regulations that show great disparities in the cost per life saved. Concern over the cost of compliance with environmental regulation pressures Congress and the executive branch to set priorities. Analytic barriers, the demands of interested groups, and Congress's decentralized structure combine to make a comprehensive, analytic approach to reducing risk unlikely.

Finally, the ultimate test of environmental policy (or any other kind of policy) is the extent to which regulated parties comply with the standards required of them. The 1990 amendments reach back to other environmental laws in devising a permit system that, used as in water pollution regulation, promises to facilitate compliance by major sources and simplify the enforcement of clean air requirements. One of the many paradoxes of clean air regulation is the attempt to clarify and facilitate compliance and enforcement by adding a new layer of regulatory requirements.

Structure of the Clean Air Act of 1970

As required by the Clean Air Act of 1970, the EPA issued health-based standards for six traditional or ambient air pollutants (sometimes referred to as "criteria" pollutants): total suspended particulates, sulfur dioxide, carbon monoxide, lead, ozone, and nitrogen dioxide. These national ambient air quality standards specified the acceptable level of concentration of these pollutants in the ambient (outside) air. (See Chapter 2.) *Primary standards* are intended to "protect the human health," with an "adequate margin of safety"; *secondary standards* are intended to protect public welfare and are aimed at crops, property, and plant and animal life. For most pollutants, the secondary standard is the same as the primary standard. The standards for some pollutants pertain to maximum levels that are permitted for one to twenty-four hours; standards for other pollutants limit average annual concentrations. Concentrations of pollutants in the ambient air are measured in micrograms per cubic meter ($\mu g/m^3$) of air or in parts of pollutant per million parts of air (ppm). Table 4-1 lists the national ambient air quality primary (health-related) standards for the six traditional or ambient air pollutants.

States are required to formulate cleanup plans, called state implementation plans, for meeting, maintaining, and enforcing the national ambient air quality standards. These plans generally impose emission limitations on existing stationary sources (industrial, commercial, and household) of pollution. They may also include transportation control measures to reduce traffic and to require the inspection and maintenance of pollution control equipment on motor vehicles. Each state is divided into air quality regions; state officials are required to identify which air regions are not in compliance with federal standards. Once cleanup plans have been approved by state officials, they become binding *state* regulations and have the force of *state* law. Once they are approved by the EPA, they become binding *federal* regulations and have the force of *federal* law.

New stationary sources of pollution, or expansions of existing ones, are expected to be cleaner than older sources. The EPA issues New Source Performance Standards for categories of industrial facilities that are generally more stringent than the state standards limiting existing sources, since the retrofitting of older facilities is assumed to be more expensive than the installation of control equipment as new facilities are built. New sources of pollution cannot be constructed until permits are granted by the state in which they will be located, and states are to issue permits only for new

Table 4-1 National Ambient Air Quality Primary (Health-Related) Standards

Pollutant	Averaging time	Maximum concentration (approximate equivalent)
Particulate matter (PM_{10})	Annual arithmetic mean 24-hour	$50 \ \mu g/m^3$ $150 \ \mu g/m^3$
Sulfur dioxide (SO_2)[a]	Annual arithmetic mean 24-hour[c]	$80 \ \mu g/m^3$ (0.03 ppm) $365 \ \mu g/m^3$ (0.14 ppm)
Carbon monoxide (CO)[b]	8-hour[c]	$10 \ mg/m^3$ (9 ppm) $40 \ mg/m^3$ (35 ppm)
Nitrogen dioxide (NO_2)	Annual arthmetic mean	$100 \ \mu g/m^3$ (0.053 ppm)
Ozone (O_3)	Maximum daily 1-hour average[d]	$235 \ \mu g/m^3$ (0.12 ppm)
Lead (Pb)	Maximum quarterly average	$1.5 \ \mu g/m^3$

Source: Environmental Protection Agency, National Air Quality and Emissions Trends Report (Washington, D.C.: EPA, 1989), 2-2.

[a] Secondary standard for SO_2: averaging time of 3 hours, concentration of 1300 µg/m3 (0.50 ppm).
[b] There is no secondary standard for CO.
[c] Not to be exceeded more than one day a year.
[d] Standard is attained when the maximum hourly average concentrations above 0.12 ppm occur no more than one day a year.

facilities that demonstrate they will meet these new source standards and will not cause the air quality area in which they are located to exceed any national ambient air quality standard. If the facility is to be built in an area that already fails to meet one or more of those standards, any new major pollution must be offset by reductions in emissions from existing sources. To achieve that result, companies proposing new construction can close down old facilities they own, purchase existing sources and reduce or eliminate their emissions, or buy from other sources part of their authorization to emit pollutants.

Motor vehicles, a major cause of pollution, are also regulated by a federal-state partnership. The Clean Air Act of 1970 specified maximum tailpipe emissions for new automobiles and authorized the EPA to enforce those standards. States are responsible for developing inspection and maintenance programs to ensure that vehicles meet the standards imposed on them at the time of manufacture. State implementation plans can include specific regulations to reduce air pollution, such as those controlling traffic and parking or encouraging carpooling.

States are also required to develop a program for the prevention of significant deterioration in areas where air quality is relatively good and meets the national ambient air quality standards (such as national parks and wilderness areas). More stringent standards are to be imposed on existing and proposed sources in these areas than in nonattainment areas.

The Clean Air Act Amendments of 1990: A Summary

The 1990 amendments to the Clean Air Act of 1970 constitute a major addition, but the basic structure of the act was not changed. Two new provisions, concerning acid rain and stratospheric ozone protection, were added, as was a workers' compensation program for those who lose their jobs as a result of compliance with the act—the first such program in any environmental statute. The main provisions of the amendments are summarized in this section and in Table 4-2.

Title I: Nonattainment

If Title I had been passed alone, it would rank as one of the most detailed and complex laws ever enacted by Congress. It is a testament to the efforts of congressional and EPA staff members and state and local regulatory officials to provide to the states all the regulatory powers that could be devised to help them meet the national ambient air quality standards.

One of the most important innovations included in Title I is an elaborate system of classifying pollutants: there are six categories of ozone nonattainment areas, from marginal to extreme, and two each for carbon monoxide and particulate matter. Deadlines of three to twenty years are set for meeting the standards. The more serious the pollution problem, the more regulatory steps states must take and the more aggressive they must be. The most difficult air quality standard to meet has been that for ground-level ozone, a main ingredient of urban smog, and Title I brings more sources of ozone under the act's coverage. Reductions are required by sources emitting 100 tons of precursors of ozone per year in marginal and moderate areas, 50 tons per year in serious areas, 25 tons per year in severe areas, and 10 tons per year in extreme areas. Furthermore, the definition of "major source" is changed so that smaller sources can be regulated in areas where there is serious air pollution. Another key provision requires establishment of annual emission reduction goals. Under the 1970 law, states were to make "reasonable further progress," but no minimum, quantitative targets were specified. The amendments state that areas of moderate to extreme ozone pollution must reduce emissions by 15 percent within the first six years and 3 percent per year thereafter. The 15 percent goal is difficult but not impossible to meet, according to state and local air quality officials, and many states should be able to meet it.[1] But one sponsor of the

Table 4-2   Summary of the 1990 Amendments to the Clean Air Act

Title I: Nonattainment
Adds new classifications of air quality areas
Imposes deadlines that vary with severity of pollution problems
Requires revised state implementation plans
Covers more pollution sources
Tightens controls on many pollution sources
Lowers thresholds for major pollution sources
Requires specific, measurable progress

Title II: Mobile Sources
Imposes new, stricter emission standards for new motor vehicles
Requires production of clean-fueled vehicles for use in fleets and pilot
  programs
Requires sale of clean fuels in severely polluted areas

Title III: Hazardous Air Pollutants
Requires regulation of 189 air toxics by technology-based controls
May require additional controls based on residual risk
Requires risk management plans for accidental release of air toxics

Title IV: Acid Deposition Control
Reduces electricity-generating power plant emissions of sulfur dioxide by
  10 million tons/year and nitrogen oxides by 2 million tons/year
Sets a cap on the amount of sulfur dioxide to be emitted by year 2000
Creates a market-based system of emission allowances to help finance
  cleanup costs

Title V: Permits
Establishes a comprehensive new state-administered permit program
Limits permits to 5 years
Requires states to charge permit fees ($25/ton)
Requires review of permits by EPA and neighboring states

Title VI: Stratospheric Ozone Protection
Phases out production and consumption of CFCs and other chemicals that
  deplete the ozone layer
Requires recycling and imposes other controls on various CFC-containing
  products

Title VII: Enforcement
Establishes $25,000/day penalties and $5,000 field citations
Establishes criminal penalties for violations knowingly committed
Expands citizen suit provisions

Source: Clean Air Act Amendments, November 15, 1990.

bill points out that "the emphasis in the bill . . . is not on the deadlines. The emphasis is on achieving steady progress before the deadlines." [2]

Title II: Mobile Sources

Title II specifies more than ninety emission standards for motor vehicles. Statutory provisions concerning use of reformulated fuels include detailed performance standards and fuel content requirements. Tailpipe emissions of hydrocarbons and nitrogen oxides are to be reduced by 35 percent and 60 percent, respectively, in some new cars by the 1994 model year and in all new cars by 1996. Beginning in 1998, pollution control equipment in all new cars will be required to have a 10-year, 100,000-mile warranty. Auto manufacturers are required to produce a fleet of experimental cars for sale in southern California (150,000 cars by 1996, 300,000 cars by 1998). Using new technologies, they are to meet even more stringent emission standards than those listed above. Oil companies are required to offer alternative formulations of gasoline that produce fewer pollutants when ignited. They are to be used in areas with the worst carbon monoxide pollution problems by 1992, and in all areas with ozone problems by 1995. In areas with serious ozone problems, fleets of ten or more vehicles that can be centrally fueled are required to use clean fuels such as methanol, ethanol, and natural gas. A new program, stage II controls, requires that equipment be placed on service station gasoline pumps to capture vapors released during refueling.

Title III: Hazardous Air Pollutants

The requirement in Title III that emission limits be established for all major sources of hazardous or toxic air pollutants represents a significant departure from the approach taken in the 1970 law. Title III also lists 189 chemicals to be regulated as hazardous air pollutants; Congress did not leave that determination to the EPA. The agency is required to list the categories of industrial processes in chemical plants, oil refineries, steel plants, and other facilities that emit these pollutants and to issue standards for each category by the deadlines specified, using as a basis minimum regulatory standards provided in the title. Within eight years of establishing the emissions standards for industrial processes, the EPA is required to establish a second round of health-based standards for each chemical that is believed to be a carcinogen and that represents a risk of at least one cancer case for every million exposed individuals. The EPA cannot impose health-based or residual risk standards on coke ovens at steel mills until 2020 if they meet interim, technology-based standards between 1993 and 1998. The major sources of hazardous air pollutants, defined as those emitting at least 10 tons per year of any one toxic pollutant or at least 25 tons per year of any combination, are required to achieve the same level of emissions reduction reached by existing sources. These reductions are to be achieved between 1995 and 2003 and are expected to reduce the emission of toxic air pollutants by as much as 90 percent by 2003. Finally, the title establishes an independent agency, the Chemical Safety Board, to investigate chemical accidents in order to determine their causes. The EPA will require industrial plants to prepare formal safety reviews to be made available to the public and will set new safety standards for plants where the bulk of toxic chemicals are used.

Title IV: Acid Deposition Control

An important innovation included in Title IV is an emissions trading program for sulfur dioxide (the major precursor of acid rain). The EPA is to allocate to each major coal-fired power plant an allowance for each ton of emission permitted; sources cannot release emissions beyond the number of allowances they are given. Allowances may be traded, bought, or sold among allowance holders. Certain midwestern utilities will receive additional allowances that they can sell to help finance their cleanup efforts. The EPA is required to create an additional pool of allowances to permit construction of new sources or expansion of existing ones. The sulfur dioxide emission allowances for each of the major power plants in twenty-one states are listed in the law; emission allowances for other power plants are to be computed by means of detailed formulas that are provided.

Sulfur dioxide emissions are to be cut in half by the imposition of these emission limitations. A 50 percent reduction from 1980 levels of 10 million tons annually is to be achieved by the year 2000. Half of the reduction had taken place, as scheduled, by January 1, 1995, when the 110 largest sulfur dioxide-emitting electric utility plants in twenty-one states were required to meet more stringent emission standards.

Emissions of nitrogen oxides, the other major cause of acid rain, are to be reduced by 2 million tons a year from 1980 levels. The first emission limits became effective within eighteen months of enactment of the 1990 amendments. Additional reductions are required by 1997.

Title V: Permits

The amendments establish a new permit program to facilitate enforcement of the Clean Air Act. All major stationary sources must have state-issued operating permits that specify what emissions they can release and at what levels, and what control measures they must employ. Major sources are defined differently for different kinds of pollution. The main thrust of this program is to bring together in one document all of the requirements with which sources must comply, to clarify for sources themselves what their obligations are, and to enable state regulatory officials and members of the public to know exactly what emissions are allowed so that compliance can be more easily monitored. The EPA is responsible for overseeing the state permitting programs.

At one level, the permitting system seeks to simplify clean air regulation. However, it actually creates a new layer of regulatory requirements. For major sources of the six criteria pollutants, permits identify the specific obligations they must meet as their contribution to achieving the objectives of their state's implementation plan. The permits require major sources of air toxics to employ specific production and control technologies. For sources of acid rain emissions, the permits specify emmissions limits and the number of allowances or tons of emissions allocated each year.

Title VI: Stratospheric Ozone Protection

The destruction of the stratospheric ozone layer was not considered a problem when the Clean Air Acts of 1967 and 1970 were enacted. The 1990 amendments are a means of implementing in the United States the Montreal Protocol on Substances That Deplete the Ozone Layer. Some sections of Title VI commit the nation to a more rapid phaseout of some of these chemicals than is required by international agreement. The title lists specific ozone-depleting chemicals and provides a schedule for the phaseout of the production and use of those chemicals. The production of chlorofluorocarbons and carbon tetrachloride is to be phased out throughout the 1990s and outlawed by January 1, 2000; methyl chloroform cannot be produced after January 1, 2002. The use of HCFCs in aerosol cans and insulating material is prohibited after January 1, 1994, and their production is prohibited after 2030. The title also requires the EPA to issue new rules for the recycling and disposal of ozone-depleting chemicals recovered from air conditioners, refrigerators, and other appliances and equipment. The current regulatory requirements for these chemicals are listed in Table 4-3.

Title VII: Enforcement

Enforcement provisions require more monitoring by sources—particularly through continuous emission monitors—and by state agencies, update the penalties imposed by the law to make them consistent with those in other environmental statutes, and increase the role of the public in enforcing the law through citizen suits to be filed against polluters and government agencies.

Title XI: Clean Air Employment Transition Assistance

The secretary of labor is authorized to establish a program to provide compensation for workers who are laid off as a consequence of compliance with the Clean Air Act, including grants for retraining and allowances for

Table 4-3   Regulating Status of Ozone-Depleting Chemicals, 1995

Chemical	Source	Lifetime in atmosphere (years)	Date production banned
Chlorofluorocarbons	refrigerators, air conditioners, solvents, sterilants	100	Jan. 1, 1996
Halons	fire extinguishers	100	Jan. 1, 1994
Carbon tetrachloride	solvents, chlorine, pesticides	50	Jan. 1, 1996
Hydrochlorfluoro-carbons (HCFCs)	air conditioners, plastic insulation, plastic packaging foam	15	2030
Methyl chloroform	industrial solvents, cleaning metal and electronics	6	Jan. 1, 1996
Methyl bromide	fumigation of soils, commodities, and structures	—	None; frozen at 1991 levels

Source: Council on Environmental Quality, Environmental Quality 1992 (Washington, D.C.: CEQ, 1993), 139.
Note: Essential uses of CFCs, halons, carbon tetrachloride, and methyl chloroform are exempted from the ban. A 99.5% phaseout of HFCs is projected to occur by 2020.

job searches and relocation. The cost of the program was expected to reach $250 million by 1995.

Other Provisions

The 1990 amendments also include a number of provisions that have been given less attention than those discussed thus far. Title VIII orders the EPA to regulate air pollution resulting from activities such as oil exploration on the outer continental shelf, to study air pollution that impairs visibility in national parks and other areas that have relatively clean air, to develop a program to monitor and improve air quality along the United States border with Mexico (a provision that became much more significant after the signing of the North American Free Trade Agreement), and to compare the environmental regulations that U.S. trading partners impose on firms within their borders with EPA regulations (a provision that took on increasing importance in light of the General Agreement on Tariffs and Trade).

The amendments also provide grants for state air pollution planning and control programs and for research on hydrogen fuel cells, and require that all sources subject to acid rain controls report to the EPA their carbon dioxide emissions to facilitate the agency's effort to gather information on gases that are believed to contribute to global climatic change. Title IX authorizes establishment of a program to monitor and analyze air pollution production and its health effects. Title X requires that no less than 10 percent of funds expended by the EPA on research be made available to businesses that are at least 51 percent owned by "one or more socially and economically disadvantaged business concerns."

Clean Air Law and Regulation: Defining the Issues

The decisions incorporated in the Clean Air Act Amendments of 1990, and the way the amendments' provisions are implemented, will have a major impact on American business and Americans' health. The precedents they establish will have important implications for environmental law and for regulation in general. Several key issues are discussed below.

Broad Goals and Detailed Provisions

The Clean Air Act as amended is a statement of broad, aggressive goals. The summary of the amendments in the preceding section does not begin to convey the technicalities and minutiae in the seven main titles. The amendments list hundreds of specific chemicals to be regulated, establish precise deadlines for virtually every regulatory step to be taken by the EPA and the states, and specify exactly how much pollution can be emitted by new and old motor vehicles. Rep. Henry Waxman (D-Calif.), a proponent of such a detailed approach, is optimistic that it will result in stricter enforcement:

To an extent unprecedented in prior environmental statutes, the pollution control programs of the 1990 Amendments include very detailed mandatory directives to EPA, rather than more general mandates or broad grants of authority that would allow for wide latitude in EPA's implementation of the CAA's programs. In addition, statutory deadlines are routinely provided to assure that required actions are taken in a timely fashion. More than two hundred rule-making actions are mandated in the first several years of the 1990 Amendments' implementation.[3]

Title I of the 1990 amendments is Congress's response to the failure of the Clean Air Act of 1977 to produce attainment of the national ambient air quality standards for the six traditional pollutants. Under the 1970 law, states were to have their attainment programs or state implementation plans in place by 1972. It became increasingly clear in the early 1980s, however, that the law was not having the intended effect. Many states failed to meet deadlines for coming into compliance and for formulating and implementing their cleanup plans. The EPA and the administration of President Ronald Reagan were widely viewed as trying to weaken the law and minimize industry compliance costs. Many members of Congress became increasingly frustrated because the EPA was slow to issue documents to guide state regulatory efforts and either failed to impose sanctions, required by law, in noncomplying states (although members of Congress representing industrial states did not want the sanctions to be imposed either), or was unwilling to enforce the sanctions as aggressively as the law seemed to require.

The challenge confronting state regulatory officials was immense. There were tens of thousands of sources to be regulated, monitoring data were usually scarce, and many states had little idea of which sources needed to be regulated and how to regulate them. Aggressive regulatory initiatives were often met by industry predictions that factories would be closed down and massive layoffs would ensue. In a series of congressional hearings, state air quality officials supported a stronger Clean Air Act and a stronger threat of federal intervention in recalcitrant states as a way to improve their regulatory position vis-á-vis other state officials who feared that environmental regulation would harm the economy.

By the mid-1980s, it was obvious that the standards for emission of ozone, carbon monoxide, and particulates would not be met unless the act was strengthened. Although the most serious problems were concentrated in large urban areas, physicians and health researchers warned in congressional hearings and elsewhere that the health of children, the elderly, and those with respiratory diseases in all areas of the country was endangered by poor air quality.[4] Members of Congress and the subcommittee staff agreed that the law needed to be more complicated because the task of regulating the different pollutants was so daunting; they also believed that Congress needed to limit the discretion of the EPA and the states. The questions they debated included what burdens, if any, should be imposed on small businesses; what kinds of sanctions for noncompliance were appropriate; how the EPA and the states were to go about enforcing compliance with the national ambient air quality standards; how far to extend the deadlines for compliance with those standards; how to determine what constitutes a major source of emissions; how to establish a new program of permits to regulate emissions from major sources; and how to prevent significant deterioration of air quality in and near national parks and wilderness areas. Most of these details were worked out in the House bill, and the House-Senate conference committee largely adopted that version.[5]

Members of Congress were constantly preoccupied with the possibility that "without detailed directives, industry intervention might frustrate efforts to put pollution control steps in place. . . . History shows that even where EPA seeks to take strong action, the White House will often intervene at industry's behest to block regulatory action." [6] The agency's actions are circumscribed by the amendments' detailed provisions; its inaction can be challenged by citizen suits (Title VII). These are usually straightforward cases that can be won simply by demonstrating that an action required by a certain date has not been taken, and their outcomes can shape the EPA's regulatory agenda. If the agency fails to act, hammer provisions go into effect. For example, after January 1, 1995, no gasoline can be sold in certain areas unless it is in compliance with EPA regulations; if no regulations have been issued, no gasoline can be sold. The petroleum industry is as interested as environmentalists in ensuring that the EPA issues these regulations. States are authorized to issue their own control technology regulations for major sources of air toxics if the EPA fails to do so, and the threat to industry of a number of different state standards will likely prompt it to support EPA efforts.[7]

Despite the widespread criticism of the traditional command-and-control form of regulation, in which Congress orders the EPA to issue regulations and the states implement them, as discussed in Chapter 1, the Clean Air Act Amendments of 1990 are based largely on that approach. The continued reliance of Congress on deadlines for state and EPA action, and the specificity of the amendments' provisions, reflect Congress's continuing distrust of the executive branch and its belief that many environmental laws are not being fully or aggressively implemented by state and federal agencies. Many of the deadlines included in the 1990 amendments have been, and will continue to be, used in citizen suits brought by environmental groups and others to force implementation of the law. Congress tried to limit the EPA's discretion in every way it could because many members, particularly Democrats, had come to believe that if the agency had any leeway, it simply would not act, or that if it tried to exercise some initiative and discretion in taking an action that was not absolutely required by law, its OMB overseers would quickly clamp down.

The EPA continues to be caught in the middle of the constitutional tug-of-war between Congress and the president over how environmental laws are to be implemented. This position poses tremendous challenges for the agency in managing its workload and setting priorities for the allocation of its resources. Agency officials have relatively little flexibility; they are committed by law to policies that reflect Congress's understanding of air pollution regulation in 1990 and that will probably impede agency adjustments as new research and new scientific developments alter our understanding of the causes and consequences of air pollution and present possible alternatives. The 1990 amendments, as they are implemented, will provide another test of whether Congress can enact laws that effectively compel agencies to pursue an aggressive regulatory agenda.

The Congress that passed the 1990 Clean Air Amendments also largely mistrusted the states. The progress many states have made in recent years in improving their capacity for environmental regulation was difficult for Congress to address. Some states had developed innovative air pollution control efforts, but their future success relied on the development of national standards so these states would not lose their industry to their neighbors.[8] States have been in the forefront of policy innovations for environmental protection in general, and clean air in particular,[9] and members of Congress looked to the experience of many states, particularly California, in devising specific provisions of their clean air bills in the 1980s. Communities throughout the country have developed innovative, cooperative regulatory initiatives. These bottom-up environmental efforts, described by one author as "civic environmentalism," hold great promise for improving environmental quality and remedying local problems.[10] Nevertheless, there are still states that resist clean air and other environmental regulatory efforts, and Congress has struggled with ways of permitting some states to enjoy some policy autonomy while forcing other states to meet minimum requirements.

Federal Regulation and the Preemption of State Efforts

Many states have developed regulatory programs that are stricter and more aggressive than those mandated by federal law, and have thus greatly complicated the compliance efforts of many industries. Industry groups have lobbied strongly for the inclusion of provisions in federal law that would preclude states from developing such regulations.

One example of state regulatory initiatives illustrates clearly the issue of preemption. Industry fears of state and local regulation of manufacturing and use of CFCs generated support for federal regulation of these ozone-depleting chemicals. Although the Clean Air Act of 1977 prohibited states from issuing such regulations, that did not keep some states and localities from taking action to limit or prohibit CFC use within their boundaries. By 1990, some two dozen ozone protection bills had been introduced in state legislatures. A bill was passed by the Hawaii state legislature that banned the sale of recharge cartridges for auto air conditioners that use CFCs as a coolant.[11] In May 1989, the Vermont state legislature passed a bill that, beginning with the 1993 model year, would prohibit the sale or registration of any car with an air conditioner using CFCs as a coolant.[12] Vermont law also required the recycling of CFCs in auto air-conditioning systems and their elimination from those systems by 1993.[13] The attorney general of Massachusetts announced in August 1988 that a foam producer had agreed to pay $700,000 in civil penalties for emitting approximately 1,300 tons of CFCs in violation of state regulations.[14] In Irvine, California, a city ordinance was enacted in July 1989 that prohibited businesses from buying, selling, or using products containing CFCs, beginning July 1, 1990. The ordinance also banned the use of halons, used in fire extinguishers, and two solvents, carbon tetrachloride and methyl chloroform. When Irvine became a CFC-free area, auto repair shops advertised their CFC-recovery equipment for servicing air conditioners. Critics predicted that the higher costs would drive business to other cities, but just the opposite happened: residents from other communities came to Irvine shops to have their air conditioners serviced, demonstrating strong public support for environmental protection and providing powerful economic incentives for other businesses to offer "green" services.[15] Maine prohibits the use in schools and government agencies of all polystyrene that is manufactured from ozone-depleting substances. Portland, Oregon, bars the service of prepared food in any polystyrene foam products.[16]

However, the Clean Air Act hearings did not address federal preemption of state and local law. The preemption provision in Title VI repealed the 1977 preemption clause and replaced it with the following provision: "[D]uring the 2-year period beginning on the enactment of the Clean Air Act Amendments of 1990, no State or local government may enforce any requirement concerning the design of any new or recalled appliance for the purpose of protecting the stratospheric ozone layer." [17] State and local governments thus are apparently free to continue to regulate the manufacturing and sale of such appliances thereafter. But new research findings concerning the risk of further ozone depletion may intensify pressure for more aggressive action.

Federal preemption of state regulatory actions is also a major theme of Title II, which establishes motor vehicle emission standards. One of the most contentious issues in the debate was whether states should be permitted to adopt the emissions standards that California already had in place for new cars sold in that state, which were more stringent than the federal requirements existing before 1990. (Five of the seven areas with the most serious ozone pollution problems in the nation are in California.) New York had adopted the California requirements before the 1990 amendments were passed, and other northeastern states planned to do so. Auto manufacturers warned that permitting states to issue their own standards would create a patchwork of requirements that would be impossible to enforce. State officials feared that federal legislation might create barriers to effective state regulation of auto emissions and make it easier for car manufacturers to challenge state enforcement decisions. Federal preemption of state programs is explored further in the next chapter.

The 1990 amendments effectively limit states to either adopting the new round of California standards or accepting the federal standards. Balancing the demand for federal standards with the urgent need to reduce emissions in California was one of the primary challenges confronting Congress and the executive branch in formulating the 1990 amendments. The California Air Resources Board's *old* tailpipe emission standards for new cars and light-duty trucks sold in that state were adopted by Congress in 1990 as the standard to be met by all new vehicles. The requirements in the 1990 amendments thus are modest in comparison with California's current program for regulating auto emissions. Title II adopts the technology-forcing approach of the Clean Air Act of 1970. The technology for lowering tailpipe emissions, however, has already been developed; consequently, the 1990 law forces more widespread use of current technologies rather than the development of new ones. The first round of controls specified in the Clean Air Act Amendments of 1990, which were phased in beginning with the 1994 model year, are the same as California's 1993 standards for new cars. A second round of controls might be imposed beginning in the year 2004. But California has launched an aggressive program requiring that, by the year 2000, all new cars sold in California must meet at least the standards for low levels of emission. By 2003, 10 percent of the new cars will be required to have zero emission, 25 percent will have to have ultralow levels of emission, and the balance must have low levels of emission. California will also require the sale of more than 1.5 million vehicles that run on alternative fuels by the year 2000.[18]

Technology Forcing

Throughout the two decades of debate over the Clean Air Act, a basic expectation has been that laws and regulations will provide clear incentives for industry to develop cleaner technologies and use them more widely. Air pollution from mobile sources has been regulated under the Clean Air Act in two ways: directly, through emissions standards, and indirectly, through transportation control measures designed to reduce traffic. One of the successes of the Clean Air Act of 1970 is that it helped force the development and use of new control technologies, such as the catalytic converter for motor vehicles. Despite its frequent praise for technology forcing, however, Congress has generally been hesitant to push industries beyond what they claim is technologically possible. Consequently, technology forcing has often meant forcing the more widespread *use* of already existing new technologies, rather than forcing the *creation* of new technologies required to meet stringent standards. Two prominent examples of technology forcing in the 1990 law include regulating tailpipe emissions and encouraging use of clean fuels.

Tailpipe Emission Standards. The Clean Air Act of 1970 established tailpipe emission standards for three pollutants: nonmethane hydrocarbons, carbon monoxide, and nitrogen oxides. To implement the standards, the EPA established in the 1970s the Federal Motor Vehicle Control Program, under which it issues national emission standards for fuel evaporation, carbon monoxide, nitrogen oxides, volatile organic compounds, and particulates. New vehicles must meet these standards; EPA officials test emissions of sample vehicles from production lines to ensure industry compliance. The states assume responsibility for enforcing tailpipe emission standards of vehicles once they are in use. Many states have included in the sections of their state implementation plans pertaining to ozone and carbon monoxide a motor vehicle inspection and maintenance program. The inspection includes an examination of the catalytic converter and other control equipment to ensure its proper functioning, as well as a test of tailpipe emissions to determine whether they meet the standards.

From 1940 to 1970, motor vehicle emissions of volatile organic compounds (VOCs) more than doubled; from 1970 to 1988 they declined by 46 percent, despite an 81 percent increase in national vehicle miles traveled in that period. Figure 4-1(a) shows the decline of motor vehicle VOC emissions from 1970 to 1988. Motor vehicle emissions of carbon monoxide nearly tripled between 1940 and 1970; they decreased by 48 percent between 1970 and 1988, as shown in Figure 4-1(b). The decrease in emissions of both VOCs and carbon monoxide was a result of the imposition of tailpipe emission standards; older cars were replaced by those using cleaner fuels. Nitrogen oxide emissions, however, peaked around 1980 due to changes in engine technology; they have since declined, as shown in Figure 4-1(c).[19]

The battle between the auto industry and clean air advocates over the extent to which cleanup can be achieved through technological controls on tailpipe emissions has dominated the debate over clean air policy for two decades, overshadowing other efforts such as the reduction of motor vehicle traffic. Aware that technological changes are easier to bring about than changes in Americans' driving habits, Congress has hesitated to impose aggressive transportation control measures. The steady increase in national vehicle miles traveled since 1980 (see Figure 4-2) has largely offset the progress made in reducing tailpipe emissions. It is clear that the imposition of strict tailpipe emission standards and the production of vehicles that emit fewer pollutants are not enough. If national ambient air quality standards are to be met, states with severe pollution problems will have to develop and enforce transportation control measures to reduce the number of vehicle miles traveled.

The progress made in the 1970s renewed demands in the 1980s that even more stringent controls be placed on tailpipe emissions. As mentioned in Chapter 3, Rep. John Dingell (D-Mich.) believed that auto company officials had borne the brunt of the effort to reduce pollution and were justified in resisting further controls. Environmental groups and state and local officials were just as adamant; pointing to the reduction in motor vehicle emissions as a cost-effective way of reducing pollution levels, they championed a new round of technology-forcing emission standards. Some

Table 4-5 Sources and Uses of Alternative Fuels

Alternative fuel	Source	Internal combustion engines	Diesel engines	Turbine engines	Electric motors	Fuel cells
				Uses		
Reformulated gasoline	Petroleum, natural gas	x				
Methanol and methyl tertiary butylether	Biomass, natural gas, coal	x	x	x		x
Ethanol and ethyl tertiary butylether	Biomass	x	x	x		
Compressed natural gas	Natural gas	x	x	x		
Electricity	Solar energy, hydroelectric power, nuclear energy, natural gas, biomass, coal, geothermal energy				x	
Hydrogen	Solar energy, nuclear energy, coal	x		x		x
Synthetic gasoline	Biomass, coal, oil shale	x				
Synthetic diesel fuel	Biomass, coal, oil shale		x	x		

Source: Adapted from Department of Energy, *Interim Report: National Energy Strategy* (Washington, D.C.: Department of Energy, 1990), 16.

Table 4-6   Advantages and Disadvantages of Reformulated and
Alternative Fuels

Methanol
Advantages:

May reduce ozone-forming hydrocarbon emissions by up to 40 percent when
used as a mixture of 85 percent methanol and 15 percent gasoline
In 100 percent concentration, may reduce ozone-forming hydrocarbon emissions by up to 90 percent
Eliminates benzene and other toxic emissions

Disadvantages:

May increase formaldehyde emissions
Requires significant expenditures for new production and distribution systems
Reduces vehicle driving range and is corrosive to engine parts
Makes vehicles difficult to start in cold temperatures

Ethanol
Advantages:

May reduce ozone-forming hydrocarbon emissions and toxic emissions to
extent and in concentration similar to methanol
Reduces carbon dioxide emissions

Disadvantages:

Emits more acetaldehyde
Would cost consumers substantially more without federal tax exemption
Requires vehicle modifications estimated at $300 per vehicle

Liquefied petroleum gas
Advantages:

Produces an estimated 50 percent fewer hydrocarbons, which have less
ozone-forming potential
May reduce carbon monoxide emissions by an estimated 25 percent to
80 percent

Disadvantages:

Reduces vehicle driving range and causes refueling inconveniences
Requires pressurized fuel tanks, which restrict vehicle cargo space
Increases new car cost by up to $1,000

Compressed natural gas
Advantages:

Reduces hydrocarbon emissions by an estimated 40 percent to 90 percent
Reduces carbon monoxide emissions by an estimated 50 percent to 90 percent
Reduces emissions of benzene and other toxic pollutants

Disadvantages:

Emits more nitrogen oxides
Requires installation of new distribution system

consequently, there are few provisions specifically requiring its use. The lesson is clear: if a powerful economic and political interest can be harnessed to environmental goals, inclusion of the relevant provisions is virtually guaranteed. Initiatives aimed at improving air quality that were coupled with subsidies generated strong political support but upset many long-standing political alliances; conservative, agriculture-oriented members of Congress were pressured to support new regulatory requirements promoted by ardent environmentalists.

Regional Politics

Much more complicated was the politics of acid rain. That the acid rain provision was included in the Clean Air Act Amendments of 1990 is remarkable, given the ten years of deadlock over the issue. An important international issue, acid rain continues to be a major source of contention between the United States and Canada, and informal discussions between officials of the two countries began in 1978. The Canadians argued that they had already taken significant steps to reduce their contribution to the problem, including a plan to reduce sulfur dioxide emissions by 50 percent of their 1980 levels (67 percent in Ontario) by 1994, and called on the Americans to do the same. But U.S. officials were hesitant to make a commitment to such reductions, claiming that the United States had already done much more than Canada to reduce sulfur emissions and that more research was necessary before making major investments in pollution control technologies. After three years of negotiations, Canada proposed reducing sulfur dioxide emissions by 50 percent of current levels in both countries, but the United States rejected that initiative.[30] A 1986 agreement called for $5 billion to be spent in the United States over five years, to be split equally by industries and the federal government, to retrofit plants with new control technologies.[31]

President Bush met with Prime Minister Brian Mulroney in February 1989 to begin discussing an acid rain agreement. Negotiations continued throughout 1989 and 1990 as the Clean Air Act wound its way through Congress. The talks culminated in an Air Quality Agreement, signed on March 13, 1991, in which Canada promised to reduce SO_2 emissions by 1994 to 2.3 million tonnes from sources in the seven eastern provinces and to impose a national cap of 3.2 million tonnes by the year 2000. The United States essentially agreed to make the reductions mandated in the Clean Air Act Amendments of 1990: a 10-million-ton reduction in SO_2 emissions from 1980 levels by 2000 and a cap by 2010 of 8.95 million tons of SO_2 from electric utilities and 5.6 million tons from industrial sources.

At least as important to Congress as foreign relations, however, was the domestic politics of acid rain, which transcended partisan politics and provides an illustrative case study of how members of Congress deal with regional conflicts. Legislation proposed in the early 1980s, as the Clean Air Act of 1977 was about to expire, called for a 40 percent reduction (10 million tons) of sulfur dioxide emissions below 1980 levels over a ten-year period. The Reagan administration and congressional opponents argued that there was insufficient information to link sulfur dioxide emissions from power plants and factories in the Midwest with acid rain damage in Canada and New England and that, in any event, the problem would be remedied as old power plants were replaced by less polluting ones.[32]

There were three central issues in the congressional debate over acid rain in the 1980s. First, how great a reduction in sulfur dioxide emissions should take place? In order to protect ecologically sensitive areas, reductions in acid deposition of 50 percent were suggested, which translated into an annual reduction in sulfur dioxide emissions of about 11 million tons. But since some areas are more sensitive than others, the distribution of reductions may be more important than an average reduction. A second divisive issue was the means of reducing sulfur dioxide emissions. If public utilities and industries were permitted to choose the most cost-effective means of reducing emissions, many would likely have substituted low-sulfur coal for high-sulfur coal. But the 1977 amendments to the Clean Air Act prohibited states from achieving national ambient air quality standards for sulfur by using low-sulfur coal and required companies to install flue gas desulfurization or "scrubbing" equipment.[33] A shift to low-sulfur coal would probably not have decreased the total number of mining jobs, and might even have increased it, but the distribution of jobs would have shifted from eastern to western coal states. Some communities in the East would have been particularly hard hit and could have lost from 20,000 to 30,000 mining jobs.[34] If scrubbers were installed to reduce emissions by 10 million tons a year, an estimated 45 million tons of scrubber sludge would also be generated each year, posing another major environmental challenge. Scrubbers also increase carbon dioxide emissions and thus contribute to global warming because they require more coal to be burned to produce the same amount of electricity, although some believe that alternative technologies will soon be available that will reduce sulfur dioxide emissions without the negative environmental by-products.[35] The third issue was who would pay for the reduction in sulfur dioxide emissions. The EPA estimated that a 50 percent reduction in the emissions causing acid rain would cost $16 billion to $33 billion over twenty years.[36] Other estimates were higher, putting the cost at $3 billion to $6 billion each year well into the twenty-first century, if utilities were to switch to another fuel, install scrubbers, and build new facilities.[37] Electric rates in Ohio were projected to increase from 8 percent to 12 percent if emission reductions were required. A shift away from high-sulfur coal would threaten as many as one job in four in some areas of Kentucky and would have adversely affected other sectors of the local economy dependent on the coal industry. States such as Ohio, West Virginia, and Indiana would face similar economic problems.[38]

Three options discussed in Congress in the 1980s were (1) to subsidize with federal tax revenues the capital expenditures required to achieve the reductions; (2) to increase taxes in the northeastern and midwestern states so that states most affected by the problem would bear the burden; and (3) to levy a tax on all electricity generated by public utilities, to be contributed to a trust fund to subsidize new investment. Midwesterners argued that federal subsidies had been used to develop sources of electricity in other areas of the country, such as hydroelectric plants in the Northwest; therefore, funds should be made available to help build coal-powered generating plants in the Midwest.

Legislation reported out by the Senate Environment and Public Works Committee in the mid-1980s required that polluters bear the burden of controls to reduce sulfur dioxide emissions. The federal subsidies that would pay for control equipment were to be funded by a surtax on electricity based on the amount of such emissions produced by each power plant. This agreement promised to protect the jobs of high-sulfur coal miners. In June 1988, a bipartisan group of twenty-eight senators proposed a compromise on acid rain that was similar to the one that had been proposed by the governors of New York and Ohio in May. Govs. Mario Cuomo and Richard F. Celeste, respectively, had proposed that the costs of the control equipment necessary to achieve major reductions in sulfur dioxide emissions be divided equally between the midwestern states and the federal government, with the federal share coming from the proceeds of a tax on oil imports.[39] By October 1988, however, despite the previous summer's heat, the most severe urban smog in a decade, and letters signed by majorities in both chambers calling for reauthorization of the Clean Air Act, Senate sponsors of the legislation abandoned their efforts. Environmentalists rejected the concessions made to industry, and some key senators on the Environment and Public Works Committee withdrew their support of the compromise. Sen. Robert Byrd (D-W.Va.) continued to refuse to bring the bill up for a floor vote in order to protect the West Virginia high-sulfur coal industry.

In the House, the Group of Nine on the Energy and Commerce Committee had begun working on a compromise bill in the mid-1980s, hoping to break the logjam between members favoring industry and those favoring environmental concerns. Rep. Jim Cooper, a Democrat from a Tennessee coal-mining district, met with the Alliance for Acid Rain Control, a group of governors led by then governor John Sununu of New Hampshire and Gov. Anthony Earl of Wisconsin, and with representatives siding with industry and environmental groups. The House compromise bill included a fifteen-year cleanup period and was a modest attempt to encourage the development of clean coal technologies instead of requiring scrubbers. One of the first bills to set a cap on total emissions, it included a minimal trading program that allowed public utilities to trade emissions allowances within their regions but did not require offsets for companies that wanted to build new plants. States that had already cleaned up or that did not really have significant pollution problems were not affected by the bill; the limits applied only to the states with high emission pollutant rates. Emissions were projected to decrease to 10 million tons by the year 2000, but could then grow over time.

Sponsors of the reauthorization legislation in both chambers blamed members favoring industry and environmental groups for taking extreme positions and causing rejection of the compromise bill. For example, Rep. Philip Sharp (D-Ind.) argued in 1988 that

advocates at polar ends of the issue prevented action this year. Some concerned environmentalists wanted more action sooner, but there is insufficient support in Congress for their position. Many in industry fear the high costs of compliance, and want fewer legal requirements. That position is insufficient to protect the public health. Together, they essentially made it impossible to move legislation.[40]

Sen. George Mitchell (D-Maine) blamed the extremism of those whose

principal weapon is the exaggerated claim that if anything is required of them to prevent pollution—anything at all—the cost will be so high that whole industries will have to shut down, whole States will suffer, whole regions will decline [and others] who say they support the Clean Air Act [but] joined with the many who oppose it. They remained rigid and unyielding, wholly unwilling to compromise, even when faced with the certainty that their rigidity would result in no action this year.[41]

The unwillingness of both groups to compromise might be attributed to their perception of the benefits of delay. The alliance between members representing the high-sulfur coal industry and environmentalists that facilitated passage of the 1977 amendments (which made mandatory the installation of scrubbers in new power plants and the use of local rather than western low-sulfur coal) was severely criticized[42] and may have discouraged subsequent compromise. Much of the progress in reducing pollution during the years immediately following enactment of those amendments was achieved by sources that were easiest (and cheapest) to control. As the control of emissions became increasingly expensive for each unit of pollution reduced, the opposition of industrial groups also increased. The decline of American competitiveness in international markets was less of a concern to these groups in 1970 and 1977 than it was in 1990. Members of Congress have been quick to give such interest groups a veto over possible compromise positions and are frequently unable or unwilling to make commitments until their assent is forthcoming. Legislators who see themselves as brokers between outside parties cannot exercise creative leadership in crafting solutions to difficult problems.

When the Bush administration released its proposed amendments to the Clean Air Act in the summer of 1989, the debate over whether new acid rain controls were necessary was essentially concluded. Environment-oriented members of Congress quickly accepted the Bush initiative as the minimum position; much of the public viewed acid rain as the worst of the environmental problems. The Bush proposal took on only one constituency, the electric utilities, and let industrial polluters off the hook. Since electric utility executives were not likely to desert the Republican party, it was a relatively safe political action to take. The proposal knocked representatives of the utilities for a loop, because they had been lobbying against a bill of any kind and their allies in Congress had demanded cost sharing before any new requirements were imposed. The president's plan was to be tough on the acid rain title and more flexible on the smog and air toxics titles. The opposition to acid rain controls was led by Democrats in both chambers; the Bush initiative disrupted these and other political coalitions in ways that opened up the legislative process.

The Clean Air Act Amendments of 1990 and Global Environmental Agreements

Once international treaties are signed, the participating nations implement them by means of their own legislation and administrative regulations. A number of bills were proposed in Congress in the late 1980s and early 1990s that addressed the global problems of stratospheric ozone depletion and global warming. The House and Senate bills that were finally agreed upon included ozone provisions, but not global warming provisions (except to require some monitoring of greenhouse gas emissions), largely because there is not the same scientific consensus on the threat of global warming as there is on the threat of CFCs to the ozone layer. The debate focused mostly on economics, however, particularly on the implications for the competitive position of U.S. industries if this nation unilaterally imposed new controls rather than waiting for global agreements to be signed.

The provisions aimed at preventing further depletion of the stratospheric ozone layer were among the most environmentally aggressive in the clean air bill; unlike other provisions, they required not merely the control but the elimination of certain substances. The opposition had claimed that the ability of the United States to encourage future international agreements would be undermined by unilateral action. Industry groups such as the National Association of Manufacturers and the Alliance for Responsible CFC Policy also argued against domestic imposition of tougher reduction schedules without corresponding international action. "Any unilateral action taken by the United States," the alliance contended, "would have an all but insignificant effect upon the global environment and severely hinder U.S. industry while placing the American economy at an unfair disadvantage in the global market, to say nothing of the loss of American jobs."[43] But industry had already demonstrated its ability to come up with alternatives, and the widespread support in both houses of Congress for more vigorous action to protect the ozone layer virtually ensured passage of the provisions.

The provisions for reducing CFC emissions contained in the Clean Air Act Amendments of 1990 and the Montreal Protocol are a sobering example of the dilemma of dealing with uncertainty. Subsequent research has identified an even further depletion of the ozone layer than was apparent in 1990. If an agreement to limit the manufacturing and use of CFCs had been concluded in the 1970s, in response to initial scientific warnings, much less damage to the ozone layer would doubtless have occurred. Many scientists fear that the Montreal Protocol is too little, too late, because the emissions released during the past decade and those that will be released in the decade to come will damage the ozone layer far into the future since CFC molecules can stay in the stratosphere for decades. Ozone depletion is a relatively simple problem compared with global warming, however. The modest progress made as a result of passage of the Clean Air Act and conclusion of the international accords is not necessarily a cause for optimism about our ability to solve other global environmental problems.

Assessing Acceptable Levels of Risk from Air Pollution

Two approaches—national ambient air quality standards and technological controls—have been emphasized at different times throughout the history of the Clean Air Act. The first approach entails determining what levels of pollution do not pose a health risk and then developing sophisticated air quality models to determine what reductions in pollution are needed to achieve those standards. The second approach—simply requiring all sources to install pollution control equipment—has usually been easier to implement. The debate then centers on the question of which technological controls should be required. Should they be reasonably effective, widely used controls? Or should they be the best controls available and those that are used by the cleanest sources? Similar questions have been debated with regard to other environmental laws as well. The Clean Water Act of 1972, for example, required every municipal and industrial source to install the best available technology; more recently, attention has shifted to the use of models to determine what is needed to ensure clean water. Critics of the national ambient air quality standards argue that they are too complicated and difficult to enforce, but unlike the technological controls approach, the air quality standards approach focuses, important-ly, on air quality and the health risks involved. The 1990 amendments maintain the national ambient air quality standards of the Clean Air Act of 1970 but also impose a wide variety of technological controls on pollution sources. Congress rejected its earlier approach to the regulation of haz-ardous air pollutants in favor of a two-tiered approach. The first round of controls imposed by the EPA are technology-based, much like those Congress has used in regulating other forms of pollution. A second round, of health-based national ambient air quality standards, will be issued by the agency if technological controls do not reduce to minimum levels the risks posed by exposure to these chemicals.

The 1970 law was widely viewed as being very stringent but underim-plemented. The addition of any provisions that weakened the requirement of meeting the absolute standard of protecting public health "with an ample margin of safety" was criticized by environmentalists as a retreat from the law. In the 1990 amendments, however, such provisions were coupled with the imposition of technological controls that were more like-ly to be enforced than the old standards and thus more likely to result in significant reductions in air toxics emissions. So the retreat was, in reality, a step forward. But environmentalists were reluctant to lose the require-ment for a commitment to the protection of public health, even though they agreed it had not always been adhered to. They saw clear indications that industry could do more than had been required of it. Because some companies were already committed to zero emissions, there was, in that respect, no need to weaken the law.

Reductions in emissions from chemical plants (the source of nearly one-half of all air toxics), for example, had begun to take place in 1984 after the chemical spill in Bhopal, India. The enforcement of disclosure laws and the imposition of fines and new regulations jolted corporate executives into realizing both that there were major economic gains to be made by reduc-ing emissions and, conversely, that pollution represented economic loss. Processes were made more efficient, waste was reduced, and uses were found for by-products. A Dow Chemical plant in Louisiana spent $15 mil-lion on waste reduction and saved $18 million within a year. A DuPont plant in Texas realized a savings of $1 million a year simply by using less of one raw material. The chairman and chief executive officer of Monsanto predicted that his company's "initiative and commitments to environmen-tal protection will, over the long term, make us more efficient, more cost effective and more competitive." [44]

Environmental regulations ultimately push companies to do what is in their own economic interest. It is no small irony that the regulations resist-ed by industry for years have led to reduced costs and may increase com-petitiveness. If regulators had been more aggressive in the past, American industry might today be more efficient and competitive. Congress might have done more in the 1990 amendments to encourage prevention of pollution than simply impose technological controls, but it has been timid in this area. Pollution fees, for example, create an immediate incentive to reduce emissions as a way to save costs. Taxing the use of virgin materials encourages recycling. Nevertheless, the costs of technological controls can create incentives to change processes.

Title III represents a significant increase in regulatory authority over the sources of air toxics. The Bush administration's bill had required regulation of only 50 percent of the source categories (smaller sources such as chemical process vents, storage tanks, and fugitive emissions) and gave the EPA discretion to regulate the remainder. But because members of Congress were hesitant to give the EPA any discretion in regulating air toxics, given the experience of the past two decades, they included in the law a list of 189 pollutants to be regulated.

The technological standards are detailed and complicated. Emission standards for sources of hazardous air pollutants require the "maximum degree of reduction . . . achievable for new or existing sources in the category or subcategory," taking into account the "cost of achieving such emission reduction" and "energy requirements." Regulations may require process changes or material substitutions, changes in design of equipment or work practices, or other measures.[45] The EPA is to consider a number of factors in establishing a compliance schedule and setting priorities for issuance of the standards: the "known or anticipated adverse effect on human health and the environment," the "quantity and location of emissions," and the "efficiency of grouping the categories by the pollutants emitted or by the processes or technologies used."[46] Congress also required the EPA to submit within six years of the amendments' enactment a report on the residual risks to public health from exposure to hazardous air pollutants—that is, the risks that remain after technological controls are installed. The study is to assess methods of calculating residual risks, the significance of the risks and of the adverse health effects likely for people living in the vicinity of the sources, and the availability and cost of additional technological controls. The EPA is also to commission a study by the National Academy of Sciences on risk assessment methodologies and is to establish a Risk Assessment and Management Commission to provide recommendations to the EPA and other federal agencies for assessing and managing risks from exposure to carcinogens and other chronic human health threats.[47] If Congress takes no action to instruct the EPA on how to assess and reduce residual risks, the agency is to promulgate, within eight years of issuing the technology-based standards for each category and subcategory of sources, health-based standards for all hazardous air pollutants to "provide an ample margin of safety to protect public health" or "to prevent, taking into consideration costs, energy, safety, and other relevant factors, an adverse environmental effect." The agency must also impose standards for sources emitting a "known, probable or possible human carcinogen" where technological controls have not reduced the "lifetime excess cancer risks to the individual most exposed to emissions from a source in the category or subcategory to less than one in one million."[48]

The voluntary reductions program included in Title III is an innovative attempt to speed up reduction of air toxics. Like other titles of the amendments, the air toxics title outlines an extended schedule for compliance. The early reduction program permits companies that agree to reduce emissions by 90 percent to obtain a six-year extension before a maximum achievable control technology (MACT) standard is applied to them. To qualify for such a waiver, companies had to make an enforceable commitment by January 1994 and achieve the reduction before the standard was proposed. Companies thus have a real incentive to inflate their emission levels in order to reduce the amount of cleanup necessary. Nevertheless, this program promises to result in immediate, significant reductions in air toxics emissions over the next few years. Even if the MACT standard were to require an emissions reduction of more than 90 percent, the early reduction program might achieve as much as four times more emissions reduction than would occur if companies waited until the MACT standards were issued before reducing their emissions.[49] Some data are available from the *Toxics Release Inventory,* and the voluntary reductions program will probably yield more detailed data, but the making of comparisons is presently difficult. The more numerous the categories, the less likely that the standards issued will be based on the best plants. The EPA may look at the emissions reduction record of plants in other countries, but there are apparently political pressures not to do so. Industry groups complain that regulations will make them less competitive with industries in other countries, but they do not want to be compared with them because foreign industries might be found to be cleaner.

Given the past problems with the attempt to develop a risk-based standard for regulating air toxics emissions, the technology-based approach may be the most effective way to gain control of air toxics. But the law presents the EPA with a tremendous challenge in preparing the technology-based standards, and Congress will likely have to review these provisions within a few years. As the EPA has begun to implement the Clean Air Act Amendments of 1990 and to establish the Risk Assessment and Management Commission, the debate over risk assessment has intensified. Skeptics charge that risk assessment is a "sham science" that can be used to justify any conclusion, usually "to justify pollution," and that it causes us to ignore potentially serious or even catastrophic problems because we lack sufficient data. Proponents argue that risk assessment is essential if we are to know "when a regulatory expenditure is not a good investment, and decide whether we want to spend money elsewhere to save a lot of lives." [50] Congressional proponents of more risk assessment and more participation by regulated industries in the process proposed legislation in 1994 to restructure EPA rule making. Both the House and Senate were expected to pass bills in early 1995, but the Clinton administration's opposition to provisions that made it more difficult for the EPA to regulate hazards made passage uncertain.

The Bottom Line: Permits and Enforcement

As is true for other environmental laws, whether and to what extent the Clean Air Act achieves its goals will be determined in large part by the effectiveness with which the EPA and the states implement and enforce it. Pollution sources may not comply with regulations if they are not given effective incentives to do so. As indicated earlier in this chapter, the state implementation plans to achieve national ambient air quality standards failed to work in many states. Some critics blamed the states' slowness in developing and approving the plans and pointed to the confusion over what exactly was required of specific sources of pollution. Others argued that the implementation process was too inefficient (since sources were not permitted to choose the most efficient way to reduce emissions), was too rigid and complicated, and failed to encourage improvements as new knowledge and new technologies became available.[51]

These criticisms led to a package of innovative reforms, introduced in the Bush administration's clean air bill and ultimately adopted by Congress, whose core proposal was the requirement that every major stationary source of pollution regulated under any provision of the law (traditional pollutants, air toxics, power plants emitting pollutants that were precursors of acid rain) have an operating permit issued by the state in which it is located. Each permit was to specify all the regulations that applied to that source, including emission limits, monitoring requirements, and maintenance procedures. Permits were viewed by EPA officials and members of Congress as a way to facilitate the enforcement of air quality provisions by the EPA, states, and communities. Because all the requirements applicable to a stationary source are conveniently brought together in one document, permits can eliminate confusion and ambiguity over which requirements apply to what sources and can facilitate efforts to assess compliance.

A permit program could be a first step in the more aggressive use of market-like incentives to reduce emissions. The permit fees to be collected under Title V, however, are not high enough alone to provide an incentive to reduce pollution; they are aimed at generating resources for state agencies to monitor emissions and administer the permit program. As states gain experience with administering a comprehensive permit program, they can experiment with other uses of permits. Polluting companies, for example, could be required to purchase an emissions permit for each unit of each pollutant they are allowed to release. The size or number of permits could be reduced each year or less often, in order that incremental reductions could be made until the national ambient air quality standard was met. Similarly, if the program was found to be inadequate because of adverse meteorological conditions or other factors, the allowable emissions or the number of permits could be reduced until the national ambient air quality standard was met. Emissions that exceeded the limit set for each facility could be taxed at a much higher rate to discourage such violations. Companies would be given the flexibility to develop the most cost-effective changes. Revenues from permit fees could be used to finance enforcement efforts and research programs.

Permits are also important because they strengthen the powers of states as the primary enforcers of environmental laws and regulations. The federal government has only about one-fifth of the enforcement resources the states have. More aggressive federal enforcement is likely to occur when federal and state officials agree that federal enforcement is the most appropriate strategy or when states have not successfully enforced major provisions of the law. A permit-based system may have significant positive implications for enforcement because it clarifies the requirements imposed on every major source of emissions.[52] The fear of permit delays (because of bureaucratic red tape) will provide a strong incentive for industry representatives to support effective implementation of the law.

The permit and enforcement provisions of the House and Senate clean air bills were seen as highly technical and detailed and initially aroused little interest. Unlike the other major titles of the 1990 amendments, they were not discussed in the negotiations between the Senate and the administration in the majority leader's office in February and March of 1990. Permits were the subject of separate but unsuccessful negotiations between members of the Senate Environment and Public Works Committee, the administration, and other senators.

Industry lobbyists came to realize fairly late in the process the possibility that permits would result in more aggressive enforcement as well as, inevitably, costs and delays arising from compliance with a new regulatory procedure. They also resisted the new enforcement provisions, but since these changes really only made the Clean Air Act's sanctions as strict as those of other environmental laws, their opposition to them was muted.

By the time the bill reached the Senate floor, the permit requirement had aroused considerable industry opposition. The permit and enforcement title was the only one opposed by the National Association of Manufacturers, which estimated that 362,000 firms would require permits.[53] Industry groups warned that if permits were to place a limit on every source of emissions, permit writers would be crushed in a mountain of detail. Permits would be unwieldy and unworkable, and moreover, companies that frequently change their processes and mix of materials would constantly have to renegotiate their permit provisions unless permits were worded to provide for operational flexibility. Some feared that regulatory requirements such as reporting and monitoring would enable competitors to discover proprietary information such as the composition of products and processes. Others charged that the inevitable delay in state and EPA approval of permits would make new construction or modification of existing sources all but impossible. This was a critical issue because if the EPA rejected a permit for being incomplete or inconsistent with the law, the source could not legally operate. The amendment was the subject of three close Senate votes, and the motion to table, or kill, the amendment was defeated by one vote. After some maneuvering, the motion to pass the amendment was also defeated by one vote. A slightly modified version was again defeated by one vote before the bill was finally passed.[54] In the House, changes were made in the Energy and Commerce Committee and in negotiations between key members before the bill was introduced on the floor.

State and local regulatory officials were opposed to EPA review and veto of permits. Environmental groups favored EPA review but feared that industries would claim that compliance with the provisions of its permit would shield a source against charges of violating any Clean Air Act regulations or standards not included in that permit. The idea of a possible "permit shield" aroused a fair amount of controversy as the bill moved through Congress. According to the conference report,

Permit compliance also may be deemed compliance with other applicable provisions of the Clean Air Act if the permit has been issued in accordance with Title V and includes those provisions, or if the permitting authority includes in the permit a specific determination that such provisions are not applicable.[55]

The uncertainty about the meaning of compliance may be cleared up only through litigation, but it is an important issue that will affect the efficacy of the permit system in reducing emissions.

The 1990 amendments updated the Clean Air Act's enforcement provisions to make them consistent with those of other environmental statutes. Under the 1970 act, all enforcement proceedings took place only in federal district courts. Calculation of penalties was to be based on the economic benefit to the source of not complying with emission limitations, which was sometimes difficult to determine. Criminal violations were considered misdemeanors and were thus of little interest to Justice Department prosecutors, who focused on felony violations.

The most important change to regulatory enforcement effected by the 1990 amendments was to make most criminal violations felonies.[56] The EPA may now initiate a civil action in a federal district court against the owner or operator of a stationary source who "knowingly violates any requirement or prohibition" included in an applicable state implementation plan, permit, or any provision of the act to obtain a permanent or temporary injunction or to assess and recover a civil penalty of up to $25,000 per day for each violation. Criminal penalties include fines and imprisonment of up to five years. Any person who misrepresents, omits, alters, conceals, fails to file or maintain information required, or tampers with or fails to install monitoring equipment is subject to up to two years' imprisonment. Any person who knowingly fails to pay a required fee can be sentenced to up to one year in prison. The maximum prison term and fine double if the person charged has been convicted of the same violation in the past. The agency may also issue an administrative order and impose a civil penalty of up to $25,000 for each day of violation if it acts within one year of the violation.[57]

Additional penalties are aimed at the release of hazardous air pollutants regulated under the act. Any person who "negligently places another person in imminent danger of death or serious bodily injury" by releasing hazardous air pollutants is subject to a fine and imprisonment of not more than one year; the maximum penalties are doubled after the first conviction. Any person who "places another person in imminent danger of death or serious bodily injury" by knowingly releasing a hazardous air pollutant is subject to fines and imprisonment of up to fifteen years. Fines assessed against an organization cannot exceed $1 million. Maximum fines and imprisonment are doubled for subsequent convictions. Serious bodily injury is defined as involving a "substantial risk of death, unconsciousness, extreme physical pain, protracted and obvious disfigurement or protracted loss or impairment of the function of a bodily member, organ, or mental facility."[58] The act defines the "operator" or person legally liable for criminal penalties as anyone classified as "senior management personnel or a corporate officer" rather than the employees who actually operate the equipment.[59]

The EPA may award up to $10,000 to any person (excluding any employee of the federal, state, or local government performing in an official capacity) who "furnishes information or services which lead to a criminal conviction or a judicial or administrative civil penalty" for any violation of the act.[60] Under the Clean Air Acts of 1970 and 1977, the EPA could require any person who may have "information necessary for the purposes" of the enforcement provisions of the act to establish and maintain records, submit reports, install and use monitoring equipment and auditing procedures, sample emissions, and submit compliance certifications and other information that the agency might need. The agency could also subpoena witnesses and relevant documentation.

Suits under the 1990 Clean Air Act may be brought in U.S. district courts by any person against state or federal officials for failing to take an action required under the law, and against any source believed to be in violation of a provision of the act, a regulation, or a permit provision. A court may enforce any emission standard or order and direct the EPA to perform any duty and to impose appropriate civil penalties. These fines are to be deposited in a special fund in the U.S. Treasury to be used by the EPA to finance "compliance and enforcement activities." A court may award the "costs of litigation (including reasonable attorney and expert witness fees) to any party, whenever the court determines such award is appropriate." [61]

The citizen suit provisions are particularly important because, as mentioned earlier in this chapter, EPA and state compliance with virtually all of the requirements and deadlines specified in the law can be compelled by court order. In addition, citizens can bring lawsuits to enforce specific permit requirements applicable to individual sources. In the past it has been difficult to file suits against sources because their emission limits were difficult to ascertain and emission data were often not available. The permit system in the 1990 law solves both problems; one document includes all the control measures the source is required to implement, and sources must monitor and report their emissions and file reports on their compliance. All provisions of the permits are to be considered "emissions standards or limitations" and are thus subject to citizen suits. Citizens can also seek civil penalties, instead of merely an injunction as under the 1970 law, and although most fines are deposited in the U.S. Treasury, courts can allocate up to $100,000 of the fines to "mitigation projects which are consistent with the Act and enhance the public health or the environment." [62]

Clean Air and the Development of Environmental Policy

The Clean Air Act Amendments of 1990 include a tremendous array of regulatory requirements. They mandate specific provisions concerning areas that have failed to attain the national ambient air quality standards for ozone, carbon monoxide, and particulates; establish research programs to be conducted or funded by the EPA; require the EPA to monitor and attempt to improve air quality of areas near the U.S.-Mexican border; order the EPA to assess the need for new regulatory initiatives to protect visibility in national parks and other areas with relatively unpolluted air; and authorize the EPA to begin collecting data on carbon dioxide emissions that contribute to the threat of global warming.[63] The 1990 law extends to a number of small sources of pollution that have never been regulated, since regulating only the largest sources is clearly insufficient to achieve compliance with national ambient air quality standards. Gas stations, dry cleaners, and consumer solvents are a significant source of ozone and air toxics emissions and will be regulated in the most polluted regions.

One potentially significant provision in the 1990 amendments is Title XI, which establishes the workers' compensation program. It brought together labor and environmental interests that have sometimes been at odds over the consequences of environmental regulation, such as job loss. Although the program may be an expensive way to achieve compromise with regard to environmental laws, it may prove to be politically powerful and may serve as a model for future environmental laws.

The expectations regarding the potential of this remarkably ambitious and far-reaching law may be unrealistically high. If regulatory history is any guide, the EPA and the states will implement it only in part. The sheer complexity of the amendments raises questions about the capability of Congress to legislate in such technical detail, but the history of limited implementation seems to provide little choice but prescriptiveness. The 1990 act clearly is an impressive accomplishment after years of deadlock, but in many ways it is only a partial, modest effort. It pushes deadlines back decades from their original dates. It falls woefully short in forcing companies to internalize their costs of production. It largely encourages the spread of existing technologies rather than the development of new ones. It fails to develop innovative solutions to the enduring problem of how much discretion should be given to states and federal agencies.

The ultimate test, however, is whether the law will lead to effective implementation, compliance, and achievement of environmental goals. Chapter 5 examines the experience of the EPA and the states in implementing the Clean Air Act Amendments of 1990 during their first four years.

Notes

1. Comments by William Becker at the Conference on Clean Air Act Implementation, sponsored by *Inside EPA* and by Morgan, Lewis & Bockius, Washington, D.C., March 26, 1991.
2. Statement of Sen. Max Baucus, *Congressional Record*, October 26, 1990, S17233.
3. Henry A. Waxman, "An Overview of the Clean Air Act Amendments of 1990," *Environmental Law* 21 (1991): 1742.
4. See, for example, James S. Cannon, *The Health Care Costs of Air Pollution: A Survey of Studies Published 1978-1983* (Washington, D.C.: American Lung Association, 1985); and U.S. Congress, House, Committee on Energy and Commerce, *Clean Air Act Amendments of 1990*, H. Rpt. 101-490, Part 1, 101st Cong., 2d sess., 1990.
5. U.S. Congress, House, *Clean Air Act Amendments of 1990*, conference on S. 1630, H. Rpt. 101-952, 101st Cong., 2d sess., 1990, 335. See also U.S. Congress, House, Committee on Energy and Commerce, Subcommittee on Energy and Power, *Clean Air Act Reauthorization (Part 1)*, Serial No. 101-111, 101st Cong.,

1st sess., 1990; U.S. Congress, House, Committee on Energy and Commerce, Subcommittee on Energy and Power, *Clean Air Act Reauthorization (Part 2)*, Serial No. 101-114, 101st Cong., 1st sess., 1990; U.S. Congress, House, Committee on Energy and Commerce, Subcommittee on Energy and Power, *Clean Air Act Reauthorization (Part 3)*, Serial No. 101-120, 101st Cong., 1st sess., 1989; U.S. Congress, House, Committee on Energy and Commerce, Subcommittee on Health and the Environment, *Air Quality Standards in Southern California*, Serial No. 100-5, 100th Cong., 1st sess., 1987; U.S. Congress, House, Committee on Energy and Commerce, Subcommittee on Health and the Environment, *Clean Air Act Amendments (Part 1)*, Serial No. 100-129, 100th Cong., 1st sess., 1987; U.S. Congress, House, Committee on Energy and Commerce, Subcommittee on Health and the Environment, *Clean Air Act Amendments (Part 2)*, Serial No. 100-130, 100th Cong., 1st sess., 1987; U.S. Congress, House, Committee on Energy and Commerce, Subcommittee on Health and the Environment, *Clean Air Act Amendments (Part 3)*, Serial No. 101-116, 101st Cong., 1st sess., 1989; U.S. Congress, House, Committee on Energy and Commerce, Subcommittee on Health and the Environment, *Clean Air Act Amendments (Part 1)*, Serial No. 101-100, 101st Cong., 1st sess., 1989; U.S. Congress, House, Committee on Energy and Commerce, Subcommittee on Health and the Environment, *Clean Air Act Amendments (Part 2)*, Serial No. 101-101, 101st Cong., 1st sess., 1989; U.S. Congress, House, Committee on Energy and Commerce, Subcommittee on Health and the Environment, *Clean Air Standards*, Serial No. 100-6, 100th Cong., 1st sess., 1987; U.S. Congress, House, Committee on Energy and Commerce, Subcommittee on Health and the Environment, *Environmental Issues*, Serial No. 99-28, 99th Cong., 1st sess., 1985; U.S. Congress, House, Committee on Energy and Commerce, Subcommittee on Oversight and Investigations, *Air Quality Standards*, Serial No. 98-189, 98th Cong., 2d sess., 1984; U.S. Congress, House, Committee on Energy and Commerce, Subcommittee on Oversight and Investigations, *EPA: Ozone and the Clean Air Act*, Serial No. 100-25, 100th Cong., 1st sess., 1987; U.S. Congress, Senate, Committee on Environment and Public Works, *Clean Air Act Amendments of 1989*, S. Rpt. 101-228, 101st Cong., 1st sess., 1989; U.S. Congress, Senate, Committee on Environment and Public Works, *The New Clean Air Act*, S. Hrg. 99-910, 99th Cong., 2d sess., 1986; U.S. Congress, Senate, Committee on Environment and Public Works, Subcommittee on Environmental Protection, *Clean Air Act Amendments of 1987 (Parts 1-3)*, S. Hrg. 100-187, 100th Cong., 1st sess., 1987; U.S. Congress, Senate, Committee on Environment and Public Works, Subcommittee on Environmental Protection, *Clean Air Act Amendments of 1989 (Parts 1-6)*, S. Hrg. 101-331, 101st Cong., 1st sess., 1989; U.S. Congress, Senate, Committee on Environment and Public Works, Subcommittee on Environmental Protection, *Health Effects of Air Pollution*, S. Hrg. 101-79, 101st Cong., 1st sess., 1989; U.S. Congress, Senate, Committee on Environment and Public Works, Subcommittee on Environmental Protection, *Ozone and Carbon Monoxide Standards: Nonattainment Issues*, S. Hrg. 100-54, 100th Cong., 1st sess., 1987.
6. Waxman, "An Overview," 1744.
7. For a fuller discussion, see Waxman, "An Overview," 1742-1754.
8. See William R. Lowry, *The Dimensions of Federalism: State Governments and Pollution Control Policies* (Durham, N.C.: Duke University Press, 1992), 121-128.

9. Evan J. Ringquist, *Environmental Protection at the State Level: Politics and Progress in Controlling Pollution* (Armonk, N.Y.: M. E. Sharpe, 1993), 61-80.

10. DeWitt John, *Civic Environmentalism: Alternatives to Regulation in States and Communities* (Washington, D.C.: CQ Press, 1994).

11. "Vermont to Ban Autos' Use of Ozone-Depleting Chemical," *New York Times,* May 10, 1989, B6.

12. Ibid.

13. Robert Reinhold, "Frustrated by Global Ozone Fight, California City Offers Own Plan," *New York Times,* July 19, 1989, A1.

14. "Ozone Depletion Penalty Set," *New York Times,* August 25, 1988, A21.

15. Comments by Jim Jenal, of Citizens for a Better Environment of Venice, California, at the Natural Resources Council of Maine/Natural Resources Defense Council clean air strategy session, Washington, D.C., May 30, 1991.

16. Nancy D. Adams, "Title VI of the 1990 Clean Air Act Amendments and State and Local Initiatives to Reverse the Stratospheric Ozone Crisis: An Analysis of Preemption," *Environmental Affairs* 19 (1991): 183-184, 187-190, 194, 203-205.

17. 42 U.S.C. sec. 7671m (1990 Supp.).

18. Presentation by Tom Cackette of the California Air Resources Board at the Conference on Clear Air Act Implementation, March 27, 1991.

19. Environmental Protection Agency (EPA), *National Air Pollutant Emission Estimates, 1940-1988* (Washington, D.C.: EPA, 1990), 56-62.

20. Comment by William Rosenberg at the Conference on Clean Air Act Implementation, March 26, 1991.

21. Thad Godish, *Air Quality* (Chelsea, Mich.: Lewis, 1991), 296-298.

22. Waxman, "An Overview," 1751-1752.

23. The following hearings held in Congress in the 1980s addressed acid rain: U.S. Congress, House, Committee on Energy and Commerce, Subcommittee on Energy and Power, *Acid Rain Oversight,* Serial No. 100-222, 100th Cong., 2d sess., 1988; U.S. Congress, House, Committee on Energy and Commerce, Subcommittee on Energy and Power, *Clean Coal Technologies,* Serial No. 100-70, 100th Cong., 1st sess., 1987; U.S. Congress, House, Committee on Energy and Commerce, Subcommittee on Energy Conservation and Power, *Acid Deposition Control Act,* Serial No. 99-153, 99th Cong., 2d sess., 1986; U.S. Congress, House, Committee on Energy and Commerce, Subcommittee on Fossil and Synthetic Fuels, *Clean Coal Technologies (Part 2),* Serial No. 99-111, 99th Cong., 2d sess., 1986; U.S. Congress, House, Committee on Energy and Commerce, Subcommittee on Fossil and Synthetic Fuels, *Future of Coal,* Serial No. 98-146, 98th Cong., 1st sess., 1983, and 98th Cong., 2d sess., 1984; U.S. Congress, House, Committee on Energy and Commerce, Subcommittee on Health and the Environment, *Acid Deposition Control Act of 1986 (Part 1),* Serial No. 99-85, 99th Cong., 2d sess., 1986; U.S. Congress, House, Committee on Energy and Commerce, Subcommittee on Health and the Environment, *Acid Deposition Control Act of 1986 (Part 2),* Serial No. 99-86, 99th Cong., 2d sess., 1986; U.S. Congress, House, Committee on Energy and Commerce, Subcommittee on Health and the Environment, *Acid Deposition Control Act of 1986 (Part 3),* Serial No. 99-87, 99th Cong., 2d sess., 1986; U.S. Congress, House, Committee on Energy and Commerce, Subcommittee on Health and the Environment, *Acid Deposition Control Act of 1987,* Serial No. 100-96, 100th

Cong., 1st sess., 1987; U.S. Congress, House, Committee on Energy and Commerce, Subcommittee on Health and the Environment, *Acid Rain Control Proposals*, Serial No. 101-25, 101st Cong., 1st sess., 1989; U.S. Congress, House, Committee on Energy and Commerce, Subcommittee on Health and the Environment, *Acid Rain in the West*, Serial No. 99-49, 99th Cong., 1st sess., 1985.

24. The EPA is also required to establish limits for emission of nitrogen oxides from utility boilers and to issue revised New Source Performance Standards for fossil-fuel-fired steam-generating facilities. Standards are to require the "best system of continuous emission reduction, taking into account available technology, costs and energy and environmental impacts." The EPA is to report to Congress by 1994 on the economic and environmental consequences of permitting the trading of SO_2 and NO_2 allowances. Clean Air Act Amendments of 1990, Publ. L. No. 101-549, 104 Stat. 2399 (November 15, 1990), secs. 406, 403(c).

25. Ibid., sec. 404.

26. Ibid., sec. 405.

27. Waxman, "An Overview," 1750. Interestingly, there are sufficient opportunities for trading, including commodities exchanges such as the Chicago Board of Trade's markets for sulfur dioxide, nitrogen oxides, and volatile organic compounds. Jeffrey Taylor, "New Rules Harness Power of Free Markets to Curb Air Pollution," *Wall Street Journal*, April 14, 1992, A1.

28. One of the most ambitious recommendations, from the Intergovernmental Panel on Climate Change's working group on the science of climate change, was for an immediate reduction in current levels of "long-lasting" greenhouse gases of 60 percent and a reduction of 15 percent to 20 percent in emissions of methane. The 1990 Interparliamentary Conference on the Global Environment, attended by parliamentarians from thirty-five countries, called on all nations to commit themselves to a 50 percent reduction in greenhouse gases from 1990 levels by the year 2010. The 1988 Toronto Conference on the Changing Atmosphere proposed a 20 percent reduction in world CO_2 emissions from current levels by the year 2005; other groups have recommended similar goals. Natural Resources Defense Council, *Slowing Global Warming* (Washington, D.C.: NRDC, 1989).

29. Richard W. Stevenson, "Trying a Market Approach to Smog," *New York Times*, March 25, 1992, C1.

30. Canadian Environmental Law Research Foundation (Toronto) and the Environmental Law Institute (Washington, D.C.), *The Regulation of Toxic and Oxidant Air Pollution in North America* (Toronto: Commerce Clearing House of Canada, 1986), 177-179.

31. Interview with Drew Lewis in *EPA Journal* 12 (June-July 1986): 4-7.

32. American Enterprise Institute, *The Clean Air Act: Proposals for Revision* (Washington, D.C.: AEI, 1981), 76-78.

33. For a history of this provision, see Bruce Ackerman and William T. Hassler, *Clean Coal/Dirty Air* (New Haven, Conn.: Yale University Press, 1981).

34. Nancy M. Davis, "Acid Rain: No Truce Is in Sight in the Eight-Year War between the States," *Governing* 2 (December 1988): 50.

35. Philip Shabecoff, "An Emergence of Political Will on Acid Rain," *New York Times*, February 19, 1989, D5.

36. Ibid.

37. Davis, "Acid Rain," 50.

38. Ibid., 54.

39. Philip Shabecoff, "Senators Announce Accord on Acid Rain Bill," *New York Times,* July 14, 1988, A30.

40. Quoted in Shannon J. Kilgore, "Muddling Through: Congressional Activity in 1988," *Environmental Law Reporter* (January 1989): 10018.

41. Quoted in Kilgore, "Muddling Through," 10018-10019, 10026.

42. See particularly Ackerman and Hassler, *Clean Coal/Dirty Air.*

43. Mike Mills, "Ratification of Ozone Pact Recommended," *Congressional Quarterly Weekly Report* 46 (February 20, 1988): 370.

44. Scott McMurray, "Chemical Firms Find That It Pays to Reduce Pollution at Source," *Wall Street Journal,* June 11, 1991, A1.

45. The maximum degree of emissions reduction is defined in different ways. For new sources, the reduction must not be less than the control achieved by the "best controlled similar source." For existing sources, if there are thirty or more sources in the same category or subcategory, the standard is the average level of control achieved by the best 12 percent. If there are fewer than thirty sources, the standard is the average level of control attained by the best five sources. Sources that met the lowest achievable emissions rate thirty months before the standard was issued are not included in the calculation of these averages.

    Source categories can be deleted if the EPA determines that, for carcinogens, no source in the category emits pollutants that result in a lifetime risk of cancer greater than one in a million to the most exposed individual in the population. For other air toxics, no source can threaten public health with an "ample margin of safety" or cause any adverse environmental effect. Clean Air Act Amendments, sec. 301(d).

46. Ibid., sec. 301.

47. Ibid., amending sec. 112(f) of Clean Air Act of 1970, Pub. L. No. 91-604, 84 Stat. 1676-1713 (December 31, 1970).

48. Ibid. Health-based standards go into effect and must be complied with as soon as they are issued, except for existing sources, which must comply within ninety days of the effective date. Existing sources may also apply for a waiver of up to two years if necessary to install controls if they agree to take whatever steps are necessary to protect the public from "imminent endangerment." These standards do not revoke or alter the national emission standards for hazardous air pollutants already issued by the EPA.

49. Comment by David Doninger, senior attorney for the Natural Resources Defense Council, at the clean air strategy session, May 30, 1991.

50. Graeme Browning, "Taking Some Risks," *National Journal* 23 (June 1, 1991): 1279-1282.

51. William F. Pedersen Jr., "Why the Clean Air Act Works Badly," *University of Pennsylvania Law Review* 129 (1981): 1059-1109.

52. Comments by Michael Alushin, EPA associate enforcement counsel for air, at the Conference on Clean Air Act Implementation, March 26, 1991.

53. Comments by Alan Eckert of the National Association of Manufacturers at the Conference on Clean Air Act Implementation, March 26, 1991.

54. U.S. Congress, Senate, *Congressional Record,* daily ed., 101st Cong., 2d sess.,

March 26, 1990, S3162-3163; March 27, 1990, S3132-3141; April 3, 1990, S3796.

55. U.S. Congress, House, *Clean Air Act Amendments of 1990*, 345.

56. Comments by Michael Alushin at the Conference on Clean Air Act Implementation, March 26, 1991.

57. Clean Air Act Amendments of 1990, sec. 701, amending secs. 113(c) and (d) of Clean Air Act of 1970.

58. Ibid., sec. 701, amending sec. 113(c) (4) and (5).

59. Ibid., sec. 701, amending sec. 113(h). Responsible officers are not to include an "engineer or technician responsible for the operation, maintenance, repair, or monitoring of equipment and facilities," or any employee "who is carrying out his normal activities" or "acting under orders from the employer," and who is not classified as "senior management personnel or a corporate officer," except in the cases of "knowing and willful violations."

60. Ibid., sec. 701, amending sec. 113(e).

61. Ibid., sec. 707(f), amending sec. 304(a). Whenever an action is brought under this provision, a copy of the complaint must be given to the EPA and the U.S. attorney general. No consent agreement can be entered into unless the EPA and the attorney general have received a copy of the proposal; they may also submit comments on the proposed agreement to the court. The EPA may intervene at any time in any citizen suit. The court may also compel agency action that has been "unreasonably delayed."

62. Clean Air Act of 1970, sec. 304(g)(2). For more on this subject, see Waxman, "An Overview," 1806-1810.

63. See, generally, Titles VIII and IX of the Clean Air Act Amendments of 1990 for these provisions.

5 Implementing the Clean Air Act Amendments

Implementation is at the heart of the policy-making process. The carrying out of public policies—the ability to achieve the results promised when policies are formulated in legislation, the capability of administrative agencies to forge the required links in a causal chain that will accomplish policy goals—is an essential part of achieving public goals.[1] How well have the EPA and the states implemented the Clean Air Act Amendments of 1990 during the first four years of their life? Although four years is an insufficient length of time upon which to fully assess the act since implementation will take place throughout the rest of the 1990s and some provisions do not take effect until the first decade of the twenty-first century, it is possible to make some judgments about what has been achieved and to offer speculation about the extent to which clean air goals will eventually be achieved in the United States.

Three questions, pursued further in Chapter 6, underlie the discussion in this chapter: (1) How well have the Clean Air Act Amendments of 1990 been implemented? (2) What does the experience of the Clean Air Act illustrate about the challenges of implementing environmental and other policies? and (3) How does the experience of this implementation illuminate the policy process and, in particular, how well did Congress and the White House formulate the 1990 law? This chapter includes a brief discussion of some of the challenges in implementing public policies, an overview of the implementation of the Clean Air Act, and an assessment of some of the key provisions of the law that illustrate in more detail the challenges of implementation. This review indicates that a great deal of implementation activity has occurred, particularly in light of only modest implementation of previous clean air laws. As a result of these efforts, much of the federal regulatory framework is in place. Whether it is well positioned to achieve the air quality goals of the Clean Air Act, however, is another question.

Implementing Public Policies

The interaction of policy formulation and implementation is central to the policy-making process. Implementation is a dynamic, ongoing enterprise. "Implementation is evolution," wrote two students of the process.

"[I]t will inevitably reformulate as well as carry out policy."[2] The problems of improving environmental quality and protecting natural resources, and other problems that are the subject of implementation, are rarely "solved": implementation is an effort to manage them, to make some incremental progress in reducing their consequences, and to adjust policy efforts in light of experience.

Public policy implementation is highly dependent upon the other components of the political process. In the United States, implementation is usually a complicated process of interpreting congressional intent, merging statutory and presidential priorities, creating administrative structures and processes, revisiting the political debates from policy formulation as administrative regulations are devised, and building political support for implementing and enforcing regulatory requirements. This model of the policy process assumes a simple relationship between policy formulation and implementation that largely mirrors the separation of powers. Congress makes the policy choices and the executive branch and states implement them. In reality, the lines between making and implementing policies are heavily blurred, there is much overlap, and those who implement laws are constantly confronted with policy choices, but the widely held perception is that major policy decisions are the responsibility of elected representatives.

Jeffrey Pressman and Aaron Wildavsky emphasize the importance of including the imperatives of implementation at the beginning of the policy-making process:

Implementation must not be conceived as a process that takes place after, and independent of, the design of policy. Means and ends can be brought into somewhat closer correspondence only by making each partially dependent on the other.[3]

Implementation efforts are often at the mercy of changed circumstances and alterations in the problems at which they are aimed. Goals may be amended. Initial energy and commitment may lag. Failure to achieve policy goals may be a result of inadequate implementation or unrealistic objectives. There may be a mismatch between the goals decided on and the means provided to accomplish them. Solutions may appear to require simple steps, but coordinating policies is often daunting, and the complexity of joint action makes most policy efforts seem impossible. While the probability of individual steps being taken may be rather high, the cumulative odds of every required action occurring can become astronomical.[4] Because of these persistent obstacles, policies are constantly being revised as implementation occurs.

The dynamic nature of implementation is well illustrated in the efforts to realize the goals of the Clean Air Act. This chapter discusses implementation between 1991 and 1994, a time period in which the Clean Air Act largely worked the way it was designed to. The Environmental Protection Agency (EPA) issued many of the regulations and guidelines required, and, even though it did not meet all the deadlines outlined in the statute, it produced an impressive number of rules, particularly in light of its history. The major shortcomings were in the preparation and implementation of state implementation plans (SIPs) and in EPA issuance of standards for air toxic emissions.

The events that led to the 1994 election of Republican majorities in state-houses and in both houses of Congress, and the initial actions taken by the new congressional leaders and governors may, however, fundamentally alter the future implementation of the act. These initial developments, and the prospects for clean air regulation, are discussed in Chapter 6.

Implementing the Clean Air Act Amendments: An Overview

The implementation of the Clean Air Act Amendments of 1990, from their passage to their four-year anniversary on November 15, 1994, has centered on a half-dozen major tasks:

- Development and enforcement of state implementation plans aimed at producing compliance with the national ambient air quality standards;
- Creation of a new operating permits system for sources of criteria pollutants and air toxics, and more stringent penalties to ensure compliance with the act's provisions;
- Regulation of motor vehicles emissions through emissions standards and the use of alternative fuels;
- Regulation of air toxics by a first round of national standards for the myriad industries and processes involved (a second round of risk-based standards will come later in the act's implementation);
- Development of the first nationwide market for trading emissions for industries that are responsible for acid rain; and
- Regulation of CFCs as required by international agreements.

The disputes that made the passage of the 1990 amendments so contentious resurfaced during implementation, as is usually the case for such legislation. The two key challenges have been the EPA's ability to issue standards and guidelines, and the ability of states to devise effective plans to achieve those standards, but other issues have also been difficult to address.

Attaining Air Quality Standards

Title I, aimed at bringing air quality regions into compliance with the national standard, is the most complicated part of the law. The EPA's primary tasks under this title are to provide guidelines for state implementation plans and to oversee state efforts to put those plans in operation. The first four years under the 1990 Clean Air Act saw EPA promulgation of a great number of regulations and guidances for states as they prepared SIPs to comply with the national ambient air quality standards. The EPA had completed the following tasks by November 1994 as part of the requirements of Title I:

- Made a number of administrative changes in the overall framework for state air pollution regulation—revised designations of air quality regions and attainment status; created additional PM_{10}, SO_2, and lead nonattainment areas; reclassified some PM_{10} areas; and established some new nonattainment boundaries for the major pollutants and new nonattainment areas;
- Created the Northeast Ozone Transport Commission to facilitate state cooperation in meeting air quality goals;
- Created the Grand Canyon Visibility Transport Commission to devise solutions to haze in Grand Canyon National Park;
- Published guidelines for states to use in preparing emission inventories for carbon monoxide and volatile organic compounds (VOCs); estimating the cost-effectiveness of controls; developing transportation control measures; placing new controls on nitrogen oxide, PM_{10}, and VOCs from bakeries and pesticide applications; monitoring ozone, NO_x, and VOCs; ensuring conformity of federally funded projects with air quality plans; and establishing economic incentives programs;
- Established general requirements for maximum achievable control technologies and for hazardous organic chemical manufacturing, as well as for case-by-case control technology determinations;
- Issued rules governing the application of sanctions to be imposed on states for failing to submit implementation plans;
- Published regulations governing emissions from sources operating on the outer continental shelf; and
- Began reviewing SIPs submitted by states.[5]

Much of the EPA's regulatory framework is now in place, although many of the standards and guidelines were issued after their statutory deadlines and the challenge has shifted to compelling states to complete their SIPs. Most states have missed most of the deadlines for submitting and implementing plans. For example, the 1990 amendments required states containing moderate PM_{10} areas to submit plans by November 15, 1991; control strategies were to be in place by December 1993 and the air quality standard was to be achieved by December 1994 (unless the state could show that this was "impracticable").[6] There are seventy PM_{10} nonattainment areas. Of the twenty-three states required to submit PM_{10} SIP revisions by November 1991, eleven failed to do so.[7] By July 1994, only thirty SIPs had

Table 5-1   Status of Ozone State Implementation Plans, November 1994

Programs in place	Some progress	Little or no progress
Alabama	Arizona	Delaware
Florida	California	Indiana
Kansas	Connecticut	Maine
Nevada	District of Columbia	Michigan
North Carolina	Georgia	Missouri
Oregon	Illinois	New Jersey
South Carolina	Kentucky	Pennsylvania
Washington	Louisiana	Utah
	Maryland	Vermont
	Massachusetts	Virginia
	New Hampshire	
	New York	
	Ohio	
	Rhode Island	
	Tennessee	
	Texas	
	West Virginia	
	Wisconsin	

Source: Clean Air Network, "Air Remains Dirty in Many States: Progress in Others; Promise of Clean Air Is in Danger" (Washington, D.C.: CAN, 1994).

been approved; the rest were in various stages of review and some had deficiencies that remained to be corrected.[8] Only a few PM_{10} SIPs were in place by November 1994; implementation of the cleanup plans was just beginning as the deadline for achieving the air quality standard arrived.

The obstacles to putting plans in place to achieve the national air quality standard for ozone have been just as daunting. Nine of thirty-five states missed the May 1991 deadline for submission of revised ozone SIPs. All areas with moderate or worse air quality were required to submit SIPs by November 1994 that included measures to reduce VOC emissions by 15 percent between 1990 and 1996. The deadline for achieving the standard ranges from 1996 for the thirty-two moderate areas to 1999 for the thirteen serious areas, 2005-2007 for the nine severe areas, and 2010 for the one extreme area, Los Angeles. By the November 1994 deadline for submitting plans, eight states had cleanup plans for ozone in place, seventeen states and the District of Columbia had initial programs in place but had failed to submit final plans that demonstrated eventual compliance, and ten states had failed to submit plans. Many of these ten states also have serious air pollution problems. The status of ozone state implementation plans as of November 1994 is demonstrated in Table 5-1. Fifteen states already meet the ozone standard: Alaska,

Arkansas, Colorado, Hawaii, Idaho, Iowa, Minnesota, Mississippi, Montana, Nebraska, New Mexico, North Dakota, Oklahoma, South Dakota, and Wyoming.[9] A 1993 General Accounting Report concluded:

Despite efforts by EPA and the Congress to address long-standing problems, delays continue in the States' submission and the EPA's review and approval of SIPs. Some States have submitted their SIPs after the deadlines established by the 1990 amendments, while other States have not yet submitted their SIPs. Also, EPA is taking longer to review and approve SIPs than the 1990 amendments allow. In some cases, SIPs have remained in the system for months without management intervention to identify and address the causes for the delays."[10]

While some plans will be submitted soon after the 1994 deadline, this part of the Clean Air Act has not worked particularly well. States have been unwilling to take steps to reduce automobile use, and some industries have resisted state efforts to devise effective cleanup plans. The EPA has been unwilling to hold states to the strict deadlines in the Clean Air Act and has rarely imposed sanctions when states have missed deadlines—perhaps at least in part because it has missed so many deadlines itself. Mandatory sanctions for failing to submit ozone SIPs, according to the Clean Air Act Amendments, should have been imposed beginning in April 1993, but the agency did not issue its rule governing the application of sanctions for failing to submit or implement SIPs until August 1994, and it refused to impose sanctions until the rule was in place. The rule provides that after the EPA finds that a state has failed to submit or implement all or part of a SIP, the state has eighteen months to require new or modified sources to gain reductions of two units for every one unit of pollution they release (a 2:1 offset); six months later, if no corrective action has been taken, federal funds for highway construction in the state are withheld.[11]

Establishing a New Permit Program and Enhancing Enforcement

The creation of a comprehensive permitting system for major stationary sources of pollutants in the Clean Air Act Amendments of 1990 was a critical step in improving enforcement of the act's provisions. The permits program is administered by state officials; the primary task of the EPA in implementing this provision has been to issue several regulations for state permitting programs. In 1992, the EPA published guidelines on state programs to assist small business and on the overall regulations for state permit programs. After states submit their permit programs to the EPA for approval, the agency must respond within one year. States are free to make their programs more stringent than required by the federal regulations. Some 34,000 major sources are required to obtain permits: 75 percent are from the manufacturing sector, 7 percent are utilities, 7 percent are mining sources, 6 percent are from the service sector, and 5 percent are from trade. An additional 350,000 sources are potentially subject to controls: 55 percent of those are gasoline stations, 33 percent are sources releasing solvent cleaners, and the balance are other sources.[12] The EPA also issued in 1992 rules of practice for administrative penalties that permitted EPA officials to carry out the new enforcement provisions of the act. During the first year of the administrative compliance program (FY 1992), the EPA issued 100 administrative complaints, referred 474 judicial and criminal-cases to the Department of Justice, and imposed fines in two cases of more than $1 million each.[13]

The permitting system got off to a very rocky start, and it is not clear how successful the program will be. A brief review of the problems the EPA encountered in formulating the permitting rule illustrates some of the challenges of implementation caused by regulated industries using the administrative process to try to win what they lost during the legislative battle.

On March 31, 1989, President George Bush established the Council on Competitiveness as part of the regulatory review process created in the administration of President Ronald Reagan. The council was headed by the vice president and included the secretaries of the Treasury and Commerce, the attorney general, the director of the Office of Management and Budget, the chairman of the Council of Economic Advisers, and the chief of staff to the president. It oversaw the regulatory review process by the Office of Management and Budget, served as an appeals board for disputes between agencies over regulations, provided a forum where parties could air their concerns about regulations with which they were expected to comply, and identified areas where it believed major changes could be made to enhance competitiveness. The council's primary goals were (1) to reduce regulatory burdens on the economy; (2) to develop strategies to improve the human resources required for an effective work force; (3) to eliminate government-imposed burdens on scientific and technological progress that threaten the competitiveness of U.S. businesses; and (4) to facilitate the free flow of investment capital necessary for economic growth. It did not really become actively involved in reviewing agency regulations until 1991.[14]

Some of the problems with the regulatory review process became clear with the first rule, dealing with municipal incinerators, proposed by the EPA under the 1990 amendments. The agency included in its draft a requirement for 25 percent recycling and the separation of lead batteries before incineration, but those provisions were deleted by the Council on Competitiveness in December 1990—despite Bush's statement in a 1988 campaign speech that "some feel the EPA's national goal of a 25 percent reduction in waste is excessive. I'd like to see us exceed that goal in my first term." The contradiction was explained away by a council staff member who said that the administration favored "voluntary recycling and market-based recycling programs."[15]

A lobbyist for local government groups that had failed to convince Congress to delete the recycling provision from the 1990 amendments explained how the regulatory review process works. "We began to think we had done everything we could do," she remarked, "when we were heartened to find the regulation was stuck—as it were—in [the Office of Management and Budget]. So we began to concentrate our efforts in the White House and OMB." An industry lobbyist complained that people at the EPA were not inclined to "focus the issue on the merits." As a result, the issue was taken to the Council on Competitiveness, which "has the unfortunate, and I think unwarranted, appearance of trying to address politically what one can't address on the merits." [16]

The experience with the permit program is another example of the Bush administration's efforts to weaken provisions of the law. The EPA submitted draft regulations to the Office of Management and Budget, as required by the regulatory review process.[17] On March 22, 1991, Vice President Dan Quayle announced that the Council on Competitiveness would assume responsibility for the review of federal agency regulations, congressional testimony, policy statements, and even press releases.[18] On April 6, the council issued a memo that described more than 100 changes it was making in the EPA's proposed permit rule. The staff of the House Energy and Commerce Committee's Subcommittee on Health and the Environment analyzed the changes and concluded that none of them "would serve to strengthen the permit program. . . . In most instances these changes are in conflict with the statute, and are therefore illegal." The subcommittee's analysis focused on the advantages industry gained from the council's review process:

The Vice President has prevailed on EPA to propose regulations substantially weaker than those mandated by Congress. The [regulatory review] process is apparently now one where polluting industries, which failed in their efforts to weaken the [Clean Air] Act as it passed the Congress, are now succeeding in undermining the law through the Vice President's Council on Competitiveness.[19]

The rule changes made by the council were substantial. With regard to a provision entitled "minor permit allowances," for example, the council would allow a source operating under a permit that did not establish emission limits to unilaterally rewrite it, and even increase the level of allowed emissions. Requirements for monitoring and inspection, since they do not directly impose emission limits, could thus be changed at will, making it difficult to determine whether sources really are complying with their emission limits. These permit changes would simply be submitted to the state regulatory agency and would go into effect unless the agency rejected them within seven days. The council also deleted from the original EPA proposal a provision requiring public notice of permit revisions and restricting the amount of increased emissions. The 1990 amendments were clear in requiring public notice (including an opportunity for public comment), EPA review, and an opportunity for judicial review of all permit revisions.[20]

The council's revised regulation would not only circumvent the law but would weaken enforcement of the law. Any source that became the subject of a citizen suit or state enforcement action could simply file for a revised permit, and if the state regulatory agency failed to respond within seven days, the source would escape legal action. The 1990 amendments require all sources to include in their permit applications a compliance plan and a schedule, enforceable by the EPA, which can be the subject of a citizen suit while the permit application is pending. The council's revised regulation would require a schedule only from facilities that were shown to be in violation of the law at the time the permit was requested, and the schedule would be enforceable only after the permit was approved.[21]

The final permit regulation was required to be issued by November 1991, but the dispute dragged on until May 1992, when the president ordered the EPA to propose the version of the regulation favored by the Council on Competitiveness and the final rule was issued.[22] Rep. Henry Waxman (D-Calif.) then notified the EPA of his intention to sue the agency for missing the permit and other deadlines. His House Energy and Commerce Committee's Subcommittee on Health and the Environment held a hearing one year after passage of the Clean Air Act Amendments of 1990 and found that the EPA had missed most of the rule-making deadlines, that the Council on Competitiveness had undermined a number of key regulations, and that the White House had directed the EPA to propose regulatory provisions that had been specifically rejected by Congress during its consideration of the Clean Air Act Amendments.[23] The council was abolished in the first days of the Clinton administration, but the dispute over the permitting system continues in the federal courts.

Reducing Motor Vehicle Emissions

The EPA has taken a number of steps to require cleaner fuels, cleaner vehicles, and better maintenance of vehicles on the road. Between 1991 and 1994, it issued a flurry of rules to achieve these goals. The agency also completed studies of non-road engines, mobile source-related air toxics, and transportation systems.[24]

As described in Chapter 4, one of the most important innovations in the 1990 act was the alternative fuels mandate. Under the old Clean Air Act, reductions in motor vehicle emissions came from tailpipe emission standards. In October 1992, the EPA put in place a program expected to eventually reduce emmissions by 17 percent by requiring the sale of oxygenated gasoline in thirty-nine cities with carbon monoxide pollution. In the summer of 1994, as required by the 1990 amendments, the agency issued regulations for the use of reformulated gas in the nine largest metropolitan areas with the most severe summertime ozone problems.[25] These nine areas include New York City; the Los Angeles metropolitan area; San Diego, California; the Chicago, Illinois/Gary, Indiana, metropolitan area; the Milwaukee/Racine metropolitan area; Baltimore, Maryland; Hartford, Connecticut; Houston, Texas; and Philadelphia, Pennsylvania. Other ozone nonattainment areas in Connecticut, Delaware, Kentucky, Maine, Maryland, Massachusetts, New Hampshire, New Jersey, New York, Pennsylvania, Rhode Island, Texas, Virginia, and the District of Columbia may opt into the program.[26] The use of reformulated gas is expected to reduce VOC and toxic emissions by 15 percent by 1995 and 20 percent by the year 2000. In addition, ethanol-blended gasoline was given a partial exemption from the federal excise tax on gasoline under energy legislation. These innovations were championed as among the most cost-effective ways of reducing air pollution.[27]

A second effort to reduce vehicle emissions—mandates for the production of cleaner vehicles—has also been implemented. More stringent tailpipe standards for new cars and light trucks were tightened significantly for the first time since 1981; as a result, hydrocarbon emissions are expected to decrease by 30 percent and nitrogen oxide emissions by 60 percent from current levels. Carbon monoxide emissions are projected to decline 20 percent to 29 percent through new controls aimed at vehicles operating in cold climates, where engine starts release relatively high levels of emissions. Standards added for heavy trucks and diesel buses are expected to reduce particulate emissions by 95 percent from uncontrolled levels. Twenty-two cities with major ozone problems were required, beginning in 1998, to reduce emissions from centrally owned and operated fleets of new vehicles by using alternative or clean fuels such as compressed natural gas or electricity. Fleet operators and vehicle manufacturers that exceed the emission reduction goals can sell their credits to others. The California clean vehicle pilot project requires 150,000 clean-fueled vehicles to be sold per year beginning in 1996, and 300,000 per year by 1999.[28]

A third major implementation effort for vehicle emissions has focused on maintenance of existing vehicles. The 1990 law requires 181 areas to institute vehicle emissions inspection programs. Cities with serious ozone or carbon monoxide problems are required to have "enhanced" inspection and maintenance (I & M) programs that are more effective than the current I & M program in identifying emission problems. Since 20 percent of the vehicles on the road are believed to be responsible for 60 percent of emissions, the EPA expects the enhanced I & M programs to reduce VOC emissions by 28 percent, carbon monoxide by 31 percent, and nitrogen oxide by 9 percent, at a lower cost than other kinds of air pollution control measures.[29]

Enhanced programs require the creation of testing-services-only facilities so that inspection and repair services are separate. Testing involves visual inspection of vehicle evaporative systems, monitoring of emissions during a simulation of city driving, and measurement of the emissions flow through the evaporative system. The equipment costs about $150,000 per test lane and is designed for 1981 and newer vehicles; older vehicles will continue to be tested with the basic, idling-only I & M test. This proposal has been one of the more controversial because of the potential impact of the cost of new equipment on the auto inspection and repair industry, and because of the possible inconvenience and delay in getting vehicles inspected. California refused to implement the enhanced I & M program (called the IM240 test procedure), offering instead to develop an alternative approach. In 1993, EPA officials rejected the initiative as weaker than the IM240 approach and threatened to impose sanctions on the state, but the White House apparently pressured the agency to retreat from the sanction threat. As a result, other states facing public opposition to the new inspection program have also tried to withdraw from it. This has become a major implementation problem for the EPA because it has set a precedent of the EPA not imposing discretionary sanctions, one of the few tools it has to pressure states.[30]

The final effort to reduce air pollution from transportation sources has also met with political and public opposition because it is aimed at motor vehicles. The Clean Air Act requires that all federally funded transportation projects in nonattainment areas conform to relevant SIPs: no federal agency may "approve, accept or fund any transportation plan, program or project unless such plan, program or project has been found to conform to any applicable implementation plan in effect."[31] Stopping popular highway projects because they are inconsistent with air quality plans has been highly controversial and has contributed to growing criticism of the Clean Air Act. The 1991 Intermodal Surface Transportation Efficiency Act (ISTEA) provides funding for transportation projects that contribute to meeting SIP requirements, and air quality standards in general, in ozone and CO nonattainment areas. (The law does not apply to PM_{10} nonattainment areas, but an argument could be made for including those areas as well.) These Congestion Mitigation and Air Quality Improvement, or CMAQ funds are distributed to states according to their share of the population living in nonattainment areas and according to their levels of air pollution.[32]

Reformulated Gasoline and Presidential Politics

Efforts to devise a new standard for reformulated gas have been particularly interesting. The Clean Air Act provides specific requirements for the reformulated gasoline program and requires the EPA to establish a rule that results in "the greatest reduction in emissions of ozone-forming and toxic air pollutants achievable through the reformulation of conventional gasoline, taking into consideration the cost of achieving such emission reductions, any non air-quality and other air-quality related health and environmental impacts and energy requirements."[33]

As indicated in Chapter 4, two additives, ethanol and methanol, are available for gasoline.[34] Ethanol has several advantages: it is made from renewable sources, it is nontoxic, and it has a higher oxygen content than methanol. Unfortunately, more energy is required to produce ethanol than is found in the product itself because farmers use gas-guzzling tractors and other equipment to grow corn, coal-fired plants are used to produce ethanol, and the fermenting and distilling processes consume energy and produce pollution. Ethanol makes gasoline more likely to evaporate (although a modification of ethanol, ethyl tertiary butyl ether or ETBE, makes it less volatile) and it costs about twice as much as methanol.[35] In addition to being less expensive, methanol does not make gasoline more volatile and does not lead to evaporation, and it has a higher energy content than ethanol. But it is largely produced from nonrenewable resources, is toxic, and does not reduce carbon monoxide emissions as much as ethanol.

A 1994 Energy Department report concluded that ethanol might result in slightly more pollution than methanol and in higher costs to consumers. Both additives have a negligible impact on motor vehicle engine parts at this level of concentration. There is little agreement on the environmental costs and benefits of the two additives in reducing ozone pollution or on their effect on global climate change.[36] Oil companies favor methanol because it is cheaper and they can produce it themselves. Agricultural interests, including the Archer-Daniels-Midland Company, which controls about half of U.S. ethanol production, have been heavy hitters in the campaign to increase the use of ethanol. Once the 1990 law was passed, the tumultuous battle over reformulated gas, described in Chapter 3, shifted to the administrative process and the EPA's efforts to write a regulation that would implement the law.

Much as it did in the legislative process, personality has played a key role in the implementation of the Clean Air Act, as demonstrated by the evolution of the reformulated gas initiative. William Rosenberg, EPA assistant administrator for air and radiation between 1990 and 1992, had long been a proponent of alternative fuels and had worked with the White House during the legislative process to develop the Bush administration's proposal. He viewed regulatory negotiations as the most effective way to produce clean air rules because they streamline the rule-making process, allow industry and government to exchange technical information, facilitate bargaining and compromise, and create incentives for affected parties to buy into rules instead of litigating them.[37] Rather than following the traditional regulatory process, in which the agency prepares a draft regulation, releases it for public comment, gains the approval of the OMB and other executive branch officials, and is then usually sued by groups unhappy with the result, the EPA decided to bring in relevant parties to hammer out compromises and fashion rules that parties will embrace and agree not to challenge in court.

The regulatory negotiation for reformulated gas began in February 1991 with an announcement of EPA's intent to negotiate the rule. The Clean Fuels Advisory Committee, comprised of representatives from the oil and automobile industries, vehicle owners, state air pollution control officials, oxygenate suppliers, gasoline retailers, environmental organizations, and citizens' groups, was established in March. Environmentalists had been hesitant to join the negotiations because they feared the White House would intervene before the final rule was published and reshape it, as the Bush White House had done in the regulation creating the permitting system. Much of the early negotiation thus focused on fashioning procedural rules for the talks that would ensure White House acceptance of the resulting agreement. As is typically provided in regulatory negotiations, the involved parties agreed not to challenge the final rule in court if it had "the same substance and effect as the consensus proposal," and agreed to oppose any who defected from the deal.[38]

Of greatest concern to industry representatives were provisions for enforcement and monitoring, as they wanted to ensure that all parties would comply. They were also concerned about the cost of the new fuel, and sought a provision permitting them to be in compliance if fuels *on average* met the standard, thereby reducing the cost of the program by two cents a gallon, or $700 million a year. Environmentalists argued that every gallon of fuel should be required to meet the standard; otherwise, fewer total emissions would result. Deals were struck that gave industry more flexibility in return for more stringent standards. Nevertheless, disputes over whether reformulated gas would increase nitrogen oxide or VOC emissions caused some participants to conclude after three months that the effort was likely to fail. As the deadline for action approached, however, parties began to see the advantages of a negotiated agreement over the delay and expense of a traditional rule-making proceeding.[39]

By August 1991, the committee produced an "Agreement in Principle" that included two steps: (1) the EPA would use a "simple model" to certify that a gasoline meets applicable emission reduction standards, based on the fuel's oxygen, benzene, heavy metal, and aromatics content and Reid Vapor Pressure (RVP); and (2) a more "complex model" would eventually be developed to supplant the simple model for certifying compliance with these standards, and a second, more stringent set of standards would also be prepared. The agreement also prohibited dumping by oil companies of cheaper, dirtier fuel to areas not required to use reformulated gas in order to recoup some of their costs of producing the cleaner, more expensive fuel.[40]

The EPA published a "Notice of Proposed Rulemaking" while negotiations continued; the proposal required the sale of reformulated gasoline to reduce emissions of toxics and VOCs in certain nonattainment areas and outlined a plan to prohibit the sale of higher-polluting gasoline throughout the country.[41] In April 1992, the EPA issued a "Supplemental Notice of Proposed Rulemaking" that described the standards and enforcement scheme for reformulated and conventional gasoline and other specific proposals. The complex model for determining compliance with the standard would be used beginning in 1998, and phase II standards would take effect in 2000. Retail sale of reformulated gasoline was to begin on January 1, 1995.[42]

The ethanol industry argued that the proposal in effect excluded ethanol from the reformulated gasoline market. At Bush's direction, the EPA proposed an ethanol incentive program to promote the use of ethanol (and other renewable oxygenates) in reformulated gasoline while maintaining the environmental benefits of reformulated gas. The increase in volatility resulting from the use of ethanol, for example, would be balanced with volatility reductions in the rest of the reformulated gas. The program would not be required in the South unless a state requested inclusion.[43] Many comments were also submitted on other aspects of the proposal. The EPA continued to develop the complex model and announced revisions in a June 1993 public workshop, and documents were made public in October 1993. The final rule was issued in February 1994, to take effect on March 18, 1994.[44]

All parties endorsed the outcome of the negotiations. The rule promised to reduce emissions of VOCs by some 95 million pounds in the nine cities with the worst ozone problems at a lower cost than had been expected under the act. Industry officials applauded the flexibility, environmentalists liked the stringent standards and enforcement commitments, and state and local regulatory officials saw the rule as helping them achieve their ozone cleanup goals.[45] However, the deal began to unravel within a few months as the ethanol industry, worried about potential problems with fuel volatility and nitrogen oxide emissions, began lobbying Congress to pressure the EPA to ensure that the final rule would expand ethanol's market share. Other participants protested, but by the summer of 1992 President Bush intervened during a campaign swing through the farm belt to grant a volatility waiver for ethanol-based reformulated gas. In order to ensure achievement of the goal of reduced emissions, volatility standards were also increased for other kinds of reformulated gas.[46]

In 1993, the Clinton administration proposed to issue the original, negotiated version of the reformulated gas regulation as well as a new Renewable Oxygenate Program that would require that at least 30 percent of reformulated gas sold be from renewable resources, guaranteeing ethanol's market share.[47] (Like President Bush, candidate Clinton had campaigned in the Midwest on a platform promoting ethanol.) The EPA issued the final rule, "Standards for Reformulated and Conventional Gasoline," in February 1994, thus formally ending the regulatory negotiation begun three years earlier.[48]

The EPA announced in June 1994 that it was issuing a separate final rule for renewable oxygenates.[49] The rule was published on August 2, and was to take effect September 1, 1994.[50] The rule's language specified that at least 15 percent of reformulated gas in 1994 and 30 percent in 1996 must include a "renewable" oxygenate; EPA administrator Carol Browner acknowledged that these percentages, at least in the near future, "will probably be from ethanol." In an unprecedented step, President Clinton issued a written statement hailing the ethanol rule as a boost to corn farmers, who could expect an increase in demand for their product of 250 million bushels a year. Environmentalists charged that this was a case of "politics replacing sound public policy." Journalists observed that the head of Archer-Daniels-Midland had contributed more than $200,000 in 1993 and early 1994 to the Democratic Party, including $100,000 at a dinner hosted by President Clinton eight days before the oxygenate rule was announced.[51] Oil industry executives called the decision "outrageous" and repeated arguments that the mandate would raise gas prices and ultimately harm the environment.[52]

The oil industry had already lobbied Congress in anticipation of EPA's ethanol ruling. Hearings had been held on the issue in May 1994.[53] In the House, Rep. Dean A. Gallo (R-N.J.) had proposed an amendment to the VA, HUD, and Independent Agencies Appropriation Act (covering the EPA and other agencies) that would prohibit funding for implementation or enforcement of "any requirement that a specified percentage of the oxygen content of reformulated gasoline come from renewable oxygenates." Efforts by Energy and Commerce Chairman John Dingell (D-Mich.), Appropriations subcommittee chairman Louis Stokes (D-Ohio),[54] and EPA officials blocked the House bill.[55]

Senators began voicing opposition to the ethanol program in February 1994, raising concerns about the increased costs and uncertain environmental benefits.[56] Environmentalists urged senators to drop the effort and rely on litigation to fight the ethanol mandate. The American Petroleum Institute and National Petroleum Refiners Association had already sued the EPA over the February 1994 standards for reformulated and conventional gasoline (the negotiated rule) because they believed the ethanol mandate violated the agreement reflected in those standards.[57] The oil industry lobbied heavily for the House Appropriations amendment. Advertising space in the *New York Times,* the *Washington Post,* and the *Wall Street Journal* became a battleground between the oil and ethanol industries. Radio commentator Paul Harvey was required to tell "the rest of the story" in defending ethanol.[58] The National Farmers Union and other agricultural interests charged that the oil industry was "polluting this clean air success story,"[59] and claimed that methanol "kills hundreds and blinds thousands."[60]

On August 3, 1994, the Senate debated an appropriations bill amendment that would "impose a limit on the use of funding to promulgate, implement, or enforce an EPA regulation mandating a specific percentage market share for ethanol oxygenates in reformulated gasoline."[61] Opponents of the EPA rule, led by Senator Bennett Johnston (D-La.), chairman of the Energy and Natural Resources Committee, expected to win the vote. But last-minute decisions resulted in a 50-50 tie on a motion to table (defeat) the Johnston amendment.[62] Vice President Al Gore then cast the deciding vote in opposition to the amendment, thus protecting the EPA's ethanol program.[63] Sen. Bill Bradley (D-N.J.) and others vowed to eliminate in 1995 the tax credits offered to ethanol producers,[64] and court challenges—some already filed and some anticipated—promised to delay the implementation of the reformulated gas program.

A few weeks later, Mobil Oil, in a *New York Times* advertisement, lamented the collapse of the effort to negotiate a reformulated gas regulation:

Remember when a deal used to be "for keeps"? Now, it seems a deal hammered out by competing interests and agreed upon three years ago, can be cavalierly deep-sixed by politics. More importantly, the failure by key participants to honor agreements casts a shadow on a relatively new method of federal government rulemaking—called regulatory negotiations or "reg-neg." Many were counting on reg-neg to smooth out the regulatory process, reduce litigation, and save money for everybody.[65]

More will be said about the idea of regulatory negotiations. But the saga of the reformulated gas provisions of the Clean Air Act is a sober reminder of how difficult it is to actually implement policies. There are unending opportunities to revisit and reverse decisions, from litigation to congressional oversight to changes in executive branch officials; few policies are ever final, and following the political trail is a daunting task. But the real challenge rests with regulated industries, who must try to devise an efficient, effective strategy to comply with a moving target.

Regulating Air Toxics

Controlling the releases, routine and accidental, of toxic or hazardous air pollutants (HAPs) has been one of the most difficult clean air undertakings. Failure to regulate air toxics was a major impetus in the 1980s to amend the 1977 Clean Air Act. As explained in Chapter 4, the primary task in implementing the air toxic provisions has been the issuance of "maximum achievable control technology," or MACT standards, for all major sources of emissions. By November 1994, the EPA had only issued three rules—for the manufacturing of hazardous organic chemicals, for steel industry coke ovens, and for dry cleaners. The hazardous organic chemical standard, aimed at reducing by 80 percent emissions of 149 HAPs from 370 manufacturing facilities, is projected to reduce air toxic emissions by 522,500 tons per year and VOCs by nearly 1.1 tons per year. The EPA also issued general guidelines for MACT standards and case-by-case MACT determinations that are required for sources if the agency fails to issue general MACT standards for those industries.[66] The issues raised in the formulation of MACT standards are discussed later in this chapter.

Despite the slowness in issuing MACT standards, the EPA has made some progress in related areas. By 1994, it had published a final list of source categories, a list of substances for the accidental releases prevention program, studies of hazards of hydrofluoric acid, statistics on hydrogen sulfide emissions from extracting oil and natural gas, guidelines for state air toxics programs, a schedule for regulating all source categories, inspection and training materials for coke ovens, an urban area strategy research report, and a Great Lakes air toxics study. New standards for large municipal waste incinerators issued in 1991 promised to reduce emissions by 90 percent by 1994. Additional reductions will come from the clean-fuel vehicle program and the more stringent tailpipe standards developed by the EPA.[67]

Several EPA initiatives that have encouraged sources to voluntarily reduce air toxics have produced impressive results. The 33/50 program, established in 1991, focused on seventeen air pollutants (such as benzene, chloroform, toluene, and xylenes); some 1,200 firms agreed to reduce their emissions of these chemicals by 33 percent by 1992 and 50 percent by 1995. A 1994 EPA study reported that emissions had been cut by 40 percent by 1992 and the 1995 goal was likely to be achieved.[68] In 1992, an "early reductions" program was inaugurated: firms that reduced emissions 90 percent to 95 percent before a MACT standard was issued for their industry would be given an additional six years to comply with the eventual standard. During the first year, some thirty-four companies agreed to make those reductions at forty-nine plants.[69]

Preventing Acid Rain

Implementation of the acid rain provisions of the Clean Air Act is a major success story. Not only are these provisions among the most ambitious clean air undertakings, they have also ignited interest in the use of market-based instruments in environmental regulation—interest that is spreading to other air pollution issues and to other environmental laws. Although the emissions reduction requirements have just begun to be implemented in 1995, the emissions trading system is firmly in place and is serving as a model for state efforts to deal with other forms of pollution as well as for global discussions over how to reduce carbon dioxide and emissions of other greenhouse gases.[70]

In 1993 and 1994, the EPA conducted the first two auctions and sales of sulfur dioxide allowances. Estimates of cost savings from using emissions trading instead of the conventional regulatory approach range from $1 billion to $2 billion. A rule issued in 1992 extended, for the first time, emission controls to nitrogen oxide emissions from coal-fired electric utility boilers, an important step in meeting the national air quality standard. Utilities can meet their obligations through averaging the annual emission rates from all of their generating units and plants, thus reducing compliance costs.[71]

As outlined in Chapter 4, the acid rain provision of the Clean Air Act Amendments of 1990 called for sulfur dioxide reductions from fossil fuel-fired power plants to be cut in half by the year 2000 but left to sources the decision about how to achieve that goal.[72] The initial allowances—permits to emit one ton of SO_2 a year—were mandated in the law and were based on the size of the power plant. The cost of reductions is determined by market forces and will differ among plants depending on what approaches they use to reduce emissions—installing scrubbers that remove sulfur dioxide and other pollutants from emissions, switching to cleaner fuels, reducing demand by promoting energy conservation, or buying and selling emission allowances. In 1994, the cost of converting to low-sulfur coal varied from $25 to $119 per kilowatt; the average cost of installing scrubbers was about $227 per kilowatt.[73] Most utilities, at least 61 percent of those involved in phase I, will reduce emissions by switching to cleaner coal rather than by installing scrubbers.

The allocation of allowances takes effect in 1995 and lasts for thirty years; they can be used in any year. Phase I of the program, to begin in 1995, affects 110 plants; phase II, commencing in 2000, will affect some 800 plants. While the initial allocation of allowances is limited to power plants, anyone can buy, sell, or own allowances, and industrial sources can voluntarily enter the market. As the total number of allowances is reduced over time, the price of allowances is expected to increase, making fuel switching or installation of pollution control equipment more attractive. Utilities must pay $2,000 for every ton of SO_2 emitted beyond their allowances.

The electric utility industry seemed to be a good candidate for experimenting with tradeable emissions because it has a relatively limited number of sources, emissions are centrally collected and released, and the aggregate rather than localized level of emissions is the primary concern.

Estimates in 1994 of the cost of achieving the emissions reductions ranged from $2 billion to $3 billion, in contrast to the $4 billion to $5 billion expected if the conventional approach to regulation were used.[74] Trading has encouraged utilities that produce the most pollution to clean up more than is required and sell their excess allowances since, because of economies of scale, it is usually cheaper to control pollution at the biggest polluters—the "big dirties." Trading has also stimulated competition among the means of controlling pollution; the possibility of trading, for example, has caused low-sulfur coal companies to offer more competitive contracts.[75] There have been numerous challenges, however, in starting up the emissions trading system. One has been to impose a market-based approach on a highly regulated industry. Since installation of new equipment takes several years, initial decisions about those investments had to be made by 1993, before the trading system was in place. Many companies, in the face of considerable uncertainty, chose to install scrubbers since that was the most familiar strategy. A heavily regulated industry, utilities are not naturally attuned to market-based actions, and state regulators have been slow to decide how allowance transactions will be accounted for as they regulate utility rates. Utilities are usually quite cautious and risk-averse, because any profits or cost savings they achieve through trading or any other effort are passed on to rate-payers rather than to the improvement of the industries' bottom line.[76]

In 1992, the first sale of emissions credits occurred when Wisconsin Power and Light sold 10,000 credits to the Tennessee Valley Authority (TVA), a utility owned by the federal government with eleven coal-fired plants. The price per allowance ranged from $250 to $400; TVA spent from $2.5 million to $4.0 million to buy the allowances, only a tiny fraction of the $750 million to $850 million it expects to spend on pollution control over the next several years.[77] The cost of allowances was significantly lower than the cost of scrubbers, and well below the 1990 estimates of allowances selling for $1,000 or so; progress in developing control technologies and other factors led to the lower price. Although only a very small deal (utilities typically emit more than 100,000 tons per year), it was heralded by trading advocates.[78]

The Wisconsin utility had already significantly reduced its emissions in response to a 1986 state law aimed at cutting SO_2 emissions, and had allowances to sell. The Bush administration apparently encouraged TVA to buy allowances as a way to jump start the market for allowances. Wisconsin Electric sold 15,000 allowances to Illinois Power Company, which amassed enough credits (433,000) that it did not have to reduce its emissions in order to meet the phase I requirements. Northeast utilities purchased and donated to the American Lung Association 10,000 allowances that were then retired.[79]

The initial trading activity in 1993 and 1994 primarily occurred as transfers within companies. Some forty to fifty customized transactions took place in private, with little public disclosure of terms. Several firms began offering their services in 1993 as brokers. Natural gas wholesalers have proposed deals where utilities pay for gas with allowances. Trades have been for cash and, as a futures market is developing, for forward delivery. Some deals involve producers of high-sulfur coal offering packages of coal and allowances to prospective buyers.[80]

The EPA sponsored auctions of allowances at the Chicago Board of Trade in March 1993 and 1994. Carolina Power and Light Company purchased nearly 100,000 allowances during the first auction.[81] The allowances were sold at the bid price, and the EPA did not set a minimum price on the allowances it sold, so the prices may be lower than buyers are actually willing to pay. Fifty thousand allowances usable in 1995 or later were sold in 1994, at an average price of $150 (the average price was $131 in 1993); 25,000 allowances usable in the year 2000 and 100,000 allowances usable in 2001 were sold at $140 each (the average price was $122 in 1993). The $150 to $200 range has become the standard price for trading allowances; trades outside that range are likely to be challenged by state utility regulators.[82]

Trading may eventually take place on a daily basis as production changes and the resultant need for more or fewer allowances depends on changes in weather, economic conditions, costs of different fuels, and decisions made by other utility companies that supply power in the same market. The market will be stimulated when nonutilities enter the market since they will sell allowances, and prices will likely drop. Increased competition in the electric utility industry, as customers will be able to choose from a wider range of suppliers (as required under the 1992 Energy Policy Act), will also stimulate trading activity as the shift to full cost pricing occurs and utilities try to more tightly manage their costs.[83]

The utility companies that have participated in trades are energetic proponents of the acid rain program. Many have saved millions of dollars by reallocating allowances within their system. However, some firms have resisted trading allowances because of fear of adverse publicity. Environmentalists in Wisconsin have challenged the trades made by Wisconsin Power and Light and Wisconsin Electric because those allowances could not have been used under the state's strict acid rain law. They fear sales of allowances to utilities in upwind states will harm lakes in their state and have pushed for legislation to require utilities to prove that trading pollution allowances will not result in pollution that will drift back to Wisconsin. New York officials have similar concerns in protecting the Adirondack lakes. Environmental groups continue to be split over trading programs: the Environmental Defense Fund vigorously promotes them, whereas other groups, including grass-roots organizations, fear they give too much discretion to polluters and allow them to comply with the law at the lowest cost rather than to make investments in the most environmentally beneficial technologies.[84]

Another barrier to implementing the acid rain program has been legislation enacted by coal-producing states that require utilities to burn a certain percentage of local coal. Legislation aimed at saving local coal-mining jobs has been challenged by governors from low-sulfur states, and they have found support in courts that have invalidated these protective laws as being inconsistent with the constitution's delegation of power to Congress to regulate interstate commerce.[85] Concerned about the impact of the Clean Air Act Amendments of 1990 on its coal industry, the Illinois General Assembly passed the 1991 Coal Act, designed "to maintain and preserve . . . the mining of coal in Illinois" and to require industry to continue "to use Illinois coal as a fuel source."[86] The statute was struck down in January 1995 by a federal court of appeals as an unconstitutional restraint on interstate commerce aimed at promoting the specific use of Illinois coal. The court found that the Illinois Act was a "none-too-subtle attempt to prevent Illinois electric utilities from switching to low-sulfur western coal as a Clean Air Act compliance option," a "discriminatory state action forbidden by the Commerce Clause."[87]

The acid rain trading system is still in its infancy. Since it takes about three years to install scrubbers, more trading activity might have occurred in 1992, in anticipation of the 1995 deadline for reducing emissions, if utilities had fully embraced the idea. Emissions trading may accelerate in anticipation of the next round of controls in the year 2000. But the promise of reducing the cost of achieving environmental goals through trading seems irresistible, and the acid rain program sets a clear precedent for future policy innovation.

The South Coast Air Quality Management District developed an emissions trading plan for reducing smog in the Los Angeles area that was approved in January 1994.[88] Other areas of the country have plans in various stages of development. Several proposals for trading schemes to reduce carbon dioxide emissions as a way to decrease the risk of global warming have also sprung from the acid rain program.[89] Chapter 6 returns to this issue in discussing the prospects for trading and other market-based approaches to regulation.

Protecting the Ozone Layer

The 1990 Clean Air Act is the instrument used to carry out the obligations the United States accepted in signing the 1988 Montreal Protocol on Substances That Deplete the Ozone Layer and the 1990 Amendments to the Protocol. By 1994, the EPA had issued a list of ozone-depleting substances; rules for phasing out CFCs and accelerated phaseout of CFCs, for recycling CFCs during servicing of mobile air conditioners, for CFC labeling, for an emissions reduction program, for procurement of CFC-related products, and for a safe alternative program; and a ban on nonessential class I and II CFC-containing products.[90] Every year since the amendments were passed, new evidence about the deteriorating ozone layer has been discovered. In 1992, the EPA accelerated the phaseout schedule of CFCs from 2000, as provided in the Clean Air Act and the Montreal Protocol, to 1995. The agency has also funded research into alternatives to CFCs and into dissemination of technology to other countries.[91]

Regulation of CFCs and other chemicals believed to harm the ozone layer has been quite successful, probably due to the lack of industry opposition to the regulations and the growing scientific research over the threat posed by damage to the ozone layer. The effort has not been without challenges, however. Two men were indicted in January 1995 for smuggling 126 tons of ozone-depleting CFC-12 (Freon) into the United States.[92]

EPA's Overall Implementation Record

Between 1991 and 1994, the EPA published more than 110 proposed rules and more than 90 final rules. The final rules affect the major sources of pollution and are expected to result in 90 percent of the total reductions in air pollution emissions—57 billion pounds—that the 1990 act was designed to achieve. While some rules were issued after the statutory deadlines, and ten rules or actions were only partially complete, almost all of the activities in the EPA's implementation strategy for the Clean Air Act had been accomplished. Despite the tremendous increase in EPA's output of regulations, more than 100 additional regulations and guidelines, and dozens of reports and studies are required by the Clean Air Act.[93] Although the EPA has fallen short of what the Clean Air Act requires, its accomplishments between 1991 and 1994, in light of the agency's history, are quite remarkable.

Two issues that have been central to the implementation of the Clean Air Act deserve additional discussion. First, EPA rule making is a critical step in implementation, in translating the hundreds of statutory provisions contained in the Clean Air Act into specific regulations. The slowness and expense of the process, the failure to meet deadlines for issuing rules, the inevitable legal challenge to virtually every major rule, and the importance of rule making for everything else that follows, have generated great interest in finding alternative ways of issuing rules. The development of the rule for coke oven emissions, a hazardous air pollutant, illustrates the way in which rule making might be changed, and is described below. The second major issue is the implementation of clean air provisions by states, and the tension between the needs for national standards and for efforts that are tailored to local conditions. This issue is discussed in the last section of the chapter.

Rule Making and Regulatory Negotiations

Rule making is an essential function of regulatory agencies as they translate statutory provisions into rules that are binding on regulated industries and state and local governments. It poses a number of challenges to agency procedures and to the conduct of government in general, ranging from procedural constraints and delays to the difficulties of setting priorities, from initiating regulations to managing intra-agency conflicts over how rules are to be written.[94]

The Role of the EPA

EPA rule making is widely criticized. Representatives of regulated industries regularly voice concerns about the inflexibility of regulatory requirements, the uncertainty that comes from a ponderous regulatory process, and the short time lines given them to comply with mandates. They seek more cooperative interaction with regulators so that they can achieve environmental improvements and still satisfy financial and other objectives.[95] Environmentalists have warned that EPA delays in issuing guidelines for states to use in developing their regulatory programs threaten to unravel some of the key provisions of the Clean Air Act.[96] The Senate Environment and Public Works Committee's 1993 report on the implementation of the Clean Air Act concluded that the EPA "must improve its regulatory process—the process of promulgating regulations is too bureaucratic; there are too many people at too many levels reviewing too many documents."[97] EPA officials have described the rule-making problem as "too many layers of management review at the end of the process, as opposed to meaningful consultation at the beginning of the process and then a commitment to allow things to move forward."[98]

Perhaps the most significant factor affecting implementation has been the impact of judicial challenges to EPA rules: virtually every major EPA regulation has been challenged in federal courts. A February 1994 tally by EPA officials listed some 120 court-ordered and settlement-agreement deadlines facing the agency; 40 of these rules dealt with clean air issues.[99] In addition to the court-mandated deadlines, the EPA has identified 147 regulations for which the Clean Air Act Amendments of 1990 gave specific issuance deadlines.[100]

The rule-making task is a difficult one: rules are expected to define administrative duties, limit administrative discretion, and facilitate administrative flexibility and managerial needs. In pursuing these competing concerns, should rules be more specific, detailed, and prescriptive, or should they give regulated parties more flexibility? Should they mandate goals and performance standards, or should they include design standards and other means by which the goals are to be achieved?[101] Regulated industries press for flexibility in devising their own solutions to regulatory requirements, and environmental advocates press for strict standards that force the development of new technologies. In turn, rules must be evaluated in terms of how well they provide the basis for compliance by regulated parties. They must include effective incentives and sanctions, and they must form, over time, an integrated and consistent regulatory program that is clearly understood by regulated industries and that is effective in accomplishing the agency's overall goals. Rules must also satisfy important procedural expectations, particularly those concerning public participation in agency deliberations.[102]

The EPA has experimented with negotiated rule making in an attempt to prevent judicial challenges to regulations and as a way to hammer out compromises and formulate regulations that all parties will accept and agree not to challenge in court.[103] The EPA had undertaken sixteen regulatory negotiations (reg-negs) by May 1994. Most of the efforts were successful in producing a consensus agreement, and the process often took only several months. Even when litigation occurred, primarily brought by nonsignatories to the negotiation, its scope appeared to be narrowed as a result of the negotiations. In some cases the final rule was issued within a year or so of the completion of the negotiations; in others, the final rule took several years to issue. Eight regulatory negotiations addressed clean air rules and eight addressed other environmental problems.[104] Reformulated gasoline and coke oven emissions are discussed elsewhere in this chapter. The following six reg-negs also addressed clean air rules:[105]

Small Non-Road Engines Emissions Controls. A committee was chartered on September 30, 1993, and was projected to terminate on May 31, 1995. It seeks to propose regulations for non-road mobile sources that are significant contributors to ozone precursors and carbon monoxide emissions.

Wood Furniture Manufacturing Industry VOC Emission Controls. A committee was chartered in 1993 and had not, as of May 1994, completed its work. The rule would regulate hazardous air pollutants that contribute to the formation of volatile organic compounds, precursors of ozone.

Architectural and Industrial Maintenance Coatings. Initial meetings began in 1992 and continued through May 1994; a proposal was expected in 1994. Architectural and industrial coatings, such as building and steel structure paints, are a major source of VOC emissions.

Fugitive Emissions from Equipment Leaks. The committee was formed in September 1989 and reached consensus in October 1990 on a rule for reducing emissions of toxic and volatile organic compounds from leaky valves, pumps, and flanges. The agreement is expected to become part of a broader EPA rule on hazardous air pollutants.

Woodburning Stoves. Chartered in 1986, the committee produced an agreement in five months, and the EPA issued a rule in 1987 that imposed New Source Performance Standards for residential wood combustion units.

Nonconformance Penalties for Heavy Duty Trucks. This was the first regulatory negotiation, established in April 1984. Agreement was reached in four months, and a proposed rule was issued by the EPA in March 1985 that permitted manufacturers of heavy trucks to pay a penalty in lieu of complying with emission standards.

The Coke Oven Negotiations

An Overview of Coke Oven Emissions. Coke oven emissions are generated when coal is distilled to produce coke, which is used as a fuel in the production of steel. Coke is used in blast furnaces to convert iron ore to iron; the iron is refined further to produce steel. There are ninety-two coke oven batteries—groups of ovens with common walls—in operation in the United States.[106] Coke oven emissions are yellowish-brown, and include some 10,000 compounds. They include both gases and respirable particulates, several of which are known human carcinogens such as beryllium, arsenic, and benzene, and other compounds that have been shown to induce cancer in animals.[107] The EPA administrator has determined that "coke oven emissions present a significant risk of cancer to the public. In addition, coke oven emissions in the presence of an air inversion also may be related to episodes of asthma, bronchitis, and other acute respiratory conditions in both children and adults."[108]

The steel industry received an extraordinary extension in the Clean Air Act Amendments of 1990 because members of Congress were quite responsive to industry fears (or threats) that if these control standards were imposed the domestic steel industry would close down. In response to these demands, the law permits the steel industry to avoid compliance until 2020 with any health-based standards the EPA might eventually issue. (For all other air toxics, industries will be subject to residual risk standards by 2005.)[109]

The Negotiations. The ambitious time table established for the EPA by Congress in the 1990 Clean Air Act for issuing technology standards for coke oven emissions encouraged the agency to look for alternatives to the traditional regulatory process. Coke oven emissions seemed a likely candidate for regulatory negotiations since there were a relatively small number of coke ovens and a limited number of groups interested in the regulations. The creation of the Clean Steel Network was an important innovation in this process. Proposed in May 1991 by David Doninger, then senior attorney at the Natural Resources Defense Council, and Blakeman Early, then Washington, D.C. representative of the Sierra Club, the network was open to any environmental, labor, or community organization "that supports strong controls on coke oven pollution."[110] The network brought together environmental and labor interests; trade associations represented the steel industry. The limited number of groups, a pressing deadline, and a relatively well-defined set of issues made the prospects for a successful reg-neg quite promising. The following groups became the major participants in the coke oven reg-neg: the Clean Steel Network, which was comprised of members of environmental groups and labor unions in Alabama, Arizona, the District of Columbia, Georgia, Illinois, Indiana, Ohio, Pennsylvania, Utah, and West Virginia, and which included Citizens against Toxic Substances, the Sierra Club, the Chicago Lung Association, local unions of the United Steelworkers, and the Group against Smog and Pollution (GASP); the American Iron and Steel Institute (AISI) and the American Coke and Coal Chemicals Institute (ACCCI), which together represented the steel industry; and state and local air pollution officials.[111]

EPA's protocol for the coke oven standards provided detailed guidelines for the membership of the committee, its operating procedures, and the standards to be developed. Any interest that would be "significantly affected" by EPA regulations governing coke ovens was allowed to join the negotiations. Additional parties were permitted to join the committee after negotiations began only if the entire committee concurred. Only committee members or designated alternates were permitted to sit at the negotiating table, but parties could bring technical or other advisers to assist them. Under the Federal Advisory Committee Act and the Negotiated Rule-making Act of 1990, the sessions were to be open to the public and announced in the *Federal Register,* and any person attending could make written or oral comments (if time permitted). Committee decisions were required to be unanimous. Committee members were expected to "represent the concerns and interests of their constituents and to ensure that any agreement developed by the Committee is acceptable to the organization or caucus which the Committee Member represents."[112]

Members were invited to form smaller working groups to address specific issues and to make recommendations. Each party was permitted to appoint members to each work group, and the committee could also invite others significantly affected by the topics addressed by the working groups to join them. The committee could move to discontinue negotiations at any time if they were not productive. Minutes of committee meetings would be prepared by the facilitator and made available to the public, but they would not be approved by the committee or used to represent the official position of the committee or of any members. Parties agreed not to withhold any relevant, nonproprietary information, and to provide needed information in advance of meetings if reasonably convenient. All parties were prohibited from releasing information shared by members in confidence. However, the information and data provided to the committee in writing were to be made part of the public record. All parties were to act in good faith in all aspects of these negotiations; specific offers, positions, or statements made were not to be used by other parties "for any purpose outside the negotiations or as a basis for future litigation" in order to "support the regulatory negotiation process by encouraging the free and open exchange of ideas, views, and information prior to achieving consensus."[113]

The protocol recognized that the EPA was solely responsible for issuing the regulations, but the agency agreed that the regulations would be based on the written agreement produced by the committee. The protocol provided that the committee was to produce a written statement, signed by all the parties, that would serve as the EPA's "Notice of Proposed Rulemaking," as long as the statement was consistent with the agency's legal obligations. The agency also agreed to consult with committee members as the draft regulations and preambles were prepared. Parties agreed they would not file negative comments on proposed regulations or their preamble, or take any other action to inhibit the agency's adoption of the regulations, as long as the final rules had "the same substance and effect as the written statement." The public comment period would be the same as for traditional rule making; the EPA would consider all relevant comments submitted and make necessary changes. If anyone sought to block the adoption of final regulations, the parties agreed to submit comments in support of the regulation and statements indicating that they participated in the negotiations and supported the regulation. State and local government representatives agreed to support the issuance of state rules that were consistent with the written statement and the final regulations. All parties were to agree that the agreement did not modify "in any way the obligations or liabilities of any person under state law, including common law."[114] The regulatory negotiations protocol was supplemented by a 1991 charter that formally established the National Emission Standards for Coke Oven Batteries Advisory Committee. In compliance with the EPA committee management manual and the Federal Advisory Committee Act, interested persons were permitted to file comments before or after meetings.[115]

The first meeting of the group was held on October 25, 1991. It was termed a discussion meeting since the parties had not yet agreed to formally participate in a regulatory negotiation. The participants made it clear what their concerns were: industry wanted "regulatory certainty" (meaning no litigation), flexibility, and numbers that were not "unrealistically low," and environmental and community groups wanted effective enforcement and emission reductions that complied with the stringent provisions of the law. The first talks were not particularly promising. Industry groups argued that the health risks of coke oven emissions were minimal, that the great variability in coke oven operations must be reflected in standards, that the cost of rebuilding the ovens would be enormous, and that the industry would suffer more than a $1.5 billion loss resulting from reduced coke oven production during the rebuilding phase.[116]

In the January 6-7, 1992, meeting the group shifted from a discussion group to a formal regulatory negotiation. It included fifty-nine people, most of whom were observers. There were a dozen EPA staff members, several state agency officials, and representatives from many of the steel companies, industry trade associations, and their law firms. The formal list of members of the negotiated rule-making committee included three EPA officials, the three network members, eight steel industry representatives, two steelworkers' union representatives, and five state and local air pollution agency officials. Industry representatives had apparently been resisting acknowledging the discussions as negotiations, perhaps because they were not yet convinced that this approach was better than the traditional rule-making/litigation mode.[117] Negotiations continued for several months. New issues continued to arise, such as the interaction of the coke oven standards with existing provisions of state implementation plans for fine particulates or PM_{10}. (Coke oven emissions are also regulated as particulates under other provisions of the Clean Air Act.) This threatened the unity of the Clean Steel Network since members in states that had been successful in getting stringent control measures for coke oven/PM_{10} emissions written into their state plans resisted any retreat in the negotiated standard.[118]

In their April 21-22 meeting, the parties focused on the "non-number" issues first, trying to get agreement on them before tackling the numbers or percentages of leaking coke oven doors and vents that would be permitted. The network group charged industry representatives with retrenching from earlier positions, and the group members expected the negotiation to collapse. Throughout the summer, industry and network members met in small groups to work out differences, and prospects improved as a result of these small sessions. The associate administrator of the EPA became involved in some shuttle diplomacy, meeting with network and industry officials to cajole them into compromising. A negotiating session took place September 15-17. After the meetings, the EPA prepared a draft regulation and preamble and circulated them to the members. Because the parties still disagreed over a number of issues, there was another session on October 8, 1992. In that final meeting, the parties resolved all outstanding issues and concurred on the draft regulation. A revised draft was prepared and circulated, and the remaining differences were worked out in small meetings that concluded on October 20.[119]

Assessment. The coke oven reg-neg appears to have been, overall, a success. The results are not in, and a final judgment will not be possible until the EPA issues the required guidelines, the industry complies with the provisions, and monitoring and enforcement occur. As industry begins to make the required investments, companies may find that they are too expensive, plead poverty, and seek exemptions. Unions may fear job loss and abandon their support for the agreement. However, the network negotiators argued that the agreement was stronger than one the Bush administration would have produced on its own, particularly in light of the role of the OMB and the Council on Competitiveness in reviewing regulations. The provisions were much more aggressive than the minimum standards mandated in the Clean Air Act, but they are very likely not sufficient to eliminate the risk of cancer from coke oven emissions.[120]

Several factors contributed to making the reg-neg work. The steel industry was anxious to have guidelines produced by the EPA, because the Clean Air Act established tight deadlines and large penalties for failure to meet them. Industry officials were also anxious to have the guidelines issued as soon as possible so that they could make financial arrangements for the required investments. Environmental groups hoped to be able to pressure the EPA into forcing industry to rebuild or replace existing coke ovens in order to reduce emissions to the lowest levels possible. The ultimate goal of the Clean Steel Network was to have companies replace existing coke oven batteries with the new, cleaner technology of "nonrecovery" coke ovens. There were incentives for both sides to participate—environmental groups could demand strong standards and industry could get standards issued early so they could plan their compliance efforts. Parties could also drop out of negotiations if they were not working, so they risked only the time invested in the negotiations.[121]

The advantages that regulatory negotiations promise in general were largely realized in the coke oven reg-neg. First, parties were encouraged to devise reasonable package deals that might be of interest to all parties rather than to take extreme positions in anticipation of adversarial proceedings. Parties were encouraged to focus on the issues of greatest interest to them, thus reducing the number of issues in dispute and permitting parties to strike deals and fashion compromises that maximized their gains within the overall constraints of the negotiations. Negotiations gave parties an opportunity to express their views to the EPA as discussions unfolded, rather than through the more cumbersome process of submitting written comments. For example, a compromise that provides a strict standard but permits gradual industry implementation may be better than the alternatives of balancing industry demands for a weaker standard and longer phase-in period and environmentalist pressures for a stringent standard quickly applied.[122]

Part of what made this negotiation successful was the possibility for win-win solutions.[123] Both the steel industry and the Clean Steel Network had something to gain from a successful negotiation. Industry got a regulation that was possible to meet with existing technology. Steel mills could begin planning to meet the standards immediately because litigation was unlikely. Environmental and union interests were able to achieve a more aggressive regulatory standard than the minimum position provided in the Clean Air Act and were able to start the process of cleaning up emissions sooner than if the traditional approach had been followed.

The negotiation was also characterized by a lack of divergence in fundamental values. Conflict among parties concerning core values makes negotiations difficult, if not impossible; negotiations are most likely to work if there is consensus over the kind of agreement needed and the range of options to be considered. Negotiations are not well suited for addressing fundamental differences or basic values but for working out compromise positions and strategies that satisfy at least some of the concerns of both parties.[124]

The selection of the parties were also critical. The formation of the Clean Steel Network helped simplify the process considerably. There were established trade associations representing the steel industry, but the limited number of large steel companies permitted direct representation by these firms as well. The EPA's support was critical; parties needed to know that the agency would implement the agreement the parties developed.[125]

The negotiations encouraged the generation and sharing of information useful to all sides in devising acceptable solutions; rather than inundating the regulatory agency with data, parties created incentives to provide information to convince other parties to accept a particular position. The negotiations made use of practical information and the need for extensive theoretical data or modeling that is often used in adversarial proceedings was reduced. Perhaps most important, the negotiations avoided the reliance on intermediaries. Intermediaries may delay decision making, separate parties, and inhibit communication and possible joint problem solving. They are expensive to hire, they may have some incentive to prolong disputes (so that they can continue working), and they may inhibit compromise since they are not authorized to make concessions or agreements but must shuttle back and forth between their clients and their counterparts. Having the parties negotiate directly helped reduce transaction costs since ideas and demands were not filtered through others.[126]

Particularly important for this rule making was the overall political context. Environmental and union groups feared the role of the Council on Competitiveness in reviewing this and other EPA regulation. The council and the OMB still reviewed the regulation, but since the review process was usually triggered by industry complaints, having industry sign off on regulations before they reached the White House review process was a critical step in avoiding problems. (This is discussed further in Chapter 6.) The good faith efforts and commitment of the parties were also critical. While some adversarial nature may be inescapable, negotiations require a spirit of joint problem solving, brainstorming to devise creative solutions, and shared research.[127]

One other issue deserves mention. Many proponents of regulatory negotiations suggest that the process should take place in private. Privacy encourages parties to make concessions on some issues, permits a frank discussion of issues with a minimum of political posturing, and allows use of confidential information that parties would not release to the public. Negotiations are facilitated if parties can provide information, agree to actions, and make statements that cannot later be used against them.[128] However, the Federal Advisory Committee Act requires that agencies organize reg-neg as an advisory committee whose meetings must be open to the public. The main sessions of the coke oven reg-neg were held in public, but much of the real work was done in small working groups that were informal and not announced to the public. The importance of these informal meetings among key parties demonstrates the value of having meetings in private, but the process also conflicts with the spirit, if not the letter, of the Federal Advisory Committee Act.[129]

Negotiated rule making does not work in every situation. Even with promising preconditions, the negotiations for the coke oven reg-neg started slowly, parties came close to breaking them off, and they lasted longer than anticipated. Reg-neg is uncertain and risky, and it takes patience and good faith on the part of the parties and the agency. The regulatory negotiations for reformulated gasoline, discussed earlier in this chapter, demonstrate some of the limitations of negotiations for issues that are particularly politically salient.

Federalism and the Challenge of Implementing Environmental Laws

The structure of federal-state relations is a key factor in the implementation of environmental regulation. Numerous problems have arisen in state implementation of environmental laws, including the Clean Air Act. State legislatures may fail to delegate sufficient authority to regulatory bodies for them to effectively implement environmental laws and may provide inadequate staffing of state regulatory agencies. Some state officials fear that effective enforcement of environmental laws will discourage investment and development. The level of compliance among regulated industries and state and local governments is often minimal, a result of ineffective implementation of federal laws by state regulatory agencies as well as federal bureaucratic problems.[130]

Environmental regulation is further complicated by provisions in federal law that preempt state regulation, such as motor vehicle emission standards.[131] Balancing the demand for national standards with the urgent need to reduce emissions in California was one of the primary challenges confronting Congress and the executive branch in the 1990 amendments, as five of the seven areas with the greatest ozone pollution problems are in California. The 1990 law effectively limits states to either accepting the California or the national standards.

The provisions of the Clean Air Act Amendments dealing with pollution from motor vehicles demonstrate some of the challenges regulatory federalism confronts in dealing with air pollution. Since air pollution in one state often affects levels in another state, cooperation among states is essential. If state policies are not consistent, economic competition can weaken environmental protection efforts. The Clean Air Act Amendments permit the creation of interstate agreements to combat air pollution, but the framework they provide is complex. When superimposed on the rest of the act, which is built on direct relations between EPA and individual state regulatory agencies, the framework is cumbersome and unwieldy. The tension between the need for interstate regulatory compacts and the basic structure of regulatory federalism poses serious challenges to the effective achievement of environmental goals.

Interstate compacts are an important means of facilitating interstate collaboration.[132] The Clean Air Act Amendments contain several provisions that recognize the interstate nature of air pollution. State implementation plans, for example, must include provisions requiring state air quality officials to notify neighboring states before the construction of new sources of pollution that may affect these states. No state may authorize the construction of a new source of pollution that would contribute to another state's failure to comply with the national standards.[133]

The Clean Air Act Amendments authorize the EPA administrator to establish interstate transport regions whenever he or she "has reason to believe that the interstate transport of air pollutants from one or more States contributes significantly to a violation of a national ambient air quality standard in one or more other States."[134] Governors of affected states may also petition the EPA for the creation of a transport region commission.[135] The commission would assess the extent to which there is an interstate air problem, explore options for reducing pollution levels, and make recommendations to the EPA about what steps should be taken to ensure states are able to implement their cleanup plans and meet their air quality goals. The experience of northeastern states in remedying their air pollution problems illustrates the challenges cooperative efforts confront under the Clean Air Act.

Regulating Air Pollution in the Northeast

The challenge in cleaning up the air in the Northeast corridor, stretching from Maine to Virginia, is daunting. According to a regional air quality model, reductions of 25 percent in volatile organic compounds and 75 percent in nitrogen oxides are required for the area to attain national air quality standards. (These two chemicals are the major precursors of ozone smog.) About 60 percent of NO_x emissions comes from motor vehicles, about 20 percent comes from utility boilers, and the balance comes from other industrial sources.[136]

The Clean Air Act Amendments of 1990 classified the New York-New Jersey-Connecticut area as a "severe" ozone nonattainment area, meaning that it has until 2007 to meet the national standard. Much of the rest of Connecticut, most of Massachusetts, part of Maine, and Rhode Island are "serious" ozone areas and have until 1996 to come into compliance. All of the available strategies for reducing motor vehicle and stationary emissions may be required. All ozone noncompliance states were required to submit to the EPA by November 15, 1994, revised SIPs that demonstrated how they would achieve the goals mandated in the Clean Air Act as well as the interim goal of a 3 percent annual decrease in ozone emissions. Downwind states will not be able to come into compliance with these goals without the cooperation of other states. Some 42 million cars are registered in the Northeast, and vehicle emissions account for 40 percent of the carbon monoxide and ozone pollution.[137]

Northeast states have created several organizations to deal with air pollution, particularly that contributed by motor vehicles.[138] One of the most important has been Northeast States for Coordinated Air Use Management (NESCAUM), formed in 1989 to facilitate interstate cooperation in meeting air quality goals. NESCAUM only makes recommendations; binding policies must be made by the states' legislatures. The Northeast Ozone Transport Commission (OTC), comprised of the governors, or their designees, of twelve northeastern states (Maine, New Hampshire, Vermont, New York, Massachusetts, New Jersey, Rhode Island, Connecticut, Pennsylvania, Delaware, Maryland, and Virginia) and the District of Columbia, was created by the Clean Air Act Amendments of 1990. It, too, lacks direct power, and was created to advise the EPA on how to improve air quality in the region.[139]

One of NESCAUM's earliest initiatives was a petition to the EPA recommending that member states be able to adopt the California motor vehicle emission standards since they believed that was the most cost-effective way to reduce carbon monoxide and ozone pollution.[140] In July and October of 1991, the OTC adopted "memoranda of understanding" supporting the adoption of the California Motor Vehicle Control Program and agreeing to lobby the EPA for permission to require that all new vehicles sold in the area meet the California Low-Emission Vehicle (LEV) standards for tailpipe emissions.[141] Three states, however, deferred a decision for consultation with their governors.[142] NESCAUM also began working to develop new efforts in inspection and maintenance programs (to ensure continuing compliance with the emission standards) and to create innovative plans to get people to drive less, since increases in vehicle miles traveled can overwhelm progress made in reducing emissions.[143] The auto industry, however, launched a major lobbying effort to discourage the states from adopting the California emissions standards.[144] As a result, only New York and Massachusetts in 1991 adopted the standards, while other states deferred action until further study. Some state officials began negotiations with representatives from the auto industry for a compromise car that was cleaner than existing ones, but not as clean as the California car.[145]

In August 1993, three states called on the OTC to petition the EPA to adopt the California LEV program throughout the Northeast.[146] The auto industry countered in late 1993 with its proposed Federal Low Emission Vehicle initiative, which would produce a vehicle capable of meeting California's standard by using clean fuels that would be made available in the Northeast.[147] The industry argued in particular that electric vehicles were prohibitively expensive and consumers would not buy them, and that other approaches to regulating mobile and stationary sources were much cheaper for each ton of pollutant avoided; it called for market-based strategies such as tax deductions and credits to encourage the purchase of alternative fueled vehicles (AFVs) and suggested that states give special consideration to AFVs in designing transportation control measures such as high occupancy vehicle lanes and parking restrictions.[148]

Other industries argued that mobile source controls were cheaper than those for stationary sources. The Edison Electric Institute, representing investor-owned utilities, argued that reducing emissions from motor vehicles costs less than half as much as reductions from utilities and other stationary sources. More than seventy environmental and public health groups wrote to the commission in January 1994, urging it to take the zero emissions route.[149]

In February 1994, the commission voted 9-4 to petition the EPA to adopt the California emission standards for new vehicles sold in the area. The petition called on the EPA to require all cars and light duty trucks sold in the region, beginning in 1999, to meet the California auto emission standards (although states could opt for earlier compliance). Five categories of vehicles would be involved: California Tier I vehicles (already in place in 1994), transitional low emission vehicles, low emission vehicles, ultra-LEVs, and zero emission vehicles. California reformulated gas and sales of zero emission vehicles would not be required.[150]

U.S. auto makers continued to campaign aggressively against adoption of the California standards in the Northeast, particularly the provision in the 1990 amendments that required 2 percent of new vehicles sold in 1999 and 10 percent sold by the year 2003 to be zero emission vehicles. Under current technology, only vehicles powered by electricity can meet that standard. The auto industry offered to accelerate its meeting of the Tier II emissions standards ahead of the date mandated in the Clean Air Act.[151] Under the Clean Air Act, the EPA cannot impose Tier II emission standards until the year 2004. The industry proposal required part of the new vehicle fleet in 2001 to comply with a modified Tier II auto emission standard; all new vehicles would meet the modified Tier II standard by 2004. This proposal would, in effect, create a new national car, and California would continue to have its own requirements.[152] The OTC rejected this proposal, however, because its projected emissions reductions were too small and would come too late to help the states come into compliance.

Policy options were expanded in March 1994 when NESCAUM proposed that state governments purchase inherently low emitting vehicles (ILEVs). ILEVs meet the California low emission vehicle standard but also have low evaporative emissions from the fuel used in the vehicles. They are expected to emit lower levels of hydrocarbons than conventional vehicles that meet the California emission standards. ILEVs run on compressed natural gas, propane, liquefied petroleum gas, neat (100 percent) ethanol, or neat methanol; electric vehicles are also ILEVs. These vehicles were required under another law, the 1992 Energy Policy Act, which requires owners of fleets of twenty or more vehicles to begin purchasing ILEVs in 1996; by the year 2000, 75 percent of those vehicles must be ILEVs.[153]

Environmental and public health advocates, utilities, industries, and producers of clean vehicles lobbied for the OTC petition, contending that the Northeast should be required to develop low emission vehicles as well as a number of other control strategies to meet air quality goals.[154] Several leading Democratic senators urged the EPA to approve the petition and argued that the auto industry proposal was inconsistent with the Clean Air Act and would "prolong the exposure of Americans to the serious health and environmental problems associated with polluted air."[155]

Utilities and manufacturers feared that without the California standards applied in the Northeast, additional controls would be required on stationary sources. Auto and stationary source industry representatives launched a barrage of studies offering widely differing estimates of the cost-effectiveness of different kinds of controls. The auto industry argued that it would be able to meet emission standards for transitional low emission vehicles and, eventually, low emission vehicles, as the California program required, but would not be able to produce ultra-low and zero emission vehicles, the other categories also required by California. One key issue was the sulfur content of fuel and the cost of shifting to reformulated gas in order to meet the ultra-low emission standard. Meeting low emission standards is harder for high-performance vehicles.[156]

The EPA was required to act on the recommendation within nine months. Caught in the middle between the OTC and industry demands, and mindful of the political fallout resulting from a regulation that might be blamed for hardship on the auto industry, it began holding a series of meetings during the summer of 1994 throughout the Northeast to aid its decision of whether to approve the OTC petition, reject it, or impose its own plan.[157] The auto industry, some state legislators, and others unhappy with the petition threatened to sue the EPA if it approved the request. Legislators in three states introduced bills to withdraw from the commission if the California standards were mandated.[158]

In August 1994, the EPA created a Clean Air Advisory Subcommittee to explore options and began to encourage OTC states and the auto industry to come up with a "49-state" car whose emissions would fall between the required amounts of the Clean Air Act and California's emission standards.[159] This would, in effect, rewrite key parts of the 1990 Clean Air Act's motor vehicle emissions provisions. A consensus among states and industry would avoid litigation and battles in each state to decide whether to accept the California standard. (Decisions to adopt the California standards in New York and Massachusetts had led to legal challenges by auto makers.) The EPA favored the 49-state approach because it would have provided for cleaner cars throughout the nation than would result under the 1990 law, but Northeast regulatory officials believed that requiring the California emission standards was an essential part of their strategy to attain air quality goals.[160]

On September 22, 1994, the EPA published a proposed rule that would approve the OTC petition as necessary for the Northeast states to achieve the national air quality standards. States would be required to revise their air quality implementation plans to ensure that new vehicles sold within their borders complied either with the low-emission vehicle program or with any new-vehicle program that the auto industry might develop that would ensure equivalent emissions reductions. States would also be allowed, but not required, to adopt the zero emission vehicle sales requirement as part of their LEV programs. States could also create economic incentives to encourage purchase of ZEVs.[161] Because of the time required to sift through the great number of comments submitted in response to its draft decision, however, the EPA failed to issue a final decision by the deadline of November 10, 1994.[162] By 1995, this issue had become entangled with challenges to the Clean Air Act's mobile source provisions. (See Chapter 6.)

The experience of the Northeast states during the first few years after the passage of the Clean Air Act Amendments of 1990 demonstrates the importance of state cooperative efforts. The Northeast's experience may serve as a model for other regions confronting air and water pollution problems. The challenge is in devising ways to simplify the regulatory process so that effective policies can be devised and implemented. As one EPA official put it, "the system is overwhelmed with checks and balances. . . . We've got to do what we do best—issue guidance and national rules and then let go. . . . If we want any environmental results out of this entire Clean Air Act the various levels of government have got to trust each other to do their job."[163]

EPA review of states' decisions, such as that to adopt more stringent motor vehicle emission standards, considerably complicates and slows down the policy process. In an ideal world, the EPA would defer to states' decisions about means, while ensuring that the goals were achieved. But the history of the Clean Air Act shows that states have often done little to remedy air pollution problems. If the EPA simply waits until deadlines for achieving air quality goals are passed, many states will do little and then use their political clout in Congress and the White House to insulate themselves against EPA sanctions.

States demand that they be given more discretion and that they be trusted more so that cost-effective regulations can be imposed and environmental protection can be balanced with other policy goals. But the lack of comity between the states, EPA, Congress, and the executive branch is rooted in decades of conflict over how to formulate and implement environmental policies. The actions of interstate organizations in the Northeast are promising and deserve support; the developmen of state and regional capacity to devise and implement effective policy is a critical element of the future of environmental regulation, and should be fostered and encouraged by the EPA and other federal actors. The regulatory tasks overwhelm federal and EPA resources, and more effective ways of harnessing available resources must be found in order to achieve the goals that are at the heart of the Clean Air Act and other statutes.

California and the Northeast states together account for nearly 50 percent of the new car market. If the OTC states are permitted to adopt the California Low Emission Vehicle program, California will, in effect, be in a position to dictate motor vehicle emission policy, and the authority of federal regulators will be diminished. Since air pollution problems differ so significantly throughout the nation, however, a more decentralized, regional approach may be the most efficient and effective way to improve air quality. That shift to a more decentralized regulatory regime will require a leap of faith for some who are convinced that only a centralized, federal regulatory effort will work. The key issues in achieving air quality goals in the Northeast include how to encourage the development of cleaner motor vehicles and how mobile and stationary sources can best be regulated together. State experimentation through regional compacts can play an important role in gaining some experience with alternative approaches to regulation. For those experiments to flourish, the EPA will need to grant more discretion to states, while at the same time monitoring their progress closely and providing effective oversight.

Assessing Implementation

The most recent air quality data, available in 1994, showed that air quality in the United States has improved since passage of the Clean Air Act Amendments of 1990. Of the ninety-eight ozone areas that were designated as nonattainment after the passage of the amendments, forty-six achieved the national air quality standards in 1992; twenty-one of the forty-one carbon monoxide nonattainment areas were in compliance with the standard. Four ozone nonattainment areas have been redesignated as having attained the national standard, and twenty-five other areas have applied for redesignation.[164] While data for one year are only of limited value since they may be greatly affected by weather patterns, levels of industrial activity, and other short-term factors, some progress is apparent. But it will take several years before the impact of the 1990 law on levels of air pollution can be assessed.

Nevertheless, looking at the first four years of implementation of the Clean Air Act Amendments of 1990, considerable progress is evident. The EPA has in place much of the federal regulatory infrastructure required by the law, a result of a strong commitment of both the Bush and Clinton administrations to issue the required regulations, of litigation aimed at pressuring the agency to meet the deadlines, and of some modest congressional oversight. While many states continue to resist making the difficult policy choices required to bring them into compliance with national air quality standards, some states have strong regulatory programs in place. Chapter 6 includes additional comments concerning implementation of the Clean Air Act.

The Clean Air Act has become a target of criticism because many of its provisions impose significant constraints on industrial and personal behavior. Criticism is expected; in fact, if people did not feel constrained by clean air regulations, the regulations would likely be too weak. This is not to say that all programs are efficient and effective; there is much room for improving the implementation of the Clean Air Act. But complaints, legitimate and not so legitimate, about specific requirements under the act have been joined with a much broader movement to cut back regulation and reduce the size of the federal government that threatens the effectiveness of the act. Given the strong support for clean air goals, the act will likely survive attacks, but there will be considerable loss of momentum and progress as the criticisms are sorted out, and implementation will suffer during the uncertainty. Chapter 6 explores the future of the Clean Air Act in light of the challenges that have been raised.

Notes

1. Jeffrey Pressman and Aaron Wildavsky, *Implementation* (Berkeley, Calif.: University of California Press, 1984): xxi-xxiii.
2. Ibid., 176, 180.
3. Ibid., 143.
4. Ibid., xix-xxv.
5. Environmental Protection Agency (EPA), Office of Air and Radiation, *Implementation Strategy for the Clean Air Act Amendments of 1990* (Washington, D.C.: EPA, 1994), 1-13.
6. See Sections 107(d)(4), 171(1), 172(c)(1), 172(c)(3), 172(c)(6), 172(c)(9), 110(a)(2)(A), 189(a)(1)(A), 189(a)(1)(B), and 189(a)(1)(C). See also 57 FR 13498 (April 16, 1992) and 57 FR 18070 (April 28, 1992).
7. U.S. Congress, Committee on Environment and Public Works, *Three Years Later: Report Card on the 1990 Clean Air Act Amendments* (Washington, D.C.: Government Printing Office, 1993), 7.
8. EPA, Office of Air Quality Planning and Standards, "PM-10 Nonattainment Area Update, July 25, 1994" (Washington, D.C.: EPA, 1994).
9. Clean Air Network, "Air Remains Dirty in Many States: Progress in Others; Promise of Clean Air Is in Danger" (Washington, D.C.: CAN, 1994).
10. U.S. General Accounting Office, Air Pollution: State Planning Requirements Will Continue to Challenge EPA and the States" (Washington, D.C.: GPO, 1993), 3.
11. Section 179(b); 59 FR 39832 (August 4, 1994), 42 U.S.C. 7905(b).
12. EPA, "Implementing the 1990 Clean Air Act: The First Two Years" (Washington, D.C.: EPA, 1992), 47-48.
13. Ibid., 49-50.
14. For an illuminating study of the council, see Jeffrey M. Berry and Kent E. Portney, "Centralizing Regulatory Control and Interest Group Access: The Quayle Council on Competitiveness," in Allan J. Cigler and Burdett A. Loomis, eds., *Interest Group Politics*, 4th ed. (Washington, D.C.: CQ Press, 1995); 319-348.
15. Ibid., 332-333.
16. Ibid., 333.
17. See, generally, National Academy of Public Administration, *Presidential Management of Rulemaking in Regulatory Agencies* (Washington, D.C.: NAPA, 1987).
18. Office of the Vice President, "Memorandum for Heads of Executive Departments and Agencies."
19. House Subcommittee on Health and the Environment, *The Vice President's Initiative to Undermine the Clean Air Act*, 102d Cong., 1st sess., May 1, 1991, 2.
20. Clean Air Act Amendments, Pub. L. No. 101-549, 104 Stat. 2399 (November 15, 1990), secs. 502(b)(6) and 505.
21. House Subcommittee on Health and the Environment, *The Vice President's Initiative*, 2-4.
22. Ann Devroy, "Environmental Presidential Politics," *Washington Post*, national weekly ed., May 4-10, 1992.
23. House Subcommittee on Health and the Environment, *Inauspicious Beginnings: A Review of the First Year of Implementation of the Clean Air Act of*

1990, 102d Cong., 1st sess., November 14, 1991.

24. EPA, Office of Air and Radiation, *Implementation Strategy*, 1-13.
25. Section 211(k)(1) of the Clean Air Act.
26. EPA, press release, "Renewable Fuels to be Included in Reformulated Gasoline" (June 30, 1994).
27. EPA, "Implementing the 1990 Clean Air Act," 33-34.
28. Ibid., 34-35.
29. Ibid., 35-36.
30. Not for attribution interview with EPA official, November 4, 1994.
31. Clean Air Act of 1990, section 176(c).
32. U.S. Department of Transportation, "Intermodal Surface Transportation Efficiency Act of 1991: A Summary" (n.d.).
33. Section 211(k)(3) provides that emissions of volatile organic compounds and toxics between 1995 and 1999 (phase I of the reformulated gasoline program) must be cut by 15 percent of the 1990 baseline emissions. For the year 2000 and beyond, the emissions must be reduced by 25 percent, although the EPA can adjust this standard upward or downward to as low as 20 percent in response to concerns of feasibility and cost (phase II reformulated gasoline performance standards). See the April 16, 1992, Supplemental Notice of Proposed Rulemaking (57 FR 13416) and the February 26, 1993, Notice of Proposed Rulemaking (58 FR 11722), the February 1993 Draft Regulatory Impact Analysis (DRIA), the Final Regulatory Impact Analysis (RIA), and Public Dockets A-91-02 and A-92-12.
34. Ethanol is produced by grinding and then fermenting corn, distilling the result, and adding it to gasoline to make up about 10 percent of the total volume of fuel. Methanol is primarily made from natural gas: the constituent parts are separated and then recombined with oxygen at high pressure and temperature. Methanol is then transformed into an ether compound, usually methyl tertiary butyl ether (MBTE). Gary Lee, "Behind Fuel Additive Decision, A Debate over Corn or Natural Gas," *Washington Post*, August 9, 1994.
35. One gallon of ethanol contains the equivalent of approximately 76,000 British Thermal Units (BTUs); to make a gallon, the Energy Department estimates that 85,000 to 91,000 BTUs are needed, although others argue that 71,000 BTUs is more accurate. Under optimal conditions of raising corn and manufacturing technology for ethanol that is not now widely used, that figure may drop to about 58,000 BTUs. Ethyl Tertiary Butyl Ether (ETBE) reduces the Reid Vapor Pressure (RVP), a measure of fuel's evaporative character, by 75 percent. Lee, "Behind Fuel Additive Decision."
36. Daniel Southerland, "U.S. Study Questions Ethanol's Effect on Pollution," *Washington Post*, August 8, 1994.
37. Michael Weiskopf, "Clean Air Power: EPA's Man With a Mission," *Washington Post*, December 7, 1990. For an interesting account of Rosenberg and the development of the reformulated gas rule, see Edward Weber, "Clean Air, Transaction Costs, and the Case of the Clean Fuels Negotiated Rulemaking," paper presented at the annual meeting of the American Political Science Association, New York (September 1-4, 1994).
38. 59 FR 7717 (February 16, 1994).
39. "Consensus Still Not Reached on Proposal for Reformulated Gas, Oxygenated Fuels," *Environmental Reporter* 22 (June 14, 1991): 333-334.

40. 59 FR 7717 (February 16, 1994).
41. 56 FR 31176 (July 9, 1991).
42. 57 FR 13416 (April 16, 1992).
43. 58 FR 11722 (February 26, 1993).
44. 59 FR 7716 (February 16, 1994). Copies of the preamble, the Final Regulatory Impact Analysis (RIA), the Responses to Comments on Enforcement Provisions (RCEP), the complex model, the simple model, and the regulations for the reformulated gasoline rule making are available on the OAQPS Technology Transfer Network Bulletin Board System (TTNBBS). The TTNBBS can be accessed with a dial-in phone line and a high-speed modem (919-541-5742).
45. Weber, "Clean Air, Transaction Costs."
46, Keith Schneider, "Bush Offers Plan for Wider Use of Ethanol in Fuel," *New York Times,* October 2, 1992; and "Bush Grants Evaporative Limit Waiver for Ethanol," *Environmental Reporter* 23 (October 9, 1992).
47. Keith Schneider, "Clinton Is Seeking to Increase Role for Ethanol in Gasoline," *New York Times,* December 15, 1992.
48. 59 FR 7716 (February 16, 1994).
49. EPA, "Renewable Fuels to be Included."
50. "Regulation of Fuels and Fuel Additives: Renewable Oxygenate Requirement for Reformulated Gas," 59 FR 39258 (August 2, 1994).
51. Timothy Noah, "EPA Came Through for Archer-Daniels-Midland Soon After Andreas's Role at Presidential Dinner," *Wall Street Journal,* July 6, 1994.
52. Gary Lee, "EPA Backs Ethanol for Fuel," *Washington Post,* July 1, 1994; "EPA to Require Cleaner-Burning Gas in Polluted Areas," *Washington Post,* July 1, 1994.
53. Hearing before the Subcommittee on VA, HUD, and Independent Agencies of the House Committee on Appropriations Regarding the EPA, May 5, 1994.
54. Letter to Rep. David R. Obey, chairman of the Appropriations Committee, from Rep. John Dingell, June 14, 1994, with an attachment containing Rep. Dean A. Gallo's amendment.
55. Letter to Sen. Thomas A. Daschle from Carol Browner, July 21, 1994.
56. See "Dear Colleague" letter from Sens. Malcolm Wallop and Bill Bradley, February 2, 1994; letter from Senators Wallop and Bradley and three other senators to Carol Browner, February 2, 1994.
57. *American Petroleum Institute v. Browner,* Court of Appeals for the District of Columbia, 94-1138 (February 24, 1994).
58. Advertisement, "Paul Harvey and . . . The Rest of the Story on Ethanol," *Wall Street Journal,* June 22, 1994.
59. Advertisement, "Truth Alert #4," *Washington Post,* July 21, 1994.
60. Advertisement, "Truth Alert #3," *Washington Post,* July 15, 1994.
61. *Congressional Record* (August 3, 1994): S 10433.
62. "Johnston Amendment to Block EPA Funding of 'Ethanol Mandate' Defeated," *Clean Air Report* 5 (August 11, 1994): 1.
63. *Congressional Record* (August 3, 1994): S 10489. See S 10433-10489 for the Senate debate over the ethanol mandate.
64. "Johnston Amendment," 3.
65. Mobil Oil advertisement, "When is a deal, a deal?" *New York Times,* September 22, 1994.
66. EPA, Office of Air and Radiation, "Implementation Strategy," 43-44.

67. Ibid., 44-45; "Update, May 1994," 1-13.
68. EPA, *1992 Toxics Release Inventory* (Washington, D.C.: EPA, 1994), 261-264.
69. EPA, Office of Air and Radiation, "Implementation Strategy," 43-44.
70. William R. Cline, *The Economics of Global Warming* (Washington, D.C.: Institute for International Economics, 1992).
71. EPA, "Update, May 1994," 1-13.
72. By 1995, utilities can emit no more than 8.9 million tons of sulfur dioxide, down from their 1980 release of 19 million tons. See discussion in Chapter 4.
73. Tom Howard, "Demand For Low-sulfur Coal Increases," *Billings (Montana) Gazette,* April 13, 1994.
74. Michael J. Walsh, "Potential for Derivative Instruments on Sulfur Dioxide Emission Reduction Credits," *Derivatives Quarterly* (Fall 1994): 5.
75. Martha M. Hamilton, "Selling Pollution Rights Cuts the Cost of Cleaner Air," *Washington Post,* August 24, 1994.
76. Matthew L. Wald, "Risk-Shy Utilities Avoid Trading Emission Credits," *New York Times,* January 25, 1993.
77. Martha M. Hamilton, "TVA to Buy Pollution 'Credits' from Wisconsin Utility: History-Making Deal to Help Giant Electric Producer Meet Clean Air Requirements," *Washington Post,* May 12, 1992.
78. Matthew L. Wald, "Utility Is Selling Right to Pollute," *New York Times,* May 12, 1992.
79. Margaret Kriz, "Emission Control," *National Journal* 26 (July 3, 1994): 1699.
80. Walsh, "Potential for Derivative Instruments," 6-7.
81. Margaret Kriz, "Emission Control," 1699.
82. Walsh, "Potential for Derivative Instruments," 3-4.
83. Ibid., 5-6.
84. Margaret Kriz, "Emission Control," 1698.
85. Tom Howard, "'Civil War' Looms Over Clean Coal," *Billings (Montana) Gazette,* November 15, 1992.
86. Illinois statute, 220 ILCS 5/8-402.1(a).
87. *Alliance for Clean Coal v. Miller,* 1995 U.S. App. LEXIS 460 (7th Cir. 1995), at 11.
88. South Coast Air Quality Management District, RECLAIM: Program Summary and Rules (1993).
89. Organisation for Economic Cooperation and Development, *International Economic Instruments and Climate Change* (Paris: OECD, 1993).
90. EPA, "Update, May 1994," 1-13.
91. EPA, "Implementation Strategy," 51-52.
92. *Greenwire,* January 19, 1995.
93. EPA, "Update, May 1994," iii.
94. For a general critique, see James DeLong, *Informal Rulemaking and the Integration of Law and Policy,* 65 VA. L. REV. (1979) 257.
95. See, generally, Bruce Smart, *Beyond Compliance: A New Industry View of the Environment* (Washington, D.C.: World Resources Institute, 1992).
96. Will Nixon, "The Air Down Here: Four Years after Its Passage, the 1990 Clean Air Act Is Coming to Crisis," *The Amicus Journal* 16 (Summer 1994): 42-45.
97. U.S. Congress, Senate, Committee on Environment and Public Works, *Three Years Later: Report Card on the 1990 Clean Air Act Amendments* (Washington, D.C.: GPO, 1993), viii-ix.

98. Quoted in Senate Committee on Environment and Public Works, *Three Years Later,* 61.
99. Declaration of EPA Associate Administrative or Mary Nichols, *Natural Resources Defense Council v. Browner,* Nos. 92-1596, 93-1004 (D.C. Cir. 1994), appendix.
100. EPA, "Update, May 1994."
101. See Theodore Lowi, *The End of Liberalism,* 2d ed. (New York: W. W. Norton, 1979), 302-303.
102. For a useful discussion of options for reforming regulatory processes, see Cass R. Sunstein, *After the Rights Revolution: Reconceiving the Regulatory State* (Cambridge, Mass.: Harvard University Press, 1990), esp. 74-110.
103. While any agency can form negotiating committees, enactment of the Administrative Dispute Resolution Act of 1990 has facilitated these efforts. 104 Stat. 2737 (1990), 5 U.S.C. 581 note. The act orders federal agencies to develop policies for alternative means of dispute resolution, outlines some possible approaches agencies might take, provides for confidentiality of negotiations, and provides for arbitration of disputes involving agencies. The Negotiated Rulemaking Act of 1990 amends the Administrative Procedure Act to provide for negotiated rule making; it outlines the major elements of the process, including publication of notice, application for membership on the negotiating committee, the formation of the committee, the committee's activities, the role of the mediator, and standards for judicial review. PL 101-648 (1990), 5 U.S.C. 581 et seq. (1993).
104. The other reg-negs include the following:

    RCRA Minor Permit Modifications: The committee met between September 1986 and February 1987; the EPA proposed a rule based on the reg-neg in September 1987. The rule created a permit modification system for hazardous waste management facilities.

    Asbestos in Schools: The committee was chartered in February 1987; the proposed rule was issued on April 30 of that year. Several nonsignatories challenged the rule in court, but the EPA prevailed. The rule established an inspection and response program for asbestos in schools.

    Recycling of Acid Lead Batteries: The committee met between January and September 1991; the EPA then concluded that the benefits to be achieved from mandating the 100 percent recycling of automotive, telecommunications, and standby power batteries did not justify the costs, and the effort was abandoned.

    Underground Injections: Chartered in 1986, the committee concluded its work seven months later without achieving consensus on how to regulate the injection of hazardous wastes into underground areas. The EPA issued a rule in 1987 that was unsuccessfully challenged by industry and environmental groups.

    Revision of the Hazardous Waste Manifest: Negotiations began in October 1992 and were completed successfully in December 1993. The rule would establish requirements for information concerning the movement of hazardous wastes.

    Disinfection By-products: The committee met between November 1992 and June 1993; the EPA is still working on final language for the proposed rule. It would regulate the use of chemicals to purify drinking water.

Farmworker Protection Standards: A committee met for four months in 1985 and produced an agreement that resulted in a proposed rule in 1988 and a final rule in 1992 mandating standards for farmworker protective clothing and other issues.

Emergency Pesticide Exemptions: The EPA created a committee in August 1984, consensus was reached in January 1985, and a final regulation was issued in January 1986.

105. The information here is summarized from Chris Kurtz, "Negotiated Rulemaking at the EPA" (unpublished report, May 21, 1994).

106. The process of producing coke includes several steps: (1) coal is loaded into the ovens (the charging phase); (2) the coal is heated by burning air and waste gas from previous cycles of coke production for 15 to 30 hours at about 1000° until it becomes coke (the coking phase); and (3) the coke is pushed out into quench cars and transported to a quenching tower, where it is drenched with water and prepared for further use (the pushing phase). Most of the gas in coke ovens is recycled and retained in the oven, but some gases escape during each of the phases through the opening of topside lids and the push and quench car side doors, cracks in the oven walls, leaks in the pipes that collect the coke oven's by-product chemicals, and emissions of the gases burned to keep the oven walls hot (these emissions are relatively pollution-free unless the oven walls have cracks that leak fumes from the coke). The most serious health risks result from leaks around the doors on the front and back ends of the oven because emissions occur during the first stage of the process when the most toxic chemicals in the coal are burned. Smoke produced when the coke is pushed out of the oven and cooled in the quenching tower is usually trapped by a hooding system and collected into a bag house, where the dust is accumulated on cloth filters, but releases can also occur here. Coke oven emissions pose a greater cancer risk for more people than any other kind of industrial air pollution. See John D. Graham and David Holtgrave, *Coke Oven Emissions: A Case Study of "Technology-Based" Regulation,* Library of Congress, Congressional Research Service (Sept. 20, 1989), 2-3; and Natural Resources Defense Council, *A New Chance to Clean Up the Coke Ovens* (Washington, D.C.: NRDC, 1991).

107. The emissions also include trace metals (cadmium, chromium, lead, and nickel) and gases (hydrogen sulfide, carbon monoxide, nitric oxide, and sulfur dioxide). Most of the regulatory concern has focused on tar pitch volatiles, particularly benzene soluble organics that are highly toxic. Graham and Holtgrave, *Coke Oven Emissions,* 4-5.

108. 52 FR 13587 (April 23, 1987). In 1989, EPA administrator William K. Reilly submitted to Congress an estimate of the health risk posed by the forty-four coke ovens operating in the United States. The level of risk depends on the volume of pollutant, its potency, and the proximity of the exposed population. Risk was estimated by projecting the number of cancer cases that might occur if individuals were exposed to a "constant ambient air concentration of one microgram of benzene soluble organics in a cubic meter of air breathed over a lifetime of 70 years," and if they lived within two-tenths of a kilometer from the facility. See EPA, "A Region VIII EPA Fact Sheet Concerning the Risk Estimates for the Geneva Coke Oven Facility in Provo, Utah," n.d. The maximum individual lifetime cancer risks associated with exposure to coke

oven emissions ranged from about 1 in 100 to 1 in 10,000. For eight plants the additional risk of cancer imposed on nearby residents is 1 case for every 100 exposed persons; for 24 plants, 1 for every 1,000; for 30 of 31 plants, 1 for every 10,000. The risk factor for the coke ovens operating in Orem, Utah, for example, was 1.1 in 100, or about one chance in 90, among the highest in the United States. The administrator concluded that "estimates of facility-specific cancer risks are highly uncertain; any risk estimate of 1 in 1,000 and greater are of serious concern." Letter from William K. Reilly, EPA administrator, to Rep. Henry A. Waxman, chairman of the Subcommittee on Health and the Environment, Energy and Commerce Committee, June 21, 1989.

109. The law specifies that MACT is to be based on the average of the best-performing, least-polluting 12 percent of existing coke ovens or the standards for coke oven emissions (specified in the law), whichever is more stringent. EPA was also required to establish work practices for coke ovens by December 31, 1992, and standards to reduce the residual risk, after MACT standards are in place, by December 31, 2001. Coke oven facilities were required to comply with the work practice standards by November 8, 1993; with the MACT standards by December 31, 1995; and with the residual risk standards by December 31, 2001 (2003 if a two-year waiver was granted). Companies choosing this approach were considered to be on the MACT track. Clean Air Act of 1990, section 112(8); EPA, Coke Oven Emissions Data (Oct. 11, 1991), 4; letter from Amanda Agnew, Standards Development Branch, EPA, Sept. 3, 1991.

110. David Doninger and Blakeman Early, "An Invitation to Join the Clean Steel Network" (May, 1991).

111. Clean Steel Network, Clean Steel Networking Group (Oct. 11, 1991).

112. EPA Negotiating Committee for Coke Oven Standards, Organizational Protocols (April 20, 1992), 1-2.

113. Ibid., 2-6.

114. Ibid., 3-4.

115. EPA Advisory Committee Charter, Organization and Functions Committees, Boards, Panels, and Councils, National Emission Standards for Coke Oven Batteries Advisory Committee (Dec. 31, 1991).

116. Memorandum from David Doninger to Clean Steel Network, October 31, 1991.

117. Memorandum from Philip J. Harter to Negotiating Committee for Coke Oven Standards, January 15, 1992.

118. Memorandum from David Doninger to Clean Steel Network, March 19, 1992.

119. Memorandum from David Doninger to Clean Steel Network, October 22, 1992.

120. Ibid., 5-6.

121. Letter from David Doninger, Natural Resources Defense Council, and Blakeman Early, Sierra Club, Oct. 4, 1991.

122. Philip Harter, "Negotiated Regulations: A Cure for Malaise," 71 *Georgetown Law Journal* (1982): 1, 19, 29.

123. See Roger Fisher and William Ury, *Getting to Yes* (New York: Penguin, 1991) for a discussion of the value of negotiations.

124. Harter, "Negotiated Regulations," 49-50.

125. Ibid., 51.
126. Ibid., 21, 30.
127. Ibid., 87-89.
128. Ibid., 84-85.
129. 5 U.S.C. alp 1-15 (1993).
130. Barry Commoner, *Making Peace with the Planet* (New York: Pantheon, 1990); Robert W. Crandall, and Lester B. Lave, *The Scientific Basis of Health and Safety Regulation* (Washington, D.C.: Brookings Institution, 1981); and John D. Graham, Laura C. Green, and Marc J. Roberts, *In Search of Safety: Chemicals and Cancer Risk* (Cambridge, Mass.: Harvard University Press, 1988).
131. For an overview of the issues involved in preemption, see Joseph F. Zimmerman, *Federal Preemption: The Silent Revolution* (Ames, Iowa: Iowa State University Press, 1991).
132. See, generally, Joseph F. Zimmerman and Deirdre A. Zimmerman, eds., *The Politics of Subnational Governance.* (Lanham, Md.: University Press of America, 1983).
133. Section 126 (42 U.S.C. 7426).
134. Section 176A (42 U.S.C. 7506a).
135. The commission is to be comprised of the governor of each affected state, the EPA administrator, the regional administrator of each region affected (each of whom may designate a representative to sit on the commission), and an air pollution control official representing each affected state.
136. Memorandum, Clean Air Network, March 15, 1994.
137. Memorandum, Clean Air Network, May 16, 1994.
138. One of the earliest efforts to organize states was the Mid-Atlantic Pollution Control Compact, created by Governor Nelson Rockefeller of New York. See Zimmerman and Zimmerman, eds., *The Politics of Subnational Governance.* In 1990, the Mid-Atlantic Regional Air Management Association was formed by Delaware, Maryland, New Jersey, North Carolina, Pennsylvania, Virginia, the District of Columbia, Philadelphia, and Allegheny County (Pittsburgh area) to develop policies for monitoring air pollution and regulating ozone and air toxics. See *Environmental Reporter,* 20 (March 2, 1990): 1818.
139. Section 184 (42 U.S.C. 7511 C).
140. "Northeast Air Administrators to Adopt California Emission Control Program," *Environmental Reporter* 20 (August 18, 1989): 687-688.
141. 59 FR 48666 (September 22, 1994).
142. "Northeastern, Mid-Atlantic States to Opt into Reformulated Gasoline Plan," *Clean Air Report* 2 (November 7, 1991): 14-15.
143. Interview with Michael Bradley, NESCAUM director, in *Clean Air Report* 2 (March 28, 1991): T-14.
144. "Northeast Transport Group to Discuss Merits of Clean Gas, Fuel Programs," *Clean Air Report* 2 (September 12, 1991): 19.
145. Matthew L. Wald, "Harder Auto Emission Rules Agreed to by Eastern States," *New York Times,* February 2, 1994.
146. 59 FR 48666 (September 22, 1994).
147. The U.S. auto industry, as of the summer of 1994, offered for sale several alternative fuel vehicles powered by methanol, ethanol, natural gas, liquefied petroleum gas, and electricity. The industry argued, however, that there was

very limited market demand for these vehicles, and government policy should not mandate their sale. Memorandum, American Automobile Manufacturers Association, "Alternative Fuel Vehicles" (June 1, 1994), 2.

148. The Chrysler Corporation, for example, indicated that converting one of its Caravan/Voyager vans to electric power would cost $83,303 (in addition to the base price of a vehicle). This is apparently the source of a widely cited figure by the auto industry that electric vehicles currently cost $100,000 to produce. While the auto industry calculates the cost of electric vehicles by using a large minivan, others propose small, subcompact vehicles that would have a much lower price. See American Automobile Manufacturers Association, "Alternative Fuel Vehicles."

149. *Electric Power Alert* (February 2, 1994): 24-25.

150. "OTC to Petition EPA for Regional Low Emission Vehicle Program," *Clean Air Report* 5 (February 10, 1994): 3-4.

151. Oscar Suris, "Regulators Back Electric Vehicles For Northeast," *Wall Street Journal*, February 2, 1994.

152. "Automakers Eye Beefed-up 'Federal LEV' Program for Northeast," *Clean Air Report* 5 (May 19, 1994): 9-10.

153. "NESCAUM Sets Plan for State Fleets to Buy Alternative Fuel Vehicles," *Clean Air Report* 5 (April 7, 1994): 13.

154. Comments to the EPA on the Notice of Proposed Rulemaking for the Ozone Transport Commission petition to adopt California Low Emission Vehicle Standards from forty-four citizen/environmental organizations, June 3, 1994.

155. Letter to EPA Administrator Carol Browner from Sens. Max Baucus, Barbara Boxer, Daniel Patrick Moynihan, James M. Jeffords, Patrick J. Leahy, and John Kerry.

156. Not for attribution interview with official of environmental group (September 20, 1994).

157. "LEV Roundtables Ready EPA for November Decision," *Northeast Air Report* (Summer 1994): 4; and "EPA to Hold Meetings on States' Request for California Program," *Clean Air Report* 5 (April 21, 1994): 17.

158. "EPA Receives Testimony on California Car Program," *Clean Air Report* 5 (May 5, 1994): 8.

159. Statement of Mary D. Nichols delivered to the Clean Air Act Advisory Subcommittee on Voluntary Vehicle Standards, September 13, 1994.

160. Matthew L. Wald, "EPA Urges an Auto Pollution Compromise, Suggesting Easier Standards for the Northeast," *New York Times*, September 14, 1994.

161. 59 FR 48664, 48667-48668 (September 22, 1994).

162. Matthew L. Wald, "EPA Seeks Compromise On Auto Emissions in East," *New York Times*, November 10, 1994.

163. Interview with John Seitz, EPA Office of Air Quality Planning and Standards, *Clean Air Report* 5 (June 2, 1994): T7-T8.

164. EPA, "Update, May 1994," 1.

6 Formulating and Implementing Clean Air Policy: An Assessment

The enactment of the Clean Air Act Amendments of 1990 was a historic achievement in the development of environmental policy. The amendments addressed many problems left unresolved by the 1970 and 1977 laws and created an exhaustive set of new prescriptions to increase the likelihood that clean air goals will be met. Area sources have been brought under regulation, and new requirements imposed to address acid rain, air toxics, and CFCs. The amendments make clean air policy more consistent with other environmental laws; penalties for violations of the law, for example, are equivalent to those under the Clean Water Act. (The permitting system aimed at controlling water pollution also served as the model for the Clean Air Act's new permitting program.)

The 1990 amendments provide an extensive set of new deadlines that take into account the seriousness of the pollution problems facing many areas, and allow more time for compliance than did the 1970 act (most of the deadlines of which were never met). Provisions of the law specify in great detail the schedule to be followed and the steps to be taken by the EPA and the states in implementing the law. Administrative discretion is further limited by the use of legislative hammers that are sufficiently stringent to provide an incentive for the EPA, the states, and the regulated industries to take action before the default provisions in the law take effect. In some areas, such as motor vehicle emissions, the 1990 amendments will force the development of new technologies in order to meet the standards; in other areas, existing technologies (such as the maximum achievable control technologies required for sources of hazardous air pollutants) will likely be adapted and employed more widely.

Act 1 of the Clean Air Act has ended. Act 2, devoted to establishing the regulatory framework, is well underway, and Act 3, implementation of clean air regulations by the states (and, to a lesser extent, the EPA) is now the primary focus of attention. The experience of the first four years of implementation, as reviewed in Chapter 5, demonstrates how much has been done to put this regulatory framework in place. In comparison with implementation efforts under previous clean air statutes and other environmental laws, the EPA's work has been impressive; the agency has issued more rules and standards than many people had thought possible. Despite

236

a slow start in 1991 and early 1992, the pace quickened considerably by the end of 1992, and a number of major regulations were completed in 1993 and 1994. The structure for many clean air programs is largely in place.

The implementation of these regulations by states, as they revise implementation plans and put in place permitting and air toxics programs, is behind schedule, however, and that delay is what the tension over clean air regulation is now focused on. Since the Clean Air Act Amendments of 1990 mandated a thirty-year program to improve air quality, the experience of the first four years can only hint at the prospects for actually achieving the goals. Given the history of implementation of the Clean Air Act, it is unlikely that the 1990 law will be an unqualified success. Its demands for action may outstrip the supply of available expertise, resources, and political will.

One way to assess the amendments more fully is to return to the basic steps of the policy-making process and seek answers to our questions: (1) How well did Congress and the executive branch understand the nature of air pollution in drafting the 1990 amendments to the Clean Air Act? (2) How well did they manage the political pressures, and to what extent did they consider the economic and scientific analyses that emerged during the legislative process? (3) How well did they provide for the effective implementation of the law by the EPA and the states? and (4) To what extent will they be willing to assess the effectiveness of the law and to make adjustments as new technologies are developed and new problems emerge? Underlying these questions is a broader one: What will be the impact of their experience in drafting and enacting the 1990 law on the capacity of government to achieve other important public policy goals?

Initiation and Definition

There is still some debate over whether air pollution problems are so serious that new regulatory controls are needed, or whether they will be resolved with advances in industrial activity (as a result of technological innovations, for example). But a rapidly growing body of literature, reviewed in Chapter 2, points to the conclusion that community air pollution is a major public health concern, responsible for tens of thousands of premature deaths and many more cases of hospitalization, illness, and lost work, as well as other social costs. People do not always choose to subject themselves to community air pollution, and the beneficiaries of the pollution-producing activities are usually not the individuals who bear the heaviest health burdens. These distributional consequences create pressure on governments to act despite limited scientific knowledge. Clean air is one of our greatest and most critical natural resources; we cannot afford to be less than vigilant in protecting it for ourselves and our children.

By reducing pollution levels, we can do much to improve health in our communities. This is the good news—in contrast to our difficulties in remedying many other diseases and health problems, we can significantly reduce disease and the number of deaths by reducing levels of air pollution, particularly PM_{10}. We can also save money by reducing health care expenditures, job losses, and other consequences of air pollution. The American Lung Association's 1995 report on particulate pollution found that nearly 2,000 premature deaths, thousands of emergency room and hospital visits, and 140,000 cases of acute bronchitis in children and 13,000 cases in adults could be prevented if the national PM_{10} standard were made as strict as the current California standard. (California adopted a PM_{10} standard in 1982, five years before the federal standard, that requires a much lower level of particulates in the atmosphere—no more than 50 $\mu g/m^3$ during any twenty-four-hour period, compared with the federal standard of 150 $\mu g/m^3$.) That would translate into a savings of some $11 billion a year in reduced medical costs and days missed at work.[1] Improved enforcement of environmental laws can help remedy the injustices that occur, as minorities and low-income individuals are more likely to be adversely affected by pollution than others.[2] The challenge is that these efforts will require effective political leadership and a great deal of energy as well as the willingness of individuals and corporations to change the way they live—they must produce less waste, use mass transit more often, and invest in more efficient uses of energy and other resources.

The economic consequences of compliance with air pollution laws and regulations continue to attract widespread attention. It is clear that, in the short run, there are some economic advantages to be gained from utilizing conventional processes that release pollution. In the long run, however, environmental degradation threatens the viability of industrial activity; investments to ensure environmental quality over time make economic sense. But an orientation to long-run concerns is not characteristic of many corporate executives and politicians.

Fortunately, we can take action to protect our health and at the same time promote a healthy economy. A high quality of life is a prerequisite for economic activity. Cleaner, more efficient industries will also, in the long run, be more profitable. Concerns about the decreased competitiveness of U.S. firms have frequently been voiced in the debate over clean air, but incentives and sanctions that encourage or force U.S. firms to become more efficient and less polluting or wasteful will in the long run yield significant economic benefits. Other countries are already moving in this direction. Japanese and German companies are very active in the market for pollution control equipment, but U.S. firms still have an opportunity to make real progress in capturing global markets. As resources become more scarce, prices will increase, and more efficient, less wasteful processes will translate into lower prices. Economic and environmental goals can be pursued together if industries and individuals adopt a creative and flexible approach.

Historically there has been little choice but to accept the inevitability of pollution as the price of economic growth. But there are tremendous opportunities for achieving environmental goals in ways that promise economic benefits as well. Regulation results in a redistribution of economic benefits and burdens, however, and the challenge facing political leaders is to manage that distribution so that it promotes both public health and economic activity. Some practices and approaches will have to be temporarily suspended or permanently ended. There will be short-term dislocations, but in the long run the reduced waste and improved environmental conditions that result will be essential to our economic future.

The real costs of improving air quality have been and will continue to be a burden for old, dirty industries, especially those that have delayed modernization, and will produce layoffs and other problems because some sources of pollution must be shut down to protect public health. Companies that are having trouble competing in global markets will readily point to environmental laws and regulations as the explanation for their difficulties, when the real problems have been poor management and the maximizing of short-run returns at the expense of long-run productivity.[3] In the short run, effective environmental regulations will be disruptive— one reason they are often not enforced. But once industries get beyond the short-run disruptions, they will find that most economic and environmental objectives are compatible. Global and domestic demand for cleaner processes and products will increase, given trends in pollution and environmental degradation, and clean companies will have more opportunities open to them.[4]

The initial successful attempts to reduce emissions of air toxics and ozone-depleting substances, discussed in Chapters 4 and 5, have emphasized the economic advantages of reducing pollution. These gains are likely to continue as more companies develop new technologies and comply with the regulations, and if some state regulatory initiatives continue to exceed federal standards. It will become more difficult to take seriously dramatic predictions by industry representatives that environmental regulation means the destruction of American business.[5]

Formulation and Enactment

From the perspective of the political process, the evolution of the Clean Air Act Amendments of 1990 is instructive. In 1988, the time seemed ripe to debate new environmental legislation. Candidate George Bush, having served as chairman of the Reagan administration's Presidential Task Force on Regulatory Relief (1981-1983 and 1986-1988), had discovered the political potential of environmental policy as a means of generating political support from the general public as well as from regulated industries. He deftly balanced accommodation to industry concerns about the costs of regulation with responsiveness to public support for effective protection of public health and the environment.[6] Considerable progress had been made in scientific research on the health effects of air pollution, and environmental protection was increasingly viewed as a public health issue rather than as the conservation of ecological systems. Concern about global air pollution had been intensified by research findings on the destruction of the stratospheric ozone layer and theories of global warming. The opening of Eastern Europe had revealed to the world the consequences of ignoring air pollution problems.

Given this promising climate, it might seem strange that Congress took so long to revise the 1970 act, even though many of its deadlines and goals had not been met, but there are so many possible points in the legislative process at which initiatives can be killed that such inaction should not be a surprise. Would there have been a clean air bill in 1990 without the president's active support? Many observers and participants in the debates have said no. The Senate came close to passing a bill in 1988; Rep. John Dingell (D-Mich.) would eventually have had to give in to Rep. Henry Waxman (D-Calif.). The president's involvement meant that the bill was probably passed sooner, and was more stringent, than it would have been if it had been the result of deliberations alone.

Although the Bush administration rightly claimed much of the credit for gaining enactment of the 1990 amendments, the 1988 Bush presidential campaign was widely criticized as a cynical attempt to manipulate and downgrade certain issues, including environmental ones, for political advantage.[7] Nevertheless, the Bush administration did move in 1989 to prepare clean air legislation, as promised in the campaign. The president's speech announcing the proposed clean air legislation was widely heralded as a strong statement in favor of protection of public health and environmental quality. But when the text of the bill was made public, praise turned to criticism, for many groups saw in the details a retreat from Bush's earlier broad claims. The administration was ever responsive to business demands to soften the impact of provisions on that sector, and furthermore, effective lobbying by the auto industry caused the White House to strike the provision requiring production of clean-fuel vehicles in its original bill when it was being considered by the House Energy and Commerce Committee.

As the discussion in Chapter 2 indicated, when the Senate was debating the bill in February and March 1990, the administration appeared to care more that the president's cost ceiling not be breached than about the content of the provisions and their consequences for air quality. Nor was there a hint of cost-benefit analysis, of a willingness to consider more stringent regulatory controls if they promised a wide range of significant health benefits. Cost is hardly the sole consideration in formulating an appropriate environmental policy, and the exclusion of other factors is rather hypocritical, given the Reagan-Bush rhetoric promising cost-benefit analysis in the review of all regulations issued by federal agencies.[8] This narrow focus led administration officials to make arbitrary and sometimes unrealistic estimates of compliance costs. The costs of complying with provisions that will almost certainly have to go into effect, such as those requiring the use of alternative fuels in the dirtiest cities, were not counted because the requirements were not expressly stated. Administration officials even seemed to be as unaware as industry executives of the tremendous economic benefits to be gained from more efficient, less polluting industrial operations. The threat of a presidential veto throughout congressional consideration of the bill also aroused in the public a sense of cynicism about the Bush administration's interest in effective environmental protection. These threats were widely discounted as a response to industry complaints: how could the "environmental president" veto the most important piece of environmental legislation in the past ten years, which had become such an important part of his domestic agenda?[9]

Another lesson from 1990 is that although the separation of powers is generally blamed for policy deadlock, the regional and ideological divisions in Congress are just as important. House and Senate efforts to amend the Clean Air Act of 1970 differed considerably. The Senate Committee on Environment and Public Works had reported out legislation several times over the years, but further action was blocked by Majority Leader Robert Byrd (D-W.Va.), who opposed acid rain controls because of their consequences for West Virginia coal miners. The election of George Mitchell (D-Maine) as majority leader in 1989 was a key development, as described in Chapter 3.

Mitchell's leadership was also instrumental in maintaining the compromise once the bill was presented to the full Senate. A number of amendments designed to strengthen the agreement, generally to replace it with the original committee provisions, were all defeated. Mitchell and Minority Leader Robert Dole (R-Kan.) skillfully used the resources of the Senate leadership. Mitchell called for his colleagues' support and explained that the bill was the best that could be done and that to demand more would doom all chances for a clean air bill in this century. His biggest challenge came when Senator Byrd, at that point the chairman of the powerful Appropriations Committee, proposed the creation of a fund to assist coal miners who would lose their jobs as a result of the Clean Air Act Amendments. Many senators were torn between offending the majority leader and offending the keeper of the purse. The measure failed by a vote of 49-50, giving Mitchell a slim but significant victory in the battle for control of the Senate. In contrast to the Senate Committee on Environment and Public Works, the House Energy and Commerce Committee had not reported out a clean air bill for nearly a decade. John Dingell, then chairman of the House committee, thought that new legislation would impose unreasonable burdens on the auto industry, which, in his view, had already done more than its share to reduce air pollution. He also argued that more stringent regulation aimed at other industries would result in widespread unemployment and reduce the competitiveness of American industry in international markets.

House subcommittee politics was also dominated by regional differences. The Subcommittee on Health and the Environment, chaired by Henry Waxman, reported out aggressive clean air legislation in the 1980s, but not without controversy. Dingell was able to pick up a few other Democratic votes and combine them with those of the Republicans to block some of the Waxman proposals. Members were constantly having to choose between supporting the subcommittee chairman and the full committee chairman. Once the Senate had acted on the clean air bill, the House Committee on Energy and Commerce was pressured to take action. Dingell continued to play a crucial role. He and the ranking Republican, Norman Lent (R-N.Y.), who had cosponsored the president's bill in the House, introduced a revision of that bill, but Dingell still sought to distance himself from it; some observers believed that he was content to sit on it and perhaps even sought to kill it. Pressures on the committee to reach an agreement came from a number of sources. Dingell and Waxman caught everyone off guard with a compromise on tailpipe emissions in November 1989. Action was again stalled until late March and early April, when the Dingell-Waxman-Lent troika began their own closed-door negotiating sessions, this time without inviting representatives from the White House, and reached a series of compromises that were accepted by the full committee.

Clearly, as noted previously, politics and personalities are intimately intertwined. The history of the Clean Air Act would probably have been much different if individuals other than Henry Waxman, John Dingell, and George Mitchell, representing different geographical regions, had held leadership positions in Congress, and someone else had been president.

The debates over the 1990 amendments also provide a useful case study of congressional politics. Environmental groups, particularly those belonging to the National Clean Air Coalition, coordinated congressional lobbying and grass-roots letter-writing and phone campaigns to put pressure on members of Congress, many of whom were sensitive to charges reported in their districts that they were taking anti-environment positions. The Senate Committee on Environment and Public Works passed its version of the bill rather quickly and with little opposition, but a major lobbying and media blitz by the Clean Air Working Group (the industry coalition) and representatives of key industries aroused such concern among senators about the costs of many proposals that the specter of a filibuster appeared. White House lobbying was also effective in raising objections to the Senate committee bill by opposing provisions that would increase projected compliance costs beyond $22 billion a year.

From a political perspective, the Clean Air Act Amendments of 1990 are a success and are evidence that divided government can work. The lesson to be learned is that breakthroughs require concentrated effort; they were achieved because the White House gave priority to the issue and Congress held exhaustive, time-consuming intramural negotiations and attended to delicate brokering of interests. But the good will engendered by passage of the legislation has already begun to dissipate in the face of congressional attempts to unravel the agreement. The success of this kind of legislative effort may ultimately lie in the ability of Congress and the executive branch to address more effectively the imperatives of implementation and the politics of administration.

From a policy perspective, the success of the 1990 act is ambiguous. The Clean Air Act Amendments of 1990 rely largely on the traditional command-and-control approach to regulation, which will likely continue to come under attack. Congress and the executive branch will continue to explore, particularly in light of the initial success of the acid rain program, how the weaknesses of the conventional approach can be overcome and whether there are more effective regulatory strategies. Some provisions of the act will become technologically obsolete and will need to be revised.

There are numerous possible explanations for the failure to enact major pieces of environmental legislation since the 1990 Clean Air Act Amendments. The support of the president and the House and Senate leadership, so evident in 1990, did not reappear in 1993 and 1994 as Congress and the president focused their attention on health care. Former majority leader George Mitchell, in reflecting on the clean air debate in Congress, observed in 1991 that "a decade is long enough for any one subject. I would like to devote the next decade to another subject. I had in mind the health care issue. I hope it doesn't take me ten years."[10] After only two years of health reform debate, however, Senator Mitchell retired. By this time, in 1993, the Senate Republicans were able to block passage of virtually every bill they wanted to, as part of their political strategy to gain control of the House and Senate in the 1994 election.

The Superfund program, for example, has been widely criticized for delays, high costs, and little environmental improvement. The Clinton administration prepared House and Senate bills, introduced early in 1994, that would have set uniform standards for site cleanups; encouraged proportional distribution of costs; used arbitration rather than litigation in settling disputes; used federal funds to pay for cleanups when responsible parties could not be held liable, rather than making other parties pay the balance; and established a new fund to pay environmental insurance.[11] The bill had been fashioned in consultation with representatives from industry, environmental, and community groups, and local governments under the National Commission on Superfund. The House Energy and Commerce Committee reported out the bill in May, with no major changes. The House Public Works and Transportation Committee added a requirement that cleanups using federal funds be governed by the Davis-Bacon Act, so that contractors were required to pay the prevailing wage rate. Senate Republicans threatened to refuse to join a conference committee if that provision remained, but House leaders were unable to remove the amendment or to deal with the more than fifty amendments offered to the bill, including major changes such as eliminating retroactive liability for companies that disposed of materials before Superfund was passed in 1980. Environmentalists pressured Congress to include groundwater decontamination requirements in the law. Advocates of cost-benefit analysis insisted on adding that provision to the law as well. The Senate failed to take action, preferring to wait and see if the House would be able to pass a bill. The House stopped work on the bill a few days before adjournment in October 1994.

In another example, the Senate Committee on Environment and Public Works reported out in February 1994 a bill reauthorizing the Clean Water Act, but left out some of the more controversial issues.[12] The House bill was introduced in March 1994 by the chairman of the Public Works and Transportation Committee, but he declined to mark up the bill.[13] Several factors led to the demise of the bill, but most important were disputes over wetlands. Environmentalists have become increasingly concerned about the loss of wetlands, whereas farmers, developers, and advocates of private property rights have charged that wetlands restrictions infringe on the rights of landowners. Other issues, such as how to control runoff from melting snow and rainwater, whether to tighten controls on discharging toxic chemicals, whether to make enforcement efforts more stringent, and whether to expand the act to include groundwater protection, also contributed to congressional failure to reauthorize the act.

The Safe Drinking Water Act requires the EPA to establish a maximum level of contamination for each regulated substance in drinking water; the standard is to be set at the level where no adverse health effects would occur, using the best available control technologies. Criticisms of this zero risk standard led to Senate passage in May 1994 of a bill that would give the EPA more flexibility to consider risk when setting standards, would require cost-benefit analysis for regulations issued under all the major environmental laws, and would give more protection to private property rights.[14] Representative Waxman led opposition to revising the law in the House. On September 27, 1994, the House passed a bill crafted by environmentalists and states that would require the EPA to consider incremental cost increases and resulting risk reductions for carcinogens.[15]

The tension that is part of divided government and political competition, together with the separation of powers and competing institutional prerogatives, poses challenges for the kind of legislation that Congress enacts. Some scholars have long argued the importance of clear statutes that give implementing agencies unambiguous direction and preserve a commitment to the rule of law and limits on bureaucratic discretion. Others argue that the price of political compromise and policy complexity is statutes that blur distinctions and permit differing interpretations.[16] The tension between the two branches of government during the 1980s and into the 1990s has focused debate on the specificity of statutes: Should they minimize discretion, so that congressional will is more likely to prevail? Should they include deadlines for executive action and legislative hammers? Or should laws give administrative officials the kind of discretion and freedom that will permit flexible and efficient administration?[17] Although such debate takes place throughout government, it has been particularly sharp in Congress for environmental legislation, given the great frustration many members had with the EPA during the early years of the Reagan administration, when the ranking agency officials defied their congressional overseers and rejected traditional interpretations of congressional intent surrounding environmental statutes.

Policy Implementation

The Clean Air Act is a quarter of a century old, but only modest progress has been made in implementing its provisions. High levels of traditional air pollutants, for example, have been partially reduced through innovations in control technologies, modernization of plants and equipment, and enforcement efforts. But in many areas, we are only, at best, keeping pollution levels from worsening. That is no small accomplishment, given the growth in population and the economy. Compliance with air quality standards depends on the weather, the level of economic activity, and other factors—as well as the efforts of regulatory agencies. But we are still far from achieving the goal of clean air that meets national air quality standards, especially for particulate and ozone pollution, and protects human health with an adequate margin of safety, as promised in the Clean Air Act of 1970.

The policy-making process cannot be understood as a series of discrete steps, but as a dynamic, "interactive process without beginning or end." It is not a rational, coherent enterprise, but is chaotic and rich in its political content. There may be little agreement over the definition of a certain problem, and some policies may emerge onto the policy agenda by accident or a failure to act. Implementation usually triggers an identification of yet another set of problems, and a solution to the problems of one group often generates a new problem for another set of interests.[18]

There are a number of reasons why environmental policies (as well as other kinds of policies) are implemented incompletely. Our limitations in remedying major social problems, whether environmental degradation or other ills, are rooted in the policy-making process. Many political scientists have argued that a critical shortcoming of implementation is the way in which it is built on permitting access to well-organized interests, which ultimately corrupts and weakens the policy-making process. Discretion in implementing agencies threatens democratic expectations of accountability, responsibility, and, ultimately, the rule of law and individual freedom. It breeds cynicism and criticism as public power is subverted for private ends. Governments become incapable of planning or taking effective action to resolve problems.[19]

Charles E. Lindblom and Edward J. Woodhouse argue that there are several reasons why we have made so little progress in attacking societal problems, and that successful implementation is ultimately a function of our ability to understand problems and develop solutions to them. They believe, however, that the problems we are concerned about are so complex that we do not understand their causes or their solutions. Part of the problem, they argue, is that such complexity simply overwhelms our cognitive abilities; we also lack effective ways to generate and debate alternative perspectives and views. While we have made some progress in measuring social problems and identifying their causes, it has been much more difficult to devise effective policy interventions. Analysis can help identify choices, but most policy questions are ultimately political and thus implicate fundamental conflicts among competing social values.[20]

Paul Sabatier and Daniel Mazmanian have argued that five factors are critical to the success of policy implementation:

- If there is a clear causal theory that connects the policy efforts with the resolution of the problem at issue, there is a greater chance that implementation will be successful.
- The integration of policy efforts across the agencies involved is critical; the lead implementation agency must be able to work with others located horizontally (other federal agencies, for example) as well as those that are vertically related (such as state and local governments).
- Policy decision can specify procedures to be followed, decision rules or criteria to be employed, and other characteristics of implementation that may make it easier or harder to accomplish the intended goals.

(Procedural requirements, for example, can slow down implementation, divert resources, or provide opportunities for opponents to defeat initiatives.)

- The level of commitment to the policy goals of the officials responsible for implementation is also critical. Changed behavior "is unlikely unless officials in the implementing agencies are strongly committed to the achievement of those objectives." New policy interventions may require special leadership efforts to develop new regulations and procedures and enforce them in the face of opposition to change.
- Statutes can also affect the influence that outside groups have on accomplishing policy objectives. Judicial standing may be given to parties to challenge administrative actions or compel nondiscretionary agency performance through citizen suit provisions, for example.[21]

The implementation of the Clean Air Act largely fails to satisfy the conditions for effective implementation. Although there is general agreement that high levels of air pollution are a health hazard, for example, there is no consensus over what exactly constitutes those high levels. A number of important studies published in 1993 and 1994 have raised new concerns about the health effects of particulate pollution. (See Chapter 2.) Strong associations between pollution and increased mortality are shown even at pollution levels below the national air quality standard. The American Lung Association and others sued the EPA in federal district court in Arizona in 1993 for failure to reassess the PM_{10} standard, as required by the Clean Air Act. In October 1994, the court ruled that since the Clean Air Act requires review of national air quality standards at least every five years,[22] the EPA was required to prepare a criteria document for review by the Clean Air Science Advisory Committee by June 1995 and to have a final rule ready for publication by January 31, 1997.[23]

There is constant tension between the EPA and the states over how the Clean Air Act is to be implemented. States demand flexibility and autonomy, and the EPA seeks to impose the same requirements on everyone. Just as difficult for the EPA are relations with other parts of the federal government. Agency officials must deal with the competing pressures of White House review and congressional oversight. Congressional reliance on detailed, agency-forcing provisions and deadlines bumps up against the need for flexibility and adaptability to respond to new scientific research and technological developments. White House officials who are determined to shape regulations according to their own policy concerns and priorities also threaten administrative flexibility and priority setting necessary to deal with complicated regulatory tasks.[24]

In November 1993, the Senate Committee on Environment and Public Works issued a "report card" on the implementation of the act. It gave the

EPA "A" grades for its acid rain and stratospheric ozone programs, a "B-" for its small business assistance program, a "C" for its management of the state implementation plan process, and "D"s for development of the MACT standard and the implementation of the California Low Emission Vehicle Program.[25] The Senate study heralded the success of the acid rain program in devising a market-based approach to environmental regulation, and emphasized the importance of environmental quality-based performance standards that create incentives for the development of new technologies. The value of setting standards and then giving regulated sources the flexibility to achieve them in the most efficient way, rather than having the EPA mandate specific technological standards, and of permitting trading of emission allowances were the two primary lessons to be learned from the first three years of implementing the Clean Air Act. However, the Senate report argued that

[T]he EPA should prioritize better—react more quickly to changes in assumptions about health effects of pollutants, and maximize the effectiveness of its resources by focusing efforts on issues with the largest potential for reducing risk to public health and the environment; and

The EPA should provide greater leadership to the states—be more aggressive in its support for state activities that go beyond the minimum requirements, be firm and fair with states to ensure they meet the minimum standards, and strictly enforce the statutory requirements and issue regulations promptly.[26]

These shortcomings in implementation were serious, but seemed manageable until the dynamics of implementation underwent a fundamental change with the election of Republicans in statehouses and as the new majority party in Congress in November 1994. A major driving force in getting the states to implement programs was the threat of sanctions, and to a lesser extent, the imposition of federal implementation plans. Governors, in response to the election, began challenging the EPA. As long as Congress was there to back up the EPA and reopening the act to weaken its provisions was not an option, the EPA could hold firm and maintain viable threats of sanctions. Since the new Congress took office in 1995, and amending the act has become a real possibility, however, the EPA has had to scramble to be accommodating to state demands as a way to forestall any congressional weakening of the act.

Regulation of stationary sources has always been contentious, as owners have warned of job layoffs and shutdowns in the face of regulatory requirements. During the first years of implementation, efforts focused on industrial polluters. But when the focus shifted to people's driving habits, opposition to clean air action took a quantum leap upward. Disgruntled citizens, joined by industry groups who saw a political opening to gain some regulatory relief, generated considerable opposition to state implementation plans. Especially intense has been the public outcry over regulations aimed at automobiles and the fuels they use. Interviews with citizens indicate a remarkable level of hostility toward requirements that they wait in line to have their cars inspected and use more expensive, cleaner fuel. One driver angrily declared, "Laws like these are meant to be broken."[27] Nevertheless, as one state air quality official put it, the "cheapest controls that will produce the greatest returns are on automobiles."[28] One environmentalist noted that "auto emissions are the only major thing left that can be cut easily and cost-effectively: it's the lowest hanging fruit."[29]

Nowhere has clean air controversy been greater than over the enhanced inspection and maintenance system, developed to replace the traditional tailpipe test required under the Clean Air Act. The test is to be performed every two years at centralized test facilities; owners of vehicles that failed the test could be obligated to pay up to $450 in repairs. (A waiver would be granted if repairs were more expensive.) The EPA required that states with ozone nonattainment areas include the enhanced program as part of their effort to reduce pollution levels by 15 percent by 1996, but in the fall of 1994, several states balked. Motorists and groups representing service station owners who could perform the original testing began criticizing the enhanced I & M program. After California was permitted to develop an alternative system of testing at both centralized locations and traditional service stations, other states began pressing the EPA for exemptions.[30]

New Jersey's pilot program for enhanced I & M was criticized because of long lines and equipment that did not always function properly. In January 1995, the EPA tentatively agreed to permit the state to test vehicles at a single, low speed, rather than at a variety of speeds, making it easier to pass the test, and to use less expensive testing equipment. Texas governor George W. Bush signed a January 1995 law that postponed his state's participation in the vehicle emissions test program for ninety days, and Texas officials promised to get for their state the same concessions given to California. (The EPA granted a ninety-day delay.)[31] The EPA also permitted Michigan to avoid testing in western parts of the state. Georgia state legislators proposed legislation in January 1995 to eliminate centralized emissions testing.[32] Maine residents complained about delays, and then led an all-out attack in the state legislature on the program after the governor permitted state officials to allow decreased emissions resulting from the testing to be offset by increases from a stationary source. Pennsylvania has placed its enhanced I & M program on hold. Maryland exempted cars manufactured before 1984 and after 1994 in its enhanced I & M program, approximately half of the cars in the state. Colorado's auto emissions testing program has been criticized for being too lenient. Arizona's emissions testing program was also mired in delay and technical difficulties.[33]

The EPA promised in December 1994 to give states more flexibility in meeting air quality goals, including the option of reducing the burdens on motor vehicles to reduce emissions, and, in January 1995 gave states an additional year to submit plans for enhanced I & M.[34] However, it is not clear how states will be able to achieve these goals since vehicles are the major source of ozone emissions. Controls on mobile sources appear to be about ten times more cost-effective than controls on stationary sources.

Other programs aimed at reducing vehicle emissions have been just as controversial. Illinois officials complained in early 1995 that the EPA had failed to provide guidance on how states were to require carpooling in companies with more than 100 employees,[35] and Pennsylvania officials excused employers in the Philadelphia area from complying with the carpool requirement.[36] There has also been some confusion as the EPA has retreated in the face of state opposition to some clean air programs. One EPA official was quoted as saying that since "emissions reductions from these [trip-reduction] programs are minuscule, there's not any reason for the EPA to be forcing people to do them from an air quality perspective." In a subsequent letter, she indicated that it was "not within the EPA's ability to make this program voluntary." A few days later, the EPA administrator indicated that enforcing those programs would be the responsibility of state officials, and the EPA "would not look over the shoulder of the states as they implement the program."[37]

The confusion spread to other areas as EPA uncertainty encouraged states and industries to ignore the law. Some EPA officials indicated the agency was exploring giving amnesty to violators of the Clean Air and Clean Water acts if they complied in the future, and was considering becoming more flexible on air pollution controls. Until November 1994, failure to comply with EPA mandates meant the possibility of EPA sanctions, but, more likely, a lawsuit from an environmental group demanding compliance with the act's requirements and accompanying deadlines. Now state officials can threaten to lobby members of Congress to repeal onerous provisions, or at least push back their deadlines, or prohibit the EPA from imposing sanctions. EPA officials indicated that they believed the accommodation on the enhanced I & M program in several states was essential in warding off hostile members of Congress who threatened legislative retaliation for EPA failure to compromise. While Administrator Carol Browner promised to hold firm on the deadlines for achievement of the air quality standards, there was still uncertainty in the states. Grass-roots groups were frustrated; they had worked hard to push their states to include I & M provisions in their SIPs and to get their state legislatures to enact the required legislation. The concessions that some states won from the EPA were demanded by others. Angry legislators began introducing legislation to repeal the aggressive regulatory programs only recently approved.[38]

What have we learned after four years of implementing the 1990 Clean Air Act? The most complicated and detailed program is aimed at helping states attain the national ambient air quality standards by preparing and implementing SIPs. Congress largely continued with the traditional command-and-control structure of federal standards and state implementation. The process has not worked particularly well: states are slow to submit SIPs, and the EPA is slow to provide guidelines and approve the SIPs once they are submitted. Part of the problem is that SIPs place controls on industries and individuals, and those unhappy with the proposed mandates have ways to slow down the process.

Regulations aimed at mobile sources demonstrate the effectiveness of technology-based standards. Clear standards force industry to develop cleaner processes. Tailpipe standards illustrate this: the new standards are much more stringent than earlier ones, but auto manufacturers, despite their threats and complaints, will be able to meet most, if not all, of them. Similarly, control technology standards for air toxics have resulted in controls on sources that have not been successfully regulated until now. The technology-based regulatory process has been much more successful than the risk-based approach used before 1990.

The acid rain program demonstrates that market incentives do cut costs of compliance. But do they solve environmental problems? New York's state government has begun to urge Congress to strengthen the federal acid rain program, and its congressional representatives, including Republicans, have pushed for more aggressive efforts to reduce acid rain emissions. A March 1995 draft of an EPA report concluded that current efforts would not stabilize areas in the Adirondacks and would at best only slow the rate of deterioration of the lakes and forests. Some 200 lakes in the Adirondacks have recently become so acidified that they cannot sustain life, and 43 percent of the lakes are expected to become acidified by the year 2040, in comparison with an estimated 50 percent if the 1990 amendments had not taken effect. The Adirondack Council, a New York environmental preservation organization, argues that, as allowed by the Clean Air Act, midwestern utilities are buying emission credits from other facilities rather than reducing their own emissions. As a result, acid rain continues to attack New York forests, lakes, and rivers.[39]

Finally, despite its shortcomings, the 1990 law energized clean air regulation and generated a great deal of activity. The structure is largely now in place, and states now need to continue and expand their efforts to put effective and efficient regulatory programs in place. This momentum is threatened, however, by the uncertain future the law faces in Congress. When federal law is uncertain and strong oversight and enforcement by the EPA is lacking (as was the case in the 1980s), many states will fail to take aggressive action to improve their air quality in response to economic demands that are oriented toward short-term concerns.

The Future of Clean Air and Environmental Regulation

The debate over the Clean Air Act Amendments of 1990 continues. In the two decades that will be required to implement them, there will be continual pressure to weaken their provisions as well as demands to achieve their goals more quickly. States will feel pressure to proceed gingerly with enforcement efforts to avoid harming industry, and the EPA will be pressured to avoid imposing sanctions for noncompliance. The grassroots interest that supported aggressive legislation will be hard to maintain throughout twenty years of the hard, less glamorous work of developing and implementing regulations.

The extent to which the Clean Air Act Amendments of 1990 achieve their goals depends on whether provisions are stringent enough to reduce or eliminate the problems at which they are aimed, whether they include sufficient incentives to ensure maximum compliance by state and local governments and regulated industries, and whether state and local governments have the political will to enforce the provisions and to go beyond what is required of them when necessary to achieve the act's goals.

The prospects for achieving clean air goals did not appear very promising as of June 1995. Thirty-one bills to amend the Clean Air Act had been introduced in the first months of the 104th Congress; one bill proposed by House Majority Whip Tom DeLay (R-Texas) would repeal all of the 1990 amendments. The biggest target was motor vehicle regulations. Several bills provided that carpooling and employer commuting programs be made voluntary; other bills would suspend the enhanced inspection and maintenance program. Five bills would suspend the EPA's authority to enforce clean air rules for one or two years, and others would end regulation of toxic chemicals, acid rain controls, and reformulated gas and would weaken SIP requirements. Riders were attached to appropriations bills that prohibited the EPA from spending money on carpooling, inspection, and reformulated gas programs. Two provisions dealing with inspections and trip reduction measures were included in a rescissions bill vetoed by President Clinton in part because of those and other cuts it required in spending for environmental regulation.[40]

Other initiatives pose a major challenge to the Clean Air Act and other environmental protection programs. In 1993, the Senate passed a bill, 95-3, that would require the EPA to assess the costs and benefits of regulations and to do comparative risk assessments to ensure that the problems addressed were sufficiently serious, in comparison with other problems, to merit regulation. The bill would also have elevated the EPA to cabinet status.[41] In February 1994, the House rejected a rule to govern debate over creating a Department of Environmental Protection, thus effectively killing the bill, because it prohibited consideration of amendments calling for comparative risk assessment.[42] Both the House and Senate passed legislation to encourage research and development of environmental technologies that included risk assessment provisions, but the two measures were never reconciled and both bills died.[43]

In January 1995, Senate Majority Leader Bob Dole promised a set of legislative initiatives aimed at requiring cost-benefit analysis of new and existing federal regulations, more judicial review of agency decisions, and more congressional oversight of "'discretionary' rulemaking that goes beyond what the law intended." Sen. Phil Gramm (R-Texas) proposed a "regulatory burden commission" to propose legislation on an industry-by-industry basis.[44] Speaker of the House Newt Gingrich (R-Ga.) proposed early in 1995 that Congress hold "correction days" to take up proposals for legislation to eliminate existing federal rules considered "obnoxious or burdensome to state or local governments." A congressional task force would identify possible regulations, confer with the relevant committees, and if there was broad support, bring them to the House floor for an up-or-down two-thirds majority vote.[45]

The Republican Party's "Contract with America" includes related provisions, particularly in the "Job Creation and Wage Enhancement Act of 1995." The brainchild of Gingrich and other Republican members of Congress and political operatives, the contract was originally designed to attract in the 1994 election the H. Ross Perot voters of 1992. It became even more powerful as an agenda for the new Congress, giving the Republicans a vehicle to channel their momentum into quick legislative successes and to avoid intraparty squabbling over what the agenda should be. The House unfunded mandates bill was carved out of the job creation and wage enhancement bill and became a separate initiative. (Unfunded mandates bills were passed by both houses and signed into law in February 1995. Congress is not prohibited from imposing regulatory mandates on states, but must go through additional procedural steps when considering bills with such provisions. The new law alters in significant ways the traditional approach to environmental regulation of shared federal-state responsibility for funding-needed investments and places a much greater burden on federal agencies to finance projects. In an era of federal budget-cutting, this approach will translate into less investment in environmental protection and more variation in environmental quality across the country.)[46] Other contract proposals included bills that would require agencies to conduct extensive, peer-reviewed cost-benefit analyses before issuing regulations, which would give regulated industries new opportunities to challenge propositions with which they disagreed.[47] A bill imposing a moratorium on recently issued regulations, strongly supported by regulated businesses, was another element of the package, as was a proposal to create a regulatory budget that would impose a limit on the compliance costs federal agencies could impose on regulated industries, require a 6.5 percent cut in those mandated costs each year, and require that agencies employ market-based approaches to regulation.

Another important initiative, which addressed the "taking" of property through environmental and other kinds of regulation, would require federal agencies to compensate regulated parties if regulations imposed on them caused a reduction in their property values of more than 10 percent. Senator Dole had already introduced legislation in 1993 that would require a "takings" impact statement for regulations.[48] But these new initiatives could make it almost impossible for agencies to issue major regulations, since they would not have the resources to reimburse regulated industries for the money they spend to limit the pollution they produce.

The strong support given to these regulatory relief initiatives reflects widespread concern and frustration with environmental regulation. Rural communities may not have the resources to meet regulatory requirements that large metropolitan areas have. Federal mandates appropriate in some areas may make little sense in other places. These problems can be addressed as they are identified, and rural areas or small businesses can be given special assistance or more flexibility in meeting their obligations. However, the broad-based, generic regulatory relief proposals threaten to undo the progress made in establishing a regulatory framework for achieving clean air and other environmental goals. Requiring cost-benefit analysis for all regulations, for example, does not provide an objective standard for assessing proposals, but actually increases the opportunities for political calculations and shifts the focus away from protection of public health. Cost-benefit analysis also provides little help in determining the advantages and disadvantages for different industries subject to regulation.

Perhaps the most frequently voiced criticism of environmental policy is that the goals established by environmental statutes and the way in which they are implemented by the EPA fail to address the most serious ecological problems. The environmental goals around which laws are constructed do not require reduction of the most serious risks, are fragmented and poorly integrated, and fail to mandate pollution prevention. The major environmental laws do not work together to reduce pollution and often result in pollution being shifted from one medium to another. Environmental goals are also criticized for failing to accommodate private property rights and for imposing burdens on state budgets that are already strained. Assessments of the goals of environmental regulation have been a major focus of reports commissioned by the EPA, as well as of other studies arising from its advisory committees. They emphasize mismatches between agency actions and the seriousness of problems, and the need to set priorities in order to maximize the benefits from the resources available for environmental protection. Given the prescriptiveness of many environmental laws, however, demands for rethinking risk assessments must also be directed toward Congress and the writing of environmental legislation.[49]

Critics have also pointed out that insufficient attention and resources have been directed toward basic research in environmental science, policy-oriented research, monitoring of emissions and environmental conditions, and other preconditions for effective regulation. Further, low morale and other problems at the EPA are rooted in the lack of political support for strong regulatory efforts. The agency has not been given adequate resources to accomplish its tasks; new programs have been regularly delegated to the EPA, but appropriations have not kept pace. The agency also has failed to engage the public and policymakers in a national debate over how we should assess and respond to risks, and what priorities are required, given the nature of risks and the limited resources available to address them.[50] These are all serious problems that must be addressed, but giving agencies both a new set of analyses to perform and procedures aimed at providing regulated industries opportunities to avoid compliance will not improve our capacity to formulate and implement effective public policies.

Environmental proposals are fraught with danger: if they are pursued by officials who have little commitment to protect public health, or if they allow polluters to take responsibility on their own time tables for the hazards they impose on others, then they will be little more than opportunities for industries to lobby for exemptions from compliance. Industries have a clear record of overstating compliance costs and blaming environmental regulations for problems that are in reality the result of other factors. If there is no commitment to a rigorous analysis of these issues, then Congress will become enmeshed in the same kinds of sweetheart deals offered by some officials in the early years of the Reagan administration to regulated industries.

As states are given more discretion in environmental regulation, clean air advocates fear that the goal of a healthy environment will be harder to reach, because some states will maintain aggressive programs but others will not. There is considerable tension in states between demands for environmental protection and efforts to promote economic growth. States may engage in bidding wars to attract new industries and sacrifice environmental quality in the process. While some states are so committed to protecting the environment that changes in federal policy may not cause them to change their own actions, they cannot escape living downwind or downstream from neighboring states less committed to environmental protection. A 1995 nationwide poll by the *Los Angeles Times* illustrates the tension between environmental protection and state discretion. The survey found that although 64 percent of the public favored (and 23 percent opposed) barring unfunded mandates, 68 percent responded that the federal government should "require states to provide sewage treatment plants even if the states must pick up the costs" (25 percent disagreed).[51]

The private property "takings" proposal, if extended to polluting industries as some members of Congress have proposed, is a reversal of common sense. Polluting industries are failing to include all the costs of production in the prices they pay when they are permitted to release their pollution. Regulation is required to ensure that true costs are included in prices; it is essential in making a system of private property and market exchanges work. Rather than being paid to reduce their emissions, polluters should be forced to pay the true costs of their production, including the cost of preventing their waste from spilling over into the communities in which they operate. Market-based approaches may remedy many of the bureaucratic and administrative shortcomings of environmental regulation, and are much more consistent with the idea of private property and markets than is the idea of paying polluters for controlling their pollution. An important advantage of market instruments is that less information is generally needed by regulatory agencies; the burden is redirected toward industry engineers to devise ways to reduce emissions efficiently, in the least costly manner. The key question becomes much simpler: Did the company's emissions exceed levels provided in its permit? The regulatory agency's tasks would still be considerable, but perhaps less demanding than its tasks under the command-and-control approach to regulation.[52]

However, market-based approaches that give sources the opportunity to buy or sell emissions allowances raise a number of questions, one of which involves calculating the volume of emissions that will fall within the limits of the ambient standards. This requires an accurate inventory of existing emissions and the selection of the baseline to be used in allocating emission allowances; however, many areas do not have accurate inventories. Industry representatives who originally supported the permit program have warned that the inventory needs to be updated and improved to account for fugitive emissions (those that cannot be traced to major smokestacks or point sources), incomplete data on some types of sources, and other shortcomings.[53] In addition, the selection of the baseline year is difficult, because emissions from sources of pollution vary considerably over time as a result of changes in overall levels of economic activity, breakdowns or problems with maintenance and operations, investments in pollution control equipment, and a host of other factors. The selection of a particular baseline year will thus be an advantage to some firms and a disadvantage to others. Firms that have already reduced their emissions may believe they are being punished when they are required to make the same level of reductions as other sources that have not taken action. The initial allocation of emission credits is similarly critical: if it is too low or based on recession year output, then companies may not be able to comply when production increases; if it is too high, real reductions may not occur for years.[54]

Opportunities for regulated sources to gain emissions credits may also inhibit the achievement of environmental goals. One of the most attractive features of trading schemes, for example, is a declining cap that requires lower total emissions each year as a way to gradually improve air quality. However, loopholes can provide opportunities to circumvent the shrinking cap. If stationary sources can purchase mobile source credits through vehicle scrappage and other programs, they may have a virtually open-ended supply of credits if increases in allocations in one area are offset by reductions in another area.[55]

Trading programs can be combined with minimum technological controls that balance the flexibility from trading with the internalization of costs that comes from technology controls. Indeed, most emission trading programs under clean air and other environmental laws require that they operate alongside technology control requirements, reasonable further progress requirements, measurable milestones, and other specific requirements. The Clean Air Act's "expeditious attainment" requirement, for example, does not permit all reductions in emissions beyond the minimum, statutorily mandated requirements to be classified as surplus. Trading programs must first identify the most expeditiously attainable reductions possible, independent of any trading. Only true surpluses that represent more rapid or greater reductions than would occur under a nonconventional or nontrading regulatory scheme can be traded. As long as the regulated sources have different marginal costs, there will be an incentive to trade. The savings from trading must be large enough to provide an incentive for trading and must also be used to reduce emissions in ways consistent with the statutory requirement that reductions be as expeditious as possible.[56]

Another critical factor in an emissions trading scheme is the scope of trading: the broader the geographic scope of trading, the greater the likelihood that permits will be traded and that "each zone contains a sufficient number of emission sources to create an active permit market."[57] Ideally, from an environmental and economic standpoint, all sources of pollution would be included in a given trading program.[58] But there are some constraints, such as the inefficiencies of trying to regulate small sources. More serious is the problem of interpollutant trading, since not all pollutants pose the same kinds of risks. Even more troubling is the distribution of pollution levels that results from trading; areas near sources that buy emission credits will have higher levels of pollutants than areas where investments in pollution control equipment permit sources to sell their excess allowances.

Precise monitoring and enforcement are critical elements of the emissions trading scheme, and, in some ways, are more important than in traditional regulatory schemes. If compliance with permitted levels is not vigorously enforced, the incentive to clean up is lost. Standards that require sources to install pollution control equipment or change procedures are, in general, easier to monitor and enforce than emissions standards, since they require less sophisticated monitoring and enforcement efforts.

Economic incentive innovations that stop with trading schemes fail to encourage the spread of the idea of true costs. One of the most important results of emissions trading programs can be to help prepare the way for emissions taxes and fees, by providing the institutional infrastructure as well as by reshaping expectations towards more effective means of regulating pollution. Although, in the aggregate, trading schemes may internalize costs for an entire sector of the economy, they do not require every source to internalize its costs. Companies that find it more expensive to clean up than to purchase emission reduction credits from others may do little to reduce their pollution. Community members who insist that major sources of pollution do all they can to reduce their emissions (while remaining economically viable) may be dissatisfied when those sources are able to escape that obligation. Trading schemes are also, in one sense, inconsistent with the "polluter pays" principle, one of the key ideas underlying environmental regulation. Trading distributes the cost of pollution controls equally rather than imposing the greatest control costs on the sources that produce the greatest emissions. It thus enables some firms to externalize some of their costs of production to other sources, rather than ensuring that they account for all of those costs.[59]

The Case for Clean Air Regulation

The public appears to be convinced that efforts to ensure clean air and water and safe disposal of hazardous chemicals are consistent with a healthy economy, and that, in the long run, environmental quality is a precondition for economic activity and for securing and improving our quality of life. In a 1992 Wirthlin Group poll, respondents offered the view, by an overwhelming margin, that a healthy environment and a healthy economy go hand in hand:

Q: Do you believe that economic growth should be sacrificed for environmental quality, should environmental quality be sacrificed for economic growth, or does it not necessarily have to be a choice between the two?

Sacrifice economic growth for environmental quality   17%
Sacrifice environmental quality for economic growth   4%
Does not have to be a choice   77%[60]

In a 1993 Peter Hart Research Associates poll, respondents emphasized that when trade-offs are required, environmental quality must be given priority:

Q: Generally speaking, in situations where there are close calls between economic development and protecting the environment, do you usually believe it is more important to promote economic development or more important to protect the environment?

More important to promote economic development   30%
More important to protect the environment   55%
Depends on specific situation   18%[61]

Responses to a December 1994 *Newsweek* poll that asked Americans "How upset would you be if many environmental regulations are seriously weakened or eliminated?" included "very upset" (40 percent), "somewhat upset" (33 percent), "not too upset" (12 percent), and "not at all upset" (12 percent).[62]

A 1995 Louis Harris and Associates poll found the following:

Q: Do you favor or oppose giving states more control and management of environmental programs?
Favor   63%
Oppose   34%

Q: If control is shifted to states, do you favor or oppose less strict health, safety, and environmental programs?
Favor   38%
Oppose   61%[63]

The evidence of the economic burdens of environmental regulation indicates only a modest increase in costs. A recent study by the Economic Policy Institute concluded that, on balance, environmental regulation has "slightly increased net employment in the U.S. economy." The report notes that "[i]n the late 1980s, an average of four manufacturing plants per year were shut down as a result of environmental or safety regulation, accounting for less than one tenth of one percent of all large-scale layoffs; [i]ndustrial firms are relocating outside the U.S. because of lower labor costs, not lax environmental regulations; and [e]nvironmental regulation provides more blue-collar jobs than government and private-sector service jobs."

Corporate downsizing, defense cutbacks, and other factors are much greater causes of job loss than are environmental regulations, and the global demand for clean manufacturing and energy technologies provides a tremendous opportunity for U.S. businesses.[64]

One of the most important contributions economic instruments can make to improving environmental quality is in helping internalize the environmental costs of producing goods and services, so that costs of production and eventually the prices charged reflect true costs. In a political economy fundamentally committed to market exchanges, regulatory strategies that help ensure that real production costs are included in prices charged can make a critical contribution. Despite the significant advantages emissions charges represent in environmental regulation, however, they have not been adopted at levels sufficient to internalize costs. One reason for this is the difficulty of calculating what levels of charges are needed to reduce emissions by the amount required to meet air quality goals. More importantly, as noted earlier, it is usually exceedingly difficult to overcome the opposition of regulated industries to new fees or charges. The Clinton administration's ill-fated effort in 1993 to impose a Btu tax on energy sources illustrates the kind of political opposition that such proposals generate. Regulated industries aggressively support emissions trading programs and other mechanisms that give them increased flexibility and reduce their costs, not regulatory approaches that might increase their costs. Shifting to a true cost economy that relies on realistic prices is the best way to limit demand and to ensure optimal use of resources.[65] If we really believe in "free markets," we ought to be willing to make them work. If we are to enjoy the freedoms that come from markets, and the economic efficiency that they produce, they have to be working markets that account for all the costs involved, including the cost of the threats imposed on those who live downwind or downstream.

Perhaps even more important than economic arguments are the public health imperatives of effective clean air regulation. As the Republican leaders in Congress are fond of saying, in a free society people need to take responsibility for their lives. Regulation of air pollution calls for people to take responsibility for the health effects they produce. People who complain about having to get their cars inspected once a year or about having difficulty handling a thick gas pump nozzle are refusing to take responsibility for their actions, as are large corporations that lobby for more studies and research when there is already ample evidence of the health effects of air pollution. If the research on the health effects of air pollution were not so conclusive, so overwhelming, one might be able to argue that compliance with deadlines could be delayed. But that is not a luxury that some people can afford, especially the elderly, children, those who already suffer from respiratory disease, and others who are particularly sensitive to air pollution.

Each month brings new studies confirming the health effects of air pollution—studies that estimate that 50,000 to 70,000 people die each year from air pollution, that show increases in mortality among children with asthma in urban areas and increases in respiratory disease among the elderly, and that calculate the cost of lost wages, medications, and hospitalization due to respiratory problems. Yet the EPA has emphasized its responsiveness to industry and governors' demands instead of aggressively making the case that public health is threatened and communicating to members of Congress, governors, and the public that effective regulation can protect lives. And no other public health agencies of the federal and state governments are out making the case for protecting public health.

The Clean Air Act of 1990 was a landmark achievement, an impressive accomplishment after years of deadlock. But it is only a partial, modest effort. It pushes deadlines back decades from their original dates. It falls woefully short in forcing companies to internalize their costs of production. It largely encourages the spread of existing technologies rather than the development of new ones. Public health and economic efficiency will both be enhanced by full implementation of the current act and continued exploration of areas in which the law can be strengthened.

Notes

1. American Lung Association, *Dollars and Cents: The Economic and Health Benefits of Particulate Matter Reductions in the United States* (New York: ALA, 1995); and California Air Resources Board, *Prospects for Attaining the State Ambient Air Quality Standards for Suspended Particulate Matter (PM$_{10}$), Visibility Reducing Particles, Sulfates, Lead, and Hydrogen Sulfide* (Sacramento, Calif.: CARB, 1991), 25-26.
2. For more on this issue, see Robert D. Bullard, ed., *Confronting Environmental Racism: Voices from the Grassroots* (Boston: South End Press, 1993); and Richard Hofrichter, *Toxic Struggles: The Theory and Practice of Environmental Justice* (Philadelphia: New Society Publishers, 1993).
3. See, generally, Ira C. Magaziner and Robert B. Reich, *Minding America's Business: The Decline and Rise of the American Economy* (New York: Vintage, 1982); and Avinash Dixit and Barry Nalebuff, *Thinking Strategically: The Competitive Edge in Business, Politics, and Everyday Life* (New York: Norton, 1991).
4. Pollution control companies in the United States sold $130 billion worth of equipment in 1991. Worldwide sales reached $370 billion. This country has a positive trade balance with all of its major trading partners for these kinds of products, and the growing awareness of environmental degradation in Eastern Europe and elsewhere will further stimulate demand for pollution control devices. Commerce Department figures cited in Michael Silverstein, "Bush's Polluter Protectionism Isn't Pro-Business," *Wall Street Journal,* May 28, 1992.
5. The Bush administration's obsession with the costs of regulation, which led to its ninety-day moratorium on new federal regulations in January 1992, is an example of short-run economic and political pressures taking precedence over

long-run concerns. The moratorium, renewed in April and August 1992, along with the president's announcement describing specific regulations that would not be imposed on industry, was widely dismissed as an election-year ploy intended to attract business support and campaign contributions. Philip A. Davis, with Mike Mills and Holly Idelson, "Outcry Greets Bush's Plan To Delay New Rules," *Congressional Quarterly Weekly Report* 52 (January 25, 1992): 164-165.

6. For more on the role of the Bush administration in clean air politics, see Norman J. Vig and Michael E. Kraft, eds., *Environmental Policy in the 1990s* (Washington, D.C.: CQ Press, 1994), 81-87, 108-113, 314-317.

7. This theme is pursued in many of the essays in Gerald M. Pomper, ed., *The Election of 1988: Reports and Interpretations* (Chatham, N.J.: Chatham House, 1989). See also Michael Nelson, ed., *The Elections of 1988* (Washington, D.C.: CQ Press, 1989), 111-122.

8. See Executive Order 12291, 46 FR 13193 (February 17, 1981); and Office of the Vice President, "Memorandum for Heads of Executive Departments and Agencies," March 22, 1991, from Vice President Quayle, reminding agency officials that proposed agency regulations, guidelines, policy manuals, and "press releases and other documents" must satisfy the "benefit-cost requirements of the Executive Order."

9. For an interesting critical analysis of the Bush administration in this regard, see "The Cynicism Thing," *The New Republic* 204 (June 24, 1991): 9-10.

10. Quoted in Richard E. Cohen, *Washington at Work: Back Rooms and Clean Air*, 2d ed. (Needham Heights, Mass.: Allyn & Bacon, 1995), 206.

11. HR 4916, H. Rpt. 103-582, parts I, II, and III; and S 1834, S. Rpt. 103-349.

12. S 2093, S. Rpt. 103-257.

13. HR 3948.

14. S 2019, S. Rpt. 103-250.

15. HR 3392, H Rpt. 103-745, part I.

16. For more on this debate see Theodore J. Lowi, *The End of Liberalism* (New York: Norton, 1979); Richard A. Harris and Sidney M. Milkis, *The Politics of Regulatory Change: A Tale of Two Agencies* (New York: Oxford, 1989); and Cass R. Sunstein, *After the Rights Revolution: Reconceiving the Regulatory State* (Cambridge, Mass.: Harvard University Press, 1990).

17. See, generally, Lawrence Dodd and Richard Schott, *Congress and the Administrative State* (New York: Wiley, 1979); Energy and Environment Study Institute, "Statutory Deadlines in Environmental Legislation: Necessary but Need Improvement," (Washington, D.C.: EESI, 1985); and National Academy of Public Administration, *Congressional Oversight of Regulatory Agencies: The Need to Strike a Balance and Focus on Performance* (Washington, D.C.: NAPA, 1988).

18. Charles E. Lindblom and Edward J. Woodhouse, *The Policy-Making Process* (Englewood Cliffs, N.J.: Prentice-Hall, 1993), 10-11.

19. See Lowi, *The End of Liberalism*, especially Chapters 5 and 10. See also David Schoenbrod, *Power without Responsibility: How Congress Abuses the People through Delegation* (New Haven, Conn.: Yale University Press, 1993).

20. Lindblom and Woodhouse, *The Policy-Making Process*, 13-22. For another very thoughtful essay on this issue, see Alice Rivlin, *Systematic Thinking for Social Action* (Washington, D.C.: Brookings Institution, 1971).

21. Daniel A. Mazmanian and Paul Sabatier, *Implementation and Public Policy* (Glenview, Ill.: Scott, Foresman, 1983), 25-30.
22. 42 U.S.C. 7409(d)(2)(B).
23. *American Lung Association v. Browner,* U.S. District Court for the District of Arizona, CIV 93-643 (October 21, 1994). See "EPA to Seek New Research Schedule for Particulates Standard," *Clean Air Report* (March 10, 1994): 3-4; and EPA (EPA), *Air Quality Criteria for Particulate Matter: Review Draft,* vol. 1-3 (Washington, D.C.: EPA, 1995).
24. *American Lung Association v. Browner.*
25. U.S. Congress, Senate, Committee on Environment and Public Works, *Three Years Later: Report Card on the 1990 Clean Air Act Amendments* (Washington, D.C.: GPO, 1993), v.
26. Ibid., viii-ix.
27. Timothy Aeppel, "Not in My Garage: Clean Air Act Triggers Backlash as Its Focus Shifts to Driving Habits," *Wall Street Journal,* January 15, 1995.
28. *Greenwire,* January 25, 1995.
29. Deborah Shprentz, Natural Resources Defense Council, quoted in Aeppel, "Not in My Garage."
30. Alex Daniels, "Tempest in a Tailpipe," *Governing* 8 (February, 1995): 37-38.
31. *Greenwire,* January 20, 1995.
32. *Greenwire,* January 18, 1995; and February 2, 1995.
33. *Greenwire,* January 4, 1995; and January 18, 1995.
34. *Greenwire,* February 2, 1995.
35. Ibid.
36. Aeppel, "Not in My Garage."
37. *Greenwire,* January 30, 1995; and February 2, 1995.
38. *Greenwire,* January 26, 1995.
39. Margaret Kriz, "Cough. Wheeze. There Goes Party Unity," *National Journal,* 27 (May 27, 1995): 1289.
40. Clean Air Network, *Clean Air Update* (Washington, D.C.: CAN, 1995).
41. S 171, S. Rpts. 103-139.
42. HR 3425, H. Rpt. 103-355.
43. HR 3870, H. Rpt. 103-536; and S 978, S. Rpt. 103-163.
44. *Greenwire,* January 27, 1995.
45. *Greenwire,* February 2, 1995.
46. Unfunded Mandate Reform Act of 1995, Pub. L. No. 104-4 (1995).
47. Timothy Noah, "GOP Pushes Bill That Lets Regulated Industries Review Regulations, to the Chagrin of Critics," *Wall Street Journal,* February 9, 1995.
48. S 177.
49. EPA, *Unfinished Business: A Comparative Assessment of Environmental Problems* (Washington, D.C.: EPA, 1987); EPA, Science Advisory Board, *Reducing Risk: Setting Priorities and Strategies for Environmental Protection* (Washington, D.C.: EPA, 1990); EPA, Expert Panel on the Role of Science at EPA, *Safeguarding the Future: Credible Science, Credible Decisions* (Washington, D.C.: EPA, 1992), 4-9; EPA, "The New Generation of Environmental Protection" (Draft, April 15, 1994).
50. For more on these issues, see Marc K. Landy, Marc J. Roberts, and Stephen R. Thomas, *The EPA: Asking the Wrong Questions* (New York: Oxford University Press, 1994).

51. *Greenwire*, January 25, 1995.
52. Bruce Ackerman and Richard Stewart, "Reforming Environmental Law: The Democratic Case for Market Incentives," *Columbia Journal of Environmental Law* 13 (1988): 171. An even more ambitious use of marketlike mechanisms in environmental regulation has been proposed by Terry L. Anderson and Donald R. Leal, who argue that markets should be created to determine the number of emission credits to be bought and sold. Persons who pollute and those who are affected by the pollution can come together and bargain for acceptable pollution levels. "Only when rights are well-defined, enforced, and transferable," Anderson and Leal write, "will self-interested individuals confront the trade-offs inherent in a world of scarcity." Anderson and Leal, *Free Market Environmentalism* (San Francisco: Pacific Research Institute for Public Policy, 1991), 22.
53. Bureau of National Affairs, "California: Problems Seen Setting Baseline Levels in South Coast Emissions-Trading Program," *Environmental Reporter* 23 (May 29, 1992): 437.
54. Letter from Gail Ruderman Feuer and Veronica Kun, Natural Resources Defense Council, to California Air Resources Board, March 8, 1994.
55. California Air Resources Board rule 2015(c)(1) provides only that the executive officer must propose to the governing board that increased allocations be offset from non-RECLAIM sources that are identified in California's Air Quality Management Plan. See letter from Feuer and Kun to California Air Resources Board, 3.
56. Sections 110(a)(2), 172(a)(2), 181(a), 186(a), 188(c), and 192(a) of the Clean Air Act, 42 U.S.C. 7401 et seq. See Natural Resources Defense Council, "Comments Before the U.S. E.P.A. on Economic Incentive Program Rules and Related Guidance" (June 13, 1993).
57. See, generally, Government of Canada, "Economic Instruments for Environmental Protection: Discussion Paper" (1992); Emission Trading Working Group, Canadian Council of Ministers of the Environment, "Emission Trading: A Discussion Paper" (May 1992).
58. Government of Canada, "Economic Instruments," 4.
59. Daniel A. Seligman, "Air Pollution Emissions Trading: Opportunity or Scam?" (Washington, D.C.: Sierra Club, unpublished paper, April 1994), 8-10.
60. These survey results were reported in the Sierra Club 1994 Congressional Platform, reprinted in *Sierra* 79 (July-August, 1994): 84A. Percentages in this poll and in those that follow do not add up to 100 due to rounding.
61. Ibid.
62. Reprinted in *Greenwire*, January 4, 1995.
63. Reported in *Greenwire*, January 18, 1995.
64. Cited in *Greenwire*, January 19, 1995.
65. Vaclav Smil, *Global Ecology: Environmental Change and Social Flexibility* (London: Routledge, 1993), 215.

Glossary

Some of the key terms used in discussions of air pollution include the following:

Acid Deposition, Acid Precipitation, Acid Rain   A complex chemical and atmospheric phenomenon that occurs when emissions of sulfur and nitrogen compounds and other substances are transformed by chemical processes in the atmosphere, often far from the original sources, and then deposited on earth in either a wet or a dry form. The wet forms, popularly called "acid rain," can fall as rain, snow, or fog. The dry forms are acidic gases and particulates.

Acute   Immediate, brief, and severe—refers to both the duration of exposure to pollutants and the effects of pollutants that follow exposure almost immediately as a direct reaction to it.

Aerosol   A gas that contains suspended solid particles or droplets of liquid able to stay suspended in air because of their very small size (usually less than 1 micrometer in diameter).

Air Toxics   Any air pollutant for which a national ambient air quality standard does not exist (that is, excluding ozone, carbon monoxide, lead, particulate matter, sulfur dioxide, nitrogen dioxide) and that may reasonably be anticipated to cause cancer, developmental effects, reproductive dysfunctions, neurological disorders, heritable gene mutations, or other serious or irreversible chronic or acute health effects in humans.

Aromatics   A class of high-octane hydrocarbons that currently constitute about 35 percent of gasoline. This percentage has increased in recent years, as refiners have blended more aromatics into gasoline to replace the octane lost as a result of lead reduction. The chief aromatics in gasoline are benzene, toluene, and xylene. The toxicity of benzene has been a cause of concern; in addition, because some aromatics are highly reactive chemically, they are likely to be active in ozone formation.

Attainment Area   An area considered to have air quality as good as or better than that required by the national ambient air quality standards as defined in the Clean Air Act. An area may be an attainment area for one pollutant and a nonattainment area for other pollutants.

Benzene   A member of the aromatics family that currently constitutes about 1.5 percent of gasoline. The EPA has identified benzene as a carcinogen and has regulated exposure to it in the workplace. The agency is currently considering limitations on the benzene component of motor vehicle emissions.

Best Available Control Measure   As determined by EPA guidelines, the best measures for controlling small or dispersed sources of particulate matter, such as roadway dust, and smoke from woodstoves and open burning.

Butane   A light hydrocarbon added to gasoline to raise octane levels and increase volume. Since butane has high vapor pressure, refiners usually add or remove it to raise or lower the vapor pressure of gasoline. Removal of butane was made necessary by the EPA's imposition of gasoline volatility limits.

Carbon Monoxide (CO)   A colorless, odorless gas that is toxic because of its tendency to reduce the oxygen-carrying capacity of the blood.

Chlorofluorocarbons (CFCs)   A family of inert, nontoxic, and easily-liquefied chemicals used in refrigeration, air conditioning, packaging, and insulation, or as solvents or aerosol propellants. CFCs are not destroyed in the lower atmosphere but drift into the upper atmosphere, where the chlorine is released and destroys ozone. CFC-12 is a chlorofluorocarbon with a trademark name of Freon, commonly used in refrigeration and automobile air-conditioning units.

Chronic   Long-lasting or long-term with reference to either the duration of exposure to a pollutant or the effect of exposure to a pollutant. (Chronic exposure to even low levels of ozone, for example, can result in permanent scarring of the lungs, causing chronic lung disease.)

Clean Coal Technology   Any technology not in widespread use as of the date of enactment of the Clean Air Act Amendments of 1990 that will achieve significant reductions in pollutants emitted in smoke from the burning of coal.

Clean Fuels   Mixtures of or substitutes for gasoline fuels; they include compressed natural gas, methanol, and ethanol.

Coke Oven   An industrial process that converts coal into coke, which is one of the basic materials used in blast furnaces for the conversion of iron ore into iron.

Cold Temperature Carbon Monoxide   A standard for automobile emissions of carbon monoxide to be met at a low temperature (such as 20°). Conventional catalytic converters are less efficient when start-up is at low temperatures.

Control Techniques Guidelines   Guidance documents issued by the EPA that define maximum achievable control technology and other technologies to be applied to existing facilities that emit certain threshold quantities of air pollutants. They contain information on the economic and technological feasibility of available techniques.

Emission   The discharge of a pollutant from a source into the environment.

Emission Standard   A legally imposed limit to the amount of a pollutant that can be discharged into the environment from a particular source. Under the Clean Air Act, emissions from existing sources are controlled by the states, which include such provisions in state implementation plans approved by the EPA. The federal government establishes maximum emission standards for new sources of pollution.

Environmental Protection Agency (EPA)   The federal agency responsible for issuing and enforcing air quality and emissions regulations and approving state implementation plans. Created by an executive order in 1970, the EPA is also responsible for regulating water pollution, toxic chemical production and use, hazardous waste disposal, solid waste disposal, pesticides, radiation, and noise pollution.

Epidemiology   An investigative approach to disease that seeks to determine the factors that account for its frequency and patterns within defined populations.

Ethanol   An alcohol produced from starch or sugar crops such as corn and sugar cane. Ethanol can be used as a fuel, as is done in Brazil, or blended into gasoline to boost octane levels and increase volume. In the United States, ethanol is usually blended with gasoline in a 10 percent mixture to form gasohol. As an oxygenate, ethanol supplies oxygen to gasoline, thus reducing motor vehicle carbon monoxide emissions. Ethanol cannot be transported in the same pipelines as gasoline, however, so it must be blended into gasoline outside the refinery. Another problem is that ethanol increases the volatility of gasoline. These drawbacks can be overcome if ethanol is converted to its ether form, ethyl tertiary butyl ether.

Ethyl Tertiary Butyl Ether   An ether compound formed from ethanol. Although it is not yet produced in commercial quantities, it could be used as a gasoline additive to boost octane levels and provide oxygen. Since it has a low vapor pressure, it would be useful in achieving compliance with volatility controls on gasoline. Unlike alcohols, the compound could be produced and blended with gasoline at the refinery and shipped in gasoline pipelines.

Federal Implementation Plan   Under the Clean Air Act of 1990, a federally implemented plan to achieve a national ambient air quality standard, used when a state is unable to develop an adequate plan. A partial federal plan containing control measures developed and promulgated by the EPA may also be issued in order to fill gaps in a state implementation plan.

Fly Ash   Gas-borne solid particles resulting from the combustion of fuel and other materials.

Gasoline Volatility   The property of gasoline that causes it to evaporate into a vapor. It is measured in pounds per square inch, a higher number indicating more gasoline evaporation. Gasoline vapor is a volatile organic compound.

Halons   A family of compounds containing bromine that are used in fighting fires whose breakdown in the atmosphere depletes stratospheric ozone.

HCFCs   Chlorofluorocarbons that have been chemically altered by the addition of hydrogen. They are significantly less damaging to stratospheric ozone than other CFCs.

Hydrocarbons with High Boiling Points   Hydrocarbons are compounds of hydrogen and carbon. Many of the hydrocarbons with high boiling points contained in gasoline are very reactive chemically and are thought to contribute to ozone formation. These hydrocarbons are the last to boil away when gasoline is subjected to high temperatures. The group of hydrocarbons being tested by the joint research project of the auto and oil industries is referred to as the "T_{90} Boiling Point Group"; it consists of the 10 percent of hydrocarbons that remain after 90 percent of the gasoline has vaporized.

Inspection and Maintenance A program for periodic inspections of motor vehicles to ensure that emissions of specified pollutants are not exceeding established limitations. Enhanced inspection and maintenance is an improved program that includes, as a minimum, coverage by vehicle type and model year, more stringent inspections, and improved management practices to ensure effectiveness. It may also include annual, computerized, or centralized inspections; under-the-hood inspections to detect tampering with pollution control equipment; and increased repair waiver cost.

Low Nitrogen Oxide Burners One of several combustion technologies used to reduce emissions of nitrogen oxides.

Lowest Achievable Emissions Reduction The most stringent standard for emission control, reflecting the highest degree of control attained by any relevant source, required of new sources built in areas that have not yet met national ambient air quality standards.

Maximum Achievable Control Technology (MACT) Emissions limitations based on the best demonstrated control technology or practices used by similar pollution sources to be applied to major sources emitting one or more of the toxic pollutants listed in Title III of the 1990 amendments.

Methanol An alcohol made primarily from natural gas. Methanol may be used as a pure (or neat) fuel, in which case it is called M100 (100 percent methanol). Because M100 vehicles are hard to start and are still in the developmental stage, some gasoline is usually added to methanol to form M85 (85 percent methanol and 15 percent gasoline), used in M85 vehicles. Methanol is not currently used as a gasoline additive for several reasons, including its adverse effects on the fuel system components of conventional vehicles. It is widely used as a gasoline additive in its ether form, methyl tertiary butyl ether.

Methyl Tertiary Butyl Ether An ether compound formed from methanol. It has been widely accepted by refiners as a gasoline additive, and its use has steadily increased in the past several years. As an oxygenate, it supplies oxygen to help reduce carbon monoxide emissions. The compound boosts octane levels but has little effect on vapor pressure. Unlike alcohols, it can be produced and blended with gasoline at the refinery and shipped in gasoline pipelines.

Montreal Protocol   An international environmental agreement, signed by thirty-one nations on September 16, 1987, to control chemicals that deplete the ozone layer. The protocol, which was renegotiated in June 1990, calls for a phase-out of CFCs, halons, and carbon tetrachloride by the year 2000, and a phase-out of chloroform by 2005. It includes provision of financial assistance to developing countries to enable them to make the transition away from use of ozone-depleting substances.

National Ambient Air Quality Standards   Limits established by the EPA for a pollutant in ambient (outside) air that are the target in local air quality improvement or protection programs. The primary standard protects public health; the secondary standard protects public welfare. Stricter standards may be established by state governments.

Nitrogen Oxides (NO$_x$)   Chemical compounds containing nitrogen and oxygen; in the presence of heat and sunlight, they react with volatile organic compounds to form ozone. They are also a major precursor of acid rain. Nationwide, approximately 45 percent of NO$_x$ emissions come from mobile sources, 35 percent are discharged by electric utilities, and 15 percent are a result of industrial fuel combustion.

Olefins   A group of highly reactive and volatile hydrocarbons that currently constitute about 12 percent of gasoline. Olefins are considered to be likely contributors to ozone formation.

On-board Controls   Devices placed on vehicles that capture gasoline vapor during refueling and route it to the engine after the vehicle is started so that it can be efficiently burned.

Oxygenate   Any gasoline additive containing oxygen. Oxygen in gasoline tends to reduce motor vehicle carbon monoxide emissions. For this reason, four states (Arizona, Colorado, Nevada, and New Mexico) require the use of oxygenated gasoline during winter months in areas with high levels of carbon monoxide emissions. Oxygenates include the alcohols, such as ethanol and methanol, and the ethers, such as methyl tertiary butyl ether and ethyl tertiary butyl ether. These compounds also boost the octane of gasoline, but their effects on volatility vary.

Oxygenated Fuels   Gasoline that has been blended with alcohols or ethers that contain oxygen in order to reduce carbon monoxide and other emissions.

Ozone   A compound consisting of three oxygen atoms that is the primary constituent of smog. It is formed as a result of chemical reactions in the atmosphere involving volatile organic compounds, nitrogen oxides, and sunlight. Ozone can cause damage to the lungs as well as to trees, crops, and materials. There is a natural layer of ozone in the upper atmosphere (or stratosphere) that shields the earth from harmful ultraviolet radiation.

Particulate Matter (PM_{10})   Solid or liquid matter suspended in the atmosphere that is more than 10 micrometers in diameter—a standard of measurement. The smaller particles penetrate to the deeper portions of the lung, affecting sensitive population groups such as children and those suffering from respiratory diseases.

Parts Per Million (ppm)   The number of parts of a given substance in one million parts of a mixture by volume.

Reasonably Available Control Measures   Technologies (such as reasonably available control technology) and other measures that can be used to control pollution. The term is broadly defined; in the case of particulate matter, it refers to approaches for controlling small or dispersed source categories such as road dust, and smoke from woodstoves and open burning.

Reasonably Available Control Technology   An emissions limitation on existing sources in nonattainment areas, defined by the EPA in a Control Techniques Guideline and implemented by the states.

Reformulated Gasoline   Gasoline whose composition differs from that of conventional gasoline (for example, lower aromatics content); it results in the production of lower levels of air pollutants.

Repowering   The replacement of an existing coal-fired boiler with one or more clean coal technologies to achieve an emission reduction significantly greater than that produced by technology in widespread use as of the enactment of the Clean Air Act Amendments (November 1990).

Residual Risk   The threat to health remaining after application of the maximum achievable control technology.

Sanctions   Actions taken by the federal government against a state or local government for failure to formulate or implement a state implementation plan. Examples include withholding of highway funds and a ban on construction of new sources.

Smog   A visible combination of smoke and fog (hence the term, coined in Los Angeles). Photochemical smog is the result of the chemical reaction of nitrogen oxides, hydrocarbons, and sunlight.

Stage II Controls   Equipment placed on service station gasoline pumps to capture and control gasoline vapors released during automobile refueling.

State Implementation Plan   A document prepared by each state, and submitted to EPA for approval, which identifies actions and programs to be undertaken by the state and its subdivisions to implement its responsibilities under the Clean Air Act.

Sulfur   A contaminant found to varying degrees in crude oil. Most of it is removed during refinery processing; the amount remaining in gasoline averages only about 300 parts per million. Industry researchers believe that even this amount may adversely affect the durability of catalyst material in catalytic converters, however.

Sulfur Oxides (SO_x)   Heavy, pungent, colorless air pollutants made up of sulfur and oxygen that are formed primarily by the combustion of fossil fuels. They are a respiratory irritant, especially for asthmatics, and are a major precursor of acid rain.

Synergism   A phenomenon in which the effect of a combination of materials is different from (usually greater than) the sum of the separate effects of the individual substances.

Thermal Inversion   An atmospheric meteorological condition in which a layer of warm air acts like a lid and traps a layer of cold air beneath it. This frustrates the normal convection of air upward that occurs when the surface of the earth is heated; the air and any pollutants vented into it are trapped.

Transportation Control Measures   Steps taken by a locality to adjust traffic patterns (bus lanes, allowing right turn on red traffic light) or to reduce vehicle use (ride sharing, high-occupancy vehicle lanes) to reduce vehicular emissions of air pollutants.

Variance   Permission by a legal body for a company or an individual to operate outside the limits prescribed by a law or standard. Industries often apply for and are granted variances to exceed air quality regulations.

Vehicle Miles Traveled A measure of both the volume and extent (within a specified geographical area during a given period) of motor vehicle operation.

Volatile Organic Compounds (VOCs) A group of chemicals that react with nitrogen oxides in the atmosphere in the presence of heat and sunlight to form ozone; includes gasoline fumes and oil-based paints but does not include methane and other compounds determined by the EPA to have negligible photochemical reactivity.

Source: Environmental Protection Agency, *The Clean Air Act Amendments of 1990: Summary Materials* (Washington, D.C.: EPA, November 15, 1990); Charles E. Kupchella and Margaret C. Hyland, *Environmental Science: Living within the System of Nature* (Boston: Allyn & Bacon, 1989); and General Accounting Office, *Gasoline Marketing: Uncertainties Surround Reformulated Gasoline as a Motor Fuel,* RCED-90-153 (Washington, D.C.: GAO, June 1990), 17-19.

Index